The Futures of European Capitalism

D0770435

San Diego Christian College
2100 Greenfield Drive
El Cajon, CA 92019

2694

26.94

330.94
S 354f

The Futures of European Capitalism

Vivien A. Schmidt

OXFORD

UNIVERSITY PRESS

Great Clarendon Street, Oxford OX2 6DP

Oxford University Press is a department of the University of Oxford.
It furthers the University's objective of excellence in research, scholarship,
and education by publishing worldwide in

Oxford New York

Auckland Cape Town Dar es Salaam Hong Kong Karachi Kuala Lumpur
Madrid Melbourne Mexico City Nairobi New Delhi Shanghai Taipei Toronto

With offices in

Argentina Austria Brazil Chile Czech Republic France Greece
Guatemala Hungary Italy Japan South Korea Poland Portugal
Singapore Switzerland Thailand Turkey Ukraine Vietnam

Oxford is a registered trade mark of Oxford University Press
in the UK and in certain other countries

Published in the United States
by Oxford University Press Inc., New York

© V. A. Schmidt, 2002

The moral rights of the author have been asserted

Database right Oxford University Press (maker)

First published 2002

All rights reserved. No part of this publication may be reproduced,
stored in a retrieval system, or transmitted, in any form or by any means,
without the prior permission in writing of Oxford University Press,
or as expressly permitted by law, or under terms agreed with the appropriate
reprographics rights organization. Enquiries concerning reproduction
outside the scope of the above should be sent to the Rights Department,
Oxford University Press, at the address above.

You must not circulate this book in any other binding or cover
and you must impose this same condition on any acquirer

British Library Cataloguing in Publication Data

Data available

Library of Congress Cataloging in Publication Data

Schmidt, Vivien Ann, 1949-
    The futures of European capitalism / Vivien A. Schmidt.
      p. cm.
    Includes bibliographical references.
      1. Europe–Economic policy. 2. Europe–Foreign economic relations.
    3. Europe–Economic integration. 4. Capitalism–Europe.
    5. Globalization–Economic aspects–Europe. I. Title.
    HC240.S3472002   330.94–dc21   2002025047

ISBN 0-19-925367-6(hbk.)
ISBN 0-19-925368-4(pbk.)

5 7 9 10 8 6 4

Typeset by Newgen Imaging Systems (P) Ltd., Chennai, India
Printed in Great Britain
on acid-free paper by
Biddles Ltd., King's Lynn, Norfolk

Preface

In the mid-1990s, when I first started writing about the impact of globalization and European integration on national economies, globalization had already become the object of tremendous public debate, with concerns raised about the unfettered powers of the financial markets and multinational corporations, about a 'race to the bottom' in terms of environmental, labour, and social standards, and even about the breakdown of the nation-state, with threats to national sovereignty and democracy. It took a bit longer for the process of Europeanization, without question the most important experiment in supranational governance today, to become a comparable object of concern, accused of exacerbating problems of unemployment and social exclusion as it imposed unrealistic economic and monetary goals on member states. But there has yet to be a balanced, in-depth assessment of the impact of globalization and Europeanization on EU member states. This is the object of this book, which uses three countries, France, Britain, and Germany, by way of illustration.

In the book, I argue that while both globalization and Europeanization have been tremendous economic, institutional, and ideational forces for change, they have not produced convergence. Since the 1980s, all European countries have indeed changed their economic policies, practices, and discourses in response to the pressures of globalization and Europeanization. But they have felt the pressures at different times, to differing degrees, with different responses, and with differing results. Although all have liberalized their economies, their policies still vary, albeit within a more restricted range; their practices continue to diverge, although much less so; and their discourses not only differ, they make a difference. Of the three countries considered in the book, I find that France has undergone the greatest amount of adjustment with the most disruption, having had to alter its traditional policies and practices more than the others in response to the pressures of globalization and European integration, and without the benefits of a fully legitimizing discourse. Britain, by contrast, began adjustment earlier, in response to the pressures of globalization, and came up with a transformative discourse that successfully legitimized changes in policies and practices that were more in keeping with its traditions as well as attuned to the coming demands of Europeanization. Germany, finally, has been the latest to adjust, given traditional policies, practices, and discourse that better meshed with global and European requirements until the 1990s, at which point it began to change its policies and practices without, so far, the benefits of a legitimizing discourse.

I had originally intended to produce an edited book with country cases. The difficulties of finding people with the time and/or the expertise were such, however, that after a couple of attempts to put together a group of six to seven specialists on major EU countries I gave up, deciding that I was better off doing this on my own. The choice of France, Britain, and Germany was a natural one, not only because they are the three biggest, most influential, and most representative of the three main forms of post-war economic governance, but also, happily, ones I already knew reasonably well. I had initially considered including Italy, but ultimately decided against. Three comparisons are hard enough for a reader to follow without adding a fourth case as complicated as is that of Italy. Throughout the book, however, I refer to Italy where most relevant as well as to other countries.

The book seeks to be both wide and deep, as befits a book on Europe. It spans major sub-fields of political science in the attempt to bridge the gaps between international relations and comparative public policy with regard to policy change, between international political economy and comparative political economy with regard to capitalism with a large C and capitalisms with a small c, and between those in the ideas/discourse literature focused on the nature and sources of policy ideas and those more concerned with their communication in the policy and political arenas.

In Part I, I address the international relations literature to show that the losses in national autonomy and control attributed to globalization and Europeanization are largely offset by gains in shared supranational authority and control. I then proceed to comparative public policy to identify the mediating factors and EU-specific institutional constraints that help explain the differential impact of globalization and Europeanization. In Part II, I add to the 'varieties of capitalism' literature in international and comparative political economy by demonstrating that European countries continue to be differentiable along lines of development from the original three post-war models of capitalism, even though they have all moved toward greater market orientation. Part III arguably represents my greatest methodological innovation by offering a new framework for the analysis of discourse to explain the political dynamics of change in national policies and practices in response to globalization and Europeanization. In the conclusion, I summarize the book's main points about European capitalisms' different pathways to adjustment, and speculate about the futures of European capitalism.

The book also seeks to balance the theoretical with the empirical. The chapters and sections focused on the development of British, German, and

French policies, practices, and discourses are written to stand on their own, as accounts of what happened, even as they serve in the more theoretical chapters and sections as evidence for the theories about why and how what happened happened. Although this may make for a bit of repetition, as the examples summarized in the theoretical chapters are elaborated at much greater length in the empirical chapters, my intention is to enable the reader to see the forest first so as better to be able to see the patterns in the trees. This balance between the theoretical and empirical should make the book fully accessible not only to an audience of specialists along with advanced under-graduate and graduate students but also to the informed public interested in the range of questions addressed in the book. For those not familiar with the 'stories' that serve to illuminate the theories, the empirical chapters offer the necessary background, and could be read first: for example, Chapter 6 on the politics, Chapter 4 on the practices, and Chapter 2 on the policies.

Although the book addresses theoretical issues in three fields, it is also heavily grounded in empirical research. Throughout, I have relied not only on the secondary literature but also on statistical data, surveys, and primary sources. I also conducted over 40 interviews with top business, government, and EU Commission officials in addition to more informal conversations and discussions in formal settings.

The book has been a longer time in gestation than originally expected. After my decision to write a single-authored book instead of an edited book, a couple of years passed before I published my first thoughts on the subject, in a piece that appeared in *Daedalus* in 1995 on the impact of globalization and European integration on the nation-state. For this, I have to thank the editor, Stephen Graubard, whose insistence on my writing an article that went beyond the French case on which I was working at the time gave me just the excuse I was looking for to range much more widely. The development of the more theoretical aspects of the argument with regard to globalization and European integration, by contrast, owes much to the impetus of two conferences organized by Alberta Sbragia at the University of Pittsburgh in 1996 and 1997, and I thank her and other participants for their thoughts. Deserving of special mention are Peter Katzenstein, who encouraged me to think more about the constructivist elements in my argument, which held the kernels of my subsequent work on discourse, and Fritz W. Scharpf, who also provided critical support for this foray into forbidden territory at the same time as we agreed that the socio-economic issues required their own separate study. (I mention this here only because our two-volume project, *Welfare and Work in the Open Economy*, is my excuse for how long it has taken me to complete this book.) Other scholars in other venues also provided valuable comments on the political-economic questions, including participants in seminars and conferences at Harvard University, the European University Institute, the London School of Economics, the University of Washington, Seattle, and at professional meetings. I thank in particular Gary Marks, Joseph Weiler, Andy Moravcsik, Mark Thatcher, David Cameron, Alain Guyomarch, Thomas Risse, Francesco Duina, Adrienne Héritier, Martin Schain, James Caporaso, John Keeler, and Jacques Le Cacheux.

The second part of this book, on models of capitalism, also benefited greatly from comments in seminars and conferences that dealt with various aspects of the issue. I would like to thank participants in seminars at the Wissenschaftzentrum of Berlin, the European University Institute, the London School of Economics, and Harvard University as well as, in particular, Wolfgang Streeck, Bob Hancké, Susanne Lütz, Mark Thatcher, Paulette Kurzer, Linda Weiss, Henry Farrell, Ulrich Glassmann, Peter Hall, Loukas Tsoukalis, David Soskice, Michel Goyer, and Pepper Culpepper, as well as others mentioned earlier.

For the third part, on the role of discourse in the dynamics of economic adjustment, I would like to thank, in addition to those already mentioned, Stephen Graubard, who once again spurred me to move beyond where I had been when he asked me to focus on the political aspects of adjustment for *Daedalus* in 1997. This first empirical piece on discourse was followed by my more theoretical explorations, which were given impetus, this time, by an invitation by Steven Weber to participate in a workshop at the University of California, Berkeley, and was further encouraged by invitations to give talks in other venues. I am indebted to John L. Campbell, Paulette Kurzer, Chris Ansell, Nick Ziegler, Elliot Posner, Vanna Gonsalez from the Berkeley workshop; Renate Mayntz and Wolfgang Streeck from the Max Planck Institute in Cologne; Yves Mény, Martin Rhodes, Maurizio Ferrera, and Philippe Schmitter at the European University Institute; Beate Kohler-Koch, Michèle Knodt, and Fabrice Larat at the University of Mannheim; and Bruno Jobert, Pierre Muller, Bruno Palier, Jean Leca, Mark Blyth, Kate McNamara, Colin Hay, Claudio Radaelli, Jonas Pontusson, Amy Verdun, and Martin Hering.

Writing this book, as is clear, took some time. For allowing me the time for research in Europe, I would like to thank Boston University for its generous leave policies. For providing research support in the form of visiting professorships, I thank the Institut d'Études Politiques, Paris; Nuffield College, Oxford University; the European University Institute, Florence; and the Max Planck Institute for the Study of Societies in Cologne.

Finally, I would also like to express my appreciation to the numbers of government and business officials as well as journalists and academics in

Brussels and in national capitals whose insights in interviews and conversations contributed to this work. Among these, I would like to thank in particular Karel Van Miert, David Williamson, Philippe de Schootheete, Dominique Strauss-Kahn, Michel Albert, Louis Schweitzer, Jean-Louis Beffa, André Lévy-Lang, Michel Bon, Jean Gandois, Michael Mertes, Joschka Fischer, Gunter Hoffman, Horst Ehmke, Wolfgang Zeh, Hans-Olaf Henkel, Albrecht Muller, Norbert Wieczorek, Hans-Ulrich Klose, Gerd Popper, Hilmar Kopper, and many others who must be left unnamed. In addition, for facilitating numbers of interviews in Cambridge as well as providing entrée in Brussels, my thanks go to Renée Haferkamp. I also have to mention the large numbers of individuals whose comments and insights conveyed in informal settings or formal talks found their way into this book. And then there are the friends who, although in some cases mentioned above, need another note to thank them for the intellectual stimulation and support as well as the patience with which they read, and reread, and read again various drafts of various chapters, in particular Fritz W. Scharpf and Paulette Kurzer. Last, but by no means least, I thank Jolyon Howorth, for all the above, and much, much more.

Vivien A. Schmidt
February 2002

Contents

PART I   The Policies of Economic Adjustment

PART II   The Practices of Economic Adjustment

PART III   The Politics of Economic Adjustment

List of Figures

List of Tables

Introduction: European Pathways to the Future

In times of great upheaval, the temptation is either to embrace change in its entirety, proclaiming the end of the old and the victory of the new, or to dismiss it by remarking 'plus ça change...' And so it is today with the debates over the political economic changes that have been seen in European countries over the last quarter of a century in response to the forces of globalization and European integration.[1] Globalization in particular has been hailed by some as a juggernaut sweeping away all national differences in its path, ensuring convergence by compelling governments to adopt the same neo-liberal policies, practices, and politics. As a result, they see global forces as powerfully undermining government autonomy in decision-making and control over economic forces and actors in the national territory; as pressing governments to monetarize their monetary policies, liberalize financial markets, privatize and deregulate business, decentralize labour markets, and rationalize the welfare state; as slowly but surely forcing the replacement of the traditional varieties of capitalism with a one-size-fits-all neo-liberal version of market capitalism; and as having converted all to neo-liberal ideas and discourse, obliterating differences between left and right. Others, however, have argued that the impact of globalization has been greatly exaggerated, with much less change in national policies, practices, and politics than assumed. Thus, they contend that such changes as have occurred have been more the product of internally generated dynamics than of externally imposed imperatives, with minimal losses in national autonomy and control; with monetarism, liberalization, privatization, deregulation, and retrenchment varying greatly from country to country; with continued differentiation in national varieties of capitalism; and with great differences in ideas and discourse, especially with regard to social justice. But regardless of scholars' views of the sources, reach, or impact of globalization, and

---

[1] See Held *et al.* (1999); Busch (2000); Weiss (1999*a*); Rhodes (1996); Waters (1995).

whether they see it as threat or opportunity, as driving force or tool for internal forces, most tend to agree that countries' responses to globalization have brought changes in policies, monetary, industrial, labour, and social; in practices, through greater emphasis on market financing, firm profits, and labour flexibility; and in politics, with changes in interest coalitions, party positions, public opinion, and legitimizing discourses.

The impact of Europeanization, although not giving rise to quite the same polemics, has been equally the subject of debate. While some scholars argue that the European Union has taken precedence over its member states, with common EU policies producing tremendous loss of national autonomy and control, others see such losses offset by greater gains in shared EU authority and control. Moreover, whereas some scholars see Europeanization as intensifying the pressures of globalization in monetary, industrial, labour, and social policy arenas, others see it as a shield against their most extreme effects. Finally, although some find the EU generating convergence not only in national economic policies but also in economic practices and politics, others suggest a more complex set of interrelationships between the EU and member states, with national policy regimes, varieties of capitalism, and ideas and discourse continuing to diverge. But again, regardless of scholars' views of the reach or impact of Europeanization and its relationship to globalization, most tend to agree that countries' responses to Europeanization have brought changes in policies, practices, and politics even greater than those related to globalization.

This book takes a middle way through the debates. I argue that, while the fears of the critics of globalization and Europeanization have been greatly exaggerated, profound changes resulting from supranational economic, institutional, and even ideational forces have indeed been at work, leading to major alterations in national economic policies, practices, and discourse, but not to convergence. National policies may now be more similar, especially where they follow from common European policies, but they are not the same. National practices, although moving in the same general direction toward greater market orientation, continue to be distinguishable into not just one or even two but three varieties of capitalism. And national discourses that generate and legitimize changes in policies and practices not only remain distinct, they matter. What were the economic and political institutional conditions that enabled some countries to respond more effectively to the pressures of globalization and Europeanization than others? What were the long-standing policy legacies and preferences that made some countries more open to neo-liberal reform than others? What were the economic practices that enabled some countries to continue much as they had in the past in response to increasing competitive pressures while others felt forced to implement major change? And how were key actors able to overcome entrenched interests and institutional obstacles to change so as to construct viable policy programmes and to gain public acceptance for reform through legitimizing discourses?

Preliminary answers to these questions can be found by examining the different pathways to adjustment of France, Britain, and Germany. The choice of these three countries as case studies of the impact of European integration and globalization is a reflection of their size as the three largest economies in the EU, of their position as the three most influential in the EU, and of their national characteristics. They have long represented ideal-typically different systems in terms of economic policies, given traditional British liberalism, French statism, and German corporatism; in terms of economic practices, given British market capitalism, French state capitalism, and German managed capitalism; and in terms of economic discourses and policy paradigms, given Britain's post-war discourses of the liberal market economy, France's post-war discourses of the state-directed market economy, and Germany's post-war discourses of the social market economy. A comparative analysis of the evolution of these three countries' policies, practices, and discourses since the mid-1970s is therefore likely to go some way toward answering the questions social scientists have become increasingly concerned with over the past two decades.

The book itself is divided into three parts. The first part focuses on the adjustment of national economic policies in response to the pressures of globalization and Europeanization; the second part considers the impact of changing economic policies on national economic practices; and the third part explores the discourses that served to generate and/or legitimize changes in economic policies and practices. In all three parts, theoretical discussions are illustrated by reference to the actual experiences of adjustment in Britain, Germany, and France.

The first chapter in Part I defines globalization and Europeanization, assesses their scope and limits, and differentiates them from one another. This chapter addresses questions about the pressures toward convergence and the loss of national autonomy and control that have been a major focus of debates in international relations and international political economy. I contend that although globalization and Europeanization, as a set of economic, institutional, and ideational forces for change, have indeed restricted national policy choices, this has not produced convergence in policies since governments continue to exercise choice within a narrower range. Although governments have experienced real losses of national autonomy and control, they have nevertheless managed to retain or regain control both individually, through the reassertion of national regulatory power or influence, and collectively, through shared supranational authority and control which, however, further increases the loss of autonomy. In the case of Europeanization—which I differentiate from European integration as the domestic impact of EU decision-making—the losses of autonomy and control are even greater than for globalization, but so are the gains in shared supranational authority and control, since the EU has served not only as a conduit for globalization but also as a shield against it.

The second chapter in Part I explores the differential impact of globalization and Europeanization on national political economic policies, with a special focus on policy adjustment in Germany, Britain, and France. In this chapter, I build on the sector-specific work of scholars of comparative public policy in an effort to provide a systematic account of the main variables involved in policy adjustment. These variables consist of the mediating factors that help explain the dynamics of policy adjustment over time, such as a country's relative economic vulnerability to the pressures of globalization and Europeanization, its political institutional capacity to adjust its economy in response to such pressures, the policy legacies that ensure a greater or lesser need for changes in its policies and policy-making institutions, the policy preferences that make it more or less open to such changes, and the discourses that enhance capacity by influencing perceptions of vulnerabilities and legacies and, thereby, preferences. In the first half of the chapter, these mediating factors provide the tools for the analysis of the sequencing of policy adjustment in Germany, Britain, and France in monetary policy, industrial policy, labour policy, and social policy in response to the economic pressures of globalization and Europeanization. These mediating factors alone, however, are not enough to explain the mechanics of countries' responses in particular policy sectors to the institutional pressures of Europeanization. In the second part of the chapter, I elaborate on how the different EU adjustment pressures—whether an EU decision is accompanied by more or less highly specified rules for compliance, suggested rules, or no rules—and potential adjustment mechanisms—coercion to a greater or lesser degree, mimesis, or regulatory competition—also affect the possible outcomes—inertia, absorption, or transformation—in a wide range of sectors including European monetary integration, financial services, telecommunications, electricity, and transport. I find that whereas Britain absorbed most Europe-related changes in these sectors with the exception of monetary integration, where it responded with inertia, Germany absorbed changes related to monetary integration but transformed itself in most other sectors, while

France transformed itself in most sectors with the exception of the public interest-related services, where it responded mostly with inertia.

The first chapter in Part II explores the changes in countries' varieties of capitalism following their policy responses to the pressures of globalization and Europeanization. This chapter addresses the 'varieties of capitalism' literature in comparative political economy. I argue that the pressures of globalization and European integration have generated tremendous change in the economic practices of countries conforming to the three ideal-typical post-war models of capitalism long identified in the literature— market capitalism, characteristic of Britain, with market-driven inter-firm relations and market-reliant management–labour relations assured by a 'liberal' state; managed capitalism, illustrated by Germany, with collaborative inter-firm relations and cooperative labour–management relations facilitated by an 'enabling' state; and state capitalism, epitomized by France, with an 'interventionist' state organizing inter-firm collaboration and imposing management–labour cooperation. But they have not led to convergence either towards one model of capitalism, as many globalization theorists argue, or towards two, as many contemporary theorists of the 'varieties of capitalism' suggest. Three varieties of capitalism remain, albeit themselves greatly altered in a market-oriented direction. Traditionally market capitalist countries have become more market capitalist, as traditionally managed capitalist countries have retained many of their basic characteristics but are nevertheless becoming more competitive through the adoption of market capitalist elements, and as traditionally state capitalist countries have changed radically by adopting elements of both market and managed capitalism but have not therefore become either market or managed capitalist. I begin the chapter with a brief discussion of the three ideal-typical models and the continuing differentiation of countries that conform(ed) to them, and then go on to an examination of the comparative advantages and disadvantages of the models that help explain the evolution of the three varieties over the past three decades.

The second chapter in this part takes a closer look at the dynamics of adjustment in economic practices in Britain, Germany, and France to elucidate the different pathways these countries took in adjusting their particular varieties of capitalism in terms of business relations, state relations with business and labour, and management–labour relations. I show that Britain, far from the ideal-typical model of market capitalism in the post-war period, comes much closer to it subsequently, as business relations become more competitive, state relations more arms' length, and labour relations more market-reliant. I find Germany, largely unchanged until the 1990s, now in transition toward a more competitive managed capitalism, with its traditional model under great strain as the network-based business relations loosen, as cooperation in labour relations diminishes, and as government struggles to enable change. Finally, I demonstrate that France, having epitomized the ideal-typical model of state capitalism in the post-war period, has undergone a major transformation in which the state has retreated significantly but is not gone as business has largely become self-directive and labour market-reliant.

The first chapter in Part III considers the national discourses that generated and legitimized the changes in political economic policies and practices in response to globalization and European integration. This chapter addresses the literature on ideas and discourse which span the fields of international relations and comparative politics, seeking to make the most of the wide range of approaches available. I show that discourse—broadly defined as consisting of whatever policy actors say to one another and to the public more generally about a given policy programme—also matters in the dynamics of economic adjustment by building a consensus for change. I suggest, moreover, that achieving any such consensus depends not only on the ideational content of the discourse—that is, on its ability to offer convincing arguments about the necessity and appropriateness of the policy programme—but also on the interactive process by which the discourse enables policy actors to coordinate the construction of their policy programme and political actors to communicate it to the general public. Different institutional contexts, however, frame the discourse, with countries in which policy construction tends to be the domain of a relatively restricted elite, such as Britain and France, more focused on communication to the general public than in countries such as Germany where policy construction is the domain of a wider set of policy actors, and the discourse is focused more on coordinating their interaction than on communicating to the wider public. Finally, I theorize about the causal influence of discourse: that is, when discourse matters over and above the interplay of interests, institutions, and culture in different discursive contexts. I argue that causal influence in countries where the communicative discourse predominates can best be seen after a new policy programme is instituted, in opinion shifts and policy continuity over time. By contrast, where the coordinative discourse predominates the discourse's influence is apparent more immediately, in whether policies are instituted in the first place.

The second chapter in this part demonstrates why discourse matters by showing how, where, and when it matters in the political dynamics of adjustment in Britain, France, and Germany. In Britain, the communicative discourse of a government of the right proved transformative early on, having served so successfully to legitimize the radical neo-liberal policy programme begun in 1979 in terms of necessity and appropriateness that the programme and the discourse are now in the process of renewal by a government of the left. In France, by contrast, governments of both the right and the left managed to convince the public of the necessity of the moderate neo-liberal policy programme begun in 1983 but not of its appropriateness, and remained in search of a sufficiently legitimizing communicative discourse until at least the late 1990s. In Germany, finally, governments of both the right and the left have had trouble generating, let alone legitimizing, change in the post-war policy programme largely because of their difficulties in recasting the coordinative discourse in such a way as to convince principal policy actors, let alone the public, of either the necessity or the appropriateness of such reform.

Overall, I argue substantively that all three countries started in different places, had different trajectories, and ended up in different places, with globalization and Europeanization having had a differential impact. Britain adjusted early to the pressures of globalization and thereby anticipated many of the policies later promoted by the EU, went farther in the direction of its traditional market capitalism, and was successful in this in part because of a transformative discourse that served to legitimize changes in policies and practices. Germany, by contrast, was little affected by the pressures of either globalization or Europeanization until comparatively late, continued to hold to the post-war model of managed capitalism until very recently, and is only now in the process of trying to recast its post-war discourse in order to legitimize change, without much success. Finally, France underwent tremendous policy adjustment in response to the pressures of both globalization and Europeanization and transformed its post-war model of state capitalism, although without the benefit of a sufficiently legitimizing discourse until very recently.

The book is methodologically diverse. Parts I and II could be seen mainly as historical institutionalist analyses of the characteristics and development of different European member states' political economic policies and practices with soft rational-choice institutionalist assumptions about the interest-motivated basis of such policies and practices and sociological institutionalist references to the differing cultural norms informing those policies and practices as well as perceptions of interest. All chapters herein deliberately use a mix of approaches because, in my view, when one's inquiry is focused on the explanation of a complex reality as opposed to, say, finding cases to prove a theory or demonstrate a methodology, one needs to use as many methods as are appropriate to a full exploration of the issues—and different methods tend to ask different kinds of questions and to provide different kinds of insights into reality. After all, we need not only to understand the interests that may motivate action but also the cultural norms and values that serve to constitute those interests and the institutional arrangements that constrain or enable the expression of those interests.

One thing is missing, however. In the explanation of political economic change, one needs to understand not only the interests that inform policies and practices, the institutions that shape them, and the cultures that frame them but also the ideas and discourses that serve to reconceptualize interests, reshape institutions, and reframe cultures.

It is in this light that I propose a new framework for the analysis of discourse in Part III to get at the politics of economic adjustment. I seek to go beyond the three institutionalisms, whether rational choice, historical, or sociological institutionalism, finding that accounts primarily in terms of interests, institutions, or culture fail to explain the dynamics of change, which can better be explored by way of an approach focused on the discursive bases of action. I chose to develop my own analytic framework, moreover, rather than rely on one or another approach in the growing literature on ideas and discourse, because most such studies seem either too limited in what they are trying to explain or too normative in their approach.

In using such a highly loaded term as 'discourse' for my central concept, I am admittedly walking into a minefield, given the wide range of philosophers and social scientists with very different definitions and purposes who also employ the term—and I therefore use it with some trepidation. But I do believe that I avoid any major misunderstandings by providing a clear definition of my use of the term, by illustrating its methodological usefulness in the elaboration of the cases of France, Britain, and Germany, by showing empirically how, where, and when discourse exerts—or fails to exert—an influence over political economic change, and by providing evidence not only of the discourse itself, that is, what is said in political speeches, party platforms, government pronouncements, opposition positions, public debates, and media commentary, but also evidence of its effect, through such things as electoral results, opinion surveys, experts' commentaries, negotiated agreements among policy actors, and so forth. My approach to discourse is not in and of itself a theory but, rather, has the same epistemological status as rational-choice, historical, or sociological institutionalism, that is, as a descriptive language or analytic framework that allows one to identify, describe, and analyse important phenomena when they occur, that applies only under certain conditions, and for which theories can be developed and tested. As such, I find it useful to call my approach 'discursive institutionalism' in order to distinguish it from the vast range of other approaches to discourse analysis and to situate it alongside the other 'new institutionalist' approaches to explanation in political science.

The book, in short, seeks to take an innovative approach to the systematic comparison of the economic adjustment of European countries in response to globalization and Europeanization by developing theoretical arguments using different methodologies spanning a number of fields in political science along three dimensions—policies, practices, and politics. The innovation was, in many ways, forced upon me by the very complexity of the task I set for myself.

In works focused on single countries, questions of change in political-economic policies, practices, and politics tend to be mixed together in a narrative of development over time. But where one's object is to compare two, three, or more countries at three different levels of economic and political activity—global, European, and national—one does best to separate one or another dimension for comparison, whether policies, practices, or politics. The problem is that these three dimensions are interdependent, and one cannot understand any one dimension fully, let alone the limits of its explanatory capacity, without reference to the other two. After all, one cannot fully explain changes in policies without knowing the politics behind them or the practices that follow from them; changes in practices without knowing the changes in policies that precede them or the changing politics that they presuppose; and changes in politics without knowing what changes in policies and practices are on offer. Moreover, policies without politics may impute an interest-based rationality and path-dependency to decisions that obscures the paths not taken and the culturally embedded reasons for action or non-action; practices without policies or politics may make change appear economically determined and path-dependent; and politics without policies or practices may bring in ideas and discourse without acknowledging the economic factors that act as an impetus to or brake on change, the institutional contexts that constrain or enable actors, and the 'objective' interests that may motivate actors, regardless of the ideas or discourse.

In what follows, we shall see how well I managed to separate the three dimensions while demonstrating their interdependence. My goal is to show that, while the separation of these three dimensions provides for greater clarity theoretically and empirically, all three dimensions are necessary to gain a full understanding of the impact of globalization and Europeanization on Britain, Germany, and France.

PART I

The Policies of Economic Adjustment

The Challenges of Globalization and Europeanization: The Impact on National Autonomy and Control

As a term, globalization has often been left vague and undefined, better to conjure up the large panoply of forces that have seemingly imposed similar imperatives across advanced industrialized countries. These forces may be understood primarily in terms of the economic pressures stemming from the internationalization of the financial markets and trade and the rise of global corporations; the institutional pressures emerging from the rules and rulings of supranational trade organizations and collective actors; and/or the ideas circulating worldwide that present those economic or institutional forces as imperatives for change. But whether seen mainly as a set of economic, institutional, or ideational forces, globalization has served as a major rationale for governments to alter their countries' monetary policies by focusing on tight budgets, low inflation, and caps on public debt, deficits, and spending; their industrial policies by liberalizing the financial markets, deregulating the rules governing business, and privatizing public sector firms; and their social policies by cutting social spending, rationalizing social services, and increasing flexibility in labour markets.

In consequence of globalization, governments have given up significant amounts of national autonomy—that is, their ability to make decisions independently, without regard to external economic forces and actors—and national control—that is, their power to influence economic forces and actors operating in the national territory, whether externally or internally based. But they have also in many instances managed to retain or regain control over those forces and actors. They have done this individually through national regulation as well as through their influence over global economic actors, given such actors' continued national grounding politically, culturally, economically, and managerially. And they have done it collectively through supranational economic governance institutions and collective actors which, although undoubtedly a further source of loss of national autonomy, in exchange provide greater shared supranational authority and shared control.

The loss of national autonomy as well as of control in consequence of global forces and institutions, however, differs in relationship to how much countries share in the decisions of supranational authorities and feel the effects of their control. The loss is minimal when the decisions are taken by governments in the context of international or EU treaty negotiations and supranational bodies, and only slightly more when the decisions are negotiated in conjunction with global or European collective actors. It is much greater when the decisions are the result of delegated powers that such supranational bodies exercise without national governments' direct participation; and greatest when by arbitration and evaluation bodies outside of any official, internationally agreed governance structures. But it also differs among countries, given that countries have liberalized to differing degrees and with differing effects, as will be explored in greater detail in the cases of Britain, Germany, and France in Chapter 2.

For European member states, Europeanization has represented an even more potent panoply of forces for change than globalization, apart from it as well as a part of it. As a set of economic pressures, Europeanization has acted both as a conduit for global forces and as a shield against them, opening member states to international competition in the capital and product markets at the same time as they protect them through monetary integration and the Single Market. As a set of institutional pressures, the European Union has gone way beyond any other international or regional economic authority with regard to the vast array of rules and rulings affecting its member states. And as a set of ideas, European integration has been driven by a common political project for economic liberalization which has been much more compelling than that of any other regional grouping of countries in the world, and which has served as a complement to the liberalizing ideas related to globalization.

European monetary integration has produced convergence in the monetary policy arena, as all member states have moved away from neo-Keynesianism toward monetarism and as most have given up national currencies and dependent monetary authorities for a single currency and independent central banks under the European Central Bank. European market integration has promoted liberalization in the industrial policy arena through EU competition policy, product harmonization, and deregulation for member states which have themselves been deregulating and privatizing also in response to global pressures. And together, these initiatives have had major spillover effects in the social policy arena, where pressures have been building to reduce social costs and for common action to increase flexibility in the labour market.

For members of the European Union, in consequence, Europeanization has not only entailed a much greater loss of national autonomy and control than for countries exposed mainly to global pressures or participating in other regional trade associations, given the greater reduction in the exclusivity and scope of national executives' decision-making. It has also ensured that these losses have been offset by much greater gains in shared supranational authority and control. The European Union has gone way beyond any other supranational economic governance organization in fostering a set of common rules governing member states' monetary and industrial policies—although not their social policies, which remain mostly within the competencies of the nation-state. Its impact on national autonomy and control, moreover, has also varied with the degree to which the exercise of supranational authority and control are shared.

This is not to suggest, however, that European member states are all converging on a single liberalized policy regime with identical sets of policies and policy-making institutions, led by the EU. Much the contrary. To begin with, European policies have tended to follow national policy responses to globalization as much as lead them, with national policies having shaped those of the EU as often as EU policies have shaped those of its member states. Moreover, despite EU policies that tend to push all member states in the same direction, national economic policy adjustment remains nationally specific and path-dependent—as will be shown in Chapter 2.

To illustrate this, in what follows we first consider globalization, in terms of both its scope and the debates about its impact, before examining in greater detail what has been lost in national autonomy and control as well as what has been retained or regained by countries individually and/or collectively through shared supranational authority and control. Next, we consider Europeanization, as the domestic impact of EU-level decision-making, by differentiating it first from globalization and second from European integration, in order then to discuss the trade-offs between losses of national autonomy and control and gains in shared supranational EU authority and control. Finally, we examine in detail the differential impact of globalization and Europeanization on policy-making in three EU member states: Britain, Germany, and France.

Globalization

At the end of the Second World War, globalization, understood at the time as the internationalization of world trade, was portrayed by many government policy-makers as an unquestioned good. The economic benefits were seen as almost boundless: growing prosperity for all would follow from increasing business efficiencies, investment opportunities, and competitiveness that would guarantee consumers products at lower prices, higher quality, and greater variety, with trans-national corporations in particular the vehicles to maximize 'the general well-being' (Wilkinson 1993: 28). The perceived political benefits were, if anything, even grander. Trade liberalization was to help ensure peace, as a frontal attack on the institution of national economic sovereignty which Albert O. Hirschman, as early as 1942, described as 'at the root of the possible use of international economic relations for national power aims' and therefore to 'be taken away from the hands of single nations' and transferred instead to an international authority (Hirschman 1980: 79–80). For the United States, the hegemonic power in the post-war period, trade liberalization as a guarantor of peace was the guiding idea behind foreign economic policy efforts and part of the fight against communism.

In the early post-war years, globalization was linked to the push for freer trade, promoted by the institutions of the General Agreement on Tariffs and Trade (GATT) and the International Monetary Fund (IMF), and justified as a means to end war and to fight communism. Today, globalization refers to the tremendous expansion of the financial markets dominated by new, non-governmental actors in the form of institutional investors, and the exponential growth of international trade dominated by seemingly 'stateless' multinational corporations. It continues to be promoted institutionally not only by the IMF and the World Trade Organization (WTO), successor to the GATT, but also through the plethora of international treaties, treaty organizations, professional associations, non-governmental bodies, and coordinated governmental actions that seek to bring some order to the international arena, even as its ideological justification died with the fall of the Berlin Wall. And it has come to mean many different things to different people.

Whereas some characterize globalization as unique in history (Held *et al.* 1999: 429), others find it a continuation of processes of internationalization interrupted by the two world wars (Bairoch 1996; Hirst and Thompson 1996). While some present it is as inexorable, as an external constraint producing desired or undesired outcomes, for others it is contingent, as an opportunity to be seized or a threat to be resisted (see Hay and Rosamund 2000). But whether as unique or more of the same, as inexorable or contingent, or as constraint or opportunity, globalization has increasingly been portrayed by governments of the left as much as the right as imposing a neo-liberal logic of the market for which there is little alternative.[1] Globalization seems to prescribe certain kinds of policies, primarily the low government deficits, debts, and inflation that are the cornerstones of monetarist policies, as well as deregulation, privatization, decentralization of labour markets, and welfare state retrenchment. And it appears to proscribe others, in particular neo-Keynesian monetary policy, government interventionism, high taxes, and high welfare-state spending. The question is: To what extent is this true? How much does globalization really circumscribe government's freedom of action? And what, if any, margin for manoeuvre is left?

Globalization and the Loss of National Autonomy and Control

Although scholars are divided over how to interpret the impact of globalization, there is little dispute over the facts related to increasing economic interdependence and internationalization of finance and trade. Globalization is first and foremost embodied in the exponential growth in the international financial markets, which have increased in magnitude, speed, and volatility while at the same time decreasing national governments' ability to control their effects. Financial globalization encompasses the rapidly expanding currency markets that in the 1970s were traded around $10–$20 billion but by 1996 traded at $1.3 trillion a day and by 1998 at $1.5 trillion; the burgeoning securities markets where the Dow Jones industrial average of the New York Stock Exchange went from 2,000 in 1987 to over the 10,000 mark in 1999; the explosive growth in cross-border transactions in bonds and equities which grew from 10 per cent of GDP in G7 countries in 1980 to more than 140 per cent in 1995; the international bank lending that grew from $265 billion in 1975 to $4.2 trillion in 1994; and the private capital flows that went from almost nothing in the 1960s to $890 billion in net new issues of international loans and bonds in 1997 (OECD 1998; UNCTAD 1997). It also includes the rise of a new, more demanding and powerful kind of institutional investor, primarily pension funds, mutual funds, and insurance companies, which in Europe expanded by 17 per cent between 1981 and 1991, to reach $3,500 billion; in North America, by 15 per cent to reach $6,400 billion; and in Japan by 24 per cent to attain $1,800 billion (OECD 1993). The influence of these institutional investors is increasingly felt in the currency markets as they demand that governments set more realistic values for their currencies or face a run on their money, and in the capital markets as they demand that firms provide not only a reasonable return on investment but

---

[1] See the discussions in Hay and Marsh (2000); Hay and Watson (1998); Weiss (1997); Zysman (1996); Kayatekin and Ruccio (1998).

also greater transparency and conformity with certain standards of corporate governance or face losses in share value and takeover threats (Useem 1996).

Globalization is also embodied in the explosion of international trade which has diminished national governments' ability to control economic actors and transactions in their own territory, let alone elsewhere, at the same time as it has heightened their awareness of the need to increase the international competitiveness of their businesses and their country's attract-iveness as an investment site. Globalization of trade encompasses the increasingly competitive product markets in which world trade tripled between 1960 and 1973 and sextupled between 1973 and 1989, from $0.574 trillion to $3.47 trillion, reaching over $6 trillion by 1996. It includes the growing competition for investment capital, with foreign direct investment stocks having nearly quadrupled in the 1980s, to reach $2 trillion in 1990, and tripled in the 1990s to $6 trillion in 2000. At the same time, foreign direct investment flows went from $60 billion in 1979 to $210 billion in 1989 to $860 billion in 1999 and topped $1.2 trillion in 2000 (UNCTAD 2001). It is also evident in the growing size, scope, and power of multinational firms as well as in the dispersion of their production locations and the diversification of their ownership. By 1993, the top 300 multinationals controlled approxi-mately 25 per cent of the world's $20 trillion stock of productive asset and the top 500 controlled two-thirds of world trade. By 1999, there were over 60,000 multinationals with over 820,000 foreign affiliates. By 2000, the worldwide annual sales of their foreign affiliates was over $15.5 trillion, up from below $2.5 trillion in 1982. Moreover, cross-border mergers and acquisitions have multiplied at an astronomical speed even in the 1990s, having gone from about $70 billion in 1992 to $236 billion by 1997, and to $1.1 trillion in 2000, with 175 transactions at over $1 billion (UNCTAD 1999, 2001). The influence of these multinationals is felt in the product markets, as they increase com-petitive pressures for all firms in terms of price and quality of goods, and in national capitals, as they press for lower taxes and better services on threat of exit.

Scholars, experts, journalists, and others have been tremendously divided over the impact of these global market forces on national sovereignty, in par-ticular when understood in terms of autonomy in national decision-making and control over economic forces and actors operating nationally. While radical globalists insist that national sovereignty has been irretrievably lost because of the transformation of the world economy, which represents a difference in kind and not just degree from the past,[2] sceptics contend that

---

[2] See, for example, Cerny (1994); Strange (1986); Wriston (1998); Greenspan (1998).

the degree of internationalization was as great if not greater in the late nineteenth century than at the end of the twentieth while sovereignty is not any more threatened now than it has been in the past.[3] With the exception of the early post-war years for the more advanced industrialized countries, so the argument goes, state sovereignty has always been under assault, whether sovereignty is understood as the government's international recognition by other states, or 'international law sovereignty'; its power to organize authority within the polity, or 'domestic sovereignty'; its ability to control activities within and across its borders, or 'interdependence sovereignty'; or its autonomy with regard to the exclusion of external authority, or 'Westphalian sovereignty' (Krasner 1999). The post-war period is quite an exception to make, however, since national autonomy and control—the most important aspects of sovereignty for our purposes—have in fact been appreciably reduced since the early 1950s, when governments could make decisions largely independently of external economic forces and could exert significant control over economic actors in the national economy, protected from financial market volatility by capital controls on currencies that were fixed in relation to the dollar by the Bretton Woods agreement and from strong competitive pressures by high protectionist barriers. But the question then remains as to how much autonomy and control has been lost since the height of post-war state sovereignty.

Radical globalists argue that globalization has so reduced sovereignty understood as national autonomy by eroding from within and without 'the authority, legitimacy, policymaking capacity, and policy-implementing effectiveness of the state' (Cerny 1995: 621) that there is no longer much difference between governments of the left and the right in terms of their liberalizing, budget-cutting policies (Strange 1995) and little to stop them from engaging in a 'race to the bottom' in regulatory policies (Cerny 1994). In response, sceptics insist that policy choices remain almost as open as they did before, arguing that deregulation does not mean no rules, just different rules;[4] that financial openness correlates with more taxation and public spending rather than less (Quinn 1997); that trade openness also correlates with increases rather than decreases in government spending;[5] and that governments of the left are largely able to pursue their traditionally redistributive goals (Garrett 1998b). Moreover, whereas sceptics also argue that sovereignty understood as national control is not lost because international

---

[3] See, for example, Hirst and Thompson (1996: 36); Bairoch (1996: 183); Bairoch and Kozul-Wright (1996).   [4] See, for example, Moran (1991); S. Vogel (1996); Trachtman (1993).

[5] See, for example, Boix (1998); Garrett and Mitchell (2001); Rodrik (1998).

organizations have served to reassert some degree of shared control over economic forces and actors,[6] the more radical globalists see this as just yet another source of undifferentiated loss of national autonomy[7] while more moderate globalists take this as proof of the transformation of state, given the division of state authority and the shifting of power to a wider range of actors and institutions at national and supranational levels.[8] In addition, while the radicals insist that governments have lost both the autonomy and control necessary to maintain the post-war commitments of the welfare state in the face of global forces that have eroded welfare entitlements and workers' rights while promoting inequality and unemployment,[9] the sceptics respond that globalization has little to do with the problems of the welfare state— which can be better explained by changing demographics, new technologies and forms of work organization, or internal economics and politics—and that the welfare state has in any case changed very little so far.[10] Finally, whereas radical globalists hail the arrival of the 'stateless' corporation as proof that governments no longer have control over supranational economic actors[11] or deplore it as the cause of unions' decline in power,[12] sceptics insist that governments still have ample means of control over what goes on in their own territory or what their own multinationals do elsewhere, that the notion of the global corporation is a myth,[13] that unions' decline is better explained by technological changes,[14] and that unions have in any event declined significantly only in some countries.[15]

Reality is somewhere in between these extremes, with choice neither entirely constrained nor completely free, the loss of autonomy and control neither total nor negligible. Moreover, not all change can be attributed to the forces of globalization. As often as not, the changes blamed on outside global forces really come from the inside, with globalization used in the political discourse as a rhetorical device to justify reforms motivated by a wide variety of purely national forces interested in the liberalization of national eco-nomies (see Hay and Rosamund 2000). The pressures for deregulation, for

[6] See, for example, S. Vogel (1996); Kapstein (1994); Helleiner (1994).

[7] For example, Stopford and Strange (1991); Strange (1996).

[8] See, for example, Held *et al.* (1999: 188).

[9] See, for example, Caporaso (1987); Tilly (1995); Greider (1997); Krugman and Venables (1995); Clayton and Pontusson (1997); Mishra (1996).

[10] See, for example, Freeman (1995); Lawrence (1997); Notermans (1993); Pierson (1996; 1998). For an overview, see Rhodes (1996).   [11] See, for example, Holstein (1990); Ohmae (1990);

[12] See, for example, Reder and Ulman (1993); Rodrik (1997); McKeown (1999).

[13] See, for example, Doremus *et al.* (1998).

[14] See, for example, Moene and Wallerstein (1993); Streeck (1993); Pontusson and Swenson (1996).

[15] See, for example, Goldin, Wallerstein, and Lange (1999).

example, have had as much of an internal pull in the desire of national businesses, financial institutions, and/or regulators to liberalize domestic cartel-like structures as they have had an external push from international trade associations and collective actors (Sobel 1994). Neo-liberal ideas and ideology have also played a major role, as national governments influenced by neo-liberal thought have sought to open up national economies to global and European markets even before actors in, and regulators of, those markets were seen to be pressing for access and openness, and as internationalizing businesses sought to free themselves from capital controls (Goodman and Pauly 1993; Helleiner 1994). Margaret Thatcher in Great Britain is the case in point. Globalization, thus, can been seen as much as an opportunity for national actors to effect desired or needed changes as a constraint forcing undesired or otherwise unnecessary change (Weiss 2002).

The changes related to globalization, in other words, result from the complex interaction of liberalizing institutions and actors, spurred by liberal capitalist ideas, pushing and ultimately, a bit like the sorcerer's apprentice, pulled by external market forces, technological innovations in communications and transportation, and so on.[16] Although national governments, whether operating alone or in concert through supranational trade organizations, are largely responsible for instituting the liberalizing changes that made globalization possible, by eliminating capital controls, reducing tariff barriers, and deregulating markets, they are increasingly subject to the globalization pressures that they have themselves set loose.

But while sovereignty may therefore indeed have been reduced as a result of globalization, this represents less an absolute loss of sovereignty than an alteration in the exclusivity and scope of national governments' competence (Rosenau 1990). National competence remains to the extent that global processes occur within national territory and, whatever the deregulatory push, continue to depend upon national legal systems in the guaranteeing of contracts and the enforcement of private property rights (Sassen 1999, 1996). What is more, national governments and actors have also often reasserted control, either individually, through national means, or collectively, whether through international trade authorities that allow for shared control over the international economy or through regional trade authorities. Rather than antinomy, in other words, interdependence characterizes the relationship between supranational and national levels (Weiss 1999a).

---

[16] See, for example, Garrett (1995: 663); Freiden and Rogowski (1996); Goodman and Pauly (1993); Andrews (1994).

What Remains of National Autonomy

Individually, governments continue to exercise policy choice, even though such choice is no doubt more restricted than in the past. The state still has a role to play, just a different role, since globalization resulting from the internationalization of both the financial markets and trade has indeed reduced governments' margins for manoeuvre. Although governments have felt pressed to give up many of the monetary and industrial policy strategies, instruments, and regulations of the past, they still have many left at their disposal at the same time as they have added new ones. Moreover, although they have engaged in significant belt-tightening with regard to government spending, this has not prevented them from continuing to spend generously in differing ways on those programmes considered of continuing value by the public, in particular in the welfare arena.

What Has Been Lost

There can be little doubt that the internationalization of the financial markets resulting from the reduction in direct controls and taxes on capital movements, the liberalization of regulatory restrictions in national financial markets, and the expansion of offshore financial markets, combined with the introduction of new technologies in the process of financial intermediation, has produced differences in kind and not just degree from the past, as the radical globalists have argued. Financial globalization has served to promote capital mobility while weakening the protective barriers around national financial systems and diminishing government's ability to pursue independent macroeconomic management strategies.[17] Because governments have feared that negative reactions from the financial markets to expansionist, neo-Keynesian monetary policies would result in economic downturn, rising unemployment, decreases in income, and, ultimately, loss of their own popularity and legitimacy, they have felt pushed to balance national budgets, diminish social spending, rationalize public services, reduce public deficits, and guard against inflation.[18]

There can also be little doubt that the internationalization of trade related to the reduction in tariff and non-tariff barriers to trade, the deregulation of the rules governing business, and the privatization of state-owned enterprise, combined with the development of new technologies facilitating faster communications and lower transportation costs and the increasing capital mobility following from financial market liberalization, have also had a

---

[17] See, for example, Pauly (1995: 369); Webb (1991); Strange (1996: 294); Andrews (1994); Simmons (1998).   [18] See, for example, Boyer and Drache (1996); Cerny (1994); Helleiner (1994).

significant impact on national autonomy. They have served to promote business internationalization while weakening the protective barriers around domestic economies and diminishing government's ability to pursue independent microeconomic management strategies or expansive industrial policies. Because governments have been concerned by the increasingly fierce competition in the product markets as well as the growing importance of foreign direct investment, they have focused on improving the international competitiveness of national goods and services while making their countries attractive to foreign and domestic firms alike. In so doing, they have not only deregulated and privatized, they have also sought to reduce wage costs, income taxes, payroll taxes, tax on corporate profits, social security payments, health-care costs, and so forth.[19] These measures, in turn, have contributed to the crisis of the welfare state, although they are not the root cause, which comes not so much from globalization as from the increasing costs related to the ageing of the population and the indexation of social security benefits.

Given the pressures of globalization, moreover, national governments are also no longer able to use the wide range of policy instruments that they formerly employed without hesitation. These include measures such as monetary and fiscal reflation to combat recessions, tariffs and import quotas to protect national producers, government procurement policies to stimulate innovation, deficit-financed investment programmes, devaluation, subsidies to declining or growing industries, credit rationing and credit channelling through nationalized banks, nationalization of industry, or even generous early retirement, disability, and unemployment compensation schemes to ease adjustment problems.

What Has Been Retained or Gained

However, despite these clear restrictions on policy choice, governments still have a wide range of policy instruments left within the narrower range allowable. To promote business competitiveness, they can still support research and development, subsidize the education and training of the workforce, invest in infrastructure, engage in active labour market policies, and create a level playing field for business through competition policy and regulation (Garrett 1998a). To ensure that their economies remain globally competitive, governments can also still use means other than welfare state retrenchment or labour market deregulation, such as promoting private or public employment in the sheltered sectors to offset losses in the exposed sectors of the economy, as

---

[19] See, for example, Garrett and Lange (1991); Leibfried and Pierson (1995); Mishra (1996); Rodrik (1997); Stephens, Huber, and Ray (1999).

in the cases of Anglo-Saxon countries such as the UK and New Zealand with respect to private sector employment and of Scandinavian countries such as Denmark and Sweden with respect to public sector employment (Scharpf 1997c).

In exchange for these and other services, moreover, governments can and do continue to tax capital without suffering from massive exit. Although the marginal rates of corporate taxation have indeed declined since the 1970s, there appears to be little causal relationship between capital mobility and corporate taxation rates (Quinn 1997; Swank 1998; Garrett 1998b) or, indeed, with taxation more generally (Ganghoff 2000), while there is even some evidence to suggest that tax burdens on corporations in advanced industrialized countries have increased rather than declined (Hobson 2002). Moreover, trade openness does generally correlate with expansion in government spending rather than with reduced government spending, as the sceptics have argued, although unusually high levels of openness have also been associated with unusually large decreases in the size of government, while the partisan effects of left-leaning governments appear modest at best (see Cameron et al. 2000). Beyond this, however, it is very difficult to make reliable causal generalizations based on large-scale, time-pooled, cross-national, multi-variate analyses, given governments' varied and changing responses to external economic pressures over time. What smaller-scale, more fine-tuned, time-sensitive quantitative analysis of advanced welfare states shows is that governments still have significant—although more restricted—margins of manoeuvre, and that, rather than convergence towards any given set of policies or spending levels, countries have continued to differ widely in what they spend, in how they spend, and in how much they spend (Scharpf 2000b).

In fact, despite the constraints imposed by tighter budgets, countries can—and do—still spend a lot on the welfare state, even as they seek to contain costs; only when public debt has been exceedingly high—that is, above 100 per cent of GDP in the cases of Belgium and Italy—can globalization pressures related to strong capital mobility be shown to be an explanation for cuts in welfare provision (Swank 2000: 23). And they spend in different ways, given differences in claiming principles, beneficiaries, financing, and services as part of different constellations of welfare states (Esping-Andersen 1990). This in turn ensures that welfare states have been differentially affected by globalization, with some more vulnerable to globalization pressures than others.[20] There is evidence to suggest that, despite the general

[20] See, for example, Bowles and Wagman (1997); Gough (1996).

trend to attempt to rationalize the welfare state, the extent of reform tends to remain in keeping with nationally based, historically endorsed attitudes toward the proper role of government, ensuring that countries that tolerated comparatively high levels of interventionism in the social policy arena in the past—for example, Italy or Germany—continue to approve of higher levels of interventionism—for instance, in government responsibility to provide jobs for all—than those that tolerated much lower levels of state interventionism—for example, the United States and Britain (Döring 1994). Moreover, the pattern of reform, whether towards greater fiscal tightening or stronger social protection, tends to depend not only on pre-existing welfare state arrangements but also on the domestic political and institutional context.[21]

There is no convergence in the welfare arena. Rather than all countries following the path taken by Anglo-Saxon countries and moving toward a 'liberal' welfare state model, with low social benefits and services and an emphasis on individual responsibility, most non-Anglo-Saxon countries retain the basic features of their traditional models even as they introduce liberalizing measures. The Scandinavian countries have remained true to the social-democratic model by respecting values of equality and universality of provision while maintaining a high level of benefits and services despite cuts in benefits and the introduction of user fees. And although Continental European countries have reformed their conservative model to varying degrees in different ways, all have retained their reasonably high level of benefits and sense of collective responsibility even as they have introduced some degree of individual recourse through pension reform (Schmidt 2000b). Poverty remains a problem primarily in the Anglo-Saxon countries, where social transfers do not bring the poverty level down as much as in the more generous Continental and Scandinavian countries (see Fig. 1.1 and discussion in Chapter 2). In Continental countries, by contrast, the problem is unemployment (see Fig. 1.2), due to much greater labour-market rigidities than in Anglo-Saxon or Scandinavian countries. For the Scandinavian countries, the problem is instead maintaining the welfare state at such a high level (see Scharpf 2000b). Within all three welfare state models, moreover, it is possible to identify ones that have reached a new sustainable equilibrium without having abandoned long-standing welfare state commitments and values of social justice: among Anglo-Saxon 'liberal' welfare states, Australia; among Scandinavian social-democratic welfare states, Denmark; and among Continental Christian-democratic welfare states, the Netherlands (Scharpf and Schmidt 2000).

---

[21] See, for example, Hemerijck and Schludi (2000); Swank (2002); Stephens, Huber, and Ray (1999).

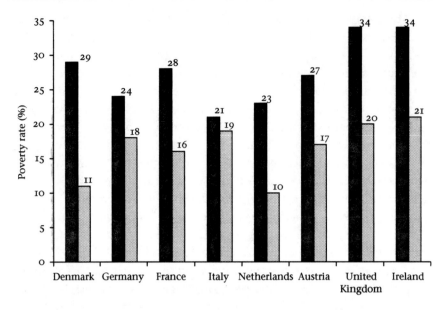

Fig. 1.1 Poverty levels and the effects of social transfers in selected EU welfare states, 1997

Anglo-Saxon (UK and Ireland), Scandinavian (Denmark), and Continental (Germany, France, Italy, the Netherlands, and Austria). Poverty rates (%) before and after social transfers with the exception of pensions; poverty is defined as income less than 60% of the median income in Europe.

Source: Eurostat (1999).

Even in those areas where national governments have clearly liberalized in similar ways in response to global pressures, such as deregulation in the financial markets, this has not meant that they have lost authority, legitimacy, or regulatory capacity. For although governments deregulated by eliminating rules limiting access and restricting tradeable instruments, they also re-regulated by replacing less formal systems of self-regulation with more formal institutionalized and codified rules enforced by regulatory agencies, supervisory bodies, or the courts in the interests of investor protection (Moran 1991; S. Vogel 1996). For the stock markets, for example, deregulation was accompanied in Britain by the establishment of a new regulatory system based on public law, in France by a structure akin to the US Securities and Exchange Commission, and in Germany by a federal agency (see Chapter 2).

The impact of globalization, in brief, has been highly differentiated. And although countries' range of economic policy choices did become more restricted, with some loss of autonomy, all managed to either retain or regain control over their economies in a variety of different ways. This was also true with respect to government control over economic actors.

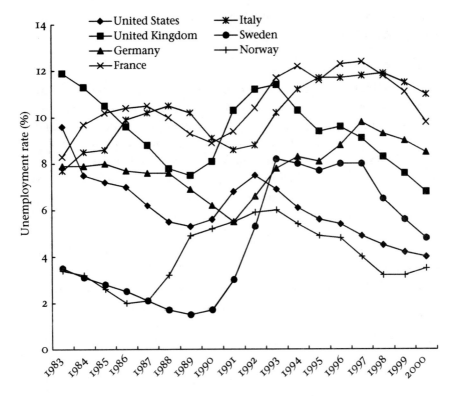

Fig. 1.2 Unemployment rates in selected EU states, 1983–2000

Commonly used definitions, in Anglo-Saxon (US, UK), Continental (Germany, France, Italy), and Scandinavian (Sweden, Norway) welfare states.

Source: OECD (2000: Statistical Annex, Table 21).

What Remains of National Control

Despite the fact that governments have indeed lost some measure of control over supranational economic actors, such actors are neither as footloose nor as fancy-free as much of the globalization literature suggests. The state, here too, still has a role to play, but again often a different role following deregulation and privatization. Moreover, although the close ties of business with governments and/or labour have in many cases eroded, multinationals nevertheless remain connected to the nation-state as a result of continuing political linkages, cultural traits, and economic base. And national environments still matter. National firms continue to vary in their levels of exposure to market pressures, in their operational practices, and in their corporate cultures; national wage-bargaining systems in their levels of coordination and decentralization; and national regulatory environments in the ways in which they inform corporate practices.

What Has Been Lost

There can be little doubt that multinational businesses have become increasingly 'stateless' (Holstein 1990) both because they are much harder for country of origin to control as they have grown in size and scope (Ohmae 1990) and because they are much more difficult to categorize by national origin in terms of either ownership or products (Reich 1991). But there is actually little new in this argument. Already in the 1960s and 1970s, scholars had hailed the rise of a new trans-national corporation that was losing all national identification as it was escaping nation-state control,[22] whether for better—because prosperity would increase outward from rich countries to less developed ones—or for worse—because wealth would instead flow from the periphery to the centre, and in particular to the United States, given the predominance of American multinationals.[23] Very quickly, however, scholars themselves found that the view of the overarching power of the multinational corporation and the concomitant decline of the nation-state was overstated. Much of it overestimated the power of the multinational corporation, underestimated the ability of the nation-state to regain control through constraints imposed by home and host country alike—for example, limits on rights to do business, special conditions for entry, buy-at-home preferences, public procurement policies, tax measures, anti-foreign bribery laws, even nationalization—and exaggerated the significance of the American ownership of multinationals.[24]

The predictions of the 1970s appear more relevant today. While home and host countries have been giving up their traditional controls over business in a wide range of areas in response to international and regional trade agreements as well as internal reform initiatives, big business has grown even larger and more global than ever before, although also more numerous and disparate in ownership. Whereas in 1970, the UN Center on Transnationals found that more than half of the 7,000 multinationals were American or British, by the early 1990s fewer than half of the now 35,000 multinationals were American, Japanese, German, or Swiss (Barnet and Cavanagh 1994: 423). And they have merged, formed joint ventures, and acquired one

---

[22] See, for example, Haas (1964); Kindleberger (1970); Vernon (1971); Cooper (1968); Galbraith (1969).

[23] On the positive arguments, see Ball (1967). On the negative, see Hymer (1972); Servan-Schreiber (1967).   [24] See Gilpin (1975: Ch. 9); Vernon (1985).

another with dizzying speed, creating cross-border alliances and international networks of firms representing the 'new competition' (Best 1990), 'alliance capitalism' (Dunning 1993), or 'post-modern global networks' (Kobrin 1997; Kogut, Shan, and Walker 1993). What is more, globalization encompasses not just the biggest corporations but also countless small and medium-sized firms (SMEs) which have been integrated into production and distribution networks globally (Castells 1996; Gereffi and Korzeniewicz 1994).

These changes in multinational business size and scope, together with their access to alternative sources of financial support through the liberalized capital market, have led to an increasing loss of loyalty to home country when it comes to jobs and operations, as multinationals relocate with an eye to lower taxes and lower wages. Business also has a greater ability to evade burdensome taxes in home and host country, in particular through transfer pricing—by posting profits or losses in countries where tax laws are beneficial to the company, although governments have taken companies to court for this: for example, Japan vs Coca Cola and Hoechst, the US vs Toyota. It has also been able to gain concessions from government and labour on threat of exit—a noteworthy case being Maytag in 1993, which closed its French Hoover vacuum-cleaner plant to move to Scotland while wringing concessions from the Scottish unions with threats to move back to France.

Moreover, as business has grown more powerful and more mobile, it has had less need of the post-war compromises brokered with governments and/or labour that aimed at maintaining national economic growth and political stability through jobs and incomes policies. In fact, while business has strengthened, labour has weakened for a variety of reasons. First, it is much less mobilizable trans-nationally than capital. Second, it is much less mobile than capital. Even in the EU, where the Single Market Act established the free movement not only of capital, goods, and services but also of people, capital mobility has far outstripped that of labour because language, culture, and family ties weigh heavily against movement, especially in the richer member states. And labour has had difficulty organizing itself at the EU level as a counterbalance to business (Ross 2000). Third, labour has lost bargaining power not only as a result of the increasing mobility of business but also because unions have been on the decline and workers generally much less militant than in the past. In many countries, this has been because they have been unwilling to risk their jobs at a time of continuing high unemployment (Marginson and Sisson 1994). Finally, labour for the most part can no longer count on government as a protector, partner, or arbitrator in its relations with business. As governments have liberalized, they have often cut off the umbilical cord with labour, although some, such as the Thatcher government with the miners' strike, have done so more brutally than others. In most advanced industrialized countries, labour has seen the end of centralized wage bargaining and the increase in wage differentials resulting from company-level negotiations. But even in countries where sector-wide wage negotiations continue, the contracts are much more flexible and often focused at the regional level, with plant-level agreements gaining greater currency (Martin and Ross 1999; Thelen 2001; and see Chapter 3).

What Has Been Retained or Gained

For all this, however, business has not become nearly as unfettered or as 'stateless' as has sometimes been argued. Although governments' traditional hold over multinational businesses for which they are either home or host country has diminished with the increasing dispersion of multinational corporations' operations, their loss of loyalty when it comes to jobs and operations, and their ability to avoid taxes, it has not disappeared. However internationalized MNCs may have become, operations are one thing, control another. The long-standing ties between multinationals and their home country continue, as do the differences between multinationals from different countries. And therefore, although national governments' control of business has indeed been loosening, significant amounts remain, with the national 'pull' offsetting much of the global 'push'.

First, all multinational enterprises retain national cultures and identity, if only in terms of leadership and control. American multinationals such as IBM Europe or Ford of Europe remain culturally American, and their top managers and directors remain mostly American despite close to 50 years in the world arena, even if foreign nationals tend to head subsidiaries: for example, in 1991 only 2.1 per cent of board members of major American companies were foreigners (*The Economist*, 6 February 1993: 69). Similarly, moreover, French multinationals remain distinctly French in culture and nationality, with French CEOs tied into top governmental circuits of power as products of elite state educational institutions who share the same set of norms, values, and sense of French interests (Schmidt 1996). German firms remain German, with German CEOs tied into the tripartite set of relations with labour and government that have made many firms more reluctant until very recently to move operations abroad. And British firms remain British, even though their CEOs are not always British, their operations are often highly international, and they are generally willing to move offshore (Egan 1997). The British, in fact, together with the Americans, tend to be better than the French and the Germans in terms of cultural diversity, to say nothing of the Japanese, where the lack of hiring of foreign managers has been a real 'Achilles heel' (Bartlett and Yoshihara 1988; Rosenzweig 1994). By the early 2000s, however, the rash of mega-mergers had made it more difficult to pin point the identity and culture of multinationals where top management and the board were from one country while the main money-making operations were in another, as in the case of Vivendi and Universal Studios.

Second, multinationals remain tied to national economic contexts through national political linkages, if only to gain government favours, whether in the form of subsidies, export support, or international leverage. Generally, the corporation has a special relationship with the home country which enables it to count on the government to come to its aid to protect existing markets and to help it penetrate new ones. This includes not only the United States— its offensive for the American movie industry against the French in the GATT negotiations being a recent example—but also that great defender of laissez-faire capitalism, Margaret Thatcher, when it came to pitching British companies' products abroad.

Third, the national environment continues to affect business competitiveness and to inform firm practice. Even such a simple thing as the home country's incorporation laws and tax laws continues to have a major impact on how multinationals operate: for example, Japan's high tax on profits that leads Japanese firms to concentrate on gaining market share, not profits; America's tax laws that favour debt over equity and also encourage exporting operations overseas; or Germany's 50 per cent tax on capital gains that has ensured industrial firms 'patient capital' from banks unable to divest themselves of large portfolios of company stocks—although this changed as of 2002. But, more importantly, the national economic environment even influences business vulnerability to global market pressures.

Although the expansion of the capital markets has made a big difference to business generally, providing ready access to new capital and diminishing industry dependence on banks and governments for loans or subsidies, market pressures on firms still vary significantly from one country to the next. This is because of the greater market capitalization of firms in countries that have long had access to larger, more active national financial markets and have therefore tended to gain their funding principally from the markets—that is, the UK and the US. This is in contrast to firms in countries with smaller financial markets that traditionally gained financing from strong banks—for example, Germany—or interventionist states—for example, France—which have only relatively recently moved toward greater market financing (see Chapters 3 and 4). Moreover, although financial market pressures have certainly been increasing for these countries as well, the more concentrated structure of ownership ensures that they are less exposed to those pressures not only with regard to the threat of takeover but also with respect to corporate governance in terms of demands for transparency and attention to shareholder value.

The national context even influences production practices, which do not necessarily all converge on a single 'best practice', despite often general agreement on what that might constitute, because of country-specific institutional, organizational, and cultural realities (Streeck 1996). For example, despite the fact that 'lean production', invented by Japanese firms and codified by American researchers, is generally acknowledged as the best manufacturing practice (Womack, Jones, and Roos 1991), Germany has not adopted it and could do so only with great difficulty. This is because of differences in model of skill and work organization, in industrial relations system, in attachment of workers to employer and involvement of workers in the firm, and in managerial discretion and the discretion of firms over the organization of work. Germany retains instead its seemingly more cumbersome pattern of organizing industrial work which has, nevertheless, served it well, even if it is currently under siege (Streeck 1996; Finegold and Wagner 1997). For similar reasons, even though French governments and firms have long recognized the superiority of the German model of industrial relations and its employment training schemes based on apprenticeship programmes and on-the-job training and re-skilling, France has never successfully replicated it despite countless government-instituted attempts in employment and training programmes (Culpepper 2001, 2002).

The seeming inability of firms in one country to adopt the 'best practices' of others has a great deal to do with the 'economic governance regime', that is, the whole complex of institutional and group relationships which differ greatly from one country to the next. These national governance regimes, or national institutional contexts, play a major role in determining management–labour relations, whether conflictual as traditionally in Britain and France, or cooperative as in Germany and the smaller European countries. They also affect management goals, whether focused on making profits, as in the UK, or on gaining market share, as in Germany and Japan; inter-firm relations, whether individualistic—for example, Britain—or cooperative—for example, Germany; production values and techniques, managerial autonomy, and so on (Hollingsworth, Schmitter, and Streeck 1994; and see Chapters 3 and 4). These regimes not only determine business practice in given countries, they also set the management patterns from which multinationals tend to generalize when they internationalize. And they make a big difference to firm competitiveness and firm responses to the pressures of internationalization, given that the organizational culture of a multinational results from the interaction between sectoral contingencies and the country of origin's institutional environment (Porter 1990).

Global competitive pressures, moreover, have brought some change in these economic governance regimes, but not as much as might have been expected from neo-liberal globalization pressures. Although one may be able to talk of a 'global spirit of capitalism' in which networks are now seen to rule supreme and management techniques popularized by US business schools are the rage (Boltanski and Chiapello 1999), words are one thing and actions—even understandings—are another. Corporate culture, as noted above, remains highly differentiated, however managers may reconceptualize their strategies and techniques over time: for example, whether in favour of decentralized systems, flat hierarchies, or networks.

Similarly, whatever the globalization pressures for labour-market liberalization, national wage bargaining remains highly differentiated. Although some countries experienced an early and emphatic end to the old compromises with labour through the radical decentralization of their wage-bargaining systems—Britain and to a lesser extent France—others revised the old compromises and systems of coordination—for example, the Netherlands and Denmark—while yet others constructed new compromises, such as Italy.[25] In the latter countries, moreover, this was less the result of institutional path-dependencies or the threat of labour resistance than of employers' own need to maintain the cooperative labour relations essential to producing high-quality products on a just-in-time basis in tightly coupled production networks (Thelen and Kume 1999; Thelen 2001). Thus, rather than globalization leading toward convergence to a single neo-liberal, deregulated model of industrial relations, it has brought continuing if not increasing divergence.[26]

Nationally based culture, control, and practices are not the only factors ensuring close ties between a multinational firm and its country of origin, however. The country of origin also remains the principal source of capital, management, and labour for most multinationals, creating their primary environment. After all, most economies remain more national than international. Only a relatively small percentage of the national economies of the larger advanced industrialized industries actually depends on international trade. In Europe, although the average international trade share in 1990 was 28 per cent, 60 per cent of this was intra-European, leaving trade with the external world at 9 per cent, the same as the US, and not much above the pre-Second World War level (Krugman 1995: 327–62). By 2000, moreover, extra-European trade had only gone up to around 12 per cent.

But while country of origin remains the primary reference point for multinational firms, their increasing internationalization especially over the course

[25] See, for example, Dore, Boyer, and Mars (1994); Dore (1994); Scharpf (2000b). On Italy, see: Ferrera and Gualmini (2000); Locke and Baccaro (1999); Regini (1997).

[26] See, for example, Kitschelt et al. (1999); Iversen and Pontusson (2000); Regini (2000); Thelen (2001); and see Chapter 3.

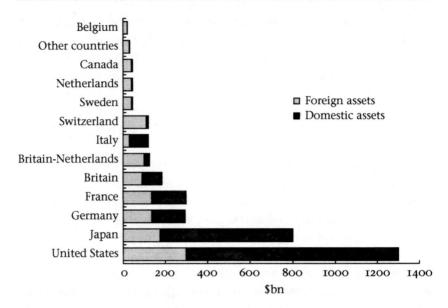

Fig. 1.3 Top 100 multinationals by home country, 1992
Source: UNCTAD 1993.

of the 1990s has reduced the weight of the national relative to the international. In the early 1990s, most of the largest multinational businesses still had most of their employees, assets, and shareholdings in their country of origin (Wade 1996; Hu 1992; Patel and Pavitt 1991). In 1992, among the top 100 multinationals, over two-thirds of the assets of US multinationals were domestic, approximately three-fourths of Japanese assets, and over half of German, French, and British-held—although British–Dutch multinationals had over three-fourths of theirs in foreign assets, also the pattern of Switzerland, Sweden, Holland, Canada, and Belgium (see Fig. 1.3). By 2000, however, the level of 'transnationality', meaning the ratio of foreign assets, sales, and employment to total assets, sales, and employment, had increased dramatically among the world's largest MNCs. Among the top 100, over half had a ratio above 50 per cent while only 10 had a transnationality ratio of under 25 per cent. The highest average scores were for European firms, with French firms leading with a ratio of 57.6 per cent followed by German and British firms at 49.6 per cent each, while US firms were trailing, at 42.7 per cent, as were Japanese firms, at 38.4 per cent (UNCTAD 2001, Tables III.1, III.5). The higher transnationality scores for French, British, and German firms are largely explainable by M&A activity in anticipation of the introduction of the Single Currency in the European Union, although these firms were equally active outside of the EU, primarily in the US. The extra-EU foreign direct investment flows between 1995 and 1999 closely matched the intra-EU flows, at an average of 52.18 per cent and 52.04 per cent respectively (UNCTAD 2001, Figure 1.8). This suggests that multinational firms still have a larger stake in their home country or, in the case of EU member-states, in the region, although they have indeed become much more transnational than in the past.

All of this taken together suggests that although the forces of globalization and Europeanization may press multinationals to be disloyal, they remain more vulnerable to national considerations than they might admit—even if less vulnerable than even a decade ago. It is telling that Renault, in response to European market pressures that dictated consolidation of its European operations, chose to close the then still-profitable but costly Vilvoorde plant in Belgium instead of two factories in France, which had been another unspoken but generally acknowledged option.

But is it then at least true that multinationals are less loyal to host countries? Even here, the answer is not so simple. Generally speaking, although businesses can refuse to invest in countries they deem over-regulated, once they have invested in a given country their mobility is much reduced since it is often relatively expensive for them to pick up and leave, given relations with suppliers, customers, local communities, and regional and national governments. For most companies—with the exception of those with the most routinized assembly operations—just-in-time production techniques that benefit from close proximity to suppliers and flexible specialization that benefits from close proximity to final markets make companies less footloose, not more so, because they ensure that they are less able to pull up roots once located somewhere, whether in home or host country (Wade 1996: 80–1). Equally importantly, businesses invest even in advanced industrialized countries with generous welfare states paid for by high tax rates, since these tend to be rich countries and as such are attractive locations for production (Baldwin and Krugman 2001). Such countries are also more likely to offer access to new technology, new distribution channels, new markets, new strategic alliances, as well as government services in stable environments, all of which are likely to offset concerns about higher taxes, even if this does have its limits.[27]

Thus, multinationals tend to remain tied not only to home country through management nationality, political ties, management culture, production practices, and source of revenues, assets, and employees, but also to host country through production techniques and market opportunities. In consequence, although national government control over multinationals operating in the national economy has indeed diminished, and national government autonomy in its policies toward multinationals has been reduced,

---

[27] See: Dunning (1988); Caves (1996); and Garrett (1998).

the losses of autonomy and control are not nearly as significant as some might argue, even if they cannot be ignored.

What is more, even if this were a slippery slope, and the current losses are only the beginning of a process of erosion that will one day make multinationals truly stateless, or even like states unto themselves, business would not end up entirely free and clear of national influence. This is because international competition remains 'powerfully conditioned' by national regulation not only in the financial markets but also in the various industrial sectors (S. Vogel 1997). National regulations still determine how companies can operate in the national arena, setting rules for competition, standards of performance, and product quality, as well as worker protections related to hiring, firing, promotion, affirmative action, and occupational safety and health. And more recent reforms, while perhaps not always constituting a form of competitive re-regulation where countries compete in regulatory subsidy by designing regulatory systems to favour national firms (Trachtman 1993), so far at least have not constituted a 'race to the bottom' through competitive deregulation, where all governments, whatever the regulatory reforms, scramble to reduce capital controls, moderate business rules, and reduce social protections in order to attract and retain global finance and business (S. Vogel 1997). In some sectors, in fact, instead of a 'race to the bottom' as a result of global pressures, there has been a 'race to the top', in many cases spurred by a US re-regulatory push akin to the 'California effect' (S. Vogel 1996; D. Vogel 1995).

Moreover, in many cases where governments can no longer exercise control individually, they have regained some shared control through the supranational authority represented by global and regional governance institutions (see Rosenau 1995; Rosenau and Czempiel 1992). However, it is a control that does come at a price, since it often serves to undermine further national governments' autonomy.

The Gains in Shared Supranational Authority and Control

Increasingly where markets and business escape national regulatory boundaries or rules of conduct, supranational governance institutions and collective actors have been instituting common rules that have enabled countries together to reassert control. These global institutions and actors are embodied in such formal, treaty-based associations such as the World Trade Organization (WTO), the World Bank, and the International Monetary Fund; in supranational professional associations in which countries indirectly participate through national regulators, for example, the International Organization of Securities Commissions (IOSCO) and the Basle Committee on Banking Supervision (Kapstein 1994; Coleman 1996; Laurence 1996); in the many different international agreements, treaties, or conferences that recommend technical standards for a wide range of manufactured products and services as well as in the areas of environmental, consumer, and labour protection (Sikkink 1986); in international non-governmental bodies that act as 'private governments' such as international credit-rating agencies or commercial arbitration houses; in coordinated action by governments or their agents, often instigated by US regulators who have been leaders of market re-regulation, as in the cases of money laundering and cross-border banking fraud (Helleiner 1999; Moran 1991); or in concerted interventions in currency markets, as in the 1992 and 1993 runs on the franc, the pound, and the lira, but also in the case of the Mexican peso (Pastor 1999) and even the 1997 Asian financial crisis—although the limits to such interventions became amply clear.

All in all, however, decisions by supranational governance bodies, together with coordinated action by national governments, provide countries with greater shared control over the international economy than they otherwise would have had. The supranational control afforded by such supranational authority, though, is not cost-free, since it comes at the expense of national autonomy, albeit at greater cost in some cases than others. Where nation-states are official and active participants in the decisions and agreements of global governance institutions, they give up national autonomy to a shared supranational authority in a close to even exchange, as in the cases of the WTO, the IOSCO, the Basle Committee, and treaties setting technical, environmental, labour, and consumer protection standards. Where global governance institutions have a supranational authority which substitutes itself for national authority by formal agreement, by contrast, as in the case of the WTO's arbitration panel, the International Monetary Fund (IMF), and the World Bank, national governments lose more autonomy because the greater supranational authority is not entirely shared and its decisions may also undermine national control. This was the case of the WTO's negative rulings on the US export tax credit and European policies on bananas and beef growth hormones.[28]

But whatever the above losses of national autonomy or control, where the supranational authority instead consists of international non-governmental bodies that act as the equivalent of global 'private governments', the losses are even more significant. This is because governments lose autonomy to such supranational authority without any compensating gain in shared control, since they do not formally participate in the agencies' decision-making and do not even have any informal influence. They accept this because the

---

[28] These losses of autonomy and control are of course nothing like those for developing nations that have chosen to subject themselves to the structural adjustment programmes of the World Bank and the International Monetary Fund, since they have little say in the supranational institutions from which they accept judgement. But this is not our focus here.

increase in supranational—but not shared—control is generally in their interest, and enables them to attain certain national goals. For example, bond-rating agencies such as Moody's and Standard and Poor's have tremendous power in determining macroeconomic outcomes and in constraining national governments' ability to raise money even as they assure potential creditors of the credit-worthiness of those governments' bonds (Sinclair 1994a,b). Similarly, in the case of international commercial arbitration, countries have accepted the creation of 'islands of private, transnational governance' because recourse to international arbitration houses rather than the national courts serves to promote transnational commerce by providing a more predictable resolution to private contract disputes, to reduce the prohibitive legal costs borne by business by avoiding preliminary adjudication on national court jurisdiction, or to free up generally overloaded court systems (Stone Sweet 2000; Dezalay and Garth 1995; Salacuse 1991).

The loss of autonomy and control results not only from substituting the oversight of supranational governance organizations for national governmental oversight but also from allowing non-governmental collective actors access to supranational decision-making. In fact, increasingly well-organized collective actors at regional and international levels, not only business and professional interests but also non-governmental organizations concerned with environmental protection, women's issues, consumer interests, human rights, and even animal rights, have had a growing impact on supranational negotiations over global agreements, rules, and standards. As such, they too have diminished not only governments' former autonomy or independence in supranational decision-making but also governments' control over national actors who participate in supranational decision-making. Business firms, however, are the primary non-governmental global players, and have alone served to alter international diplomacy, which has now become triangular as governments negotiate with other governments, governments negotiate with firms, and firms negotiate with one another, such that international trade and production much more than inter-governmental institutions have become the 'transmission mechanism between the world market economy and the state system' (Stopford and Strange 1991; Evans 1993).

Complicating the situation even further is the fact that such formally recognized actors are supplemented by informal, supranational networks or associational linkages of global and regional economic actors that also increasingly undermine national autonomy and defy national control as they set new, informal rules of the game alongside the more formal agreements reached through supranational organizations. These are generally national economic actors who belong to global networks and who interact in a variety of settings, not only work-related but also professional meetings and governmental conferences such as the G-7 meetings of finance ministers, OECD committees that bring together top bankers, economists, government officials, and the Davos seminar, which CEOs of major firms pay upwards of $20,000 each to attend—and is more significant for the informal networks created than the formal purposes of the meeting, even when the topic is social responsibility, as in 1997. Even international crime syndicates qualify as informal, supranational networks.

In some cases, these global networks are territorially situated within a given nation-state, even though they escape its control, leading to the 'denationalization' of national territory (Sassen 1999, 1996, 1991). Such 'global spaces in local places' are epitomized by Wall Street in New York and the City in London which, although they operate according to nationally devised rules, have essentially become global institutions with global players who operate within global networks increasingly according to non-formalized global rules that develop alongside the formal rules set down by national governments. These global networks encompass not only the stockbrokers and traders but also the whole panoply of financial, accounting, and legal services that surround the financial markets and that serve as the go-betweens, fixers, and the like, for corporations, pension funds, institutional investors, and others. More-over, the increasing number of global actors, as the new 'jet-setters' who circle the world not only via jet but also by cellular phone and e-mail, serve not only to promote the international circulation of financial products and industrial goods, they also serve to promote the circulation of liberalizing ideas.

Thus, although national governments have been able to retain or regain control over global economic forces and actors through supranational institutions and agreements, they have lost autonomy through those very institutions and agreements as authority has moved up from the national to the supranational level, where other non-governmental actors also have an increasingly powerful voice in, and/or influence over the shape of, the rules governing global finance and commerce. Globalization, in other words, has indeed transformed the rules of the game, reducing governments' traditional autonomy and control in exchange for gains in supranational authority and control shared with other supranational and national governmental and non-governmental actors.

Europeanization

For most European countries, the changes related to globalization cannot be considered in isolation from those related to the regionalism concerning

European integration.[29] The European Union is the most advanced of all regional trade associations. It has gone much farther than the Asia-Pacific Economic Cooperation (APEC), which relies on more informal and inclusive network structures than on the formal and exclusive European structure of integration (Katzenstein 1996), as well as the North American Free Trade Association (NAFTA) which, as little more than a free trade zone, at best resembles the earliest incarnation of the EU in the European Economic Community (EEC) but without the larger European ambitions or the institutions. In fact, only Europe exhibits a 'deep regionalism' characterized by 'the sophistication and intensity of its institutional fabric underpinned by an organic system of law' and normative underpinnings that have contributed to a redefinition of collective identity and a redistribution of responsibility for public policy (Laffan 1998). As a result, while Europeanization has served to moderate the impact of globalization, it has even further diminished national autonomy and control in exchange, however, for much greater shared supranational authority and control.

For scholars who relate the loss of autonomy and control as a result of European integration to questions of national sovereignty, international law sovereignty is not so much the issue here, since, by agreeing by treaty to share certain responsibilities that in the past were the purview of individual nations alone, European member states essentially 'pooled their sovereignty' (Keohane and Hoffmann 1991). This agreement for pooled sovereignty, however, entails the acceptance of limits to all types of sovereignty: to 'Westphalian sovereignty', since the state has agreed to subordinate its autonomy and freedom from external incursions to the EU; to 'interdependence sovereignty', since the state now necessarily shares control over activities within and across its borders; and to 'domestic sovereignty', since the state is no longer the exclusive organizer of domestic authority, given the impact of EU institutions such as the EU Commission and the European Court of Justice. For our purposes, the most important aspects of sovereignty are those regarding governmental autonomy— 'Westphalian' sovereignty— and control— 'interdependence' sovereignty—since these are most clearly linked to political economic change. This is not to deny that the loss of internal organizing authority—'domestic sovereignty'—is also an important question, since it concerns the state's ability to structure the economy or even to manage the polity as it sees fit. But this falls for the most part outside the purview of this study, since it is more in the realm of political institutions and democracy, and focuses more on questions of 'popular sovereignty'

[29] See, for example, Katzenstein (1996); Ohmae (1993); Oman (1994); Lorenz (1992).

involving democratic access to decision-making and 'divided' or 'shared' sovereignty through the transfer of certain state competencies to different institutions at different levels of government (Newman 1996: 12–15).

Globalization, Europeanization, and European Integration

Europeanization has been inextricably linked to globalization in the set of liberal, capitalist ideas that have gained increasing currency and significance in the post-war period. Europeanization, like globalization, was designed to end war and fight communism, in this case by embracing Germany while containing the Soviet Union and its Eastern Bloc allies economically as well as militarily, through NATO. For the countries that were to form the European Community, regional integration represented not only a way of ensuring peace, it also appeared the only answer to the problems of international and inter-European competition (Garrett and Weingaast 1993). Europeanization was initially promoted by the institutions of the European Coal and Steel Community (ECSC) and subsequently the European Economic Community (EEC), as its mandate grew from a rather narrow focus on coordinating structural adjustment in the sectors most linked to the problems that helped precipitate the Second World War to coordinating trade liberalization and economic development across sectors of industry.

Since then, the pressures related to Europeanization have grown rapidly to include the impact on member states not only of European market liberalization and capital mobility but also of the increasingly ambitious political programme for European integration. And like globalization, it continues despite the fact that part of its original justification also died with the fall of the Berlin Wall. With the European Union, Europeanization has essentially moved from the modest effects of the early, post-war programme for little more than a customs union to the dramatic changes related to today's programme for common defense, economic, and monetary policy along with enlargement to the east.

Thus, if globalization can be most simply defined as a set of international economic, institutional, and ideational forces for change affecting national policies, practices, and politics, then Europeanization can be equally simply defined as a set of regional economic, institutional, and ideational forces for change also affecting national policies, practices, and politics. What this means is not so simple, however, given the complex set of interrelationships between globalization, Europeanization, and European integration.

Herein, for purposes of clarity, I distinguish Europeanization from European integration to highlight two separate but intertwined aspects of a single phenomenon. I define European integration as the process of EEC/EC/EU construction and policy-formulation by a wide range of actors—representative of governmental as well as non-governmental entities, of member states as well as of the EU—engaged in decision-making at the EU level. Such decision-making, including both the EU-level process and its outcomes, generates the economic, institutional, and ideational forces for change in member states' policies, practices, and politics which I term Europeanization. In contrast to many definitions of Europeanization, then, this one separates out European-level decision-making and institution-building from its domestic impact[30] as opposed to putting the two together[31] or concentrating primarily on the European level.[32] In my formulation, whereas European integration can be pictured with vertical arrows going up from the member states to the EU, along with horizontal arrows at the EU level representing the complex EU decision-making processes among actors, Europeanization can be pictured as consisting of vertical arrows going down from the EU to member states, with a feedback loop into the vertical arrows going up, as member state responses to Europeanization affect their further positions on EU level decision-making (see Fig. 1.4). But before developing this explanation of Europeanization further, it is necessary first to elaborate on the relationship between Europeanization and globalization.

Most importantly, one cannot say that Europeanization has principally been a regional variant of globalization, even if one can say that it has been the most advanced such variant. For although the developments related to Europeanization meet if not surpass the ideas and ideals of globalization for the progressive opening of capital and product markets, these developments are also part of a complex set of regional dynamics accompanying, but not subsumable under, the set of international dynamics related to globalization.

Europeanization as a Distinct Set of Ideas

At the European Union level, Europeanization rather than globalization has been at the centre of policy-makers' ideas and projects. Their discussions have remained focused on all aspects of European integration, from the 'community method' to subsidiarity, the quandary of 'widening vs deepening',

---

[30] This is much like the approaches of Ladrech (1994); Radaelli (2000a); Kohler-Koch (1997); Héritier, Knill, and Mingers (1996); and Wallace (2000).

[31] The approach of Cowles, Caporaso, and Risse (2001); Rometsch and Wessels (1996).

[32] The approach of Jupille and Caporaso (1999). See Featherstone (2001) for a review of the range of definitions of Europeanization.

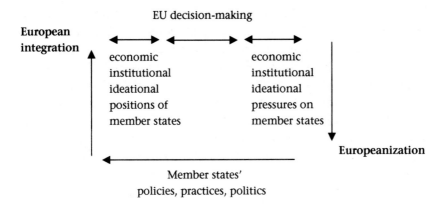

Fig. 1.4 Europeanization vs European integration

the extent of enlargement, and the extension of the '*acquis communautaire*'.[33] Globalization instead seems to have been so much part of background assumptions about the necessity and appropriateness of economic openness and market-driven policies of budgetary restraint in the process of European integration that the term itself has appeared comparatively infrequently in the discourse of the EU Commission. And where it has appeared, it has been 'little more than a largely "empty signifier" ' denoting challenge or change for the EU and its member states, even if sometimes it has been presented as an opportunity, other times as a threat, but in all cases as a spur to further Europeanization (Rosamund 1999; see also Hay and Rosamund 2000). The concept of 'European competitiveness' (Jacquemin and Pench 1997), however, although also a 'meaningless notion of dubious significance' in economic terms (Strange 1998; Hay and Rosamund 2000), has been used by the EU Commission in much the same way as globalization has been used by national governments in the national context, as a discursive construct focused on the challenges from exogenous imperatives (Rosamund 1999) used to persuade of the necessity of reform.

For EU member states, Europeanization as a set of ideas or ideals is not only separable from those attached to globalization, the two concepts also have different meanings in different countries. To begin with, the ideas behind EU member states' support for the renewed push for European integration in the mid-1980s, which came around the same time as the intensification of

---

[33] These are all the accumulated rights and obligations of member states as expressed in the perhaps 100,000 pages of legal texts in the laws, conventions, agreements, and procedures of the European Union.

globalization pressures, differed greatly (Ross 1998). The French, for example, saw European integration as a source of *grandeur* and freedom from US domination as much as a shield against globalization. Globalization itself, moreover, which in the 1980s was primarily portrayed as a competitive challenge for French business, by the late 1990s had also become synony-mous with homogenization via Americanization, the producer of bad foods and bad films, and therefore a danger to French culture and identity (Meunier 2000). All in all, the French have been much more concerned with the threat to governmental control over national economic activity posed by globalization—interdependence sovereignty—than with any threat posed by European supranational authority to governmental autonomy—Westphalian sovereignty.

The British, by contrast, have feared more the challenges to govern-mental autonomy from European supranational authority—Westphalian sovereignty—than the challenges to governmental control over national economic activity from globalization—interdependence sovereignty. In Britain, globalization as Americanization has never been seen as bad, given the transatlantic relationship, and has been presented either as an accom-paniment to neo-liberal policy—for Thatcher—or as a driver of it—for Blair—while Europeanization has been more questionable (Hay and Watson 1998; Schmidt 2001a). While the British have been largely supportive of European market integration, hopeful that it would produce a deregulated quasi-free trade zone, monetary integration has been perceived as a threat to national sovereignty and its openness to globalization—although less so with Blair (Hay and Rosamund 2000; Hay and Watson 1998; Ross 1998).

Germany, unlike either France or Britain, has generally presented both globalization and Europeanization in positive terms in the discourse. The Germans were happy to use European integration as a political cover for the country's rising economic power, global as much as European, while 'being European' was a way of avoiding the problematic national identity of 'being German' after the Second World War (Ross 1998; Risse *et al.* 1999). Moreover, unlike the British or the French, the Germans worried little about the loss of autonomy or control, having had little conception of either 'Westphalian' or 'interdependence' sovereignty as such in the post-war period—given institutional arrangements and history—while globalization as much as Europeanization were seen as enhancements of the social market economy until the mid-1990s.

Finally, Italy and Greece, by way of further comparison, were looking for the rescue of the nation-state, with European integration seen as assuring modernization and 'normalization' in both economic and institutional terms and representing a promise of greater governmental autonomy and control rather than any threat to it.[34] This was equally true of Spain and Portugal, which sought an anchor for democratization as much as a spur for modernization (Ross 1998).

Moreover, while the ideas that acted as a spur to European integration differed greatly among countries, the policies implemented also did not necessarily follow from the liberalizing global ideas of the moment. These were instead for the most part grounded in earlier European ideas about integration: for example, the completion of the Single Market and monetary union which were broached in 1969 at the Hague Summit in order to carry out the 'finalities' of the Rome Treaties. And yet Europeanization, despite being the unintended, path-dependent product of strategic choices meant to confront problems which had little or nothing to do with globalization, has nonetheless ensured that the economic impact of globalization has been more pronounced in Europe than elsewhere (Ross 1998: 175).

The Differentiable Economic Impact of Europeanization

This does not mean, however, that Europeanization is simply a regional extension of globalization, and has therefore engendered for the EU all the same dangers enumerated by the critics of globalization. Much the contrary, mainly because Europeanization has represented a regional foil to globalization as much as a regional variant of it in the areas of monetary and industrial policy. Economically, Europeanization has not just been a force accompanying globalization—in the international financial markets by promoting further liberalization and in international trade by ensuring the progressive reduction in tariff and non-tariff barriers; it has also been a countervailing force in its own right.

Europeanization does not simply add to the global a layer of Europe-specific financial market pressures, by promoting openness in the currency markets through reductions in national capital controls as well as liberalization in the capital markets; it also serves to contain those forces by reducing European member states' exposure to the currency markets through convergence in the monetary policy arena. Coordinated action through the European Monetary System (EMS) softened the impact of the increasing volatility that came with the end of the Bretton Woods agreement for a fixed dollar exchange rate—and the inadequacies of the 'snake'—although clearly

[34] See, for example, Ferrera and Gualmini (1999; 2000); Featherstone (1998).

it could not regulate currency flows, given the new liberalized environment. Through the 1980s, the EMS, with its Exchange Rate Mechanism (ERM) in which the value of currencies were to fluctuate within a given band around the Deutschmark, was in fact quite successful in reducing the detrimental effects of global financial market speculation for those countries that also adopted the 'right' set of monetary policies, that is, monetarism. In the early 1990s, however, it proved only partial protection against such speculation, as evidenced by the two monetary crises that involved major runs on European currencies, the first of which in September 1992 pushed Britain and Italy out of the ERM of the EMS and the second of which nearly destroyed the EMS altogether in summer 1993, and forced the widening of the band of fluctuation allowed within the ERM, from plus or minus 2.25 per cent to plus or minus 15 per cent. The drive toward a single currency within the context of European Monetary Union (EMU), with the Maastricht Treaty's convergence criteria targeting a budget deficit of no more than 3 per cent of GDP, a public debt at or below 60 per cent of GDP, and an inflation rate of at no more than 1.5 per cent above the average of the lowest three countries, was undertaken to provide greater protection against such speculative forces as well as greater currency stability and a euro that would rival the dollar as a world reserve currency (see Forder and Menon 1998; Temperton 1997). This greater protection was bourne out already in the second half of 1998, when the shock waves from the financial crises in Asia and Latin America did not force a change in the exchange rate parities that had just been fixed irrevocably by EMU members in May—whereas it did force change in the rates of the pound against both the dollar and the euro (Jones 2001). Since then, the unexpected weakness of the euro, although potentially dangerous with regard to inflation, has nonetheless been a boon to exports and helped Germany in particular stave off recession from 1999 to late into 2001.

At the same time as the euro provides a shield against the vagaries of global market forces, however, it also brings risks of its own. The problems are first of all ones of coordination among euro-zone members and the European Central Bank (ECB) in the face of global markets, and encompass such issues as how to confront adverse supply-side shocks that hamper growth and fuel inflation; how to convince the markets that member states share common understandings of the economic policy objectives of the euro-zone; how to develop a consensus on the national use of monetary, fiscal, tax, and structural policy instruments; and how and/or whether to develop common EU policies in these areas (Jacquet and Pisani-Ferry 2001). Individually, moreover, euro-zone members face additional EU-generated pressures when their inflation rates are either above or below the European average, given the one-size-fits-all monetary policy of the ECB, or when they suffer from asymmetric shocks, which by agreement they must handle on their own but without the flexibility of the past, given the stability Pact. In both cases, their problems would only be increased if euro-zone members were to fully harmonize fiscal and tax policies, since this would deny them one of the few areas of flexibility they have left (Enderlein 2001).

Finally, countries with coordinated patterns of wage-bargaining face an additional challenge: whether business and labour will successfully negotiate wage restraint without the national independent bank—or monetary authority—to set monetary targets backed up by a clear threat to raise interest rates if wage rises appear inflationary, with instead the ECB as a much more remote and unknown entity (Soskice 1997a). In the absence of an EU-wide wage-restraint bargaining system—and the unlikelihood of any being established—the potential problems can be avoided only if bargaining itself is increasingly focused on branch-by-branch negotiations rather than on coordinated national level agreements, with the euro acting as the reference point. In this case, the credibility of the ECB is less relevant. Its actions will affect the environment of negotiation, but wage costs will be directly comparable across countries from sector to sector, and unions and management will have to base their wage negotiations on branch competitiveness Europe-wide.

Moreover, Europeanization does not only add a set of Europe-generated competitive challenges to the global ones by adding the competitive pressures of the Single Market to those of the single currency and thereby exerting further pressures on firms to restructure and consolidate their operations. It also serves to contain those forces in the industrial policy arena by improving the competitiveness of European member states' economies through the reduction in tariff and non-tariff barriers to trade, through the economies of scale afforded by the Single European Market, and through protection from the dangers of unfair competition and the costs of inefficient regulation. Over the course of the post-war period, European integration together with the GATT succeeded in greatly lowering tariff rates: the average tariffs on manufactured products in 1990, at 5.9 per cent in France, Britain, and Germany, were lower by at least 12–20 points than in 1950 or in 1913 (see Table 1.1). Since the inception of the Single Market, moreover, the EU has speeded up the elimination of non-tariff barriers as well through the development of common rules in the domains of competition policy and health, safety, and environmental protection; the harmonization of standards and/or the 'mutual recognition' of manufactured goods; and the deregulation of a large number of sectors, including the financial markets, telecommunications,

Table 1.1 Tariffs of major advanced industrialized countries over time

	1913	1950	1990
France	21	18	5.9
Germany	20	26	5.9
Italy	18	25	5.9
Japan	30	—	5.3
Holland	4	11	5.9
Sweden	20	9	4.4
Britain	—	23	5.9
United States	44	14	4.8

Sources: The Economist, 24 June 1995; Bairoch (1996); UNCTAD (1995).

electricity, and air transportation.[35] The results can be seen in the figures on trade openness—exports plus imports divided by GDP—between 1960 and 1998, which rose from 30 per cent to 50 per cent for the EU-15, almost all accounted for by trade with other EU countries (Sapir 2001). Moreover, the Single Market programme has had a substantial pro-competitive effect in European markets, with significant reductions in price-cost mark-ups (Allen *et al.* 1998). Additionally, the EU has continued to protect a wide range of industries through anti-dumping measures, multilateral as well as bilateral trade agreements, and common agricultural and fisheries policies.

Europeanization, then, rather than intensifying global forces of competition, may very well have attenuated them. This is even evident in such things as European taxation levels, despite the fact that there has been no fiscal harmonization since the post-war period—and may very well never be if the UK and other member states have their way. Although the differences in tax rates between the richer, traditionally high-tax, high-wage EU member states and the poorer, low-tax, low-wage ones have narrowed, this has constituted not a 'race to the bottom' but rather something of a 'race to the top', with the richer countries little affected by the low wage rates in the poorer ones, despite continued higher corporation as well as general taxation rates.

---

[35] See, for example, Keohane and Hoffmann (1991); Dinan (1994); Majone (1996); Sbragia (1992); Egan (2001).

While France, Germany, Italy, and the Benelux countries together had aggregate tax rates of around 40 per cent in 1967 which had increased to around 45 per cent by the mid-1990s, Greece, Portugal, Spain, and Ireland increased more dramatically, from around 20 per cent to over 35 per cent. With the single currency, of course, it is harder to do without some kind of fiscal harmonization, but there are a range of possibilities that would insure against any move to the lowest common denominator without, at the same time, forcing the poorer member states to lose competitiveness, for example, setting a tax floor that is just below the initial tax rates of the poorer countries (Baldwin and Krugman 2001).

Finally, the competitiveness of European firms has also been enhanced by the end to borders and the commitment to free movement of capital, goods, and services, which have been an impetus for the consolidation and concentration of European firms through mergers, joint ventures, and acquisitions. In 1999, European cross-border mergers and acquisitions (M&As) accounted for close to half of all global cross-border M&A-related sales and 70 per cent of purchases (UNCTAD 2000). In 2000, EU member-states alone were responsible for 67 per cent, or $770 billion, of world foreign direct investment outflows while they attracted 50 per cent, or $617 billion of inflows. Significantly, intra-European investment was a major component of these flows, with 50 per cent of outflows to and 80 per cent of inflows from other member-states (Fitoussi and Le Cacheux 2002: 157–8). However important the global and European dimension of these M&As, though, the national dimension was the more significant from the mid-1980s to the late 1990s, with the majority of acquisitions by national firms of other national firms, and the rest close to evenly divided between acquisitions of other European firms and of firms outside Europe (see Table 1.2). Extra-European acquisitions were greater between 1986 and 1990 and towards the end of the 1990s, mainly when European economies were booming and firms searching for new investments, whether to gain hi-tech expertise from the United States, to take advantage of the privatizations in eastern Europe, to gain a hold in developing markets, or to distribute risks. In 1999 and 2000, however, a boom in European mergers followed the introduction of the euro (Sachwald 2001).

Thus, although member states have lost autonomy in industrial policy-making as a result of the Single Market programme, the Single Market has promoted European firms' competitiveness by facilitating cross-border business mergers and acquisitions and eliminating the unnecessary or unwarranted costs stemming from over-protected and/or over-regulated capital and

Table 1.2 Acquisitions by European firms as percentage of the value of the operations

Period	National targets	European targets	Extra-European targets
1986–90	48.4	22.3	29.3
1991–3	61.6	26.5	11.8
1994–8	52.6	23.1	24.2
1998	44.5	23.0	32.5

Source: Sachwald (2001).

industrial markets while avoiding any 'race to the bottom' through regulatory competition in these markets. In exchange for the loss of national autonomy and control, in other words, they have gained a shared control by way of the shared supranational authority of the EU. Similarly, moreover, despite the fact that in joining EMU member states necessarily gave up the last vestige of national autonomy in monetary policy-making to the ECB with regard to such things as the printing of money and the setting of interest rates (see Wincott 1994), they gained a supranational authority that provided greater shared control, again outweighing any losses in national autonomy (Cameron 1998).

Only in the social policy arena is Europeanization not so protective. Here, in the absence of common policies, and the difficulty of instituting them because of the tremendous diversity in the concepts, priorities, policy instruments, and funding of social security systems (Hantrais 1995; Scharpf and Schmidt 2000), European member states have been left to cope largely on their own with social security deficits, unemployment, and/or poverty in a climate of budgetary austerity (Leibfried and Pierson 1995: 74). Moreover, while European monetary integration may have reduced globalization pressures on member states' currencies, it may simply have displaced these onto their economies through the even greater demands for budgetary austerity related to the restrictive criteria for EMU (Martin 1997; Pierson 1998). And because countries will no longer have the monetary flexibility of the past in times of economic downturn to cushion its effects by, for example, lowering interest rates, adjusting the money supply, loosening credit, or devaluing the currency, they are likely to feel economic problems more intensely and/or more immediately—and without much help from the EU, since, as President of the Bundesbank, Hans Tietmeyer, explained it in an address in Dublin on 15 March 1996, 'In the event of an asymmetric shock, the countries in the monetary union must, on a point of principle, be responsible themselves for achieving the necessary flexibility through internal measures' (cited in Laffan 1998).

European market integration has also added pressures. The 'negative integration' represented by liberalization and deregulation may act as a source of regulatory competition among member states with rising pressures for reductions in such things as payroll taxes and labour protections in order to increase firms' competitiveness and the country's overall attractiveness to investors (Scharpf 1996; 1997a; 2000a). What is more, deregulation in the 'service public' sectors, that is, infrastructural services such as telecommunications, energy, and transport, has represented a special challenge for countries where these services are linked to cherished notions about the welfare state, that is, how best to ensure public access to essential services in order to promote the general interest—especially France.

In fact, although common efforts at resolving problems have developed recently, such as the new benchmarking exercises with regard to employment and social policy following the Luxembourg and Lisbon summits through the open model of coordination, these rely on voluntary efforts in which countries are expected to learn from one another's 'best practices' and to be 'named and shamed' into meeting their self-set targets. There is no significant 'positive integration' promoting European-level social regulation, and certainly no European welfare state in the offing.[36] Nor is there likely to be. This is not only because of the near-impossibility of such a task, given the diversity and complexity of national social security systems, but also because of the fact that policy-makers of Britain, France, and Germany deliberately accepted an 'asymmetrical' EMU in which the monetary was highly developed and the economic only minimally. They did not want to consider national fiscal and social policies or the issues of wealth distribution at the European level, convinced that the issues were too politically sensitive and better left to piecemeal, national-level changes in response to the pressures of market forces (Verdun 1996). Member states, as a result, have largely retained their autonomy with regard to social policy to the detriment of their capacity.

Europeanization, in short, has served to enhance many of the beneficial effects of globalization for EU member states while avoiding many of its negative effects through common monetary and industrial policies, although not social policy. But these gains in shared supranational authority and control have come with added losses of national autonomy in the

---

[36] See Majone (1996: 159–63); Leibfried and Pierson (1995); Rhodes (1995).

monetary and industrial policy arenas, at the same time as the continued autonomy in the social policy sphere has entailed a loss of capacity.

The Greater Institutional Impact of Europeanization

EU member states' loss of autonomy is related not only to the fact that European economic policies replace national economic policies but also to the fact that European governance institutions increasingly take precedence over national ones. Member states are now enmeshed not only in a European economic system that ties national currencies to a single European currency, turns national markets into European markets, and encourages national firms to become European firms but also in a European multi-level governance system that transforms national executives into European decision-makers; turns national parliaments, judiciaries, regions, and administrations into implementers of European decisions; and makes of nationally organized interests European lobbies that increasingly operate as part of highly fluid European governance networks (Marks, Hooghe, and Blank 1996; Kohler-Koch 1996). Europeanization, in other words, is a process as much of political institutional adaptation to EU governance structures and policy-making processes as of economic policy adjustment to EU economic policy and policy-making requirements (see Schmidt 1999a,b). Together, these processes have had a much more significant impact on EU member states in terms of loss of national autonomy and control than the processes of either economic adjustment or political institutional adaptation related to globalization alone. But the question is: how much loss of national autonomy and control in exchange for how much gain in shared supranational authority and control?

The question that has most divided European scholars with regard to the losses of national autonomy and control in response to European integration and Europeanization has been more related to political institutional adaptation than economic policy adjustment. It focuses on whether the nation-state has traded national autonomy for significant shared supranational authority through the Council of Ministers, the European Council, and the many summits and Intergovernmental Conferences or whether other EU bodies such as the Commission, the European Court of Justice (ECJ), and, to a lesser extent, the Parliament are instead predominant. The debates between the intergovernmentalists[37] and the supranationalists[38] are legion, and encompass such questions as whether the process of integration has

---

[37] See, for example, Hoffmann (1966; 1982); Taylor (1983; 1991); Moravcsik (1991); Garrett (1992).
[38] See, for example, Haas (1958); Sandholtz and Zysman (1989); Marks, Hooghe, and Blank (1996).

been primarily neo-functionalist, with European institutions slowly encroaching on nation-state powers through the effects of spillover as well as through Court activism and Commission entrepreneurialism (Alter 1998; Cram 1993), or whether member states remain in charge and have even been strengthened (Milward 1992; Moravcsik 1993).

These 'ontological' debates about the evolution of the balance of power at the supranational level as a result of the process of European integration cannot be dealt with at any length here, since our focus is on the 'post-ontological' issues related to the impact of European integration on the national level (Caporaso 1996), that is, on Europeanization. Moreover, within the context of Europeanization, since our topic is restricted to the impact of EU economic policies on national economic policies and policy-making, we also do not have room to explore other aspects of Europeanization, in particular the impact of the EU on 'polity' (see Morlino 1999) rather than policy, that is, how EU governance structures affect national ones;[39] how EU policy-making processes impinge on national ones;[40] how national administrations have responded to EU membership;[41] how political parties have shifted in response to the EU;[42] and how national interest-group activity has altered in response to EU interest intermediation.[43] Nonetheless, the political institutional debates about European integration are significant enough for our purposes to merit brief consideration, since the national political institutional losses of autonomy that follow from who decides at the EU level also entail losses of autonomy and control with regard to national economic policies and policy-making.

In the debates about European integration, suffice it to say that both sides of the intergovernmental/supranationalist divide are partially right, since much depends upon what aspect of European decision-making is emphasized. Very generally speaking, the more we go in the direction of 'high' politics and treaty-making, the more intergovernmental the policy-making process and the less the loss of national autonomy and control by member states; while the more we go toward 'low' politics and everyday policies, the more supranational the policy-making and the more the loss of national autonomy and control by member states. Moreover, whereas in the first pillar of the EU, concentrating on economic policies, supranationalism is

[39] See, for example, Mény, Muller, and Quermonne (1996); Schmidt (1999a); Rometsch and Wessels (1996); Marks, Hooghe, and Blank (1996).

[40] See, for example, Schmidt (1999b); Kohler-Koch and Eising (1999).

[41] See, for example, Harmsen (1999); Wessels (1998).

[42] See, for example, Ladrech and Marlière (1999); Morlino (1999).

[43] See, for example, Cowles (2001); Coen (1997); Aspinwall (1999).

increasingly the rule, in the second and third pillars of foreign and security policy and justice and home affairs intergovernmentalism remains primary. But even with regard to the economic matters dealt with in the first pillar, member states lose differing amounts of national autonomy and control largely in relation to how much they share in the exercise of supranational authority and control.

The amount of loss of autonomy and control is similar to that related to global institutions and actors. How shared that supranational control and, concomitantly, how great the loss of autonomy vary according to whether (1) EU decisions result directly from member state governments' deliberations, as with the major treaty negotiations for the Single Market or Maastricht and EMU, and in deliberations in the Council of Ministers where unanimity decision rules apply. Here, there is a fairly even exchange of autonomy for shared control, given that all member states have a veto; (2) decisions are agreed to in the Council of Ministers by qualified majority voting, but which come from deliberations among all interested parties, including business and other groups, government representatives, and EU officials, as in standard-setting, where the loss of autonomy is only somewhat greater than in the first case; or (3) decisions are taken by EU officials alone based on previously agreed-to rules, regulations, or precedents that follow from the Treaties, as in many EU Commission decisions in the area of competition policy and most ECJ judgments, as well as all decisions by the ECB.

In this last instance, the independent actions of EU officials greatly diminish member state autonomy, since they are taken without member state involvement and may even go against a member state's own actions or expressed preferences, thereby also undermining its control. The ECB by treaty agreement makes monetary policy decisions for all member states, regardless of governments' views whether expressed individually or collectively as part of the Euro group of finance ministers in the Council, as evidenced by ECB head Wim Duisenberg's express refusal in early 2000 to countenance calls for a reduction in interest rates. The EU Commission, moreover, on advice from the Directorate-General on Competition, has authority independent of the Council of Ministers to make judgments on violations of competition law, on state aid to business (M. Smith 1996; 1998), and on the largest business mergers and acquisitions.

In competition law, for example, the Competition Directorate has been increasingly active in using its powers since 1990 to oversee the biggest mergers and acquisitions—where companies have a combined global turnover greater than £5 billion and European turnover of £250 million. Its investigations have served to alter or even derail proposed mergers that looked as if they would lead to near-monopolist global power in such sectors as accounting, telecommunications, pharmaceuticals, and high technology. This began under Commissioner Leon Brittan in 1989 with the refusal to allow Aérospatiale to acquire de Havilland, much to the dismay of the French, for whom it symbolized the loss of state sovereignty and not simply of government autonomy (Schmidt 1996); it continued under Commissioner Van Miert with the abandonment of the merger between Glaxo and Welcome; and it culminated under Commissioner Mario Monti in the 2000s with a large number of decisions affecting non-European as well as European firms (see below).

The Competition Directorate has also often questioned governments' grants to business on the grounds that they were disguised subsidies. Its insistence that Volkswagen give back a good portion of the money it had been granted by Saxony was protested by the *Land* as well as by the federal government as an attack on national sovereignty. Moreover, its condemnation of the low-interest rate lending practices of the *Landesbanken*—the States' regional savings and loan banks—to the *Mittelstand*—medium-sized enterprises—as unfair competition has been a matter of great concern to the *Länder* as well as the federal government, since it calls into question the 'enabling' role of the (regional) state in the economy and could undermine a very basic element in the operation of the social market economy (M. Smith 2001b).

Moreover, in its extension of competition rules to areas not explicitly covered by the Treaty, the EU has also undermined national autonomy. In air transport, for example, which has been difficult to deregulate because it comes under unanimity rules, ECJ decisions, followed by Commission action, ultimately forced deregulation on a number of reluctant governments (Kassim 1998), while the mere threat of ECJ action in the telecommunications and electricity sectors helped bring all parties to the table (S. Schmidt 1998; Eising and Jabko 2001). A similarly significant loss of autonomy has also occurred in standard-setting, where the Commission has used standards in one area to extend its jurisdiction to another or, even more significantly, to extend the standards to a country which has gained an opt-out in the area—as in the case of the 48-hour working week, which was applied to Britain as an occupational health and safety requirement.

This is not to suggest, however, that all is just 'negative integration' where the EU tends to follow a liberalizing, deregulatory logic as set out by the treaties (Scharpf 1996) and imposes its choices on reluctant member states. For deregulation has been moderated in instances where some member states have been able to persuade other member states and the Commission that deregulation would affect questions of the general interest and not simply more narrow economic self-interest—as in the case of the French defence of the 'service public' in a variety of sectors (Héritier 2000b). Moreover, in many instances, even without appeals to the common good, deregulation has been stopped by strong opposition from member states able to rally support from other member states, as in the cases of postal services liberalization and the opening of public procurement markets (M. Smith 2001a). Member states through the Council of Ministers, in other words, can moderate the loss of autonomy to, as well as the deregulatory push of, the Commission in order to exercise choice with regard to the nature and content of EU policies.

Finally, European integration has created a whole new dynamic of collective action which has served to diminish EU member state control over those national constituencies that have European-level access and/or are involved in European competition, in particular national businesses with global or European operations and/or ambitions. However extensive the global networks, in fact the European ones are even more so. This is because in Europe, in addition to the mainly informal networks and associational linkages that define the global sphere of activity, there are the more formal EU governance-related networks and associational linkages that recreate a European sphere of activity separate from the global, although often also complementary to it. The sheer density of these European networks has ensured that the European level is more privileged in most business sectors except the most internationalized, such as the financial markets or long-internationalized industries such as chemicals. And it also means that the loss of national control by European governments over national business constituencies may be, depending upon the industry, a result of CEOs' networks being, on top of the national, primarily European, primarily global, or European and global at one and the same time. Whereas a member of the governing board of the Bank of France, Michel Albert, saw himself as both global and European as much as French in his activities, with meetings with the IMF or the OECD interspersed with meetings with the EU and the French Ministry of Finance as well as with the banks of other European countries, investment banker André Lévy-Lang saw himself as primarily French and global, given much less personal contact with EU officials and the placement of Paribas' activities, Louis Schweitzer saw himself as French and European, given the locus of Renault's main operations, and Jean-Louis Beffa saw himself as primarily global, given how far-flung Saint-Gobain's operations were.[44]

---

[44] Interviews with author, Paris, June 1997.

For all this, however, European multinationals are no more 'stateless' than non-European ones. The national environment clearly still matters, in the European as much as the global context, in all the ways enumerated above with regard to management leadership, control, culture, and practice. Moreover, despite the denser European networks of formal as well as informal relationships, European MNCs retain close national ties. The nation-state continues to act as a 'travelling salesman' for home-grown companies by promoting the purchase of domestic products and services by foreign governments and corporations; as a 'seducer' for foreign investment by providing incentives for foreign companies to set up operations in-country; as an 'advocate' in the EU by promoting regulations and standards that benefit its own industries and opposing those that do not; and even occasionally as a 'shield or protector' for strategic industries as well as a 'cushion' for major firms in need of subsidies or tax relief, although nothing like in the past (Wright 1994).

What is more, European member states' businesses also do not escape regulatory control. This is true not only at the purely national level, since deregulation still means that companies are subject to different forms of regulation rather than no regulation at all, or at the European level, where greater product harmonization, common regulatory standards, and EU and national competition policies have increased rather than decreased regulations for European firms generally, but also at the global level. In competition policy, for example, the Commission has ruled on mergers and acquisitions not only of European firms but also of non-European firms that have European operations—for example, the merger of the American Kimberley Clark with the Canadian Scott Paper and of the American firms GEC and Honeywell, where it set conditions that led GEC to abandon the merger—or even those only with European sales—for example, the merger of Boeing and McDonnell Douglas or of Time-Warner and AOL. They have also promoted increasingly close relations, if not coordination, with the US Federal Trade Commission and the Anti-Trust Division of the Justice Department, according to former Competition Commissioner Karel Van Miert[45] as well as current officials. These represent the beginnings of a near-global set of regulatory relationships in the interests of enhancing global competition by protecting it from one of its most deleterious effects, the creation of monopolies. Moreover, in other areas such as technical standard-setting, environmental protection, and health and safety policies, the European Commission has also had an ever-increasing global influence.

---

[45] Interview with author, Cambridge, MA, 27 April 1998.

Conclusion

Thus, EU member states' losses in national autonomy and control clearly go way beyond those for countries subject only to globalization pressures, but so do the gains in shared supranational authority and control. At the same time as governmental authority may have been diminished by being subordinated to the EU, it has been enhanced by virtue of being part of a larger Europe-wide authority that commands global respect. As a regional authority, the European Union not only serves to constrain national governments, undermining their autonomy and control, it also serves to contain global economic forces, stepping into the breach where national institutions and actors have little or no power or authority to intervene—as in international trade disputes and mergers of US firms with a large share in European markets. Moreover, with these institutional gains come economic ones, as countries benefit from larger European financial markets, more intra-European trade, higher general European standards, better protections for all citizens of the EU, and greater European economic stability—to say nothing here of the gains from the beginnings of a European political entity and a collective European identity.

Europeanization, in brief, has if anything been an even greater force for change for EU member states than globalization, greatly diminishing national autonomy and control in exchange for much greater shared EU supranational authority and control. To understand this more fully, however, it is necessary to look in much greater depth at the differences among countries in the dynamics of change over time in monetary, industrial, labour and social policy arenas as well as in the mechanics of adjustment in response to EU decisions in a wide range of policy sectors. These are the focus of the next chapter.

2

The Dynamics and Mechanics of Policy Adjustment in Britain, Germany, and France

When considering the actual policies national governments institute in response to globalization and Europeanization, as opposed to the relations of power and influence between national and supranational authorities, the concepts of sovereignty, autonomy, and control, as the terms of reference of international relations, do little for us. In the realm of comparative politics, where our focus is on the intricacies of the policy process, we require other concepts as well—ones that enable us to analyse the differences among countries' responses by reference to the factors that influence policy adjustment. In this context, the very language of losses and gains in sovereignty, autonomy, and control can be misleading.

The language of loss and gain, first and foremost, tends to underplay the complexity of the trade-offs involved in a country giving up sovereignty, understood as national autonomy and/or control, to a supranational authority. The trade-offs are best differentiated in Weberian or Parsonian terms[1] according to whether the giving up of autonomy is experienced as an absolute loss of nation-state power because the supranational authority exerts coercive power over the national authority or as a gain in power because the national authority is now better able to achieve its goals, even if autonomy is lost and control is now shared. Often, the impact of globalization and even more so Europeanization represents a mix of these, for, at the same time as change may be coercive to the extent that it imposes new policies or institutional arrangements that the national authority may not have initially desired, it also may enable governments to further other national goals and/or to gain power at the supranational level. This 'enabling' role has been increasingly emphasized by scholars interested in exploring national

[1] My thanks to Gary Marks for suggesting this line of argument.

responses to globalization in detail, who have found that discussions in terms of autonomy and control or convergence cannot capture the complexities of how new policies develop that better meet the desires and needs of multiple actors in different national institutional contexts in a changing global environment (see Weiss 2002). This has also been true of scholars of Europeanization.[2] It almost goes without saying that European integration has progressed as far as it has because countries' concerns about Weberian losses in power and the EU's coerciveness have been offset by their Parsonian gains in attaining national goals and enhancing national power through joint EU-level decision-making.

The language of the mainstream international relations literature, in other words, does not allow us to appreciate sufficiently the differences either in kinds of powers lost and gained or in how these are experienced by different countries. But there are other problems as well. By treating states as rational actors pursuing their interests, the international relations mainstream implies not only that they know what their losses and gains are but also that they are consciously calculating these at any given moment, whereas they are in fact in the midst of a continuous process of adjustment where the actual gains and losses as such may be unknown or obscure. Most importantly, however, the very use of the terms of sovereignty, autonomy, and control in the mainstream international relations literature implies that states are single entities comprised of governmental actors representing closed systems with clear boundaries between the world 'outside' and the nation 'inside'. But in fact, states represent much more open systems made up of multiple actors—non-governmental as well as governmental— with permeable and even overlapping boundaries between inside and outside, with national actors also operating as supranational actors and/or as part of networks that straddle the lines between the domestic and the international (Ansell and Weber 1999). In this view, globalization and Europeanization also represent spurs to internal adaptation and transformation by and within states (see Weiss 1998) rather than only external constraints on sovereignty, autonomy, and control.

In short, the international relations literature is at a higher level of abstraction than is necessary or useful in comparative politics, where our focus is not on theoretical questions about whether state sovereignty is eroding and national autonomy or control lost in the face of globalization and Europeanization but, rather, on the more empirical questions about how

---

[2] See, for example, Héritier, Knill, and Mingers (1996); Knill and Lehmkuhl (1999); Börzel and Risse (2000); Cowles, Caporaso, and Risse (2001).

actors in nation-states respond to the pressures of globalization and Europeanization in different policy arenas in different countries across time. And for this we need to consider a whole host of other intervening variables.

These variables encompass, first, the mediating factors that shed light on the dynamics of policy adjustment: that is, on when, how, and why countries altered their policies in response to the economic pressures of globalization and Europeanization. These factors include countries' economic vulnerability to global and European forces, their political institutional capacity to alter their policies as necessary, the extent to which the policy initiatives went against their policy legacies and policy preferences, and the discourses that may have enhanced their capacity to respond by changing perceptions of vulnerabilities and legacies and ultimately, therefore, preferences.

Within the context of Europeanization, moreover, additional variables are needed to explain the mechanics of adjustment: that is, when, how, and why countries altered their policies in response to the specific institutional pressures tied to European decision-making. For this, we need to consider the adjustment pressures and mechanisms, that is, how constraining EU decisions are on member-states because the EU defines highly specified and therefore highly coercive rules for countries to follow in implementing the decision; sets less specified and therefore less coercive rules; proffers only suggested rules where adjustment proceeds—or not—on the basis of mimesis; or offers no rules at all, with regulatory competition the expected pressure because barriers to trade are simply removed.

Only with these additional variables, considered together with the mediating factors, can we hope to explain countries' differential policy outcomes in response to EU decisions over the course of the 1980s and 1990s in different policy sectors. These ran the gamut from inertia because of resistance to EU decisions, to absorption because such decisions resulted in minimal policy change, to transformation because such decisions resulted in radical policy change.

Although each policy sector is necessarily different in the mechanics of adjustment, certain patterns of responses nevertheless emerge for the three countries in our study, in part as a result of the economic dynamics of adjustment. Britain, having felt the economic pressures of globalization early and transformed its policies in response, anticipated many of the institutional as well as economic pressures of Europeanization and subsequently absorbed most of the policy changes related to EU decisions. Germany, having felt the economic pressures of globalization and Europeanization late, responded first with inertia to EU decisions but ultimately transformed itself in most policy sectors. France, finally, having felt the economic pressures of globalization as early as Britain, transformed itself early in some sectors with policies that then led EU decisions but responded late and with inertia to EU decisions in a number of other sectors.

To elucidate the above, the chapter first explores the dynamics of policy adjustment to the economic pressures of globalization and Europeanization, using the mediating factors to help explain the different sequencing of responses among European member states in monetary policy, industrial policy, labour, and social policy. Then the chapter examines more closely the mechanics of policy adjustment in response to the institutional pressures of Europeanization in such sectors as European monetary integration, the financial markets, telecommunications, electricity, transport, and employment to elucidate how general EU adjustment pressures and adjustment mechanisms interact with the mediating factors to produce different outcomes in different policy sectors.

The Dynamics of Policy Adjustment to Globalization and Europeanization

Countries have felt the economic constraints of globalization and Europeanization to varying degrees at differing moments, and have responded at different times to differing effects, depending upon five main mediating factors: economic vulnerability, political institutional capacity, policy legacies, policy preferences, and discourse (see Table 2.1). To illustrate this, in what follows I set countries' choices of monetary, industrial, labour, and social policies in a temporal context, against the sequencing of pressures from

Table 2.1 Mediating factors in policy adjustment to globalization and Europeanization

Economic vulnerability	Presence or absence of economic crisis; competitiveness in capital and product markets
Political institutional capacity	Principal policy actors' ability to impose or negotiate change depending upon political interactions and institutional arrangements
Policy legacies	'Fit' with long-standing policies and policy-making institutions
Policy preferences	'Fit' with the old preferences and/or openness to new
Discourse	Ability to change preferences by altering perceptions of economic vulnerabilities and policy legacies and thereby enhance political institutional capacity to impose or negotiate change

globalization and Europeanization as they presented themselves across the 1970s, 1980s, and 1990s.

The Mediating Factors

Of the five mediating factors that help explain countries' responses to the pressures of globalization and Europeanization, economic vulnerability is probably the most straightforward.[3] Countries generally tend to be more open to policy change when they are faced with economic crisis, that is, when recessionary pressures hit and business investment lags, competitiveness decreases, unemployment rises, and consumption declines. Even without crisis, however, they may be open to change depending upon the extent to which they find themselves vulnerable to the pressures from increasing competition in the capital and product markets, with some countries more vulnerable than others depending upon the strength of their currencies, the size of their financial markets, and the scope of their businesses. Germany in the 1980s, for example, as the lead European economy with the lead currency and the leader of European monetary policy, was much less vulnerable to globalization or Europeanization pressures than Britain or France, whereas increasingly over the course of the 1990s it appeared more vulnerable than either of these other two countries, as the costs of unification added to the competitive pressures from globalization. It should not be surprising, therefore, that Germany began serious industrial policy reform efforts only in the 1990s, whereas both Britain and France had already made significant changes in the 1980s.

Economic vulnerability, however, although an impetus to change, cannot on its own be a predictor of it. Adjustment also depends upon countries' political institutional capacity to respond to the external economic pressures. Such capacity depends primarily upon the political interactions and institutional arrangements that affect principal policy actors' ability to impose and/or negotiate change. This is related to the political powers of principal policy actors—based on party politics, elections, interest coalitions, and the like (Huber, Ragin, and Stephens 1993)—as they play themselves out within different institutional contexts.

These institutional differences can be conceived in terms of single-actor and multi-actor systems following a rational choice institutionalist approach, that is, as political systems with few veto points on executive leadership or

[3] In sectors other than political economy, vulnerability would not be economic but, say, military as in the security and defence arena, or ecological as in the environmental arena.

with many, where 'veto-players' facilitate or constrain reform efforts (Tsebelis 1995; Scharpf 1997*b*); or in the more historical institutional terms of unitary and federal states with statist, corporatist, or pluralist policy-making processes that affect the relative concentration or dispersion of power and authority. More specifically, in single-actor systems with few veto-players such as France and Britain, as unitary states with a concentration of power in the executive and 'statist' policy-making processes that allow the executive to formulate policy largely without societal interest intermediation, a restricted group of primarily governmental policy actors have the capacity to impose their decisions—subject, however, to electoral sanctions and protest in the streets, especially in France (Schmidt 1996). By contrast, in multi-actor systems with many veto-players, such as Germany, as a federal state with a diffusion of power among different branches and levels of government and 'corporatist' policy-making processes that include the social partners, the *Länder*, and even the opposition in decision-making, the executive cannot impose, and therefore must negotiate with a wide range of policy actors.

The ability to impose or negotiate reform in turn may depend upon a variety of other elements that are more political than institutional. These include the resources of domestic actors, whether material, informational, legal, or other, that enhance actors' capacity to act; policy learning from past mistakes; culturally grounded patterns of interaction; and collective understandings making up national decision-making or policy styles, whether conflictual or cooperative (Scharpf, Schmidt, and Vad 1998; Hemerijck and Schludi 2000). Ability to implement the decisions once taken is another matter, not dealt with here, but also part of political institutional capacity— as in the case of air pollution (see Duina and Blithe 1999).

Perhaps the best examples of countries' political institutional capacity to respond to economic vulnerability are the smaller European countries such as the Netherlands, Austria, Switzerland, Denmark, and Sweden. These countries, although by their very nature more vulnerable to international economic pressures than the larger countries as well as more complex institutionally, proved themselves in many cases better able to adapt across monetary, industrial, labour, and social policy arenas because of their ability to negotiate change cooperatively among the wide range of policy actors involved in their dense multi-actor systems (Katzenstein 1985; Scharpf and Schmidt 2000). Although multi-actor Germany had great political institutional capacity to negotiate change in monetary policy, it had less with regard to industrial policy, and almost none with regard to labour or social policy. Single-actor France had by comparison great capacity to impose change when it came to labour and industrial policies as well as monetary policy, but little with regard to social policy, although still more than Germany. Among the larger countries, only single-actor Britain has had great political institutional capacity to impose reform across policy arenas (see below).

Political institutional capacity, however, is a necessary but generally not a sufficient condition for explaining a country's ability to respond in the face of economic vulnerability. This is because countries' policy legacies have made it harder for some to adopt and adapt to liberalizing reforms than others while their policy preferences have made some less amenable to such reform than others. Policy legacies involve questions of 'fit', that is, whether a country's long-standing policies and policy-making institutions are compatible with the new, whether in terms of the substantive content of policies or the regulatory structures and processes.[4] Policy preferences are less fixed, and depend upon how readily principal policy actors and/or the public are able to countenance change to policy legacies. This may be primarily a question of interests, especially those of well-entrenched interests against newly formed coalitions whose interactions are analysable through rational-choice institutionalism and game theory (Scharpf 1997b). But these are likely also to be based on certain shared cognitive and normative structures, that is, supported by ideas about the necessity of particular policies and beliefs about their appropriateness (March and Olsen 1989), and therefore interpretable through sociological institutionalism. In the negotiations leading up to the Maastricht Treaty, for example, explanations of countries' differing positions by reference to economic interests (Moravcsik 1998) are best complemented by reference to countries' desires to preserve the differing policy legacies that inform those interests: that is, their differing varieties of capitalism (see Fioretos 2001).

Where reform initiatives largely fit long-standing policy legacies and long-established policy preferences, political institutional capacity to adjust is barely at issue and economic vulnerability not a significant threat since little change is required. But where a major transformation is demanded, political institutional capacity is of the essence, either to impose or to negotiate change. Economic policy adjustment in France, for example, which went against its monetary, industrial, labour, and social policy legacies and preferences, demanded much greater political institutional capacity for change than Germany with regard to monetary policy, where the policy changes largely fit with its long-established policy legacies and long-standing preferences, or than Britain with regard to industrial policy, where the policy

---

[4] The notion of 'fit' has been variously conceptualized as a problem of 'misfit' (Börzel 1999; Börzel and Risse 2000; Duina 1999); 'mismatch' (in Héritier, Knill, and Mingers 1996) or 'goodness of fit' (in Cowles, Caporaso, and Risse 2001).

changes fit with new preferences and old, pre-Second World War legacies. For Germany, the changes in industrial, labour, and social policy demanded greater capacity since these went against policy legacies and preferences, which it had for industrial policy in the 1990s but lacked for social policy, and for Britain, in monetary policy with respect to EMU, which it still lacks.

One question remains: how do we explain changes that go against long-established policy legacies and long-standing preferences? The answer brings us back to questions of economic vulnerability, with economic crisis a spur to reform. But it also takes us forward to the politics of adjustment, and in particular the discourses that may serve to enhance policy actors' political institutional capacity to impose or negotiate reform by altering perceptions of economic vulnerabilities and policy legacies and thereby influencing policy preferences. The discourse serves to alter perceptions and influence preferences through cognitive arguments about the logic and necessity of new policies in the face of the failures of previous ones and normative appeal to values, whether ongoing or newly emerging, that suggest why the new policies are not only sound but appropriate, even if they go against narrow self-interests. Moreover, it enhances political institutional capacity by contributing in single-actor systems to the executive's ability to gain public acquiescence for decisions that it imposes and in multi-actor systems to principal policy actors' ability to reach agreement for decisions they negotiate (see Schmidt 2000a,b, 2001a, 2002a).

This added variable is the focus of Chapters 5 and 6, where it will be elaborated on at greater length. It is nevertheless important to note here that this variable is different from the others, since discourse cannot be readily separated from the preferences which find expression through it or from the cognitive and normative structures that shape its perceptions of economic vulnerabilities or policy legacies. While discourse may serve to change perceptions and preferences through the reconceptualization of interests and the reframing of cognitive and normative structures, it may instead merely reinforce them. Discourse, in other words, sometimes matters and sometimes does not, sometimes exerting a causal influence on policy change, sometimes not (see Schmidt 2001a, 2002a). For example, while in Britain discourse played a major role in solidifying monetary, industrial, labour, and social policy reforms from the late 1970s on, in France the absence of a sufficiently legitimizing discourse from the mid-1980s to the late 1990s contributed to difficulties in instituting social policy reforms, while in Germany such a lack beginning in the mid- to late 1990s has also been problematic. In different policy sectors, moreover, discourses linked to globalization as well as Europeanization have often but certainly not always been a powerful ideational force for change, tipping the balance in favour of reform in Germany in a wide range of sectors in the 1990s, while many fewer in France.

The Sequencing of Policy Responses to Globalization and Europeanization

Over the course of the 1970s, 1980s, and 1990s, the policy responses of France, Britain, and Germany to the pressures of globalization and Europeanization in the monetary, industrial, labour, and social policy arenas were highly differentiated (see Fig. 2.1). These differences are best explained with reference to the mediating factors described above, given differences not only in these countries' levels of economic vulnerability but also their political institutional capacity to reform, the fit of such reforms with existing policy legacies and preferences, and the persuasiveness of their discourse (see also Scharpf and Schmidt 2000).

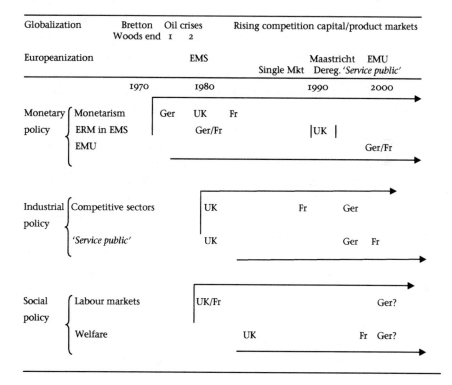

Fig. 2.1 Policy adjustment time line

Countries' positions are approximate times when first significant reforms start.

The pressures of globalization begin for most countries in the early 1970s with the collapse of the Bretton Woods system of fixed exchange rates, followed by the two oil shocks, and continuing with the rising internationalization of markets for goods, capital, and services. Although all advanced industrialized countries had to deal with floating exchange rates while adjusting to the sudden, astronomical rise in the price of crude oil during the first oil shock of the mid-1970s and then the second one of the late 1970s, their monetary policy responses made the difference in terms of how they weathered the storm. This in turn affected how they were able to compete in the product markets and for capital, and how and when they changed their industrial policies through deregulation and privatization. Finally, reforms of monetary, industrial, and labour policies influenced when and how they addressed the structural and financing problems of the welfare state (see Hemerijck and Schludi 2000).

The pressures from Europeanization begin around the same time as those related to globalization, often intensifying the competitive pressures from globalization. With regard to the internationalization of trade, the end to tariff barriers between European countries by 1969 made European countries even more susceptible to rising competition in European product markets than countries subject only to the tariff reductions related to the GATT agreements. Moreover, growing product market integration related to the increasing reduction in non-tariff barriers with the Single Market programme beginning in the mid-1980s only intensified competition, as did deregulation in competitive industrial sectors, whether nationally or EU-led, along with privatization—whether spurred by ideology or market pressures related to globalization and Europeanization. Finally, the EU Commission's push in the 1990s for deregulation of 'service public' sectors also had a major impact, since it opened up to global and not just European competition sectors that had in many EU member states been essentially closed to competition. Deregulation represented a challenge not only because it paved the way to the transformation of these formerly protected sectors but also because in some states it also threatened notions about linkages between the 'service public' and the welfare state, that is, how best to ensure public access to essential services in order to ensure the public interest (see Chapter 1).

Europeanization also intensified the pressures of globalization with regard to the internationalization of the financial markets. Even as the EMS served to protect against the increasing volatility of the financial markets, it added institutional pressures to the economic—as noted in Chapter 1—while the phased elimination of capital controls together with the deregulation of the rules limiting market access and tradable instruments opened them up to greater competition in the capital markets. In addition, the belt-tightening related to national efforts to meet the convergence criteria for EMU had a direct effect on the crisis of the welfare state, by contrast with the indirect effects of globalization or the spillover effects of other changes in monetary and industrial policies related to less money—from austerity budgets—and higher unemployment—for France and Germany—or poverty—for Britain. The most direct pressures, however, came from the changing demographics related to the ageing of the population—which made the pay-as-you-go systems with which all three countries had started increasingly unsustainable—as well as from changing family patterns, with women eager to enter the workforce and increasingly needed given more precarious employment conditions.

Countries' economic vulnerability to the pressures of globalization and Europeanization varied greatly, especially at first, with their policy responses achieving varying degrees of success. Some countries 'got it right' with regard to monetary policy earlier than others, by turning to monetarism following the first oil crisis, in response to an environment of increasing currency volatility and of 'stagflation', where the traditional Keynesian solutions no longer seemed to work as unemployment rose while inflation threatened. Others 'got it right' following the second oil crisis, in response to an environment of rising real interest rates and growing costs of public debt, where the turn to monetarism appeared almost inevitable for most countries once the Federal Reserve Bank had turned to tighter monetary policies (Scharpf 2000b). The creation of the European Monetary System in 1979 added to that inevitability, given the established bands of currency value fluctuations allowable for countries that chose to join, although not all recognized this at the time—France, for example. But 'getting it right' in the 1970s or early 1980s with regard to monetary policy did not guarantee 'getting it right' in the 1980s or the 1990s with regard to industrial policy as global and European economic pressures to deregulate and privatize in competitive sectors increased, while European institutional forces also promoted deregulation not only in the competitive sectors but, increasingly throughout the 1990s, in the *service public* sectors. Welfare systems and labour markets were also coming onto the agenda of all countries, as social security deficits rose while the ratio of workers to retirees declined, as unemployment remained stubbornly high in some countries while poverty became a problem in others, and as growing numbers of women entered the workforce, increasing demand for family and elderly services, for part-time and temporary work, and for more individualized pension arrangements (Daly 2000). At all junctures, moreover, 'getting it right' depended upon a whole host of factors, and turned not only on countries' economic vulnerabilities but also on their political institutional capacities, policy legacies, policy preferences, and discourse as well as, of course, on events.

The Dynamics of Adjustment in Germany

In Germany, monetary policy change came very early, industrial policy change came late, and labour and social policy change came hardly at all. In the face of high economic vulnerability, policy actors were able to muster the necessary political institutional capacity to negotiate monetary policy reform in the 1970s and industrial policy reform in the 1990s, but not labour or social policy reform until the 2000s, hindered by the absence of a sufficiently persuasive discourse to legitimize policies that would reverse policy legacies and preferences.

German Monetary Policy

In the monetary policy arena, Germany in the mid-1970s at the time of the first oil crisis 'got it right' from the outset when the Bundesbank shifted away from a focus on growth, which required coordination from government, to one emphasizing economic stability, through a non-accommodating, hard money policy. The Bundesbank's turn to monetarism fitted with the country's traditional preference for stability above all else, with policies focused on combating inflation first and foremost even if it meant risking rising unemployment. The non-accommodating monetary policy essentially forced the government to switch to a more conservative fiscal policy, and the unions by 1976 to agree to wage restraint as the way to reduce escalating unemployment. It worked, however, not only because of the political institutional capacity of the Bundesbank to impose change, the result of its postwar independence as a central bank much like the United States' Federal Reserve Bank, but also because of the ability of the social partners—business and labour—to deliver on wage moderation (Scharpf 2000b: 32–3, 45–6; and see discussion in Chapter 4).

When the second oil crisis hit, since Germany had already turned to monetarism, with a non-accommodating monetary policy and accommodating unions, it managed to weather the recession linked to the oil crisis reasonably well, with its goods highly competitive internationally, even though initially unemployment rose moderately (Scharpf 2000b: 58–9). Moreover, Germany's elimination of capital controls as early as 1981, pressed by the need for capital inflows because of a precipitous drop in its current accounts and by the interests of the rapidly internationalizing German banks, ensured that the Deutschmark would become the reserve currency for the rest of Europe, and the Bundesbank therefore the EC's proxy for a central bank (Goodman 1992; Goodman and Pauly 1993). The EMS consecrated this. As a result, the Europeanization of German monetary policy—or shall we call it the Germanization of European monetary policy through the Bundesbank's de facto control over European monetary affairs from 1979 to 1999—represented more a reinforcement through European enlargement of Germany's post-war macroeconomic hedge against globalization than any new protection against it, as it was for many other member states.

Even German unification in 1990, which represented perhaps the single greatest shock for the economy since the end of the Second World War (Czada 1998), had minimal effect on German monetary policy given the Bundesbank's central monetary role in Europe. But it did have a major impact on the value of East German money given the conversion of the East German Mark on a one-to-one ratio with the West's, as well as on German industrial, labour, and social policies. The extension of the German model to East Germany of 'socially circumscribed markets, negotiated firms, enabling state intervention, and market-regulating associations' in the attempt to recreate the West German high-wage economy in the East resulted in the immediate collapse of the East German command economy and an exponential rise in unemployment (Streeck 1997; and see Chapter 4).

German Industrial Policy

While the switch in monetary policy came earlier in Germany than other EU member states, industrial policy change came much later, mainly because Germany experienced little economic vulnerability to global or European pressures in the 1980s. The strength of Germany's currency and its industry together ensured that it felt little need to change its industrial policy legacies or preferences, or its labour or social policies for that matter, whether to deregulate, privatize, or increase the flexibility of its labour markets, although it did tighten social expenditures (Manow and Seils 2000). In fact, in the absence of any clear economic imperatives for change, the Kohl government, which had been elected in the early 1980s on a modestly neo-liberal platform, had little political institutional capacity to reform since it had to negotiate this with a wide range of other policy actors, including the *Länder* which predominate in providing subsidies to business and the 'social partners'—business and labour that coordinate a wide range of industrial activities—all of whom resisted change at the time (see Chapter 6). Despite efforts to promote deregulation in such areas as telecommunications, to cut costs in health care, or to diminish restrictive regulations on business—for example, shop closing hours, licensing, environmental rules, and other red tape—the sectoral fragmentation of the ministries, the resistance of organized interests, and the concerns of the *Länder* ensured that reform came very slowly if at all in the 1980s. Neo-liberal labour market policy reforms were also not very extensive, mainly because Kohl backed off in response to electoral sanctions from *Länder* elections subsequent to legislation that sought to deny unemployment compensation to workers laid off as a result of a strike in another region (Lehmbruch 1999).

Only in the 1990s, faced with decreasing competitiveness in the capital and product markets, did the Kohl government begin significant deregulation and privatization of business. In addition to the massive privatization programme in East Germany, major monopolistic public service providers in telecommunications and air and rail transport were privatized while highly regulated markets such as the stock markets, electricity, and road haulage were deregulated (see below). Although this went quite slowly, it was remarkably successful, the result of the political institutional capacity of government to negotiate reform cooperatively with business, labour, and the *Länder* in such a way that it transformed a wide range of policy sectors with little disruptive impact on the traditional patterns of cooperative economic governance (Esser 1995; see Chapter 4). In Germany, in fact, the country's 'hidden flexibility within stable institutions' continued to ensure that change involved a subtle process of shifting power and responsibilities without altering existing structures (Katzenstein 1989), so much so that even EU competition policies that had initially appeared to jeopardize the role of Germany's public sector banks and the postal services in the social market economy were resolved in symbiosis with the EU (M. Smith 2001*b*). Moreover, discourses that spoke of the necessity of change due not only to global economic pressures but also to European policy imperatives enhanced the political institutional capacity to alter preferences and reverse policy legacies in most public service sectors (see below). But while Germany managed to negotiate significant changes in industrial policy, it was much less successful with regard to labour flexibility or social policy, which by the year 2000 remained largely to be negotiated.

German Labour and Social Policies

In the 1990s, high rates of unemployment and growing social security deficits as a result of the costs of unification and of the pressures of international competition seemed to leave Germany little choice other than to overhaul the structure and financing of the welfare state and increase labour flexibility. Unemployment, having been relatively low in the 1980s, had

skyrocketed to 11 per cent in the mid-1990s—its highest rate since Hitler—
while welfare spending, which had remained reasonably steady in the 1980s,
going from 25.7 per cent of GDP in 1980 to 24.8 per cent in 1990, jumped to
29.6 per cent of GDP in 1995 (OECD 1998). This is when it became clear that
reform was needed for a social security system which relied on high payroll
taxes that discouraged internal investment and in which the relatively high
wages of the lowest paid and the high social assistance levels encouraged
'welfare without work' while discouraging the move toward service-sector
jobs (Manow and Seils 2000).

But the country was largely stymied in reform efforts throughout the
decade. Almost nothing was done to reduce payroll costs, whether by shifting
some of the burden from payroll taxes paid for by employers and employees
to more general taxation—as the French began to do—or by reducing the
levels of payroll tax and increasing federal outlays (see Manow and Seils
2000; Hemerijck and Schludi 2000). Moreover, government cuts in the social
security system in the mid-1990s were minimal, such as measures changing
employees' rights to a stay at a spa from four weeks every three years to three
weeks every four years as of 1996, while companies in the face of union
protest ultimately did not use a highly contested 1996 law allowing them to
lower the minimum amount they must pay employees on sick leave from full
salary down to 80 per cent of workers' pay. In the face of a lack of agreement
among the social partners, the Kohl government did not have the political
institutional capacity to impose welfare and work reforms that went against
post-war policy legacies and preferences while it largely lacked the persuasive
powers to reframe the terms of the discourse. And the Schröder Government,
elected on promises of reform, did not have much more such capacity or
a much more persuasive discourse to speak to either the necessity or the
appropriateness of reform (see Chapter 6).

In a welfare system founded on the Bismarckian model, where the reasonably generous level of state provision was focused on male breadwinners
working full-time for a lifetime in order to ensure adequate family support,
successive governments experienced great resistance to any decrease in
benefits as well as to any increase in labour flexibility with regard to part-time
and temporary jobs—thereby perpetuating the pattern of gender discrimina-
tion with regard to women in the workplace. Moreover, in a country where
social security contributions were regarded as property rights, any cuts in or
marketization of pensions would be strongly resisted. Only in the year 2000
did the Schröder government manage to institute freezes on pension
increases—for two years, later renegotiated down to one—and only in 2001
was it able to negotiate in conjunction with the unions and employers

modest reforms in pension systems by way of their partial privatization (see Chapter 6). The government did, however, succeed in imposing one tax cut which could have a major impact on the German model of capitalism as a whole. The late December 1999 tax reform proposal to eliminate the 50 per cent rate of capital gains tax on firms selling shares in other firms, slipped into the budget without discussion or negotiation, could do more to undermine the network-based inter-firm relations that underpin the traditional German social market economy than any other of Schröder's reform initiatives once its goes into effect in 2002 (see Chapter 4).

The Dynamics of Adjustment in Britain

Britain changed its monetary policies later than Germany, but then proceeded almost immediately to alter its industrial, labour, and social policies way ahead of other member states. High economic vulnerability, combined with great political institutional capacity to impose reform and a persuasive legitimizing discourse, enabled the government to make major changes in the country's policy legacies and preferences in the 1980s while setting the stage for further social policy reform in the 1990s.

British Monetary Policy

In the monetary policy arena, Britain, by contrast with Germany, 'got it wrong' in response to the first oil crisis when it chose Keynesian reflation in keeping with long-standing policy legacies and preferences. This proved to be no solution at all, given rising inflation in a situation where the government did not have the capacity to impose wage moderation, nor could the unions ultimately ensure it (see Chapter 4). The result, after a short period of 'incomes policy', was a complete loss of control, evident in exploding wages, double-digit inflation, and major strikes, followed by Prime Minister Thatcher's victory in 1979 and the introduction of monetarist policies that put strict controls on the money supply and reduced public spending to combat inflation and limit monetary volatility (Walsh 2000).

With the switch to monetarism following the lead of the Federal Reserve Bank and the example of Germany, Thatcher remained true to long-standing British policy preferences for a strong pound as an international reserve currency—although not, clearly, to policy legacies of neo-Keynesianism. Moreover, she maintained British preferences with regard to monetary autonomy by joining the EMS but not participating in its key component, the European Exchange Rate Mechanism (ERM), fearful of the possible negative effects of membership. Because Thatcher had just eliminated the country's exchange controls, had the country participated in the ERM, it would have had less control over its monetary policy than France or Italy, which continued to have an added measure of protection until the phase-out of exchange controls in 1989–90, and it would therefore have exposed its more widely traded sterling to more serious speculative stress (Artis 1998: 42).

Britain limited its commitment to the EMS for other reasons as well. These included political concerns about the loss of national sovereignty as well as economic doubts about the ability of a common monetary policy to combat inflation or to work effectively, given Britain's poor experiences with fixed or near-fixed exchange-rate systems from the gold standard to Bretton Woods and the Snake. Britain also did not need monetary integration as much as France for economic reasons nor want it as much as Germany for political reasons. In monetary policy in particular, in fact, the British tended to perceive Europeanization as more of a threat than globalization. And the British experience with European monetary integration seemed only to confirm this view, since once Britain did finally join the ERM, in 1990, it had to bail out shortly thereafter, in 1992, after suffering the worst single loss in monetary history as a result of the run on its currency. Moreover, Britain's exit from the ERM in 1992 was a kick-start to renewed growth at a time when most other countries that stayed in the ERM, such as France and Germany, remained in recession. Its negotiated opt-out from EMU at this same time meant that it could maintain its traditional policy preferences with regard to monetary autonomy—something which continued into the 2000s, despite the promises of the Blair government beginning in 1997 seriously to consider entry into EMU 'as long as the economic conditions were right'. In the face of negative public opinion as well as political opposition, the Blair government had yet by 2002 to make any irreversible policy decisions or even broach a legitimizing discourse that spoke to the necessity, let alone the appropriateness, of change (see Chapter 6).

British Industrial and Labour Policies

Changes in industrial and labour policies began in the early to mid-1980s following the changes in monetary policy. These were pushed not only by continued economic vulnerabilities despite monetary policy reform but also by the ideological commitments of the Thatcher government to spur industrial competitiveness through deregulation and privatization and to reduce labour's powers through restrictive rules governing union action and a return to a hands-off policy in pay settlements. Such changes were made possible by Thatcher's ability to exploit the full institutional capacities of the Westminster model, given the political powers that came with her electoral impregnability—the result of a divided opposition. And this capacity in turn was enhanced by Thatcher's discourse about the appropriateness, and not simply the necessity, of neo-liberal reform (see Chapter 6).

While the coming on stream of North Sea oil ended the balance of payments crises that had bedevilled all previous post-war governments, Thatcher's switch to an extremely restrictive monetary policy, together with North Sea oil, produced such a sharp rise in the value of the pound that it engendered a precipitous drop in the international competitiveness of British goods. This, together with the elimination of most protectionist barriers to trade, led to the near-destruction of British industry (see Chapter 4). Moreover, inflation remained high while wages continued to escalate along with job losses until the mid-1980s, when the combination of mass unemployment, the defeat of the coal miners' strike, and anti-union legislation effectively radically decentralized wage-setting and deregulated the labour market more generally. The new laws, beginning with the Employment Acts of 1980 and 1982, followed by the Trade Union Act of 1984 and culminating in the Employment Act of 1988, made strikes and union organizing more difficult by diminishing labour's ability to organize workers in closed shops, limiting strike action, lifting unions' immunity from damages for work actions that were not strictly related to industrial relations disputes, increasing non-union workers' rights and protections, and loosening the rules with regard to hiring and firing.[5]

The resulting greater labour flexibility and lower wages set the institutional conditions for greater business competitiveness, which was also promoted through ideologically driven policies of privatization of firms in both competitive and public services sectors, deregulation of business, and liberalization of the financial markets (see Chapter 4). Privatization was highly laissez-faire, with companies freely floated on the stock market, and was focused as much on monopolistic public service enterprises such as telephone, gas, water, electricity, and air transport as on firms in the competitive sector, such as steel and oil companies. Deregulation, moreover, served as an accompaniment to privatization, replacing voluntary self-governing arrangements and informal government-industry relationships with independent regulatory agencies for the financial markets and public service enterprises such as telecommunications, gas, and later the railways (see Chapter 4). With these policies, moreover, Britain anticipated many of the deregulatory initiatives of the European Community, going farther faster than any other European member state in dismantling state control of an economy that had in any

---

[5] See Auerbach (1990); Davies and Freedland (1993); Dickens and Hall (1995); Brown (1994); Howell (1995; 1999).

case been less state regulated than those on the Continent. But although Thatcher's policy programme set the stage for the dramatic economic turn-around of the country, the price was very high in the short term with respect to the rise of poverty and unemployment. And Thatcher's social policy reforms did little to cushion these effects.

British Social Policy

In Britain, the major battles with regard to social policy were fought in the 1980s. And even though the reforms were less extensive than promised in elec-tion campaigns, Thatcher did make significant inroads on the welfare state as she sought to reduce social expenditures while altering the manner of welfare provision. The cumulative effect of incremental welfare reforms moved British pension arrangements toward a more marginal model of welfare, moderated the pace of growth in expenditures, and began the turn to the market through the introduction of private pension schemes and competition in health pro-vision and tertiary education (Fawcett 1995; Rhodes 2000). Moreover, social expenditure as a percentage of gross domestic product remained virtually the same after ten years of Thatcherism (Klein 1989). It went from 18.3 per cent of GDP in 1980 to a high of 21.4 per cent in 1986, and back down to 19.6 per cent in 1990, when Thatcher left office. It increased somewhat only under Major, going to 22.8 per cent of GDP in 1995 (OECD 1998).

The Thatcher government went farthest with cuts in social assistance, unemployment compensation, and housing allowances for the unemployed, single mothers, and youth. Because Britain has been a liberal welfare state founded on the Beveridge model, where the low level of state provision for individuals entailed that the many had to pay for the few while having to rely on themselves for social security above the minimum level, Thatcher did not encounter significant opposition to cuts in areas where the 'haves' paid and the 'have-nots' benefited. There was much greater resistance to proposed cuts in universal benefits and services. In consequence, Thatcher did not cut the basic pension, although she reduced its redistributive effect by de-linking pen-sions from earnings; and she partially privatized pensions above the basic minimum by allowing individuals to opt for defined-contribution schemes as an alternative to the existing company benefit schemes in order to enable con-tributors to have individual control over the capital asset and greater job mobility (Waine 1995; Timmins 1995: 396–7). Moreover, plans for radical reform of the National Health Service were abandoned when they were found unpopular with the Conservatives' own constituency (Pierson and Smith 1993: 513). But Thatcher did introduce market principles and competition into the health sector by changing the resource-allocation mechanisms with the separation of providers and purchasers, with health authorities purchasing health care from hospitals, and with general practitioners having greater powers in relation to hospitals and hospital consultants. In higher education, moreover, she instituted competition through periodic reviews of academic and teaching performance linked to increases or decreases in funding.

By the 1990s, in consequence of both labour and social policy reforms plus an expanding economy, Britain had largely solved its problems of high unemployment—which had plummeted to around 7 per cent as of the mid-1990s, by contrast with Continental countries which had unemployment figures in the double digits—as well as brought its social security deficits under control. But it still suffered from problems of poverty and indigence which began to be addressed only in the late 1990s by Blair's 'New Labour' government. The reforms, which were facilitated by Blair's discourse of the 'third way' and resonated better with the British public, remained neo-liberal in their market orientation even as they sought to promote greater social equality and opportunity (Schmidt 2000*a*; and Chapter 6). New Labour went way beyond anything Thatcher had proposed with welfare-to-work programmes for social assistance recipients, 'New Deal' youth employment programmes later generalized to single mothers and the unemployed of all ages, and tuition fees for students in tertiary education. Moreover, it continued means testing in social assistance and the marketization of pension systems. Health care, by contrast, has seen no cuts or imposition of significant fees, only promises to increase funding and decrease waiting times for operations. And the Blair government has also been somewhat more generous and redistributive in its social policies with regard to the very poor by raising the level of social assistance and by instituting a minimum wage for the first time ever (Rhodes 2000). But the problems of poverty remain, with British levels of poverty far higher than in either Germany or France—and with social transfers doing much less to make up the difference. Whereas in Britain 34 per cent of the population fall below the European definition of poverty—lower than 60 per cent of the median income in Europe—with social transfers bringing the rate down to 21 per cent, in Germany only 24 per cent of the population fall below the poverty line, while social transfers bring the rate down to 18 per cent. In France, by comparison, 28 per cent of the population fall below the line, but social transfers bring the rate to 16 per cent (Eurostat 1999; and see Fig. 1.1).

The Dynamics of Adjustment in France

France changed its monetary policies much later than either Germany or Britain, but then proceeded as quickly as Britain to alter its industrial and labour policies but not its social policies. Economic vulnerability combined here too with great political institutional capacity to enable governments to reverse the country's policy legacies and preferences in the 1980s with regard to monetary, industrial, and labour policies; but the lack of a sufficiently legitimizing discourse proved an impediment to social policy change in the 1990s.

French Monetary Policy

In the monetary policy arena, France in the mid-1970s, like Britain, 'got it wrong' when it chose neo-Keynesianism in response not only, briefly, to the first oil crisis but also, more importantly, to the second. The mid-1970s neo-Keynesian revival proved only a short-term fix, since the government switched to moderately restrictive monetary and fiscal policies by 1976 to combat the resulting double-digit inflation, which in turn led to a concomitant rise in unemployment which was contained only by the government's use of the nationalized firms as buffers as well as by early retirement programmes (Schmidt 1996; Scharpf 2000b: 36–40). France's joint effort with Germany at the end of the 1970s to create the European Monetary System along with its emulation of the German monetary policy programme represented its attempt to regain control over a monetary situation it saw as getting increasingly out of hand (Boltho 1982; McNamara 1998), with French leaders Raymond Barre and Valéry Giscard d'Estaing repeatedly invoking the German model in their political discourse to legitimize austerity measures to the public (Hayward 1982; McCarthy 1990).

In 1981, however, at a time when both Germany and Britain had already fully committed themselves to monetarism, the new Mitterrand government in France chose neo-Keynesian reflation instead, engaging in a counter-cyclical 'relance' in the expectation of an economic upswing that never came, with all that that entailed in terms of rising wages, social spending, and public deficits. By early 1983, faced with an economy out of control as a result of double-digit inflation, high debt, runaway spending, capital flight, continually rising unemployment, and plummeting industrial competitiveness, as well as in danger of having to pull out of the European Monetary System, the government had seemingly little choice other than to take the 'great U-turn' to monetarism (Boltho 1996; Schmidt 1996).[6] In so doing, it abandoned its preferences for neo-Keynesian monetary policies and the legacies of

---

[6] David Cameron (1996) makes the point that, although by 1983 the French government did indeed have little choice, there were actions it could have taken earlier to avoid such a radical shift in policy, such as an earlier devaluation of the currency.

a state-controlled system of credit allocation in which, until the collapse of the Bretton Woods system, French governments had used the central bank in a zigzag course against the fixed dollar exchange rate through inflation and devaluation in order to promote economic growth (Loriaux 1991; Hall 1986).

In place of France's traditional monetary *dirigisme*, the Mitterrand government adopted a more German-style monetary liberalism, instituting tight monetary policies, austerity budgets, and a policy of 'competitive disinflation' focused on damping inflation and maintaining a strong currency, the *franc fort*. Such policies were intended to counteract the increasing vulnerability of the French economy to external, global market forces, and in particular to the currency exchange markets (Favier and Martin-Rolland 1996). Until the advent of the euro, the franc was consistently adversely affected by dollar instability since investors regularly moved to the mark when the dollar weakened and vice versa (Dillingham 1996; Thiel 1982; Van Ypersele 1985). This vulnerability was also related to the elimination of capital controls of which France had begun a phased reduction starting in the mid-1980s as an accompaniment to growing financial liberalization— after having increased its capital controls in the early 1980s in order to contain capital outflows—but which had taken full effect only in 1990 (Goodman 1992; Goodman and Pauly 1993).

French governments' commitment to continued liberal economic transformation through increasing European monetary and economic integration had everything to do with their desire to protect the country against global forces, and helps explain every subsequent move in European integration. Thus, the creation of the single market in finance was to increase the amount of capital while decreasing its cost in France and Europe. The commitment to a common European currency was to create a counterweight to the dollar while eliminating the exchange rate premium attached to the franc. The agreement to create a European central bank was to give France a voice in European monetary policy while diminishing German dominance. And the commitment to the Maastricht criteria for EMU was to combat the potential volatility of intra-European capital flows and their increasing exposure to the pressures of the international financial system (Gros and Thygesen 1992; Dillingham 1996; Reland 1998). Adherence to the rather strict Maastricht convergence criteria was to ensure the quickest progress toward monetary and economic integration while serving as a clear message to the markets about the stability and investment-worthiness of EMU-linked European economies generally and that of France specifically (Dillingham 1996; Reland 1998).

None of these integrating moves, however, was enough to rid France of its vulnerability to the international financial markets, which was dramatized in the 1992 and 1993 runs on the franc. This continuing vulnerability, however, merely reinforced French governmental elites' conviction, which they reiterated in word as well as deed, that only full European monetary integration could be an effective shield against the economic instability generated by the global financial markets, even if this meant giving up some measure of national autonomy in exchange for greater shared supranational control (see Chapter 6). As a result, successive French governments have been solidly behind monetary integration since the signing of the Maastricht Treaty, although they have sought to counterbalance the independence of the European Central Bank by strengthening the 'voice' of the euro-group of ministers in various ways.

French Industrial Policy in Competitive Sectors and Labour Policy

In 1981, the Mitterrand government accompanied its neo-Keynesian mone-tary policy with a renewal of state *dirigisme*—interventionism—in industrial policy through large-scale nationalizations and extensive industrial restruc-turing and re-capitalizing of public enterprises (Schmidt 1996; see Chapter 4). In 1983, the Mitterrand government accompanied its abrupt switch to monetarism with an equally radical reversal of its *dirigiste* industrial policy legacies and preferences. Financial market liberalization, business deregula-tion, and privatization, moreover, came along with a French push for greater European market integration to complement its push for European monetary integration (Schmidt 1996). Once French leaders had decided to liberal-ize and deregulate the competitive sectors of the country's economy, they sought to ensure that such liberalization would extend to the rest of Europe, in particular with regard to the financial markets. The *service public* or public utilities and infrastructural services sectors were another matter, how-ever, and successive French governments resisted deregulatory initiatives by the EU Commission in the 1980s and well into the 1990s, at which time they only reluctantly agreed to liberalize in the face of strong EU pressure (see below).

Deregulation of business from the mid-1980s on by successive govern-ments of the left and the right significantly diminished traditional state control over business by stripping it of its traditional policy instruments, in particular through the opening of the financial markets, the lifting of price controls, the abrogation of barriers to competition, the easing of sectoral rules governing business, and so forth. Moreover, the independent regula-tory agencies set up to supervise the financial markets, the radio and televi-sion industries, and, in the 1990s, the liberalized public service sectors only added to the loss of governmental power. EU Commission limits on state aid to industry, combined with the state's lack of money to subsidize business as it had in the past, also reduced government ability to influence business investment and development (see Chapter 4). Privatization, finally, beginning in 1986 and continuing intermittently but increasingly through the 1990s until today—in which governments of the right but also later of the left sold off long-nationalized companies as well as ones more recently nationalized by the Mitterrand government in 1981–2—naturally reduced state control at the same time as state ownership. But, unlike in Britain, privatization focused primarily on public enterprises in the competitive sector, and was highly *dirigiste* in approach, as the government decided how the shares were to be distributed among a hard core of investors and others (Schmidt 1996; and see Chapter 4).

The changes in labour policy began in the early 1980s even before those in industrial policy, and resulted by the end of the decade in the radical decentralization of wage bargaining. Laws in the early 1980s—the Auroux laws—that established more direct worker-management dialogue in the firm and at the shop-floor level started the process of labour market deregulation by inadvertently weakening the unions (see Chapter 4). These were followed in the mid- and late 1980s by a string of measures promoting flexibility in hiring and firing, such as the 1986 law abolishing the administrative authorization of lay-offs for fewer than ten workers and later laws reducing restrictions on part-time and temporary work. By the 1990s, moreover, the government had abandoned the entire system of state-organized wage bargaining, thereby ensuring that most private-sector negotiations would be decentralized to the firm level.

Not all labour policies were deregulatory, however. Socialist governments in the 1990s also occasionally made efforts to 'moralize' the labour market. The Aubry law of 1993 required employers to have a 'social plan' for laid-off workers, and allowed the courts to reverse lay-offs on grounds of firm profitability, moves overseas, or imprecise plans. Moreover, the 35-hour work week announced in 1997 and which took effect in 2000 sought to reduce the numbers of working hours in order to protect labour and increase jobs, although it actually did more to increase labour flexibility than jobs by enabling companies to use the negotiations to revisit most company working-time rules (see Chapter 4).

The results of such changes in labour policy, together with those in industrial and monetary policies, were greater currency stability, decreasing inflation, and increasing business competitiveness and labour productivity, although unemployment continued to climb and France's economic recovery had been delayed by the comparatively late turn to budgetary austerity, giving it less time to benefit from the world economic expansion beginning in the mid-1980s. French governments, faced with serious economic crisis, had had the political institutional capacity to impose all of these reforms without significant public protest, due to discourses that spoke to the necessity of such reforms while appealing mainly to national sacrifice and pride (see Chapter 6). Social policy reform was another matter, however, despite the fact that it too had become imperative, given mounting social security deficits, continued high unemployment, increasing competitiveness problems related to high payroll taxes, and growing budgetary pressures related to the Maastricht criteria of EMU (see Ross n.d.).

French Social Policy and Industrial Policy in Public Service Sectors

Although France had seemingly resolved the major problems related to the structure of the economy and of work in the 1980s, it still confronted significant problems with the structure of welfare and the *service public* sectors intimately linked to it. Unemployment had risen steadily since the 1980s, reaching 11 per cent in late 1993 and hitting a post-war high of 12.8 per cent in February 1997, to go below 10 per cent not before 2000. Social security costs, moreover, had expanded significantly, going from 23.5 per cent of GDP in 1980 to 26.7 per cent in 1990, and up to 30.1 per cent in 1995 (OECD 1998). In addition, France was at a competitive disadvantage and in danger from 'social dumping' by corporations unwilling to pay its high payroll taxes which, at around 40 per cent, were funded through employer and employee contributions at a higher rate and with less state support than other such insurance-based systems in Germany, Belgium, Italy, the Netherlands, and Luxembourg, let alone universalist systems which fund social security through taxation, such as Britain, Denmark, Ireland, Sweden, and Finland (Hantrais 1995; Korpi 1995). Finally, in the public services sector tied to the welfare state France was under increasing pressure from global economic forces at least to rationalize if not also to privatize and from EU institutional forces to deregulate. EU deregulatory policies promoting competition and the opening of the market in sectors such as telecommunications, electricity, and transport have been especially difficult for France to absorb, since they undermined the central role of national champions in infrastructural services and have been difficult to legitimize in the context of discourses that had consistently presented the *service public* as central to the welfare state responsibilities of the 'Republican State' (see below). And although successive French governments certainly had the political institutional capacity to impose reforms in both the *service public* and welfare arenas that went against policy legacies and preferences, in the 1990s at least until the Jospin government—with the exception of telecommunications—they lacked the discursive powers to convince the public of the appropriateness of reform, and retreated time and again in the face of protest (Schmidt 2000*b*; and Chapter 6).

In the 1980s, French governments, unlike their British and German counterparts, actively expanded welfare state benefits as well as spending, bringing France up to the level of other reasonably generous Continental welfare states. This began with the Socialists' 1981 reforms which provided a wide range of social benefits, such as retirement at 60, an extra week of vacation—to 5 weeks—and a reduction of the work week from 40 to 39 hours, with the extra hour's pay staying in workers' pockets. These continued with generous early retirement, unemployment, jobs creation programmes, and youth training and employment initiatives as the Socialists sought to cushion the impact of their industrial policies after 1983 (Levy 2000). None of these benefits or programmes was in any way reversed by the right in 1986–8, despite its expressed admiration for Thatcherite neo-liberalism at the time (see Chapter 6). And when the Socialists returned to power in 1988, they continued to expand the welfare state by addressing problems of 'exclusion' through the *Revenu Minimum d'Insertion* (RMI), which provided a minimum income for those who did not qualify for unemployment compensation or other forms of social assistance. They also set the groundwork for the eventual reform of the contribution system, however, by introducing a general social security tax—the *contribution sociale généralisée* (CSG)—which was progressive in that it taxed all forms of income rather than only wage earnings, even if, at 1.1 per cent of income, its revenue was insignificant in amount at the time.

Only when the right came to power in 1993 were there any serious attempts to cut social spending or reform the social security system. But these met with mixed results. Prime Minister Balladur's one major success, which passed without consultation, legitimizing discourse, or protest, was the reduction in the pension benefits of private sector employees through raising the years needed for full retirement benefits from 37.5 to 40 years, calculating benefits on the basis of the best 25 rather than the best ten years of salary, and indexing pensions to the rise in prices rather than wages (Levy 2001). But when Prime Minister Juppé sought to extend this reform to the public sector in 1995 while eliminating the special pension schemes of various public sector employees—which allowed some to retire at 50—without any consultation or legitimizing discourse, he was confronted with massive strikes, and retreated (see Chapter 6). He nevertheless succeeding in restructuring French social security by subjecting the social security budget to parliamentary vote and reducing the influence of the social partners in the management of social security funds (Bonoli and Palier 1997). Neither Balladur nor Juppé, however, made much progress in the partial privatization or rationalization of the public services sector, as employees struck against restructuring plans for Air France and the railway system and against share flotations for France Télécom—although deregulation of the telecommunications sector was successful. Both did, however, begin to shift the burden away from payroll taxes through increases in the CSG—Balladur to 2.4 per cent and Juppé to 3.4 per cent—although these were made regressive because deductible, thereby benefiting wage earners in high-income brackets (Levy 2001).

The Jospin government had greater success with social welfare and public service reforms than its predecessors, mainly by speaking to its appropriateness as much as to its necessity with a discourse about balancing equity with efficiency in policies that mixed progressive and neo-liberal elements (see Chapter 6). For example, although the Jospin government kept in place Juppé's partial marketization of pensions, it made it more financially compatible with public pensions—as a supplement, not a future substitute—more widely available through extension to smaller companies—through inter-company plans—and not just large corporations, and more democratically managed through administration by the social partners rather than by private companies. Moreover, the Socialists ensured that higher-income groups would pay more of the costs of austerity budgets through higher taxes or reduced tax credits—such as the child income tax—while providing tax relief to lower-income groups. It did this by increasing the CSG to 7.5 per cent from 3.4 per cent while decreasing worker contributions to health insurance from 5.5 per cent to 0.75 per cent, by providing targeted tax cuts reducing the per capita habitation tax, lowering tax rates for the two lowest-income brackets, and by dropping the regressive value-added tax (VAT) by one percentage point. However, it also promised to cut the overall tax burden—taxes plus social charges—by 2003 to 43.5 per cent, down from a peak of 45.7 per cent (*Le Monde*, 2–3 April 2000: 7).

Finally, at the same time as it cut costs in health care by funnelling patients through primary care physicians, with higher reimbursement rates for those who saw their general practitioners first, it inaugurated a universal health insurance programme—the *couverture maladie universelle* (CMU)—that made health care free of charge for lower-income groups by providing supplementary health insurance on a means-tested basis to an estimated 6 million needy individuals (see Levy 2001). The one thing the Jospin government did not do, however, was reform public sector pensions. And here the problem remained a question of political institutional capacity, given the difficulty of imposing reforms without crippling protests in the streets.

France, in short, just as Germany and Britain, altered its monetary, industrial, labour, and social policies at different times in different ways to differing
effects in response to the differently experienced pressures of globalization and
Europeanization. All three countries followed their own internal logics related
to national economic vulnerabilities, political institutional capacities, policy
legacies, policy preferences, and policy discourses, rather than some external
logic related to globalization or Europeanization. These internal logics also
help explain the differential mechanics of policy adjustment in response to
the adjustment pressures of Europeanization in specific policy sectors.

The Mechanics of Policy Adjustment to Europeanization

Other variables must be considered in conjunction with the mediating
factors when explaining the differential effects of Europeanization on EU
member-states in specific policy sectors. This is because Europeanization has
been a major institutional force in addition to the economic, having exerted
different adjustment pressures on member states depending upon how
constraining decisions taken at the EU level have been in their implementation at the national level, however they were arrived at.[7] Such constraints are
related to whether an EU decision proffers a highly specified set of rules for
compliance, less specified rules, only suggested rules, or no rules at all, and
whether the adjustment mechanisms involve coercion, mimesis, or regulatory competition. In the end, such adjustment pressures and mechanisms,
considered in conjunction with the mediating factors, lead to differential
outcomes, whether inertia, absorption, or transformation.

EU Adjustment Pressures, Adjustment Mechanisms, and Outcomes

It is important to note that regardless of how little or much loss of autonomy
occurs with regard to EU-level decision-making, that is, whether a decision
comes out of treaty negotiations, Council directives, or of the ECJ, once it is
decided it becomes an adjustment pressure for all member states since all
must implement the decision. The amount of pressure however, differs
according to the degree of constraint related to member-state compliance
with the EU decision and the adjustment mechanisms that this entails.
Where an EU decision requires member states to follow a highly specified set

---

[7] I speak here only of decisions in the regulatory arena. In distributive policies, such as research
and development or structural and cohesion policies, there is probably not the same set of dynamics or mechanics. Moreover, these are areas in which the arrows go up as much as down.

of rules when complying with it, the adjustment mechanism potentially involves a high degree of coercion, as in the case of the Maastricht criteria in the run-up to EMU. Where the rules are less highly specified, leaving leeway in their transposition into national rules, the adjustment normally entails a lower degree of coercion, as when the EU sets targets for the date, kind, and amount of liberalization of a formerly highly regulated sector such as telecommunications or electricity, but leaves the country to specify many of the details of liberalizing policies and regulatory arrangements. By contrast, where the EU decision only suggests rules, which member states can choose to follow closely, loosely, or not at all, the adjustment mechanisms are primarily ones of mimesis, since member states are free to imitate or not as they see fit, as in the case of rail transport or road haulage. Finally, where an EU decision specifies no rules to follow, as in cases such as the mutual recognition of products, where it simply lifts barriers to trade, then the adjustment mechanism generally involves regulatory competition and in principle no coercion, since no change in rules is demanded, even if there may be significant economic pressures for change resulting from competition (see Table 2.2).[8]

Potential adjustment pressure, however, is different from actual pressure, and any decision rule may in practice be linked to any one of the adjustment mechanisms in any given case. This is because, even if a rule is highly specified, it may not be experienced as coercive to a member state for which it fits policy legacies and preferences, while even a suggested rule may seem coercive to a member state that feels pressured to conform if only by the force of ideas. Similarly, moreover, whereas mimesis can occur even with rules that are specified to a greater or lesser extent, as countries search for the best solutions to regulatory specifications, even mutual recognition may be experienced as coercive when domestic actors feel empowered to press for national regulatory change. The differences between member-states' expected and actual experiences of compliance with EU decisions can best be explained by reference to the mediating factors, which also serve to explain member-states' differential outcomes in response to EU decisions.

In different policy sectors, one can differentiate among three kinds of outcomes in response to the pressures of Europeanization—inertia, absorption, and transformation[9]—as a result of the mediating factors discussed above

---

[8] On the constraints related to European decision rules, Knill and Lehmkuhl (1999) refer to 'positive integration' in what I term cases of highly or less specified decision rules, to 'negative integration' in cases of no rule, and to 'framing' where a rule is suggested. On adjustment mechanisms, see Radaelli (2000a,b).

[9] See Héritier (2000a); Cowles, Caporaso, and Risse (2001); Börzel (1999); Radaelli (2000a).

Table 2.2 EU adjustment pressures and potential adjustment mechanisms

Adjustment pressures	Potential adjustment mechanisms	Examples
Decision rules highly specified	Coercion at a high level	European monetary union, some environmental policies
Decision rules less specified	Coercion at a less high level	Deregulation of financial services, telecom, electricity, air transport
Decision rules only suggested	Mimesis	Rail transport, road haulage
No decision rules	Regulatory competition	Mutual recognition of products

(see Fig. 2.2). Inertia—that is, slowness or resistance to change—appears where actors feel little economic pressure to change, see little 'fit' in terms of long-standing policies or policy-making institutions, would prefer not to change, have little capacity to negotiate or impose change, and/or have no discourse that could persuade of the necessity and appropriateness of change. With inertia, policy legacies and preferences are maintained at the price of adjustment. Absorption is when accommodation occurs without significant change, given a good 'fit' with national policy legacies and preferences as well as institutional capabilities for adaptation (see Héritier 2001a).[10] Here, policy legacies and preferences are maintained at virtually no cost at all, and neither politics nor economics is at issue. Transformation is when changes occur that reverse policy legacies and go against traditional policy preferences, which often assumes significant economic vulnerability and political institutional capacity to impose or negotiate reform, which in turn presupposes a transformative discourse.[11] Only here is the price of adjustment the reversal of policy legacies and preferences. And this is the only place where it makes sense to talk of a significant loss of autonomy, albeit often in exchange for gains in power in the Parsonian sense.

---

[10] Börzel and Risse (2000) further differentiate between absorption and accommodation, where absorption provides for no change to existing policies or policy-making institutions, accommodation for modest change due to readjustments that have little real effect on existing policies or policy-making institutions. Similarly Knill and Lenschow (2001) differentiate between 'confirmation of the core or compliance without change' and 'change within a static core'. For purposes of simplicity, I use 'absorption' to include both meanings.

[11] In the terms of Knill and Lenschow (2001), this would be 'change within a changing core'.

Adjustment pressures from Europeanization	Factors mediating impact of Europeanization pressures	Potential outcomes
Rules highly specified	Economic vulnerability	Inertia
Rules less specified	Political institutional capacity	
		Absorption
Rules suggested	Policy legacies	
No rules	Policy preferences	Transformation
	Discourse	

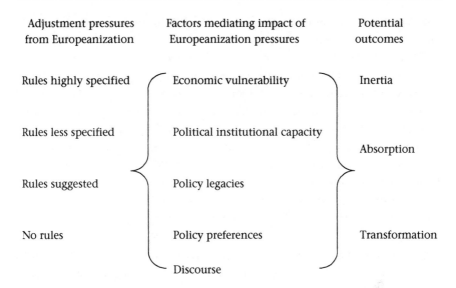

Fig. 2.2 Europeanization flow-chart

The Mechanics of Adjustment to Highly Specified EU Decision Rules

The coerciveness of an EU decision is in principle highest where member states must implement a highly specified rule. In practice, however, member states are not likely to experience coerciveness if the rule fits with long-standing policy legacies. In such cases, the outcome of policy adjustment will be absorption. But even where a rule appears highly coercive, by going against a country's policy legacies and preferences, transformation may not always be the end result, given inertia for some, whether through opt-outs or failure to comply.

European Monetary Integration

In European monetary integration, for example, although the adjustment mechanism is in principle coercion—given that with EMU all countries participating are required not only to meet the specific macroeconomic targets related to public deficits, debt, and inflation rates but also to bring their macroeconomic management systems in conformity, in particular with regard to the independence of the central bank—the actual outcomes vary. Here, the political institutional capacity to change has not been so much at issue. Not only has monetary policy-making tended to be the exclusive purview of the state or state-delegated bodies, with government capacity to impose change generally higher than in most other policy areas, but in most countries by the 1980s it had been 'captured' by a highly restricted policy elite dedicated to monetarism (Dyson and Featherstone 1999). However, vulnerability to intensifying global economic pressures was an issue, although it was greater for some member states than others, given very different levels of exposure to the currency markets as well as very different macroeconomic management systems—some of which worked better than others in a rapidly internationalizing economic environment (as noted earlier). The decision to join the European Monetary System in 1979 and later the European Monetary Union, with all that this meant in terms of changes in monetary policies and institutions, was more difficult for some countries than others, depending upon questions of 'fit' in terms of policy legacies and preferences and the ability of the discourse to persuade major policy actors and/or the general public of the necessity and appropriateness of changes in monetary policies and institutions to promote monetary integration.

In Germany, Europeanization beginning with the European Monetary System of 1979 and then with the run-up to EMU beginning in 1992 has been little more than an extension to Europe and its member states of Germany's own traditional macroeconomic patterns and prejudices—despite initial resistance by other founders of the EMS (Ludlow 1982)—in particular its emphasis on the importance of a strong currency, of price stability, and of the dangers of inflation. In consequence, Germany has essentially been able to absorb most policy changes related to monetary integration up until the euro without any sense of coercion, having maintained its own long-standing policy preferences and legacies—as noted above.

By the same token, however, Germany was itself a coercive force with regard to other member states' national economies through the Bundesbank's role in setting interest rates up until EMU (McNamara 1998; Thiel and Schroeder 1998). This was particularly problematic for other member-states in the early 1990s at the time of German unification, when the Bundesbank, mandated by law to focus on domestic price stability even if this meant the sacrifice of the EMU or harder times for fellow member states' economies, raised interest rates to avoid inflation in Germany, given government unwillingness to raise taxes any higher. This thereby forced other member states to raise their own interest rates even higher to maintain currency exchange rates in line with the Deutschmark, slowing their own economic growth and deepening recessions more than would otherwise have been necessary (Sperling 1994; McNamara and Jones 1995).

Only with the advent of the euro and the transfer of responsibility for monetary policy to the European Central Bank did Germany also undergo a transformation in the monetary policy arena, and thereby experience coercion. The loss of the Deutschmark in particular presented difficulties in the discourse in the late 1990s, given public concerns about the loss of one of the closest things to a symbol of national sovereignty in Germany (Schmidt 1997a). And yet, in most other ways, the transformation has so far been symbolic at best, since the shared control exercised by the ECB as supranational authority has reflected German policy legacies and preferences with regard to inflation, just as was expected, given central bankers' apprenticeship in Bundesbank methods in the run-up to EMU.

In Britain, European monetary integration also has had relatively little effect, but mainly because the country responded with inertia. By joining the EMS but not the ERM in 1979, Britain managed to maintain a large measure of monetary autonomy, something given up only briefly subsequently between 1990 and 1992, with the—disastrous—foray into the ERM. No European regulations or directives have had any significant impact on monetary policy in Britain (Artis 1998). Moreover, economic management institutions remained unchanged, most notably state control of the Bank of England, until the June 1997 decision of the Blair government to seek membership in EMU, which involved starting the central bank down the path to independence along with other measures. But although Blair started the transformation process, he kept his options open with regard to EMU.

This inertia with regard to European monetary integration has meant that Britain has maintained its policy legacies and preferences at the price of adjustment. The inertia itself stems not only from the fact that policy elites remain divided over whether European monetary integration would make Britain more or less economically vulnerable to globalization. It is also because they have been paralysed by the lack of a persuasive public discourse capable of convincing the public, and even more importantly the media, not just of the necessity of change but even more importantly of its appropriateness, given concerns about encroachments on national sovereignty (see Schmidt 1997a; 2000a).

In France, finally, by contrast with German absorption and British inertia, European monetary integration has been transformative. Although the country made an early and full commitment to European monetary integration by joining the EMS in 1979, the country's real transformation came in 1983, in response not just to global economic pressures but also to the institutional constraints imposed by the EMS, which essentially demanded the turn to monetarism if the country were to stay in (see above). With this switch, France transformed its monetary policies and policy-making institutions completely in the face of European monetary integration, going against long-standing policy legacies and preferences for neo-Keynesian demand-management and a state-directed credit allocation system (Loriaux 1998; Boltho 1996). But in giving away much of the state's autonomy in monetary affairs, it was able to regain control over the evolution of fundamental monetary quantities (Loriaux 1991: 270). Moreover, although the switch was initially experienced as coercive and thus a loss of power in Weberian terms, the end result served new national economic and political goals, and thereby also represented a gain in power in Parsonian terms. France's subsequent leadership of monetary integration through the Maastricht Treaty and the euro, in partnership with Germany, is testimony to the country's gain in power in political terms—and was the focus of the government's legitimizing discourse. Economically, moreover, it was also a way of insuring against further vulnerability to global currency markets, by exerting a control that was to be fully shared, however, only once the ECB took over from the Bundesbank (see above).

Other Policy Arenas

Another set of examples illustrative of the impact of highly specified EU decision rules, albeit in a domain outside our immediate subject of study, is in the environmental policy arena, where highly specified rules for a wide range of environmental protection decisions have also been potentially highly coercive. Here again, however, the actual results have been mediated by the amount of fit with policy legacies and preferences, as well as political institutional capacity—economic vulnerability not being a factor here. For example, both France and Britain—initially—responded with inertia to the 1980 Water Directive, where the EU prescribed uniform standards and formal, legalistic patterns of interest intermediation. In France, this was because the new EU rules went against the traditional higher-level civil servants' administrative discretion in implementation and, thus, against the legacies of its policy-making institutions; in Britain, similarly, because it went against its own legacies of industry self-regulation—until the British government changed its policy preferences with regard to the water industry, and transformed the regulatory system to follow the EU model as it privatized the water industry. Germany, by contrast, responded with absorption to the Water Directive, given that the EU's prescribed legalistic and interventionist patterns fitted with its policy legacies, although its demand for higher water-quality standards, which conflicted with the preferences of some groups—polluters—but was in keeping with those of others—water providers and environmental associations—meant that it took government some time to negotiate (see Knill and Lenschow 1998; Knill 1998; Knill and Lehmkuhl 1999).

Fit with policy legacies or preferences, however, is not always sufficient to predict the results. This is because political institutional capacity is also a major mediating factor, with principal policy actors' ability to impose or negotiate reform often determining the outcome, whether or not an EU decision is compatible with long-standing policies or preferences. In the Waste Packaging Directive, for example, where the EU also prescribed relatively high, uniform environmental protection objectives and formal, legalistic patterns of interest intermediation, the 'misfit' with British policy legacies and preferences for self-regulation and low standards did not stop the transformation of the sector. This was mainly because the British government, intent on guaranteeing the free movement of goods and in favour of harmonization, was not only willing to go against its traditional preferences but had the political institutional capacity to impose an innovative set of changes in conformity with the EU rule that industry was unable to stop. In Germany, by contrast, where the EU rule seemingly fitted with long-standing German policy legacies since it required an equally legalistic approach which did not challenge the regulatory style, inertia rather than absorption was the result. This was mainly because the larger number of actors with a say in decision-making were able to resist the much more minimal Europe-led changes—and no amount of government discourse focused on the necessity of conforming to EU decisions could persuade them of the appropriateness of watering down the higher German environmental protection targets (Haverland 1999).

In other words, in a multi-actor system such as Germany where a highly specified EU decision rule goes against principal policy actors' preferences for higher standards, inertia may result from the political institutional incapacity to negotiate reform. By contrast, in single-actor systems such as Britain or France where non-governmental policy actors are often weak and where the political institutional capacity to impose is strong, the outcome tends to depend on national policy legacies and government preferences. This was the case of the Equal Pay Directive, which was in keeping with French governmental policy legacies and preferences and led to absorption, having been transposed fully on time and applied almost fully but late; whereas it went against British policy legacies and government preferences and led to inertia, having been transposed late and never applied (Duina 1999). This suggests that even where an EU decision provides a highly specified rule for member-states to implement, the outcomes may vary significantly.

The Mechanics of Adjustment to Less Specified EU Decision Rules

By comparison with highly specified rules, the adjustment pressures from EU decisions are less great when the rules are less specified, as is their coerciveness because countries are freer to choose how to implement the decision.

Moreover, the actual outcome of adjustment depends upon countries' policy legacies and preferences as well as institutional capacities and economic vulnerabilities. Equally importantly, the amount of coercion countries feel with regard to the institutional pressures from EU decisions may vary across industrial sectors, depending upon the sector's level of vulnerability to global and European economic pressures. For where economic vulnerability is high, the EU institutional pressures may represent more an accompaniment to national change than a leader of it. Sectors such as financial services and telecommunications in fact changed more in response to intensified economic pressures from international competition and Europe-wide industry consolidation, as well as advances in technology, than other sectors of the economy which have been less vulnerable to global competition because they are more strictly European—for example, electricity—or even national—for example, the railroads or road haulage—in scope, and less driven by technological change, competitive pressures, or potential profits. These latter sectors are where the EU has more often led reform efforts rather than followed them.

Financial Services

In the financial services sector, for example, the internationalization of the financial markets, which was facilitated by rapidly changing technology, made attractive by high profit potentials, and spurred by the 1979 US stock market deregulation, represented the main pressure for change in Britain and France, way ahead of any European decisions in the area. Britain transformed its financial services sector with the 'big bang' in 1986, having had the political institutional capacity to impose deregulation in response to concerns about the City's ability to meet the competitive challenges following from the US stock market deregulation. It subsequently absorbed the changes related to EU decision rules—although not without protest at their statutory as opposed to voluntary nature (see Chapters 4 and 6). France's transformation, with the 'little bang' of the same year, resulted from an equally high political institutional capacity to impose reforms that went hand in hand with privatization, as a means to ensure the successful sell-off of public enterprises while also providing alternative sources of capital for businesses no longer able to turn to the now cash-poor state, given the turn to monetarism. What is more, European integration in financial markets in some sense followed from French financial market liberalization, given that it was the key to French support for an integrated European market for financial services, and a sine qua non of the Single Market (Mélitz 1993). Germany, in contrast to both France and Britain, did not reform its stock market until 1995, with inertia explicable in terms of its lack of economic vulnerability in the 1980s to either global or European economic forces and its lack of political institutional capacity to change given opposition by the large national banks and the regional governments. Transformation came in response to the growing competitive pressures from European capital market integration (Story 1996), and was spurred not by the European Commission but by domestic actors once the banks began internationalizing through the acquisition of British investment houses in the late 1980s, having recognized that Germany would be left behind if it did not liberalize (Lütz 1998).[12]

In all three countries, then, transformation came primarily in response to economic vulnerabilities to global and European economic pressures rather than EU adjustment pressures; and all countries absorbed any further changes related to European decisions, such as on investment services, without significant alteration in their basic institutional arrangements or policies.[13] Moreover, while all three countries have liberalized in similar ways, the distinctiveness of national policy-making institutions remains. Britain's 'big bang' of 1986 replaced the informal rules and gentlemen's agreements of the past with a regulatory system based on public law. France's 'little bang' of 1986 substituted an independent regulatory commission akin to the American Security and Exchange Commission (SEC) for its hidebound, oligopolistic system of the past. And Germany's much later liberalization of 1995—which was also in response to the lack of foreign investment in the German market due to the costs of transactions and the 'opaqueness of the self-regulatory system' as well as the refusal of US, British, and French stock markets to list German shares because of their lower regulatory standards—replaced a regionalized, self-regulatory, cartel-like arrangement with a more centralized, federal supervisory agency (Lütz 1998).

Telecommunications

In telecommunications, much as in financial services, change has also been driven mostly by the increasingly intense global competitive pressures, the technological possibilities, and the potential profits, spurred by US deregulation in the 1970s and early 1980s. Here, however, EU decisions did play a greater intermediary role in transmitting, channelling, and amplifying global pressures, and in structuring the resulting regulatory systems of most

---

[12] European policy pressures were evident only in the case of the European insider trading directive of 1989, which Germany originally tried to block, capitulating only when it saw itself likely to be overruled.

[13] Such changes have been modest, however, because EU legislation has been hampered by political disagreements and cumbersome legislative processes (see Murray 2001).

member states (Schneider 2001; S. Schmidt 1998). This was least the case for Britain, however, which transformed its telecommunications sector early, ahead of EU adjustment pressures, having deregulated and privatized in 1984. Britain, therefore, simply absorbed most subsequent changes resulting from the increasing importance of EU decisions in the 1990s. For Germany and France, the EU was a much more significant force, not only as a source of adjustment pressure but also as a source of legitimization for change through national discourse, especially by governments of the left faced with opposition from political allies as well as from telecoms trade unions and employees (Thatcher 2000).

Germany transformed its telecommunications sector later than Britain, over the late 1980s to the early and mid-1990s, but before or at the same time as European decisions, some of which it was instrumental in passing. The changes in policy preferences were related to the costs of unification as well as to the coming challenges of competition in European markets. Deregulation and privatization were the result not only of changing preferences, however, but also of Germany's political institutional capacity to engage in a slow, politically initiated, pragmatic, and consensus-focused process of negotiation with the wide range of affected actors, including Deutsche Telekom management and workers, which ensured the successful 1989 restructuring and the 1994 agreement to privatize the company by 1996. France's experience was different, with incremental reforms in the late 1980s followed by inertia in the 1990s, mainly because French governments were stymied by the lack of political institutional capacity to change in the face of strong union opposition and public attachment to the ideas of *service public* as the obligation of the 'Republican State'. Transformation ultimately came as a result of a shift in the preferences of the French government and France Télécom's top management, fuelled by ideology, technological innovation, and interest in pursuing global and European alliances. The government's 1993 reversal of its long-standing opposition to opening the market to competition translated itself into cooperative negotiations at the EU level. This in turn produced European decisions that the government and top management were then able to use domestically in the discourse to justify reforming France Télécom, including partial privatization as of 1997 (Thatcher 1999, 2000; Schneider 2001).

In all three countries, again, then, change came primarily in response to global economic vulnerabilities, although EU adjustment pressures played a greater role in structuring the responses, with all having introduced competition in traditional telephony, at least partially privatized their former public operations, and created independent regulatory agencies for the tasks of monitoring, licensing, and regulating. But here, too, distinctiveness remains in the policy-making institutions, with the British set-up granting greater freedom to the regulatory agency in terms of licensing and retail pricing than those of France or Germany (Thatcher 1999).

Electricity

In electricity, by contrast with the telecommunications and financial services sectors, economic vulnerability was not much of a factor, given that there was little pressure from globalization in a sector with few technological changes and little competition in highly protected markets. Here, Europeanization was the main—institutional—pressure for liberalization, with the EU Commission the principal instigator of reform and the EU decision-making process crucial in getting member states to accept changes which for some went completely against their policy legacies and preferences.

This was not the case for Britain, which absorbed the reform without any loss of autonomy, given that it had deregulated already in 1990. But for France and Germany, the countries which had been largely responsible for the inertia in the sector through the 1980s and early 1990s, major changes followed from the electricity liberalization directive of December 1996—which was not applied until 1999—although without as much loss of auto-nomy as one might have expected (Eising and Jabko 2002). This is because, although both agreed to open up highly protected markets to phased-in competition, they both managed largely to maintain the institutional arrangements of the past. France kept its single, dominant, nationalized player, even though Electicité de France (EDF) lost its monopoly, and Germany kept its highly decentralized market. Moreover, France managed to insert in the directive an article (3.2) that recognized the rights of states to impose public service obligations in the general interest.

The difference in the experiences of the two countries, however, is that whereas Germany transformed its electricity sector by liberalizing much more than the EU directive demanded, France resisted transformation, with inertia largely the outcome. In Germany, in fact, federal government actors and industry supporters changed their preferences while the directive was being negotiated, and then gained in political institutional capacity to negotiate reform by using the EU in the discourse to persuade all of the appropriateness of change (Eising and Jabko 2002). The reasons for this were multiple: the example of the successful liberalization in Britain had had an effect, promoting a general sense that liberalization could reinforce the German model by reducing prices while ending regional monopolies, some-thing the bigger companies favoured and the smaller operators opposed.

Moreover, the EU-level policy proposals were largely viewed as compatible with the idea of the social market economy.

In France, by contrast, EU deregulation was mainly seen as incompatible with the idea of the *service public* which the government defended, concerned about opposition from EDF—after initial support in the late 1980s—as well as negative public reactions, in particular strikes by the public service unions. Thus, not only did the reform remain largely against French policy preferences, the French government was also unsure of its political institutional capacity to impose reform in the face of opposition—a fact that was born out by the protracted approval process in Parliament which delayed implementation until 1999 (Eising and Jabko 2002) and which the French Secretary of State for Industry explained was a result of 'the seriousness of desired democratic debate' (*Le Figaro*, 19 November 1999). Thus, although competition has been introduced into the French electricity sector, there has so far been no transformation of the sector—although this may be an ultimate consequence of the sector's being opened up to competition.

Air Transport

In air transport, much as in electricity, reform was driven by the EU Commission, despite the fact that global competition has exerted some pressure and US deregulation acted somewhat as a spur for change. In France, much as in the case of electricity, the response was mainly inertia, as the government sought to do as much as possible to maintain the dominance of its single nationalized player, Air France. But it was forced to abandon its traditional preference for a public service monopoly that provided an extensive air services network within a protected domestic market, and to allow foreign competitors into the domestic market. In Germany, by contrast, as in the cases of telecommunications and electricity, the response was transformation. But the process was very slow, given initial opposition from some federal States worried about the impact on the airline's relationship with German aerospace firms located in their regions and the need to work out the specifics between labour and management. Moreover, here as in the telecommunications case, the EU push was not as significant as internal pressures for change that came from actors' concerns about firms' global competitiveness. The privatization of Lufthansa in the mid-1990s, although certainly spurred in part by the creation of the Single Market, was much more related to domestic concerns about the performance of the public enterprise and pressures on public finances. In Britain, finally, where privatization came in the mid-1980s, the response to the EU was mainly one of absorption since the UK was little affected in the substance of policy, the availability of traditional policy instruments, or the introduction of new ideas, although it no longer enjoys absolute discretion over market access, capacity, tariff-setting, or licensing (see Kassim 1998). In fact, whereas one can ascribe a significant loss of autonomy to France in this case, given that reform went against national policy preferences and legacies, one could argue that the UK has enhanced its autonomy, given that the UK regime was in many ways generalized to the rest of the EU.

The Mechanics of Adjustment to a Suggested EU Model or No Model

In areas where EU decisions provide only suggested rules for compliance or no rules at all, coercion is generally low compared to EU decisions with specified rules. Suggested decision rules mainly occur in areas where the EU provides 'soft' framing mechanisms, such as minimalist directives, non-compulsory regulations, and EU policy recommendations that serve to legitimize and/or influence national plans for reform; or where it establishes high-level EU policy committees that serve to socialize national policy-makers into accepting or rejecting certain policy practices. In these cases, the adjustment mechanisms involve primarily mimesis, as countries are expected to consider the EU's ideas and suggestions for liberalization and to learn from them as well as from one another on the liberalizing possibilities. Where there is no decision rule at all, generally the case of mutual recognition, the adjustment mechanisms involve primarily regulatory competition as barriers to the free movement of goods, capital, services, and/or people are lifted. But although there is no EU-related institutional coercion in either case, countries can nevertheless experience coercion as a by-product of the psychological pressures related to group processes or of the economic pressures from regulatory competition. EU decisions, however, may represent not just constraints but also opportunities, providing governments with legitimizing arguments and empowering new coalitions for reform.

Rail Transport and Road Haulage

In rail transport, the lack of economic vulnerability with regard to global pressures, together with decision-making based on unanimity in the Council of Ministers, ensured against any major EU regulatory overhaul of the sector, despite pressure from the EU Commission. Nonetheless, the railways directive, which outlined a series of deregulatory recommendations but was compulsory only in terms of changes in national accounting systems, has been a powerful ideational mechanism of adjustment for some countries. The EU's suggested rules provided the British government with extra legitimization for its radical privatization programme, thereby enhancing its political institutional capacity to reform. For the German government, the directive gave it the necessary legitimacy to negotiate domestic-driven reforms that had been stymied. By contrast, the EU had comparatively little effect on the French government, which resisted any radical reform while maintaining its long-held policy preferences and long-standing policy legacies in this *service public* area, as in it had in electricity and air transport (Knill and Lehmkuhl 1999; Héritier 2000*a*, 2001*b*).[14]

In the case of road haulage, the driver of change came more from domestic groups empowered by the EU decision than from the ideational uses of the decision. Again, though, the EU decision was relatively limited: the cabotage directive introduced the right of non-resident transport haulers to operate in foreign markets but allowed quantitative restrictions and price controls to remain, which acted as a spur for change where domestic coalitions were able to use the EU rule to challenge the existing equilibria. This has led to highly differentiated results. In Britain and France, which already had liberalized regulatory regimes, absorption was the result. In Germany, by contrast, transformation toward a more liberalized regime came after a long period of inertia, with the EU rule acting as a spur to the formation of new domestic coalitions for reform. In Italy, by comparison, the domestic coalitions united against liberalizing European trends ensured that the resulting inertia could be seen as retrenchment, given a move toward greater protectionism in the sector (Héritier, Knill, and Mingers 1996; Knill and Lehmkuhl 1999).

Mutual Recognition of Goods and Services

Mutual recognition in principle involves the least amount of coercion, since it imposes no EU decision rules on member states as it provides for the acceptance throughout the EU of products that meet the standards of one member nation, as long as national provisions do not violate primary Community law. One can safely say that the ECJ decision enabling French beer to be sold in Germany even though it did not meet German beer brewing requirements originally set in the sixteenth century has not involved any coercion of German beer-drinkers, nor has it altered German beer-drinking habits one whit. Because mutual recognition simply allows for a good to be sold in a country, but does not oblige consumers to buy the product, coercion

---

[14] The importance of ideas has similarly been evident in television policy, where the EU's use of the instrument of audience share in media ownership policy served both Germany and Britain as inspiration for their reform initiatives (Harcourt 2000). And in tax policy, the Council of Ministers group dedicated to the peer review of harmful tax practices led to the shelving of certain bad practices already in the pipeline (Radaelli 1999*a*).

is not at issue—unless one wants to argue that simply introducing a product into the market is problematic, which one could conceivably do only in the case of British beef in France.

However, the economic pressures related to regulatory competition even in the absence of direct EU-related institutional pressures can themselves be a coercive force for change. The danger is that they lead to competitive deregulation, most notably by triggering a 'race to the bottom' in standards in such areas as environmental protection, labour regulation, and even occupational safety and health, where these are not covered by EU law (Sun and Pelkmans 1995; Majone 1996). Mutual recognition in theory at least would encourage competition among member states' regulatory activities by enabling firms to allocate their resources in such a way as to avoid heavy regulatory burdens. By moving or even just threatening to move their production facilities to countries with the lowest wages and lowest worker safety and product quality standards, firms would thereby push member states to lower standards regulating the workplace and rules with regard to workers' pay and protections (McGee and S. Weatherhill 1990; Dehousse 1992: 395). In practice, however, such a race to the bottom has yet to materialize, even though some did argue that Renault's closing of the Vilvoorde factory in Belgium in 1997 to open one in Spain represented the beginning of one.[15]

Conclusion

Thus, there are no simple generalizations to be made about the mechanics of member states' adjustment to Europeanization, given the mediating factors influencing outcomes and the differential losses of autonomy and control in different policy sectors at different times in response to different EU decision-making constraints. Country-specific patterns of adjustment nevertheless emerge, once one considers responses across political economic sectors (see Table 2.3).

For Britain, the pattern of policy adjustment is one of early response to globalization, with absorption of EU decisions in areas where Britain anticipated Europe-led liberalization, that is, in financial services, telecommunications, electricity, air transport, railways, and road haulage, but with inertia in European monetary integration. For Germany, by contrast, we find absorption

[15] Louis Schweitzer, CEO of Renault, however, when asked about this, insisted that he was not against 'social Europe'. After all, he said, we planned a move to Spain, which is part of a social Europe, not to the UK or Ireland. Interview with author, Paris, June 1997.

Table 2.3 Impact of adjustment pressures on policy sectors

	Monetary integration	Financial services	Telecom	Electricity	Air transport	Railways	Road haulage
UK							
Timing	Not yet	Early	Early	Early	Early	Early	Early
Pressures	Global	Global	Global	Global	Global	Internal/Eur	Internal
EU response	Inertia	Absorb	Absorb	Absorb	Absorb	Absorb	Absorb
France							
Timing	Early	Early	Late	Late	Late	Late	Early
Pressures	Global/Eur	Global	Global/Eur	European	European	European	Internal
EU response	Transformation	Absorb	Inertia/Transf	Inertia	Inertia	Inertia	Absorb
Germany							
Timing	Early	Late	Mid	Late	Late	Late	Late
Pressures	Global	Glob/internal	Glob/unification	European	European	European	European
EU response	Absorb	Transform	Inertia/Transf	Transform	Transform	Transform	Inertia/Transf

only with regard to European monetary integration, the result of a very early response to globalization, and transformation in all the other political economic policy sectors, coming late in response to European decisions and pressures. In France, finally, the pattern is more mixed, with early transformation in response to globalization pressures in European monetary integration, financial services, and road haulage, late transformation in telecommunications, but with inertia in all other areas which are traditionally seen as part of the *service public*: electricity, air transport, and railways, where reform has been harder to legitimize as appropriate in public discourse.

Across time, moreover, the dynamics of policy adjustment show that, although these three countries did move in the same general policy directions, globalization and Europeanization have not produced convergence. First of all, they reformed at different times in different sequencing. Germany, for example, shifted earliest to monetarism but deregulated and privatized last, while it has yet to decentralize its labour market in any significant way or to retrench the welfare state. Britain, by contrast, shifted to monetarism five years after Germany, decentralized its labour markets shortly after this, began deregulation and privatization not long thereafter, then made efforts to retrench the welfare state. France, meanwhile, shifted to monetarism nine years after Germany and five after Britain, began the decentralization of the labour markets even earlier than its shift to monetarism around the same time as Britain, and proceeded to deregulate and privatize shortly thereafter, while it waited very much later to begin reform of the welfare state and the deregulation of the public services sector.

Second, these countries have ended up in different places, with all three monetarist but Britain still out of EMU; with Britain's business more deregulated and privatized than that of France or Germany; with Britain and France's industrial relations systems far more decentralized than that of Germany; and with Britain's welfare state far less generous than those of Germany and France. And finally, the changes experienced by these three countries with respect to Europeanization from the 1980s to the late 1990s were very different, given that French adjustment involved transformation with respect to monetary and industrial policy—in the competitive sector—and inertia in social policy and '*services public*', German adjustment involved absorption with respect to monetary policy, late transformation in industrial policy, and inertia in labour and social policies, and British adjustment involved absorption in industrial policy and inertia in monetary and social policy.

The mediating factors help explain these different experiences. While economic vulnerability to globalization was an impetus to monetary policy change in Germany in the mid-1970s and to industrial policy change only in the 1990s, it was a force for change in Britain beginning in the late 1970s, while additional vulnerability to Europeanization also pushed France to begin reform in the mid-1980s. Political institutional capacity to impose or negotiate change was less likely when governments were faced with protest in the streets—France with regard to industrial policies on public services and social policies until the late 1990s—or strong union resistance—Germany in industrial policy until the mid-1990s and social policy until the 2000s—than when they met with citizen passivity and union demobilization—Britain beginning in the mid-1980s. Policy legacies and preferences with regard to industrial and social policy made it somewhat easier for Britain to reform than France or Germany, while they made it easier for Germany with regard to monetary policy. As for discourse, in the reform of social policy in particular, all three countries experienced difficulties in convincing the public of the appropriateness of reform, even when they were able to show its necessity (see Chapter 6).

Given these policy adjustments in response to the pressures of Europeanization as well as globalization, the next question is: what impact on national practice? For this, we need to look more closely at changes in relations of business, government, and labour from the post-war period, where three basic varieties of capitalism are discernible, even up to today.

PART II

The Practices of Economic Adjustment

3

Still Three Models of Capitalism? The Impact of Changing Policies and Growing Pressures on Economic Practices

The political economic policies which have brought convergence in the monetary policy arena, liberalization in the industrial policy arena, decentralization in the industrial relations arena, and retrenchment in the social policy arena have also had a significant impact on political economic practices. European countries that conformed to the 'models of capitalism' of the postwar period have changed. But how? The main questions here are: Are European countries now converging on the model of market capitalism, as proponents of globalization insist? Do they, instead, now divide into two varieties of capitalism—market capitalism and managed capitalism—as much of the 'varieties of capitalism' literature suggests? Or do they remain divisible into three, despite all having moved in a more market-oriented direction, as I argue here?

Up until the early 1980s, capitalism in Europe was generally seen as conforming to one of three ideal-typical models: (1) market capitalism, where the liberal state allows economic actors to operate autonomously and to decide for themselves on the directions of their economic activity; (2) managed capitalism, where the 'enabling' state encourages economic actors to operate cooperatively and to coordinate the direction of their activities with one another and the state; and (3) state capitalism, where the interventionist state organizes cooperation among autonomous economic actors and directs their economic activities.

These models have three main distinguishing components that generally require separate elucidation: (1) the structure of business relations, encompassing interactions among firms and between industry and finance, which tend to be driven by the market in market capitalism, managed outside the market in managed capitalism, and organized by the state in state capitalism; (2) the structure of government relations, involving the interactions between state and firms and state and labour, which tend to be at arms' length in market capitalism, negotiated in managed capitalism, and state-directed in state capitalism; and (3) the structure of industrial relations, including wage bargaining, management-labour relations, and the government role in labour regulation, which tend to be market-reliant in market capitalism, coordinated in managed capitalism, and state-controlled in state capitalism.

These models are essentially ideal types, that is, inductive sets of generalizations based on groupings of countries with similar characteristics, and in no way are they meant to represent some ideal or idealized set of forms of capitalism. Although one can argue quite convincingly that all countries have their own distinctive variety of capitalism (Crouch and Streeck 1997), this threefold comparison is useful not only as a heuristic device to illuminate similarities among individual countries' models of capitalism but also as a key to understanding the direction of reform undertaken by governments in response to global and European pressures. This is because these idealtypes have themselves been idealized—or demonized—by policy-makers as models to emulate—or to avoid. As such, they represent at one and the same time empirically grounded ideal types of the past and normative ideals for the present and future.

Although no one country has entirely fitted any of these ideal types, certain countries have come closer than others, if not always because of their structural organization then because of their philosophical ideals. The United States has long been seen as representing the ideal-typical model of market capitalism, while in Europe Britain has represented the closest approximation to it, especially since Thatcher.[1] The smaller European democracies such as the Netherlands, Denmark, Sweden, and Austria are instead closest to the ideal-typical model of managed capitalism, with the 'third Italy' qualifying as a regionally based equivalent of it.[2] But among the larger advanced industrialized countries, Germany's 'social market economy' comes closest to the managed capitalist model, and is generally used in illustration of it, despite its more decentralized, regional patterns of interaction.[3] Finally, France until the 1980s has been the ideal-typical model of state capitalism, although Japan could also be cited here with regard to its close business-government relationship, even if the structure of business relations better matches the model of managed capitalism.[4] The 'developmental state'

---

[1] See, for example, Coates (2000); Soskice (1991); Lane (1995). On the significant differences between the US and the UK, see Lazonick and O'Sullivan (1997).

[2] For the smaller European countries, see Katzenstein (1985); Kurzer (1993). For Italy, see Locke (1995).   [3] See Streeck (1997); Katzenstein (1989); Soskice (1991); Lane (1995).

[4] For France, see Hayward (1973); Zysman (1983); Hall (1986); Schmidt (1996). For Japan, see Dore (1997).

as found in Korea and Taiwan also fits under state capitalism, although it too has been in the process of change.[5] Even Italy until the early 1990s, in particular the 'first Italy' of large firms and nationalized enterprises with highly unionized workforces, albeit the weakest case of state capitalism, approximates the model, although it has mainly been state-led by indirection.[6]

In the last quarter of the twentieth century, there can be no doubt that the pressures of globalization and Europeanization combined with the policies instituted in response have altered the environment in which business, government, and labour interact, pushing countries conforming to all three models of capitalism in the direction of greater market orientation. But this does not mean that they are now all converging on the model of market capitalism. Although some countries have indeed gone very far down the road to market capitalism, generally these are the ones that were already market capitalist in their traditional economic management systems, such as Britain. Countries that traditionally conformed more to the model of managed capitalism, by contrast, have been incorporating elements of market capitalism into their economic management systems in order to become more competitive without, for the moment at least, destroying the model, as in the case of Germany, although its system has admittedly been under great strain. By comparison, countries that conformed more to the state capitalist model such as France have transformed their economic management systems through reforms that borrow from managed capitalism as well as market capitalism but that continue to leave a greater role to the state or state-related actors.

There are still three varieties of capitalism, in other words, even though these have evolved significantly from the post-war ideal-typical models. This view contradicts the globalization literature which assumes convergence toward the market capitalist model of the United States and Britain. But it also does not accord entirely with much of the 'varieties of capitalism' literature which assumes contemporary capitalism to be divided into two main kinds: market capitalism, alternatively called the 'liberal market economy', and managed capitalism, otherwise called the 'organized market economy' or the 'coordinated market economy' (Soskice 1991; Hall 2000). State capitalism, in fact, is hardly ever mentioned as an alternative model, and, when countries such as France or Italy are considered at all, they are either lumped together as part of a 'Mediterranean' form of capitalism with Spain, Portugal, Greece, and Turkey (Rhodes 1997; Hall and Soskice 2001: 21) or they are subsumed under managed capitalism as less successful forms of 'coordinated

---

[5] See Weiss (1999b); Woo-Cumings (1999).   [6] See Lange and Regini (1989).

capitalism' or 'network-oriented capitalism' (Rhodes and Van Apeldoorn 1997). Only a few scholars see a distinctive pattern for France, Italy, and others along the same lines discussed herein.[7] And yet, in the earlier literature, this third model was very clearly identified, finding pride of place as 'statism' next to 'liberalism' and 'corporatism' (Katzenstein 1978; Shonfield 1965).

The reason for the elimination of state capitalism stems mainly from scholars' assumptions that today this model has lost its empirical validity as much as its normative value. Although such assumptions are not wrong with regard to the post-war model, they tend to overlook the continuing import-ance of the state or state-related institutions in the economic management systems of countries which have evolved from post-war state capitalism to what one might today call 'state-enhanced capitalism'. There is much to be learned from comparative analyses of those countries in which the state, having played a highly directive role in the past, continues to exercise signi-ficant albeit less direct influence. But the distinctive patterns of such 'state-enhanced' capitalism tend to be lost when scholars put the firm at the centre of their analyses, with labour an important secondary preoccupation and the state only a relatively insignificant and distant third, relegated to the legal and regulatory environment in which firms act. Such an approach risks privileging countries where the state has long played only a secondary or tertiary role—that is, countries conforming to the managed or market capit-alist pattern—and treating as outliers those countries in which the state has played and continues to play a larger role.

This is not to suggest that the firm-centred, dualistic approach to capitalism should be rejected out of hand. Much the contrary. It is in fact a useful cor-rective to approaches of the past which, concerned with modernization, focused almost exclusively on the role of the state;[8] which, concerned with inflation, focused on neo-corporatist patterns of industrial relations;[9] or which, concerned with industrial innovation, focused on sectoral or regional patterns of interaction.[10] At a time when firms have become central players in contemporary capitalism, given the loosening of ties to government and labour as a result of liberalizing reforms, concern with business-led growth makes the firm-centred approach the natural successor to earlier approaches.

---

[7] For example, Boyer (1996) who identifies four models of capitalism and Coates (1999) who identifies the same three models described herein.

[8] See, for example, Shonfield (1965); Katzenstein (1978); Skocpol (1985).

[9] See, for example, Schmitter and Lehmbruch (1979); Lehmbruch and Schmitter (1982); Goldethorpe (1984).

[10] See, for example, Piore and Sabel (1984); Putnam (1993); Locke (1995). For more detail, see the discussion in Hall and Soskice (2001).

Moreover, this approach has a lot to teach us about the interactive dimensions of the relationship between firms and other actors as well as how to conceptualize such relationships (Hall and Soskice 2001)—even with regard to formerly state-capitalist countries.[11] The discussion of the three models of capitalism at the beginning of this chapter owes much in its definitions of market capitalism and managed capitalism to the interactive conceptualizations developed in the firm-centred approach, while the definition of state capitalism builds on these conceptual foundations. And imitation is, after all, the highest form of praise.

I do have one significant critique of the firm-centred approach, however. It runs the risk of presenting reality as static, with the two varieties of capitalism as systems maintaining a kind of homeostatic equilibrium as they adjust to external economic pressures.[12] Approaches that take each country as having its own system of capitalism are less prone to this danger, since they tend to see national capitalisms as evolving over time, becoming hybrids as they take on aspects of other varieties, in particular the Anglo-Saxon.[13] I too see great change over time, as countries have sought to overcome the disadvantages and build on the advantages of their post-war models by incorporating elements of the other models. But rather than characterizing such change as hybridization, I see clusters of countries still differentiable along lines of development from the original three models, with traditionally market capitalist countries having moved toward intensified market capitalism, managed capitalist countries toward more competitive managed capitalism, and state capitalist countries to state-enhanced from state-led capitalism.

Thus, while my classification of European capitalism relies heavily on the 'varieties of capitalism' literature, in particular on the definitions of market and managed capitalism, it adds to it in two basic ways. First, it defines a third variety of capitalism, state-enhanced capitalism, as an alternative to the two that are the focus of the current literature. And second, it focuses on the dynamics of change in economic practices by showing how changes in economic policies in response to the pressures of globalization and European integration have affected the structures of business, government, and labour relations without, however, necessarily producing convergence on a single

---

[11] See, for example, Culpepper (2001); Hancké and Soskice (1996); Hancké (1996; 2001); Lehrer (2001).

[12] This is in particular a problem for Hall and Soskice (2001). Some of the contributors to their edited volume have a more dynamic, firm-centred approach, such as Thelen (2001) and Culpepper (2001).

[13] See, for example, Crouch and Streeck (1997); Crouch (2001); Streeck and Yamamura (2001); Jackson (2001).

model of market capitalism or a binary division into market and managed capitalism.

In what follows, I first define the three ideal-typical models of capitalism and outline the different national pathways to adjustment in response to globalization and Europeanization of countries that more or less conformed to those models in the postwar years. Next, I show how the three varieties of capitalism have remained distinct despite the increasing importance of the international financial markets, as revealed through countries' differentiated finance-related indicators; despite the general retreat of the state through deregulation, as seen through continued differences in state relations with business and labour; and despite the increasing competitiveness of the product markets, as revealed through countries' different production-related indicators. Then, I outline the comparative advantages and disadvantages of the three varieties of capitalism under pressures of globalization and Europeanization. In conclusion, I consider where countries that conformed to the three models in the 1970s seem to have ended up as of the early 2000s. Throughout, I illustrate with examples from Britain, France, and Germany, although these cases are elaborated in the next chapter, which takes a closer look at the trajectories of France, Britain, and Germany from the post-war period to today.

The Three Ideal-Typical Models of Capitalism

In the three ideal-typical models of capitalism—market capitalism, managed capitalism, and state capitalism—business, government, and labour relations are all closely interconnected, leading to distinctive systems (see Table 3.1). As ideal types, moreover, the models encompass various characteristics that in most countries gradually developed over time, with some elements already present pre-war, others established in the early post-war years, and yet others evident only in the 1970s or even later (see Chapter 4). What is more, although ideal-typical market capitalism can be seen as practised still today, ideal-typical state capitalism remains very much a post-war type which is no longer practicable as such, while the practicability of ideal-typical managed capitalism has only recently come into question.

In market capitalism, the structure of the business relationship is market-driven, with inter-firm relations individualistic, competitive, and contractual. Industry-finance relations are similarly distant, with industry dependent on the financial markets for capital, and therefore short-term in view because of the markets' focus on quarterly reports and profits. Government relations

Table 3.1 Ideal-typical characteristics of the models of capitalism

	Market capitalism (US, UK)	Managed capitalism (Ger, NL, Swed)	State capitalism (Fr, It)
Business relations	Market-driven	Non-market managed	State organized
Inter-firm relations	Individualistic, competitive, contractual	Mutually reinforcing, network-based	State-mediated, competitive
Industry-finance	Distant	Close	State-mediated
Investment	Short-term view	Long-term view	Medium-term view
Government relations	Arms' length	Negotiated	State-directed
State characteristics	'Liberal' arbiter	'Enabling' facilitator	'Interventionist' leader
Labour relations	Adversarial	Cooperative	Adversarial
Wage bargaining	Market-reliant	Coordinated	State-controlled
Government role in labour regulation	Bystander	Co-equal or bystander	State imposes

with business are also at arms' length, with the state limited to setting rules and settling conflicts, often leaving the administration of the rules to self-governing bodies or semi-independent regulatory agencies. Otherwise, the state deals with business reactively, providing aid on an ad hoc basis through supply-side measures such as tax credits for investment. Finally, industrial relations tend to rely on the market, with the state a bystander in highly decentralized, often fragmented wage bargaining consisting of negotiations between individual employers and employees while management-labour relations are at best neutral if not adversarial.

Among European countries, only Britain approximated this model in the post-war period. But before the 1980s, it was in fact far from the market capitalist ideal (see Chapter 4). Although inter-firm relations were individualistic and relations between industry and finance distant, competitive behaviour tended to be moderated by 'gentlemanly' agreements. Moreover, despite the fact that the state was generally 'hands-off' in its relations with business, this did not stop governments from intervening through planning experiments, subsidies to declining industries on an ad hoc basis, nationalized enterprises, or the sanctioning of privately regulated cartels. What is more, although the state also tended in principle to respect management's and labour's preference for 'voluntarism,' or free collective bargaining, this did not keep it from intervening through wage controls when the pound was under pressure or from attempting social concertation experiments and 'incomes policies' in failed attempts to coordinate wage restraint. Finally, wage bargaining was itself not as market-reliant as in the ideal because it involved not individual contracts between employer and employee but rather collective bargaining agreements which, given fragmented employer associations and unions, tended to lead to the kinds of inflationary wage rises that compelled governments to intervene in order to ensure the macro-economic health of the country. This was largely responsible for the 'stop-go' pattern of economic policy-making so detrimental to business competitive-ness and ultimately also to employment. Moreover, the constant strike activity only contributed to the adversarial nature of management-labour relations at the same time as it reduced labour productivity and, thereby, further affected business competitiveness.

Much of this was to change with the advent of Thatcher in 1979 as the shift to monetarism together with the radical decentralization of wage-bargaining, privatization, and deregulation ended the stop-go pattern of macroeco-nomic adjustment, the gentlemanly business arrangements, and the state's interventionism in business and labour (see Chapter 2). Labour-management relations became more neutral, wage-bargaining more individualized, inter-firm relations more individualistic and competitive, industry-finance rela-tions even more distant, and state relations with business and labour more arms' length (see Chapter 4). As such, Britain came to epitomize the ideal-typical model only beginning in the 1980s. This is quite different from countries conforming to both managed and state capitalism, which epitom-ized the ideal-typical models in the post-war period up until the 1980s and/or 1990s and diverged from them to varying degrees thereafter.

In managed capitalism, the business relationship is non-market managed, inter-firm relations are mutually reinforcing, and interaction among firms is coordinated through a network-based sharing of information and corporate strategies. Industry-finance relations are close. Industry depends more on the banks than the markets and thus takes a more long-term view because the banks are more focused on increasing market share and company value rather than profits. Government relations with business, moreover, tend to be negotiated: the state acts as an 'enabler' of business activity, taking action not simply to arbitrate among economic actors but to facilitate their activities, often leaving the rules to be jointly administered by them. Finally, management-labour relations tend to be cooperative, with the state either a co-equal or a bystander in labour regulation as well as in wage-bargaining that results from coordinated decision-making between self-organized, cohesive management and unions.

Among the several European countries that fit this model in the post-war period, the smaller countries like the Netherlands—until the 1970s—Sweden—until the 1980s—and Austria—until the 1990s—have come closer to the ideal type than Germany. German business' network-based interrelations have been more loosely constituted and regionally differentiated than in smaller countries where national rather than regional economies are primary. The German government's 'enabling' relations with business and labour are less closely integrated and less influential than in the smaller managed capitalist countries where the central state has been directly involved in all manner of economic policy. In Germany, the federal state has largely left monetary policy to the independent central bank, industrial policy to the *Länder*, and labour and social policy to the social partners. Moreover, German wage bargaining and management-labour relations are bipartite rather than tripartite, since government is generally kept out of business-labour relations rather than let in as a co-equal; wage bargaining is only informally centralized because regionally patterned; and it is generally more conflictual, even if the outcomes are equally consensual. German labour-management relations, finally, are distinctive for the system of co-determination which puts labour on the board of directors.

But whatever the differences from other managed capitalist countries, these are nothing compared with those with regard to market capitalist Britain. The close, network-based relations of German firms have ensured them greater stability and strategic cooperation than the competitive, arm's length relations of British business while the close business-banking relationships have provided German firms with more 'patient capital' and greater protection from takeover than British firms, which rely for financing on the 'impatient capital' of the more profit-oriented, takeover-friendly capital markets. Moreover, German governments'—federal and regional—relations with business have been much more supportive and 'enabling' than the more 'hands-off' and liberal policies of the British government through more targeted aid to industry in areas such as education, apprenticeship and training, and research and development. And although the system of autonomous wage bargaining between management and labour that by law has kept the government out of the process has made it in this sense even more voluntarist than the British, German labour-management relations have nevertheless been much more organized and cooperative than the decentralized and confrontational—until the mid- to late 1980s—or neutral—since the late 1980s—interactions of British business and labour. In Britain, voluntarism meant having barely any rules governing labour-management interaction, decentralization entailed comparatively little coordination, and the conflictual relations prevented agreements on wage restraint of the kind routinely agreed to in Germany.

Little of this was to change for Germany until the 1990s, when the pressures from increasing international competition as well as the costs of unification and the deregulatory push of the EU promoted liberalization in the capital, product, and labour markets (see Chapter 2). The time of reckoning came earlier for most of the smaller managed capitalist countries, especially with regard to labour-market coordination, where many have moved toward greater flexibility through decentralization from the industry-wide level to the plant level in terms of wage structures and work organization.[14] These kinds of labour-related changes have been much slower to be instituted in Germany. Beginning in the mid-1990s, however, German firms increasingly went to the financial markets for capital, with business-banking relations becoming more distant as a result. Moreover, the growing focus on profits has strained cooperative relations with suppliers while the demands for flexibility along with lower wage rises have led to more contentious relations with labour (see Chapter 4). But although Germany has moved toward greater market orientation, the major outlines of the post-war model remain, albeit with modifications around the edges. This cannot be said for state capitalism, where no country now conforms to the ideal type of the post-war period.

In state capitalism, the business relationship tends to be state-organized. Inter-firm relations are mediated by the state, while interaction between firms when not mediated by the state is generally as competitive and distant as in market capitalism except where there are ties through cross-shareholding akin to the managed capitalist model. Industry-finance relations are similarly state-mediated. Industry is more dependent upon the state than the banks or the markets for financing and takes a more medium-term view due to the state's greater focus on national politico-economic priorities than on firm value or profits per se. Therefore, business-government relations tend to be state-directed, with the state influencing business development through planning, industrial policy, or state-owned enterprises. It often picks winners and losers rather than only arbitrating among economic actors or facilitating their activities. Government relations with labour also tend to be state-controlled although more distant than its relations with business. Wage bargaining is largely determined by the state, which often imposes its decisions on fragmented unions and business, while labour-management relations are mostly adversarial.

---

[14] See Thelen (1993; 2001); Soskice and Schettkat (1993); Scharpf and Schmidt (2000, Vol. II).

Among European countries, France until the 1980s was the ideal-typical state capitalist country, with the *dirigiste*, or directive, state predominating through its leadership of business activity and it control over labour (see Chapter 4). Italy, by comparison, fell far short of the ideal as a kind of failed state capitalism in which the state was unable to control the unions or provide leadership to business, given a weak regulatory framework and nationalized enterprises headed by individuals appointed more for their party loyalty than their competence. In France, business relations were state-organized and state-financed rather than firm-managed and bank- or self-financed as in Germany or capital market-driven and financed as in Britain. In contrast with the British state's 'hands-off' approach to business or the German state's 'enabling' role, the French state had a close, 'hands-on' approach, whether through planning, industrial policy, or the nationalized enterprises—even though this typically meant that, however 'directive' the state, business mostly got its way. The story was different with labour, where the relationship was more distant and the state sought to control wage bargaining centrally in a situation where labour-management relations were as confrontational as the British. Moreover, unlike the Germans, French labour had no role in state-sponsored programmes or in the state-led industrial policy-making process—for which business was the state's privileged interlocutor—let alone in managerial decision-making.

Much of this changed beginning in the 1980s, as successive governments began to dismantle state power and control through liberalization of the financial markets, deregulation of business activity, privatization of nationalized firms, and decentralization of the labour markets (see Chapter 2). The state has given up its organizing role along with its financing of business, leaving firms to chart their own strategies and to arrange their own financing from the capital markets; and it has abandoned its control of wage bargaining, leaving labour relations highly decentralized, much as in Britain today. But, for all this, the state continues to exercise leadership, albeit in a more indirect and often supply-side way, whether through the informal relationships among state-trained business elites, through state support of industry in a more centralized and active way than in Germany, through labour policies that seek to 'moralize' the labour market, and in social policies, where the state has redirected its most *dirigiste* efforts (see Chapter 4).

Although France has moved quite far away from the ideal-typical state capitalism of the post-war years until the early 1980s, in short, it retains certain distinguishing characteristics that continue to differentiate it from Germany, which has itself only recently been experiencing significant market-oriented changes in its post-war managed capitalism, and Britain, which has moved even farther in a market capitalist direction from its original market capitalist starting point. These continuing differences can best be seen by comparisons of the profiles of the three countries in business and financial market activities, state activities, and labour market activities in the mid- to late 1990s.

National Pathways of Adjustment

Britain, Germany, and France are relatively closely matched on the most general macroeconomic indicators (see Table 3.2). In Gross Domestic Product, although Germany is the largest economy, the GDP per capita figures show that the three countries are not that dissimilar, with Britain only slightly behind Germany, and France slightly behind Britain. Moreover, while Germany is ahead in manufacturing in terms of value-added as a percentage of GDP, France and Britain are ahead in services. Disposable income per capita also shows comparatively little variation.

The differences among the three countries are much more significant once one turns to specific economic indicators, where countries differ along the expected lines discussed above. Britain scores high on all the indicators related to market capitalism: for example, in degree of financial market capitalization, in amount of takeover activity, in levels of internationalization of finance, and in the breadth and strength of share ownership. But whereas Germany scores lowest on most of these indicators, it comes out on top—and Britain on the bottom—when it comes to investment in production

Table 3.2 Macroeconomic indicators

Indicator	Britain	Germany	France
GDP: $US billions at current prices and purchasing power parity in 1998	1,201	1,819	1,246
GDP per capita: US$ at current prices and purchasing power parity in 1998	22,272	23,554	21,875
Value-added in industry as % of GDP (1996 for France/ Germany; 1995 for Britain)	27.6	36.2	26.1
Value-added in services as % of GDP (1996 for France/ Germany; 1995 for Britain)	70.8	62.7	71.5
Disposable income per capita in 1996 (US$)	12,471	13,512*	12,559

* Data refer to West Germany only.

Source: OECD National Accounts (various years).

activities, relative unit labour costs, product quality, skills, and the like. France sits somewhere in between the two on most indicators: closer to Britain in terms of market capitalization but even higher in terms of foreign penetration of the stock market, closer to Germany with regard to skills but even higher on productivity. It remains distinctive in terms of the role of the French state despite its neo-liberal turn, which is more active in both business and labour than the German, let alone the British.[15]

The Differential Impact of the Financial Markets

Although the liberalization of the financial markets has ensured that firms in all three countries have increasingly turned to equity financing, the three remain clearly differentiated, with Britain the most finance-led and Germany the least (see Table 3.3). British firms have much higher levels of market capitalization than either French or German firms: in 1997, over double the French capitalization and closer to triple the German; and Britain also has a much larger number of large firms capitalized on the financial markets, with more than twice as many as either France or Germany for close to double the amount of money. Britain also comes out ahead on the availability of venture capital for business development, ranked 8 in a survey by the *World Competitiveness Report* (2000) by comparison with Germany's rank of 15 and France's of 17. And it has the greatest number of mergers and acquisitions, for amounts that are over double the percentages of GDP of either Germany or France in 1999. Moreover, Britain has been the unquestioned leader in foreign direct investment in the 1990s. Inward investment flows in 1998 were over twice the percentage of GDP of those of France and more than four times those of Germany, while inward investment stocks were a third larger than those of Germany and close to double those of France. Outward investment flows in 1998 were over twice the percentages of GDP of those of France and triple those of Germany while outward investment stocks were close to a quarter larger than of Germany and twice as large as France. In addition,

[15] There is no room, here, to provide the data to show the clustering of all the countries into the three varieties of capitalism. This is in any event not necessary for Britain or Germany, since there are now numerous studies that show how Britain fits perfectly into a cluster with other market capitalist countries such as the US, Australia, New Zealand, Canada, and Ireland, while Germany is in the same grouping as Austria, Belgium, Denmark, Finland, Iceland, Netherlands, Norway, Sweden, and Switzerland (Hall and Soskice 2001). What remains to be done is to show how France, Italy, Spain, Korea, Taiwan, and Japan—generally put in the managed capitalist camp—make up another variety of capitalism. For the moment, the demonstration that France represents a distinctive case, with occasional references to other countries that conformed to state capitalism in the post-war period, will have to suffice.

Table 3.3 Financial market indicators of the differences in the three countries' capitalisms

Economic indicator		Britain	Germany	France
1. Stock market capitalization in 1997 (% of GDP)		100.9	31.4	40.6
2. Firms capitalized on financial markets, among Europe's top 500 in 2000	Number	146	60	67
	$ billions	2.27	1.1	1.8
3. Availability of venture capital in 1999 (survey ranking)		6.970	6.118	5.685
4. Mergers and acquisitions in 1999 (% of GDP)		25	12.3	11.4
5. Direct investment flows in 1998 (% of GDP)	Inward	4.7	0.9	2
	Outward	8.4	2.8	4
6. Direct investment stocks in 1998 ($ billions)	Inward	326.81	228.79	179.19
	Outward	498.62	390.09	242.35
7. Households' equity holdings as a percentage of annual disposable income in 1998		82	22	19
8. Size of pension funds in 1996 (percentage of GDP)		74.2	5.8	5.6
9. Pension fund holdings of international bonds and equities in 1993 (% of total holdings)		27	3	5
10. Ratio of international debt securities to domestic securities in 1996		51	8	15
11. Foreign assets as percentage of total assets of commercial banks in 1996		47	16	30.9
12. Foreign holdings of equities in national stock exchange in 1997 (% of total holdings)		9	10	35

Sources: 1, 5, 7, and 8: OECD National Accounts (1996–1999); 2: *Financial Times*, 4 May 2000; 3 and 6: *World Competitiveness Yearbook* (2000); 4: Sachwald (2001); 9, 10, 11: Hirst and Thompson (2000); 12: Morin (2000).

share ownership is more widely distributed in Britain, with British household equity holdings as a percentage of disposable income around four times greater than that of either German or French households, while Britain's pension funds are among the largest of all advanced industrialized countries[16] and those of France and Germany are among the smallest. The size of

---

[16] Second only to the United States, at 169% of GDP, to Britain's 82%.

British pension funds has in turn contributed to their global power: they are not only much more internationalized than those of France or Germany but also add to the globalization pressures on these and other countries. All in all, these figures, combined with others such as Britain's ratio of international debt securities to domestic securities and its foreign assets, make only Britain appear to be truly internationalized, as 'globalization in one country' or as an 'over-internationalized economy in an under-globalized world' (Hirst and Thompson 2000).

Although French and German firms' levels of market capitalization have been rising rapidly and will continue to do so—as increasing numbers of French and German businesses go to the New York and London exchanges, as their national stock markets develop, as European stock markets consolidate, and as liberalizing policies promote further business recourse to the capital markets—it is not simply a matter of time before they begin taking on all the other finance-driven characteristics of market capitalism. Although British firms' reliance on the capital markets for financing does promote finance-led patterns of growth, German and French firms' similarly increasing turn to the financial markets will not necessarily lead to the same outcomes, mainly because of differences in the structure of stock ownership and of corporate governance.

To begin with, the financial markets are much greater drivers of corporate strategy and investment in Britain than in Germany or France. The figures discussed above alone show the much greater development and internationalization of British finance next to French or German. Moreover, British firms derive more of their corporate investment funds from the markets than do French and German firms, which rely more on retained earnings for investment, with both turning to the primary markets mainly for the financing of restructurings and mergers and acquisitions. British firms also have much more developed rules on corporate governance promoting transparency and accountability than Germany, although France has also increased its rules in recent years, and now even leads Britain and Germany in stock option plans (see Chapter 4). Equally importantly, there are significant differences in the structure of stock ownership, with much greater dispersion of ownership in Britain than in France, let alone Germany, and with differing resulting constraints on CEOs.

In Britain, the dominant ownership structure consists of small shareholdings by portfolio investors and households. In 1997, they held 50 per cent and 30 per cent of all shares in the markets respectively, leaving strategic investors at a paltry 7 per cent (Vitols 2001). Thus, the interests of portfolio investors, generally focused on a high return on their investment and, therefore, on firm profitability, are predominant, with CEOs tending to gear their discourse and their strategies to maximizing 'shareholder value'.[17] Moreover, employees have little say in this shareholder model except, of course, when they themselves hold shares directly in the firm—but this constitutes a relatively small percentage other than top management through stock options. The CEOs tend to dominate the boards of directors and to be solely responsible for the decisions for which they will be held accountable by the financial markets (Lane 1998; Vitols 2001), and they have a relatively low degree of interconnectedness with other firms in terms of interlocking directorships or ownership, especially by comparison with Germany (Windolf and Beyer 1996). Their operations, which are often far-flung, tend to reflect this, with a comparatively low percentage of employees, turnover, and assets in home country (Lane 1998).

In Germany, by contrast, the dominant ownership structure consists of large shareholdings by strategic investors. In 1997, corporations, financial companies, and the public sector controlled 57 per cent of all publicly traded shares whereas portfolio investors and households together came only to 35 per cent (Vitols 2001). This high percentage of concentration is likely to diminish in consequence of the changes in the tax laws as of 2002, when the end of the 50 per cent capital gains tax will enable German corporations and financial companies to sell without penalty shares long tied up in strategic investments. Pension funds will also get a boost as a result of the partial privatization of pensions. But, although these changes are likely to inject new liquidity into the primary markets with the concomitant increase in pressures for profits, how much they will serve to unravel the system of strategic shareholdings remains open to question. But even if they were to do so, this would not in any event in and of itself push German firms to become as financial market-driven as British firms. It is true that German CEOs now pay a great deal of attention to shareholder value. But it is important to note that the major changes in industrial firms' structures and practices, including the turn to 'shareholder value' in managerial language and techniques, came in the early 1990s in response to the competitive pressures in the product markets rather than from the finance-driven imperatives of the capital markets (Vitols 1999; Jürgens, Naumann, and Rupp 2000: 73).

Moreover, despite the greater emphasis on shareholder value, the network-based relationships remain alive and well.[18] Because the large majority of German firms remain closely held, and the *Hausbank* relationship between

---

[17] On the shareholder value discourse in Britain, see Froud *et al.* (2000).

[18] See Windolf and Beyer (1996); Lane (1995); Adams (1999).

regional banks and small and medium-sized firms continues to be significant, the bedrock of the system has so far not changed much, even if the larger banks have gone off to global conquest and the larger firms, as well as some of the smaller ones, to the German and foreign stock exchanges (Griffin 2000; Vitols 2000). But however internationalized the larger firms have become, not only in who holds their shares but in how far-flung their operations, they remain much more closely connected to and invested in their home base than British firms (Lane 1998).

What is more, even for the larger German firms the system of corporate governance serves to reinforce a 'stakeholder' rather than 'shareholder' view of value. After all, employees still sit on the supervisory boards of directors as a result of the system of co-determination, as do the strategic shareholders, while management is in control only of the management board of directors and, thus, is in principle constrained in its decisions by the supervisory board on which it does not sit although it does have a voice. In this context, profitability, although of central concern to CEOs with companies quoted on the financial markets, is only one among a number of 'stakeholder' interests involved—with firm value, strategic business interests, and employee concerns also significant (Vitols 2001; Lane 1998).

France differs in its patterns of ownership and corporate governance from both Germany and Britain. France, like Germany, also has a greater concentration in share ownership than Britain, with strategic shareholdings that, in the case of industrial companies, have even been ahead of the Germans, let alone the British.[19] This particular pattern of ownership by strategic investors is of recent vintage. It followed upon the privatizations beginning in the mid-1980s, when the controlling interest in most large firms came to be held by hard-core groups of investors in a set of network-based relationships the state had hoped would reproduce German managed capitalism (Schmidt 1996). These relationships established only a very partial and weak imitation of managed capitalism for a decade at most. And they have been breaking down since the mid-1990s as a result of divestment by some hard-core investors and a concomitant rise in foreign investors—which as of 1997 held over a third of shares in French firms compared with no more than a tenth in Germany or the UK (see Table 3.3) and which by 2001 had increased to around half of shares.

For some commentators, these developments, together with CEOs' discourse of shareholder value, new corporate governance rules, a greater focus on profitability, and an increase in takeover activity, are proof of the victory

[19] In France, 58 per cent of shares were held in other companies in 1995 vs 42 per cent in Germany and 4 per cent in the UK (Deutsche Bundesbank 1997: 29; Jürgens, Naumann, and Rup 2000).

of Anglo-Saxon market capitalism over managed capitalism in France (Orléan 1999; Morin 2000). But in fact, these developments do little to alter the continuing differentiation of French capitalism from both market capitalism and managed capitalism. The ownership structure of French firms remains much more concentrated than the British, corporate investment much less dependent upon the financial markets, and CEOs much less vulnerable to the pressures of institutional investors and much more interconnected than the British, although in a much more informal way than the Germans.

Although there is no doubt that French CEOs, like the Germans, now pay a lot more attention to the financial markets and to 'shareholder value', in France, too, the changes in industrial firms' structures and practices also came much earlier than the foreign investors' presence in the financial markets, in response to competitive pressures in the product markets. For the French, however, those pressures led to an earlier internationalization of operations without, however, any greater disconnection with or disinvestment in their home base than German firms (Schmidt 1996).

Moreover, while French CEOs have also talked the talk of shareholder value, they have not walked the same walk as the British or the Germans. For French CEOs, shareholder value, corporate governance, and profitability means not only increasing their own credibility and their firms' capitalizability vis-à-vis the markets but also ensuring their autonomy vis-à-vis other stakeholders in the firm—for example, labour, suppliers, customers—as much as the state (Hancké 2001; O'Sullivan 2001). The breakdown of the hard-core shareholders has only increased that autonomy by reducing CEOs' direct accountability and mutual obligations to them, something which continues to constrain the Germans. French CEOs by the mid- to late 1990s no longer needed the hard cores as much they did initially, given the mergers and acquisitions that have increased their size and scope, while they have needed the money tied up in the hard cores to remain competitive in the product markets. Moreover, their autonomy is only enhanced by the vertically integrated system of coordination between large firms and small ones, where the CEO in the Paris headquarters typically sets the strategies for operations in the French regions and elsewhere (Amable and Hancké 2001; Hancké 2001).

French CEOs as a result of the changes since the mid-1980s now have an unprecedented level of autonomy: from the financial markets, from one another, and from the state. But this is not to suggest that French CEOs are therefore as little interconnected as British CEOs. Much the contrary, since they remain interconnected as a result of the informal networks based on their elite state education and state career paths, albeit increasingly abbreviated (Schmidt 1996). This elite coordination system ensures French

CEOs greater access to high-level advice and coordination than the British (Hancké and Soskice 1997; Hancké 2001), although with more interpersonal competitiveness than the Germans, given the culture of competitiveness bred by the meritocratic state exams system.

The Differing Role of the State

In France, then, the state still plays a more significant role than in Germany or Britain, if only in terms of its infusion of a set of values and experiences (Schmidt 1996). But this is not the only reason it is more significant since, although it has retreated, it still seeks to influence the direction of the economy more than either of the other two states. This is reflected in particular in the three countries' differing ideas about the role of the state in the economy: whether to preserve the market as in Britain, to protect non-market coordination as in Germany, or to do both, depending upon the circumstances, as in France.

In British market capitalism today, business expects the state to act as an agent of market preservation by providing framework legislation to locate decision-making power in companies and limit the power of organized labour (Wood 2001). The neo-liberal reforms of the 1980s that consecrated this role were made possible by the combination of a right-wing government with the political institutional capacity to pass the requisite legislation and a business community that had grown increasingly hostile to attempts to coordinate supply-side public goods policies—for example, training systems, incomes policies, industrial planning—with labour and/or government, given the failures of the post-war years (King and Wood 1999). Because employers viewed unions as inflating the costs of production by demanding higher wages, they sought to deregulate labour markets and weaken unions as far as possible in order to have maximum 'managerial freedom' in adjustment to changing market conditions. This strategy has also led to a 'segmentalist' approach to the retention of labour, as employers sought to shield themselves from competition through internal career ladders, seniority wages, and in-house training (Thelen 2001: 75–80).

In German managed capitalism since the early post-war years, by contrast, business has seen the state as protector of the production system's non-market coordinating institutions by establishing and periodically renewing the framework laws that invest regulatory authority in private bodies, including employers' associations and unions (King and Wood 1999). The employers here sought to maintain organized labour markets and strong unions in order to ensure continued coordination in the adjustment process and to reinforce the collectivist approach to labour retention through coordinated wage formation, shared costs for skill formation costs, and sanctions on labour poaching (Thelen 2001: 75–80). Because the employers saw unions as potentially reducing the costs of production by promoting wage restraint, they were to be maintained in a balance of power with employers (King and Wood 1999). This helps explain employers' resistance to government efforts to impose neo-liberal reforms that would have undermined the coordination system, such as the government initiatives limiting strike benefits in the 1980s and sick pay in the 1990s (King and Wood 1999; Wood 2001; and see Chapter 6). And it also sheds light on why market-oriented reforms have been so slow in coming, given that they have been negotiated in a cooperative manner in order to ensure that the coordinating institutions would not be negatively affected (see Chapter 2).

In post-war state capitalism, finally, business expected the state to act *in loco mercatis* where necessary, that is, in place of the market, by setting up wage coordinating mechanisms, buying labour peace through various welfare and labour market programmes, using the nationalized industries to maintain employment or to create industrial capacity, and orienting business investment through planning exercises and industrial policies. Neo-liberal reforms beginning in the 1980s changed the state's role to part creator-preserver of the market, part creator-protector of non-market institutions. This mixed role has been the result of a combination of governments of the left and the right with the political institutional capacity to reform but without the coordinating partners willing and/or able to make the reforms work in the intended manner. As a result, although the French state tried to create the coordinating institutions of managed capitalism in business relations and in labour relations, it ended up creating the uncoordinated institutions of market capitalism. In business, the creation of hard-core shareholdings linked to privatization provided elements of network coordination which, weak to begin with, are already unravelling. In the labour markets, laws to increase direct worker-management dialogue in the early 1980s ended up giving more decision-making power to companies by paving the way to radical decentralization of wage bargaining from national sectoral to regional, local, and/or firm levels when unions proved unable to take up a coordinating role.[20] The 35-hour work week beginning in the late 1990s has been another opportunity for business to increase labour market flexibility. Business' view of the role of the state today is therefore mixed, hopeful that the state will continue market-preserving legislation but apprehensive any time the

---

[20] See Kesselman (1989); W. R. Smith (1988); Howell (1992); Schmidt (1999c).

state chooses to intervene to 'moralize' the financial markets or the labour markets. The state's view is no less mixed, as it seeks to preserve the market functions that exist even as it continually seeks to create greater coordination.

Other former state capitalist countries have been more successful than France in creating greater coordination in the labour markets. In France, the radical decentralization of bargaining may be less a necessary consequence of reform than of the particular circumstances of French industrial relations, namely, the weakness of the employers' associations and the unions. Where unions and employers' associations have been stronger, the move has been in the opposite direction, towards a recentralization of bargaining with unions, employers' associations, and government at the table. Italy, which had also had a state-controlled wage bargaining system similar to the French—albeit much less effective given the Italian state's weakness, politicization, and permeation by interests—has since 1992 instituted incomes policies coordinated between social partners and facilitated by the state. Spain has similarly turned to more corporatist, tripartite patterns of bargaining, as has Australia, while New Zealand followed the French pattern for similar reasons.[21]

The direction of reform towards either greater market reliance or greater coordination, in other words, depends on the relative levels of unionization and central organization of employers' associations as well as unions. The resulting industrial relations systems, however, are less fully market-reliant than in market capitalist countries or less stably coordinated than in managed capitalist countries. The state still plays a larger role. In countries which recentralized wage bargaining between employers and labour, such as Italy, this may take the form of an ever-vigilant, highly proactive state which, in words and actions, seeks to ensure successful wage-bargaining rounds, to dampen conflicts, and to involve the social partners in pension reforms. Or it may, as in France, involve continuing legislative efforts to shape the labour market.

The Differences in Production Profiles

These differing patterns of business interrelationships, state relationships with business and labour, and labour relations, can be clearly seen in the production-related economic indicators. On indicators where managed capitalist countries would be expected to score high, such as product quality, capital investment, state aid to manufacturing, skills, long-term employment

---

[21] On Italy, see Treu (1994); Regini (1997); Regini and Regalia (1997); Locke and Baccaro (1999); Ferrera and Gualmini (2000). On Spain, see Perez (2000). On Australia and New Zealand, see Schwartz (2000).

and the like, Germany comes out way ahead of Britain, while France comes in between the two on most measures other than productivity, where it outdistances both (see Table 3.4). Moreover, although Britain scores better on red tape, levels of workforce participation, and unemployment, Germany nonetheless remains highest in location attractiveness.

German products, to begin with, are generally better than comparable French products, and much better than the British. On the ratio of price to quality of domestic products by comparison with foreign competitors, a survey in the World Competitiveness Yearbook (2000) ranks Germany among the highest, at 5, France at number 14, at the lower end of the advanced industrialized countries, while the United Kingdom is down at number 28, with many less developed countries. This can be explained by the high levels of investment—gross fixed capital formation—in Germany, with France following and Britain lowest. The same is true for state aid in manufacturing, where Germany provides over three times more support than France and over seven times Britain, the result of the key enabling role played by the *Länder*, by contrast with France, where the central state has found itself more constrained than Germany in providing aid because of EU strictures (see Chapter 1), or Britain, which has sought to reduce all aid. On red tape,

Table 3.4 Production-related indicators of the differences in the three countries' capitalisms

		Britain	Germany	France
1. Price/quality ratio of domestic products (1999)		5.2600	6.711	6.1573
2. Relative unit labour costs in manufacturing (1999) (1995 = 100)		141.5	88.8	92.6
3. Overall productivity (PPP)—GDP per person employed (1999)		$44,852	$51,487	$56,356
4. Investment (gross fixed capital formation as % of GDP in 1997)		15.6	19.9	17.1
5. State aid to manufacturing 1995-7 (EU 12)		5%	37%	12%
6. Location attractiveness rankings in survey (2000)		15	8	19
7. Workforce participation rates	Male	83.9	79.2	74.1
(%) in 1999	Female	67.8	60.9	60.8
8. Unemployment rates	Total	6.5	8.6	11.9
(percentages in 1999)	Youth	12.3	9.4	25.4

Sources: 1, 3, 6: *World Competitiveness Yearbook* (2000); 2, 4: OECD National Accounts (2000); 5: Eurostat (1998); 7, 8: Confederation of British Industry (1999).

however, Britain comes out in better shape than the other two countries, with the number of weeks its takes to register a firm only four in Britain by comparison with eight in Germany and 15 in France—as against only two in the United States (*The Economist*, 8 July 2001). This did not affect Germany's high score on 'location attractiveness' though, by contrast with that of Britain, but it could explain France's even worse results, despite its having attracted more inward investment than Germany in the 1990s.

Germany comes out equally well on relative unit labour costs in manufacturing, with France only slightly behind, but Britain far worse. On overall productivity, however, France ranks highest among the three countries, at 6, slightly ahead of Germany at 8, while the United Kingdom is way down at 21. France's high rating is testimony not only to a slower progression of wage increases since the 1980s but also to the re-skilling and replacement of workers through early retirement programmes. This has brought France closer to the German model in manufacturing than the British (see Chapter 4)—although also with one of the lowest rates of male workforce participation in Europe, way behind Britain and even Germany. Female workforce participation is another matter, however, as is unemployment—where Britain does much better than both Germany and France, the result of such factors as lower wages, greater availability of part-time jobs, more labour flexibility, and a pension system that discourages 'welfare without work'.[22]

Germany's high production profile is also reflected in comparisons on the basis of indices of employment protection, unemployment protection, and skills profiles, where it consistently scores at the top, with France in the middle and Britain at the bottom (see Table 3.5). In Germany, the high levels of employment and unemployment protection, reinforced by long-term employment and high investment in vocational training by state and employers alike, all underpin a production system of flexible specialization based on high skills, high wages, and high product quality. In Britain, the low levels of employment and unemployment protection, together with comparatively short-term employment and little vocational training, underpin a production system of mass production based on low skills, low wages, and low product quality.[23] In France, the still reasonably high levels of employment and unemployment protection, reinforced by more medium-term employment and middling investment in vocational training, underpin a production system of modified mass production—flexible Fordism—based on medium skills, wages, and product-quality.

[22] For the full story, see Scharpf and Schmidt (2000).
[23] See Lane (1989; 1995); Streeck (1997); Soskice (1997b); Hall and Soskice (2001).

Table 3.5 Indices of employment protection, unemployment protection, and skill profiles

Country	Employment protection[a]	Unemployment protection[b]	Skill profiles		
			Length of tenure[c]	Vocational training share[d]	Vocational training system[e]
Germany	0.86	0.77	10.7	34	Dual apprenticeship
France	0.61	0.54	7.7	28	School-based
Britain	0.25	0.11	5.0	11	Weak

[a] Based on weighted averages of indexes of employment protection legislation, collective dismissal protection, and company-based protections (higher numbers mean more restricted regimes).

[b] Based on average of net unemployment rates for a 40-year-old unemployed worker, generosity of benefits, restrictiveness definition of 'suitable' job in the administration of benefits to unemployed.

[c] Median length of enterprise tenure.

[d] Percentage share of an age cohort in either secondary or post-secondary vocational training.

[e] Character of training system, with 'weak' involving a combination of on-the-job training and school-based training.

Source: Estevez-Abe, Iversen, and Soskice (2001).

In sum, the differences among countries continue along the lines of the three main post-war models, despite tremendous change. Britain's market capitalism is more pronounced, with more recourse to the financial markets, more competitive business relations, radically decentralized labour markets, and even less interventionism by the state. Germany's managed capitalism remains network-based, although the ties between among firms are loosening and labour market coordination is decentralizing. Finally, although France is no longer state capitalist, given the autonomy of firms, the market-reliance of labour, and the less interventionist role of the state, it is still neither market nor managed capitalist.

The Comparative Advantages and Disadvantages of the Three Models of Capitalism

But if all three varieties of capitalism clearly persist, one therefore might ask which of these three is best suited for today's global economy. There is no easy answer. Economic performance, to begin with, is difficult to compare since it depends upon a whole host of factors that may have little to do with the model per se, such as a country's historical inheritance, material as well as human resources, levels of social cohesion or fragmentation, configuration of political institutions, and economic conjunctures. Even if one leaves this problem aside, however, the question remains as to what one would measure in order to have a fair comparison. If one were to consider corporate profits alone, one would necessarily privilege market capitalism, while rate of productivity growth might push the balance in favour of managed capitalism, and so on. One recent study, which tries to consider all factors related to differences in corporate performance among Anglo-Saxon, Germanic, and Latin firms in Europe—with reference to, for example, net surplus value, size ratios, productivity, employment, and shareholders' returns over the long term—finds that Anglo-Saxon firms do a bit more poorly than either Germanic or Latin firms (de Jong 1997). But this focuses only on the dimension of the structure of business relations and does not concern itself with the dimensions of state relations or industrial relations, which have an effect on the economic environment of firms more generally and which are much more difficult to quantify. Most importantly, however, one can argue that these kinds of comparisons beg the main issue, which is that countries' differences in institutional structures and interactive processes ensure that they do well in different markets, and that, so long as they remain in the markets for which their institutional structures afford them a comparative advantage, they will all do well (Soskice 1999).

This suggests that there are no better or worse varieties of capitalism, just different ones with different comparative advantages or disadvantages. But even if there were better or worse ones, the fact is that countries still conform largely to the three varieties discussed herein, for better or worse, and that it is therefore useful to consider their comparative advantages or disadvantages in the context of their adjustment to the twin forces of globalization and European integration.

The Comparative Advantages and Disadvantages of Market Capitalism

The comparative advantages of market capitalism centre around business' responsiveness to the market, with few constraints from government or labour. The structure of business relations, to begin with, tends to promote radical innovation and high responsiveness to changing market conditions. Firms' ready access to open financial markets, in particular with regard to venture capital, facilitates the kind of risk taking and entrepreneurialism that tends to generate great innovation in terms of product development as well as in corporate strategies. Firms' arms' length relations with customers and suppliers means that they can react quickly to changing markets and needs. And their arms' length relations with providers of finance, where investors' greater concern with share price than corporate strategy puts pressure on firms to make steady profits or risk takeover, encourages firms to invest in projects with the potential for high yields in short time frames.[24] In this context, moreover, the liberal state's relations with business, by creating a fair playing field but otherwise maintaining a hands-off approach, means that firms often avoid the rigidities of highly regulated environments. Finally, the decentralized wage-bargaining system ensures management the kind of flexibility in hiring and firing that enables it to alter its employee profile swiftly in response to changing market preferences as well as to weather economic downturns without significant loss of profits. And such flexibility, combined with financial market pressure, means that it tends to gain the most from production strategies focused on low-cost, low-skilled labour.

The advantages of such a model are especially apparent in sectors where success depends upon radical innovation, that is, in areas of fast-paced, research-led product development such as biotechnology, semiconductors, and software development, or of complex production systems such as defence and telecommunications as well as high-end services such as airlines, advertising, corporate finance, and entertainment (Hall and Soskice 2001: 39). Most of these sectors have been high-growth areas that have also shown high levels of profit and financial market-led increase in firm value. British firms have done well in some of these sectors, such as high-end services and biotechnology. Otherwise, British firms' investment patterns have mainly been in industries demanding low workers' skill and low research and development, where it has also done well, such as foods, beverages, tobacco, and other low-tech goods, although it has also done well in the chemical and oil industries (Lane 1998).

Market capitalism, however, also has certain disadvantages by comparison with the other two varieties of capitalism. For one, the structure of business relations promotes greater instability in times of economic downturn, with the larger firms at greater risk from takeover and the smaller from bankruptcy than companies in the more supportive environments of managed or state capitalism. And this is only aggravated by the state's laissez-faire approach which leaves firms to fend for themselves even when they might benefit from the kind of coordination facilitated by managed capitalism or the interventionism provided by state capitalism. The end of the British automotive and electronics industries are cases in point.

[24] See Hall (2000); Soskice (1991; 1999); Hall and Soskice (2001).

For two, the focus on short-term profitability often engenders a loss of market opportunities that come only with investment focused on the medium or long term, while financial market control also causes problems with regard to innovation and industrial development. This is mainly because strategic managers have aligned their interests too much with the stockholders, and have thereby become too removed from the organizations in which 'the development and utilization of productive resources occurs' (Lazonick and O'Sullivan 1997).

For three, not only does the emphasis on labour flexibility lead to a loss of skill-based knowledge in consequence of high employee turnover but the preservation of managerial prerogatives in the organization of work also means that such firms do not profit from other kinds of work coordination based on employee-led innovation in production processes, as is typical in managed capitalist systems (Hancké 1996). And therefore, what firms gain in low wage costs they may lose in productivity. Moreover, the emphasis on low-wage, low-skilled labour may deny companies the higher profits that come with the value-added production of higher-waged, higher-skilled employees in managed capitalist systems at the same time as it may leave them vulnerable to competition from lower-waged, lower-skilled countries, especially as workers in such countries become increasing skilled and achieve higher product quality. Finally, in market capitalism there is always the potential of labour strife and strike-induced loss of productivity, especially where labour is more organized, given the distrustful labour-relations environment in which the costs of firm flexibility and profitability as well as of training and education generally fall on the employees.

In market capitalist Britain, then, as British governments have over the course of the 1980s and 1990s deregulated financial markets, product markets, services, and labour, British firms have gained even greater advantages with regard to quicker response times, easier access to capital, less state interference, more flexibility in the workforce, and higher profits. But they also have suffered from greater disadvantages such as higher firm instability, more losses of medium- or long-term investment opportunities, even less state support in times of trouble, increasing competition from low-wage countries, and, in some cases, even lower-skilled, potentially less productive, more distrustful employees. Although such disadvantages have been counteracted to some extent as numbers of British firms have imitated foreign transplants in adopting more modern human-resource management techniques, more cooperative relationships with suppliers as well as with competitors through joint ventures, and longer-term investment commitments, these have not served to alter the overall pattern of British market capitalism.

The Comparative Advantages and Disadvantages of Managed Capitalism

In ideal-typical managed capitalism, firms generally have less of the innovativeness, flexibility, quick responses to changing market conditions, and high short-term profits that characterize market capitalism. Instead, they have greater stability in the business environment, greater reliability of firm and labour interrelationships, and steadier profitability over the long-term (Soskice 1994; de Jong 1997). The non-market institutions that organize market activity by way of networks of firms linked through supervisory boards, cross-shareholding, close customer and supplier relations, and close business-banking relations create a more stable environment for firms generally due to the extensive exchange of information and cooperation on the setting of corporate strategies (Hall and Soskice 2001). Although the density of the networks and the need for consultation among a number of partners greatly slows reaction time, the supportive business interrelationships and cross-shareholdings enable firms better to weather economic downturn while protecting big firms against takeover and small firms against bankruptcy. Moreover, although the traditional reliance on bank rather than market financing is an impediment to the kind of risk-taking that often leads to radical innovation and high short-term profits, the more conservative, 'patient' capital supplied by the banks or from retained earnings enables firms to take advantage of market opportunities that come only from investment over the long haul, where the primary emphasis on market share can ultimately lead to steadier and sometimes even larger profits.

In addition, the state's enabling role facilitates interactions between business and labour through mediation and arbitration, while in times of economic downturn it can offer necessary support and leadership.[25] Therefore, although the state's greater involvement in the functioning of the economic system than in ideal-typical market capitalism may increase rigidities and slow adjustment to changing market conditions, its involvement at the same time can serve to grease the wheels, making the economic system run more smoothly, especially with regard to management-labour relations. In fact, the state's facilitating role here, along with the more organized, long-term cooperation among firms, are together conducive to more coordinated action with regard to national or sectoral wage bargaining, to industry-wide, in-house vocational training and apprenticeship programmes, and to longer-term employment patterns (Culpepper 2001). The result is better trained, more

---

[25] The term 'state' must be understood rather loosely here when it comes to Germany, where government 'enabling' action occurs more at the regional than at the federal level.

highly skilled workers better able to work in teams, to take autonomous responsibility, and thereby to sustain competitiveness in higher value-added markets where technological developments demand just such a workforce (Soskice 1997b). Although this comes with higher wages than in the more mass production-oriented market capitalism, it brings with it higher productivity for higher quality products, such that firms in managed capitalist countries compete on quality rather than cost. Moreover, the incremental, employee-led innovation that follows from a high-skilled, highly productive, high-wage labour force focused on high value-added product lines in managed capitalism may offset the lack of radical product innovation found in market capitalism.[26] Finally, the more organized and cooperative nature of unions, combined with that of business, helps promote the consensual patterns of bargaining that can go as far as 'incomes policies', that is, agreements on wage restraint by management and labour.

The advantages of this model are most apparent in sectors where success depends on incremental innovation, that is, in areas where the emphasis is on maintaining high quality while holding down costs, whether in machine tools, consumer durables, electric/electronic engineering, automobiles, chemicals, or other precision-engineering products.[27] The patterns of investment of Germany's largest firms reflect this, with concentration in industries demanding high-skilled workers and medium-to-high technology and which depend on stable, long-term links with customers (Lane 1998).

By contrast, the disadvantages of German institutional arrangements result from their difficulty in developing high-risk innovation strategies in newly emerging technologies. There is evidence, however, to suggest that German enterprises have found high-tech market niches in the 'platform technologies' of biotechnology and in business software and systems integration services in the software industry, where incremental innovation proves highly successful (Casper, Lehrer, and Soskice 1999). Moreover, the German 'insider-dominated' financial system works much better in the mechanical and electrical engineering industries as well as in auto vehicles, where innovations are lower in visibility and therefore require greater 'firm-specific perceptiveness' from banks, family shareholders, and customers and suppliers. By contrast, 'outsider-dominated' financial systems work better where innovations are higher in visibility and where there is high 'industry-specific expertise' among institutional investors,[28] leading to the

---

[26] See Finegold and Soskice (1988); Soskice (1994); Streeck (1997); Culpepper and Finegold (1999).

[27] Porter (1990); Soskice (1997); Hall and Soskice (2001).

[28] This capacity is generally more developed in the United States than Britain except in pharmaceuticals.

UK being ahead of Germany in electronics, drugs, and bio-chemicals (Tylecote and Conesa 1999).

In the context of intensifying global and European competition, countries which conform to the managed capitalist model have for the most part been able to adjust their systems without major institutional change. Firms in these countries have the advantage of greater stability, greater long-term investment opportunities, greater state facilitation of firm activity, and higher-skilled, more productive, and more trustful employees. But they also have the disadvantage of slower response times, less easy access to capital, a more rigid regulatory environment, less flexibility in the workforce, and lower profits. Such disadvantages, of course, can also be counteracted, and have been by firms which have adopted more market capitalist ideals and practices, gained quicker and easier access to capital via the global financial markets, and reorganized operations to focus more on shareholder value and profits while seeking to contain high wage costs.

The question for countries which conformed largely to the managed capitalist model in the post-war years is whether, as increasing numbers of firms are adopting such market capitalist practices, can the managed capitalist model survive? So far, under pressure from such firms, most managed capitalist countries have been adjusting. In business structure, changes include the loosening of network-based, inter-firm relations in response to the reorganization of production systems and the weakening of the business-bank partnership in the wake of greater opportunities provided by the rapidly expanding financial markets, dom-estic and international. In industrial relations, they involve primarily the decentralization of wage-bargaining institutions, the differentiation of wages, and the introduction of greater flexibility in employment in response to the pressures of international competition. These adjustments have slowly been moving most managed capitalist countries from the post-war 'social market' ideal to a more 'liberal market' ideal, albeit still within a more 'managed' context. But how much farther can they go without engendering a breakdown of the managed capitalist model as a whole, and thereby lose the advantages of the model without necessarily gaining those of the market capitalist? In other words, on top of the slower response times and the lesser employment flexibility typical of managed capitalism could be added: lost long-term investment opportunities due to marketized firms' greater emphasis on short-term profits; less inter-firm and business-banking cooperation due to greater inter-firm competition and distance between self-financing business and capital-market-focused banks; and less cooperation, more labour strife, lower productivity, and lost employee-led innovation from less trustful employees in response to employers' profit squeeze on salaries and benefits.

The questions, then, for all countries which conformed to the post-war model of managed capitalism, are: Can managed capitalism adapt enough to survive by liberalizing the system as a whole? Or can the various components of managed capitalism be decoupled, such that it continues in management-labour relations and even inter-firm relations while business-finance relations become increasingly market capitalist? Can the state—or, in Germany, the *Länder*—continue to play an 'enabling' role within the limits imposed by European competition authorities and more restricted budgets? In short, will managed capitalist countries' economic practices evolve into a more 'competitive' managed capitalism? Or will they simply become failed managed capitalism under the pressures of adjustment? These remain open questions for Germany, although countries such as the Netherlands and Denmark seem to have successfully moved toward competitive managed capitalism, with still-networked but more market capitalist inter-firm and business-finance relations underpinned by still highly cooperative management-labour relations facilitated by an enabling state.[29]

The Comparative Advantages and Disadvantages of State Capitalism

The questions confronting countries which conform to the managed capitalist model are nothing, however, compared with those which since the 1980s have confronted countries which conformed in the post-war period to the state capitalist model. For whereas managed capitalist countries have been able so far to retain the outlines of the classic model largely intact, state capitalist countries have seen a major transformation of their economic management systems in response to global and European pressures.

In the ideal-typical state capitalism of the post-war period, the state provided the kind of financing that the banks provide in managed capitalism, by underwriting business investment through subsidies or loans; organized the kind of exchange of information generated by networks of firms in managed capitalism through planning; offered the kind of guidance in corporate strategies that the banks do in managed capitalism by way of industrial policy; and managed alone the kind of coordination in industrial relations that business and labour do together with the help of the state in managed capitalism. Where the state had leadership capacity, the result was an economic development model that had the market model's faster reaction time and the managed model's ability to coordinate action. Moreover, in times of economic downturn, the state could intervene more quickly and effectively

---

[29] See Visser and Hemerijck (1997); Hemerijck and Schludi (2000); Benner and Vad (2000).

than either the market or managed models of capitalism, protecting big firms from takeover and small firms from bankruptcy by providing the necessary financial or strategic support. What is more, rather than the 'impatient' capital of market capitalism that demands quick returns on investment or the 'patient' capital of managed capitalism that is in it for the long haul, firms in state capitalism depended on the capital of the state. And this sometimes demanded no financial return at all if other state goals were being fulfilled, such as continued employment or production in government-targeted strategic areas.

The state, however, was not always a good substitute for either market or non-market coordination. The state-organized business relationship still lacked the innovative capabilities of the market-driven relationship, where entrepreneurialism is encouraged through the risk-taking of market-financed investment. But it still probably had more innovative capabilities than the non-market managed structure, since state financing could often be less risk-averse than bank financing. Moreover, the state-directed nature of business-government relations, where planning exercises and industrial policies sought to coordinate the direction of corporate strategy from the outside, was often no replacement for the inside, network-based cooperation among firms that makes for internally-coordinated corporate strategies. The problem was that the state necessarily had less of a sense of market needs than business, and therefore may have intervened even where it should not have, moving business in directions that may have gone against market preferences, choosing losers rather than winners, and consequently in such cases spending taxpayers' money with little or no return on state investment.

In industrial relations, moreover, state control often confronted the same labour problems as the market-reliant approach of market capitalism, without its flexibility in hiring and firing, while it could not achieve the same kind of organizational success as the cooperative approach of managed capitalism. Although the state could coordinate management and labour negotiations from the outside, it could not instil the kind of labour-management trust and coordination found in the more cooperative industrial relations systems that lead to employer commitments to long-term employment and sector-wide vocational training and apprenticeship programmes that ensure the high-skilled labour necessary to employee-led innovation (Culpepper forthcoming). Moreover, the state-controlled national or sectoral wage bargaining necessarily reduced the kind of wage flexibility that helps keep wages low in more market-reliant systems while it was harder put to achieve the kind of wage restraint agreed to in coordinated systems (see Scharpf 2000b). In addition, state-imposed labour regulation reduced the hiring and firing flexibility that facilitates the quick responses to changing market conditions of market-reliant systems, and all this without diminishing the potential for labour strife. This model, therefore, in many cases led to worse problems than the market-reliant and coordinated approaches to industrial relations combined, since the result was higher-waged, lower-skilled, more contentious labour, the worst of all possible worlds.

It has been no wonder, then, that in response to the pressures of globalization and European integration countries that have traditionally conformed to the state capitalist model have been transforming themselves. Whereas countries conforming to either market or managed capitalist models have so far found their model reasonably well adapted to the new competitive environment, countries conforming to the state capitalist model found their model particularly ill-adapted to the new environment, and therefore in need of change. Disadvantages remained disadvantages, while advantages turned into disadvantages. In an increasingly complex and competitive environment, the state could no longer ensure economic growth or firm stability, substitute for the market effectively, direct industry efficiently, or coordinate industrial relations successfully. In an increasingly tight budgetary context, moreover, the state could no longer afford to disregard firm profitability or underwrite industry investment as it had in the past. And industry still lacked sufficient technological innovativeness, employment flexibility, inter-firm coordination, and labour-management cooperation, while it continued to have to deal with high labour costs, low-skilled employees, and high levels of labour strife.

Major reforms have led to the retreat of the state from active direction of industry in all but a few strategic sectors, to the reorientation of business towards the market through privatizing and deregulatory reforms, to an increase in employment flexibility and a decrease in labour contentiousness through the decentralization of wage-bargaining relations, as in France, or through their greater coordination, as in Italy. Business has gained greater access to capital through deregulated financial markets, greater inter-firm coordination through cross-share holdings and alliances, and better labour-management relations through greater focus on re-skilling of workers and the use of other modern management techniques.

Business coordination, instead of being state-organized, is now business-based, led by autonomous firms loosely connected through informal networks of state-trained elites (Schmidt 1996). Although this system comes with certain risks (see Chapter 4), it provides a workable solution to some of the greatest potential problems of coordination. The system allows for greater inter-firm coordination, sharing of information, and cooperation on corporate strategies than that found in market capitalist countries such as Britain, even if it is no substitute for the deep network linkages of managed capitalist countries such as Germany (Hancké and Soskice 1996; Hancké 2001). Moreover, although the partial unravelling of the hard core of investors has increased business exposure to the markets, the presence of hard-core investment from the mid-1980s to the late 1990s ensured the kind of stability and protection necessary for newly privatized firms. The retained earnings represented by those hard-core investments, moreover, subsequently proved a welcome source of cash for exporting firms trying to stay ahead of the product markets. Because French firms have rapid model cycles, they needed increasing amounts of investment in centralized product development, machinery, and marketing, which could come only from the money tied up in the cross-shareholdings. Moreover, because they also needed foreign investors, given that the French capital markets alone could not absorb their needs, the end of the hard-core investors would also help increase the transparency expected by foreign investors (Hancké 2001).

Finally, with regard to innovation, France remains somewhere between Britain and Germany. Its most notable capacity for innovation has been in sectors that are still heavily state-dominated and based on networking capacities provided through the state and cross-shareholdings in sectors such as telecommunications, high-speed trains, and nuclear-powered electricity (Hancké 2001). But it also does well in some aspects of mechanical and electrical engineering and auto vehicles—ahead of Britain although behind Germany—as a result of a financial system which continues to be largely 'insider-dominated' in these areas and where lower-visibility innovations have gained from the 'firm-specific perceptiveness' and industry-specific expertise of state-related circuits of influence (Tylecote and Conesa 1999). Moreover, it has used mergers and acquisitions to gain sources of radical innovation, particularly in the United States—in great contrast with Germany, which used American subsidiaries to complement domestic core competencies (Cantwell and Kotecha 1997; Goyer 2001). The comparative figures on foreign shares in US patents tells it all, whereas France's share tripled between 1983–86 and 1991–95—from 9 to 33 per cent—Germany's increased by only a third—from 15 to 21 per cent. The UK, by comparison, started out much higher, at 47 per cent, and went even higher, to 56 per cent (UNCTAD 2001, Table II.9).

Countries that have traditionally conformed to the model of state capitalism, in consequence of all of these changes, have become at best pale shadows of their former selves, since most have transformed themselves by taking steps in the direction of market capitalism, although they have also adopted elements of managed capitalism. But whatever the additions from market or managed capitalism, these countries retain a core element of traditional state capitalism, mainly because the state remains a significant, albeit much lesser, element in the mix, taking action where business and/or labour do not or cannot act for themselves. From traditional state capitalism, then, these countries' economic practices have moved at the very least to 'state-enhanced' capitalism. This has certainly been the case for France, where the state has retreated very far indeed, as well as for Taiwan and Korea (Weiss 1999b). Italy is a harder call, since it may very well have moved from failed state capitalism toward competitive managed capitalism.

Still Three Varieties of Capitalism

Thus, although all three countries have been liberalizing in response to the pressures of globalization and European integration, they have not converged on the market capitalist model even if they have all become more market-oriented. Their patterns of business, government, and labour relations remain distinct, even if somewhat less so than in the past (see Table 3.6).

Traditionally market capitalist Britain has become, if anything, more financial market driven in business relations, more liberal in state relations with business and labour, and more market-reliant and decentralized in industrial relations. Traditionally managed capitalist Germany has not lost its main characteristics, although its non-market managed business relations are suffering from erosion in the close network-based inter-firm and business-banking inter-relationships while its cooperative industrial relations are under pressure. Traditionally state capitalist France, by comparison, has been transformed by the radical reduction in state interventionism, the dramatic increase in firm autonomy, and the radical turn to market reliance in industrial relations.

But while firms in all three countries have become much more market-oriented as they have adjusted to the pressures of globalization and Europeanization, they remain distinct. To begin with, British firms continue to be more financial market-driven, given higher levels of market capitalization, greater dispersion in share ownership, and greater dependence for capital investment on the markets. German firms are instead more stakeholder focused, given network-based relationships that, although loosening, remain important and employee participation on corporate governance boards. French firms, by comparison, are more autonomous than either their network-linked German or financial market-dependent British counterparts, let alone the state-led French firms of the post-war period. But they are nevertheless more exposed to the financial markets than German firms, given the high level of foreign institutional investors, and more coordinated than British firms through informal elite networks.

Table 3.6 Changes in characteristics of models of capitalism by 2000

	Market capitalism (Britain)	Managed capitalism (Germany)	State capitalism (France)
Business relations	More market-driven	Still non-market managed	More market-driven and less state-organized
Inter-firm relations	More individualistic, competitive, contractual	Erosion of mutually reinforcing and network-based relationships	End of state mediation, more competitive, and more network-based
Industry-finance	More distant	Erosion of closeness	No longer state-mediated, closer
Investment	Even shorter-term view	Somewhat less longer-term view	Less medium-term view
Government relations	More arms' length	Still negotiated	Less state-directed, more arms' length
State characteristics	More liberal arbiter	Still 'enabling' facilitator	Much less interventionist, much more liberal
Labour relations	Less adversarial, more neutral	Still cooperative	Less adversarial, more neutral (France) Cooperative (Italy since 1992)
Wage bargaining	More market-reliant, more decentralized	Still coordinated but more decentralized	No longer state-controlled, now market-reliant, decentralized (France) or coordinated (Italy since 1992)
Government role in labour regulation	Still bystander or state imposed (UK)	State still co-equal or bystander	No longer state-imposed, now bystander (France) Co-equal (Italy since 1992)

Moreover, despite the general retreat of the state, France retains a more active role for the state than in either market or managed capitalist countries. While the British state acts primarily to preserve the market and the German to protect non-market coordinating mechanisms, the French state continues to intervene, albeit in a more limited, supply-side way, through laws and incentives intended not only to make the economy more competitive but also to 'moralize' business and labour relations—even though as often as not its intervention has served only to further marketize those relationships.

In addition, although all three countries have increased their competitiveness in the product markets, Germany remains the most competitive in terms of the price/quality ratios of its products, its relative unit labour costs in manufacturing, the level of corporate investment and state aid, and the high skill levels of its workers, all of which provide an environment which encourages incremental innovation and steady profits over the long haul in sectors such as high-precision engineering. But Britain has been much better at cutting red tape, at female as well as male workforce participation, at instituting labour market flexibility, and in providing an environment which encourages radical innovation in high growth, high profit areas, although competitiveness continues to suffer from a manufacturing system based on low skills, low wages, and low product quality. France sits somewhere in between, with a higher productivity rate than the Germans and higher skills than the British, a production system based on medium skills, wages, and product quality, and a higher capacity than Germany for radical innovation—in particular in formerly state-dominated sectors—and than Britain for incremental innovation.

Finally, in each of the three countries, adjustment has been the function of very different mechanisms for change. In today's more intensively market capitalist Britain, change is driven by the financial markets and led by autonomous firms acting on their own, with comparatively little input—whether positive or negative—from the state or labour. In today's more competitive managed capitalist Germany, change is led by firms and negotiated cooperatively between business, labour, and the state, by contrast with the unilateral actions of autonomous firms in Britain. In the state-enhanced capitalist system of France, change is firm-led in those domains where business now exercises autonomy—in business strategy, investment, production, and wage-bargaining—but change is still state-driven in those domains where neither business nor labour can exercise leadership—in labour rules, pension systems, and the like—or where the state sees a need to reshape the general economic environment to promote competitiveness. In either case, the interaction is one of hierarchical direction rather than joint-decision or unilateral action.

In Fig. 3.1, I have provided a rough idea of how the changes in the three countries might be plotted in three different time periods—the 1970s, the late 1990s, and a few years hence—as a projection of current trends. I drew a triangle rather than the usual fourfold table in order to illustrate how the different countries have evolved along continua between market, managed, and state capitalism in terms of business, state, and industrial relations.[30]

---

[30] This triangular approach was inspired by that of Coates (1999).

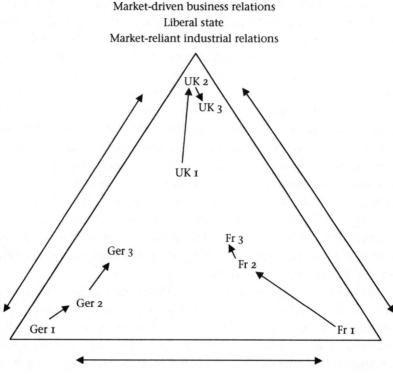

MARKET CAPITALISM
Market-driven business relations
Liberal state
Market-reliant industrial relations

Non-market managed business relations   State-organized business relations
Enabling state   Interventionist state
Coordinated industrial relations   State-controlled industrial relations

MANAGED CAPITALISM   STATE CAPITALISM

Fig. 3.1 Changing models of capitalism

1: country circa 1970; 2: country in the late 1990s; 3: speculates on next few years based on current trends.

I naturally put market capitalism at the top, given the pressures from global-ization and European integration that tend to favour reforms in this direc-tion. What comes out most clearly is that there is no necessary convergence, although all three countries have moved up closer to market capitalism. Britain, which started out the closest in the 1970s, although still reasonably far from the ideal, came much closer by the 1990s. But I suggest that it may be moving a bit down again, with a little more state intervention coming through increasing state regulation of business—whether pushed by the EU or the Blair government—and of industrial relations, with the minimum wage already introduced by the Blair government in 1997 an example along with increasing EU rules. Germany, which began in the 1970s at the bottom left of the triangle as highly managed capitalist, moved not very significantly up from this by the end of the 1990s. But I foresee a major jump in the next few years toward market capitalism as firms increase their exposure to the financial markets and wage-bargaining becomes more decentralized. Finally, France, which found itself in the 1970s at the bottom right of the triangle as the ideal-typical state capitalist country, moved radically up toward the centre of the triangle as business was deregulated and privatized and wage bargaining decentralized by the 1990s. But I don't see it going much farther in the direction of market capitalism in the next few years.

What then is the future of Europe's three capitalisms? The most I can say is that advanced industrialized countries are most likely to remain distinguishable along the lines of the modified varieties outlined above, at least for a while, although they will continue to progress in response to the demands for greater competitiveness and market orientation in a more internationalized and Europeanized economic environment. But even as these countries strive to become increasingly competitive in their very different ways, they will continue to exhibit significant differences in business, state, and industrial relations. Convergence along market capitalist lines is highly unlikely, and is not simply a question of time, because countries' different economic and political institutions are path dependent, providing different constraints or opportunities for change, while countries' different histories and cultures frame actors' differing conceptions of what can or should be done in the context of globalization and European integration, creating different possibilities and limits to change.

This is not to suggest, however, a kind of institutional or cultural determinism that insists that countries are forever stuck in a particular pattern of business, government, and labour relations and practices. In fact, countries can change variety, as in the cases of New Zealand, which seems to have moved from a version of state capitalism to market capitalism; Australia, which appears to have moved from state capitalism to a mix of market capitalism in business relations and managed capitalism in labour relations (Schwartz 2000); and even Italy, which may very well have moved from a kind of failed state capitalism to managed capitalism.[31] Moreover, it is conceivable that even Britain, despite its long history of liberalism, might have

---

[31] My thanks to David Soskice for this insight. Marino Regini qualifies this, however, by suggesting that while the 'first Italy' may be moving from failed state capitalism towards managed capitalism, the managed capitalist 'third Italy' of the 1980s may in fact be moving in the direction of market capitalism, although still closer to the centre of the triangle than the top.

moved toward managed capitalism at least in the industrial relations arena had the experiences of the 1970s not been so disastrous. But there is no doubt that that history made it easier for Thatcher to legitimize policy reforms that moved Britain toward greater market capitalism by contrast with France, where Mitterrand had much greater difficulty legitimizing the retreat from post-war state capitalism, or Germany, where Schröder continues to struggle to generate, let alone legitimize, reforms that would move German managed capitalism toward greater market competitiveness (see Chapter 6).

To understand this fully, however, it is necessary to focus on the politics of adjustment and the distinctiveness of the national discourses that seek to generate and legitimize changes in political-economic policies and practices in terms of nationally based ideas and values. But before this, the next chapter will develop in greater detail the dynamics of change in the political-economic practices of Britain, France, and Germany.

4

The Dynamics of Adjustment in Economic Practices in Britain, Germany, and France

In the early post-war years, in the context of the international regime of 'embedded liberalism' (Ruggie 1982) which allowed countries to develop under the protective barriers of capital exchange controls, fixed but adjustable exchange rates, and optional barriers to trade, Britain, Germany, and France consolidated very different systems of economic management and development. These differences were apparent in the interrelationships of business, government, and labour: in the varying degrees of business interconnectedness, of government interventionism, and of labour cooperation. The three countries' post-war configurations of capitalism worked, for better or for worse, relatively unconstrained by major external pressures until the 1970s, when the end of the Bretton Woods system of fixed exchange rates followed by the first and then the second oil crisis threw all three countries' capitalisms into question. In the face of increasing competitive pressures in the capital and product markets, whether from global or European forces, all three countries sought to adapt and adjust their systems. For Britain, this entailed, beginning in 1979, radical therapy in the country's quasi-market capitalist system that brought the system closer to the market capitalist ideal, with business relations more distant, government relations more arm's length, and labour relations more market-reliant. For Germany, instead, the competitive challenges spurred little deep-seated change in the country's ideal-typical managed capitalism until the 1990s, at which point incremental changes began in the effort to make the system more competitive, with the loosening of business interconnections, with still coordinated but more decentralized labour–management relations, and with government seeking to facilitate the adjustment. For France, finally, the government's responses to the challenges brought a major transformation in the country's ideal-typical state capitalism beginning in the mid-1980s, with the move away from state-led capitalism to a more state-enhanced variety where business is more autonomous and labour more market-reliant, but the state still has a role to play.

Britain: The Deepening of Market Capitalism

Of all the member states of the EU, Britain has probably gone the farthest in instituting reforms promoting a market capitalist system in a country that was already far and away the most market capitalist in Europe even prior to the reforms. Britain's economy has long been more liberal and open than most of its Continental European counterparts, given its nineteenth-century history of empire which established the pound sterling as an international currency and ensured that British businesses would be among the most internationalized and outward-looking. And while British business relations have always been more individualistic and competitive, the government's relationship with business and labour has always been much less close, and the management-labour relationship has often been much more adversarial.

By the late 1970s, moreover, the country's greater exposure to global forces, the declining competitiveness of its business, and the crisis of its economy, combined with the accession to power of Margaret Thatcher with her ideological commitment to bringing Britain closer to the market capitalist ideal, meant that Britain introduced market capitalist reforms earlier than other EC member states. Moreover, it also in many ways acted as the impetus for the spread of market capitalism in Europe more generally by leading the charge for the deregulation of markets and privatization of industry. The reforms that followed Thatcher's election in 1979 and that continued through the 1980s and into the 1990s have brought Britain much closer to the ideal-typical model of market capitalism than before at the same time as the Thatcherite market capitalist reform project has served as the market capitalist ideal for other countries to emulate and even, in certain instances, for the EU Commission to generalize to the EU as a whole.

The Post-war Model

Market-driven business relations and the split between industry and finance, the more or less hands-off approach to business of a liberal state, and decentralized, adversarial labour relations were already present prior to the Thatcherite reforms. Yet Britain fell far short of the ideal-type of market capitalism outlined earlier. Business relations tended to be much less market-driven than they were to become as a result of deregulation and privatization. In many areas, although the structure of inter-firm interaction remained highly individualistic, arms' length, and contractual, the behaviour often belied the structure. A 'gentlemanly' style tended to moderate competitive behaviour, leading to a softer kind of capitalism characterized by tacit understandings and cartel-like arrangements. Nevertheless, industry and finance remained separate: industry gained much of its financing either through retained earnings or through the sale of equity and bonds, and relied on the banks only for short-term operating funds. As such, industry and finance were 'autonomous bargaining partners' (Zysman 1983: 70), with finance having little understanding of or concern for the long-term needs of industry, focusing more on quarterly reports and profits rather than on any longer-term questions of firm value or market share.

Within this context, the government's focus on maintaining the pound sterling as an international currency, regardless of its deleterious effects on business investment, ensured an alliance with the financiers often against the interests of business (Shonfield 1958). The reasons for this approach have their foundations not just in policy preferences, in particular the desire to serve national pride through the pound's role as an international reserve and trade currency or the national interest through its reinforcement of currency and trade linkages with Commonwealth countries. They also stem from economic vulnerabilities, in particular the need to service the extraordinarily high debt load left by the war—with a debt–income ratio of 175 per cent—which, added to continuing balance of payments crises, left the pound consistently vulnerable and in need of shoring up (Eichengreen and Ritschl 1998). At the same time, however, governments were committed to maintaining full employment at almost all costs, making it unable to pursue a hard-money policy long enough to solve its balance of payments problems once and for all. This dual commitment to full employment as well as a strong pound led to the 'stop-go' economic policies that so adversely affected business throughout the post-war period (see Pollard 1992; Tomlinson 1990: 257–61).

Whenever a balance of payments and/or sterling crisis threatened, the government would put on the brakes by cutting budgets, reducing demand in order to lower imports and raise exports, thereby increasing unemployment until such a time as the balance of payments situation eased and unemployment grew to an unacceptably high level. At this point, the government would step on the accelerator by increasing demand and expanding employment until imports rose and potential exports were diverted to the home market, so much so that another balance of payments and sterling crisis threatened, at which time the brakes were put on yet again. For business, the 'stop' periods in which government intermittently held back investment as part of its policy of controlling the level of demand greatly limited their expansion while the 'go' periods were generally not long enough to ensure the kind of confidence or sustained profits necessary to investment. Add this to the financial markets' preference for liquid, short-term investments, and it becomes clear why business investment lagged behind that of other countries throughout this period.

Government macroeconomic policies that discouraged investment, however, were not the sole cause of business decline. Rather, they only added to the problems of an industrial structure plagued not only by low investment but also by ageing plants, poor management, and poor labour relations (see Coates 1994). All of this contributed to the decreasing international competitiveness of British products, which tended to be low in quality and high in cost—in particular when the pound was strong.

The lack of competitiveness began with the fact that, despite the openness of the economy from very early on, British manufacturing firms still felt comparatively little pressure to cut costs or improve quality because of guaranteed Commonwealth markets as well as import and price controls and subsidies in the early post-war years—that lasted well into the 1950s in some areas.[1] This was compounded over time by the comparative lack of improvement in managerial practice, given the 'amateur tradition' that valued generalist knowledge over the technical.[2] In addition, the lack of capital investment in manufacturing meant that plants were ageing rapidly, while the focus on financial controls rather than, say, technological prowess, as in France, meant that profits were squeezed out at the expense of investment in new machinery and technologies. Research and development expenditures were some of the lowest in Europe, and, even where R&D occurred, the production system was not likely to get the new products to market fast enough, with high enough quality or low enough prices, to make them competitive. The problems with prices had much to do with escalating wages that did not match productivity gains, a result in part of the conflictual labour relations system (see below), while the problems with quality followed not just from the low capital investment in machinery and technology but also from the lack of investment in human resources (Lane 1989). Workers remained low-skilled, as well as poorly motivated, in large measure because employers were reluctant to pay for training programmes that they viewed as a risky investment, given that they saw employees as free agents, likely to move if offered a better job, and in any case possibly to be laid off at the next economic downturn.

Successive governments did not do much to solve the problems, even though they were not unaware of them. Early post-war governments did

---

[1] See, for example, Broadberry and Crafts (1996); Eichengreen and Ritschl (1998); Schenk (1994).

[2] See, for example, Weiner (1981); Lane (1989); Tiratsoo and Tomlinson (1998).

little because of their reticence to challenge management practice or to upset the consensual relationship between government and the private sector (Middlemas 1986: 12). Moreover, even though subsequent governments were sometimes more interventionist, in particular in the 1960s and 1970s, such efforts generally came to naught. This was related to the fact that post-war British governments' approach to economic development generally was one in which the government sought to control the total level of economic activity rather than intervene in particular sectors of activity through detailed plans and industrial policies, as was the case with the state capitalist approach of the French. And when they did intervene, whether through planning experiments similar to those of French state capitalism or social concertation ones similar to those of the managed capitalism of the smaller European countries, they tended to fail.[3] Similarly, moreover, the nationalized industries which were to control the 'commanding heights' of the economy rarely did very well, and remained quite marginal to overall economic policy-making, which was largely focused on the macroeconomic.[4]

British governments' preference for the macro-management rather than the micro-management of the economy is reflected in the traditional pattern of government relations with business, which has been one in which the British 'spectator state' maintained a 'hands-off' approach to business (Grant 1995). This often meant allowing business to organize its own regulation through 'private interest governments' in which business essentially set its own rules and policed itself. This in turn served to reinforce the 'gentlemen's agreements' mentioned above, and the cartel-like relationships, clubbishness, and cosy understandings that pervaded many sectors of business. Business accommodation was also promoted through the informal relationships between civil servants and businessmen in many spheres as well as through the ministerial departments that acted as the semi-official sponsors of given businesses within the machinery of government (Grant and Sargent 1987). Altogether this allowed for a comfortable, often not very competitive, capitalism in which insiders remained inside and outsiders were kept out.

But however much post-war Britain's sometimes interventionist and not-so-competitive business-government relationship departed from ideal-typical market capitalism, British industrial relations departed even more. Although it fitted the model in terms of the fragmentation of management and unions, the adversarial nature of labour–management relations, and the decentralization of wage-bargaining, the particularities of the industrial

[3] On planning experiments, see Shonfield (1965); Hayward (1973a); Cairncross (1985). On social concertation experiments, see Middlemas (1979); Winkler (1976).

[4] See, for example, Tomlinson (1990); Chester (1975).

relations system ensured that the state itself would have to take a much more active role than the ideal allowed. Because decentralized wage-bargaining involved not individual contracts between employer and employee but rather collective bargaining agreements; because union fragmentation did not prevent their centralized organization or density of membership; and because management fragmentation hindered the creation of a united front against labour demands, Britain experienced the kinds of wage rises that forced successive governments to intervene in order to ensure the macro-economic health of the country (see Scharpf 1991: Ch. 5). Whereas British governments may have largely maintained a hands-off approach with regard to relations with business, they maintained no such approach to labour.

Moreover, although the interventionist role of the British state with regard to labour might appear to come close to that of to state capitalism, it was in fact far from it. In Britain, there was almost never any question of attempting to organize and control the negotiations or set targets for wage rises, although there was the occasional imposition of agreement through wage controls. Such micro-management was ruled out from the start by successive governments' care to respect both management's and labour's preference for 'voluntarism', which meant free collective bargaining—and even the absence of laws to structure and limit labour–management conflict, such as no-strike rules subsequent to an agreement or a 'duty of peace' in negotiations, as in Germany. What is more, British governments ruled out in advance any attempt to create the conditions for the corporatist approach to wage-setting of managed capitalism, given the general sense that a long-term incomes policy could not be built on anything other than voluntary cooperation—as it had been between 1948 and 1950—and a recognition that any formal incomes policy would demand a recasting of the whole industrial relations system (Middlemas 1986). In consequence, in the face of its almost consistently failed efforts to moderate wage rises, British governments' only effective tool with regard to wage-bargaining settlements was used after the fact, through the macro-management of the economy.

The Enhancement of Market Capitalism

With the advent of Margaret Thatcher, Britain moved back toward its market capitalist roots, with Thatcher seeking to bring the British economy in line with her idealized view of market capitalism and to strip away what she saw as the twin evils of 'socialism' and 'corporatism'. The Thatcher government was, if anything, more interventionist than previous governments. But it was so with the intent of dismantling government interventionism in the economy in order to create a truly market capitalist economy. And it ultimately ensured that the limited role of the state would be diminished even further, with the 'spectator state' becoming even more of a spectator.

The Changing Profile of the British Economy

The government's interventionism began, as always, with macroeconomic policies; and, as always, these policies had a deleterious impact on business. The tight monetary policies that very quickly led to a major appreciation of the pound sterling had a devastating effect on manufacturing firms. Almost overnight, manufacturers found their goods priced out of foreign markets, while domestic markets were flooded with lower-priced foreign goods. Thatcher had assumed that her monetarist policies, together with the reduction in subsidies to nationalized industries, would force firms to become more competitive through cost-cutting and labour-shedding (Howe 1994; Lawson 1993: 56–9). Instead, British firms went bankrupt or were bought by foreign companies.

Since the late 1970s, in fact, the British state has exposed business to greater international competition and the vagaries of the market without the level of government support and government-initiated restructuring of France or the level of business cooperation and labour concertation of Germany. In Britain, unlike in France where the state led business transformation, the laissez-faire nature of privatization made certain that privatized business would be without government-arranged acquirers or protection from takeover, leaving it more vulnerable to foreign acquisition. It also ensured that the deregulated stock market rather than the state, as in France or other state capitalist countries, would lead the moves toward industry concentration and consolidation. And it facilitated a situation in which foreign acquirers would more often than not impose modernization and internationalization from the outside.

Having been left to sink or swim on its own, British industry has sunk more often than not. The policies that invited foreign competitors in on the mistaken assumption that British industry would rise to meet the challenge, together with the more arms-length relationship between business and its stakeholders as well as government, seems to have left much of British industry less competitive than Continental counterparts that benefit from the advantages of a more stable economic governance environment promoted by government, the banks, or even the unions. As proof, one need only look at Britain's share in world exports, which is far below that of Germany, although not that much lower than that of France (see Fig. 4.1). Labour productivity has also remained consistently behind Germany's since the 1960s

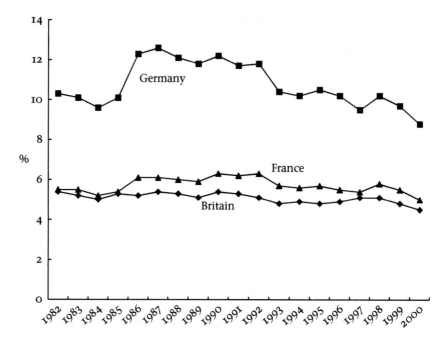

Fig. 4.1 Shares in world exports, 1982–2000

Percentage, values for total goods, customs basis.

Source: OECD Historical Statistics (various years).

and France's since the 1970s, at 26 points behind Germany in the 1980s and 11 points behind France in the 1990s in terms of value added per hour worked in manufacturing (see Table 4.1). In manufacturing more specifically, Britain no longer has a nationally owned automotive or electronics industry. This can be explained by the example of the electronics industry. Faced with the Japanese challenge, predicated on better products at cheaper prices, British governments chose to encourage inward investment by Japanese firms on the assumption that British companies would seek to meet the competitive challenge through reinvestment. They did not, with all having chosen to exit the industry instead of following any other alternatives, which might have included offshore assembly or diversification (Cawson 1994).

And yet foreign-owned industry in Britain has done reasonably well, as have some large British multinationals such as ICI and British Airways. One of the reasons for this has been the welcoming investment environment and, in particular, the low tax rate on business—30 per cent for large companies when profits are above £300,000 and 21 per cent for small and medium sized companies—by contrast with the French rate of 40 per cent for large

Table 4.1 Relative labour productivity levels in manufacturing (US = 100)

	1960: Value added per		1973: Value added per		1985: Value added per		1995: Value added per	
	person hired	hour worked	person hired	hour worked	person hired	hour worked	person hired	hour worked
Germany	60.6	56.0	72.5	76.1	75.6	86.4	63.1	81.4
France	47.5	45.9	66.0	70.0	72.3	85.8	70.1	85.1
United Kingdom	48.6	45.0	52.0	53.6	54.7	59.7	59.6	69.7

Source: OECD (1996).

firms—which dropped to 36.6 per cent in the year 2000—and 36.6 per cent for small and medium-sized firms (*Le Monde*, 11 May 1999). The marginal rate of taxation on income has also been lower in Britain, at 40 per cent, than the French 54 per cent.

The reasons also have to do with the low wage costs, high labour flexibility, and comparatively low labour militancy. This transformation in British labour rates, rules, and relations results from a combination of harsh Tory policies toward labour that virtually crushed the unions in the early 1980s and of the amelioration in management practices with regard to labour, led in large measure by foreign manufacturing firms, Japanese in particular. And it means that Britain, having been disdained for years for its failing industries and low productivity, has now become a preferred host for foreign direct investment and its industries worthy global competitors, even if there are many fewer of them, with a large number of them foreign owned. Britain has consistently way outdistanced Germany in investment inflows since the mid-1980s, and it has also been ahead of France for much of that period (see Fig. 4.2). Britain has also, however, been the unquestioned leader in direct outward investment flows throughout this period. This is testimony to its long history of more internationalized firms with less embeddedness in the home environment, plus its greater willingness to go offshore for production (see Fig. 4.3).

Britain's turnaround can also be seen in its unemployment rates. Although the harsh medicine of the early Thatcher years greatly increased unemployment, the rates headed steadily down thereafter. While in the early 1980s the country was in worse shape than France and Germany, it fell below France in unemployment by the mid-1980s and Germany in the mid-1990s (see Fig. 4.4). Since the mid-1990s, its unemployment record has been a major advertisement for the market capitalist model in Europe.

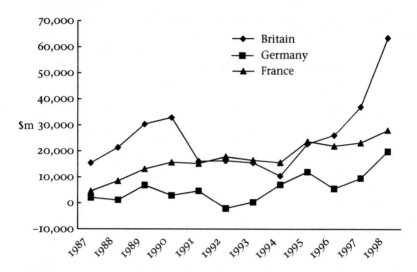

Fig. 4.2 Direct investment inflows, 1987–1998
Source: OECD National Accounts (various years).

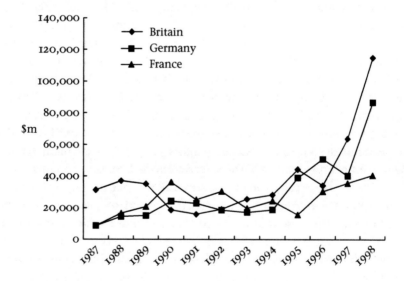

Fig. 4.3 Direct investment outflows, 1987–1998
Source: OECD National Accounts (various years).

The Greater Distance in British Business and Business-Finance Relations

How did Britain's transformation come about? First and foremost, if we leave aside the macroeconomic policies that created a crisis for British manufacturing, was the restructuring of business relations through the liberalization

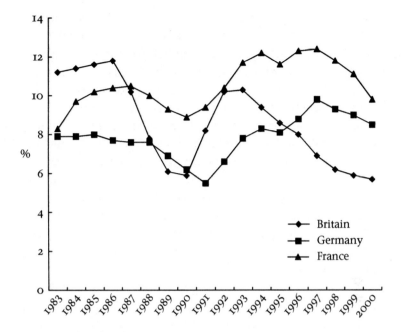

Fig. 4.4 Unemployment rates, 1983–2000

Source: OECD Labour Force Statistics (various years).

of the financial markets and the privatization of major monopolistic public enterprises. The 'big bang' of 1986, to begin with, produced not only a tremendous expansion in the financial markets, with a concomitant change toward more competitive patterns of behaviour within the City, but it also pushed industry-finance relations farther in the traditional direction, towards greater separation. The exponential growth of the liberalized financial markets simply reinforced business' reliance on the markets for capital and decreased even further its bank borrowing, with the traditionally high level of market capitalization of firms having grown while bank financing dropped even further. The changes in the culture of the financial markets, from a more 'gentlemanly' set of attitudes to the rough-and-tumble of takeover artists and the like, also imposed greater pressures on firms for corporate performance, meaning positive quarterly reports that showed profits and promised dividends. Moreover, the rise of institutional investors has added pressures in terms of corporate governance, in particular with regard to greater transparency and attention to shareholder value.

The changes in the capital markets most importantly led to a rapid rise in British firms' market capitalization—from 77 per cent of GDP in 1985 to 142 per cent of GDP in 1996 and to 197 per cent in 2000. Firms' high levels of market capitalization, together with the fact that they have a large percentage of their equity freely traded in the markets—as opposed to their being closely held, or held in friendly hands or by the banks—ensures that they are highly exposed to financial market pressures. This in turn generally entails a greater corporate focus on profit-making and on profit-taking. It is telling that among the 25 most profitable companies in Europe of the top 500 in 1996, a large majority were British (16), with only one French company on the list and no German (*Financial Times*, 24 January 1997).[5] And with higher profits come not just higher dividends to investors but also higher salaries for CEOs. British CEOs have some of the highest pay packages in Europe, although they still come nowhere near the Americans. And much as the American CEOs, the British sometimes continue to collect their high salaries and large bonuses even when their companies have been doing poorly, as in the case of British Gas. This has been the subject of much public outcry, as it has in the United States, and has served as the impetus for new—voluntary—rules on public reporting of executive pay.

Pressures for attention to corporate governance issues have been particularly strong in the UK, much as in the US. This is largely because of British firms' high levels of market capitalization, which means that they are necessarily subject to pressures from institutional investors. Britain, along with the US and Japan, has one of the largest holdings in pension funds, amounting to $US775 billion or 76.5 per cent of GNP in 1996. Predictably, therefore, given the size of its pension funds and exposure to the capital markets, shareholder activism is very powerful in the UK, although not as much as in the US. In the UK, as in the US, a number of large pension funds have been publishing their voting guidelines and making public their corporate governance policies. And in response, British companies have been changing their corporate governance practices, for the most part voluntarily complying with recommendations for reform by official business committees. The increase in supervisory committees is impressive, with a massive increase between 1985 and 1998 in audit, remuneration, and nomination committees (see Table 4.2).

But, although the reforms constituted a major change from the traditional British system of private conversations between fund managers and companies by adding to board powers and to the transparency of corporate accounts, they have not led to any revolution in British corporate governance: institutional shareholders continue to wield significant power that tends to counter that of smaller, more activist shareholder groups, illustrated most notably by their defeat of a move to scrap directors' large pay increases in the

---

[5] By 2001, however, French and German companies were catching up, with four each by comparison with Britain's eight companies in the top 25.

Table 4.2 Percentage of firms with specialized board committees

Country	Audit		Remuneration		Nomination	
	1985	1998	1985	1998	1985	1998
UK (FTSE 350)	21	100	23	100	7	73
Germany (DAX 30)	0	7	0	3	0	7
France (CAC 40)	0	90	0	70	0	43

Source: Goyer (2001).

1996 British Gas annual meeting; and the profiles of directors are still more inside than outside or independent. It is telling that the Blair government announced in 2001 a bill to allow shareholders to vote on executive pay.

These changes in industry-finance relations have in turn affected inter-relationships among firms, which have given up much of the clubbishness and gentlemanliness of the past, and have become more competitive and individualistic as a result. For the large, highly market capitalized firms, moreover, they have also diminished firm stability by encouraging takeover activity as the solution to performance problems. For the small and medium-sized firms, unable to take advantage of the financial markets and without the banking-industry partnerships or the close supplier relationships of managed capitalism, they have done little to resolve their problems related to a lack of cash (see Sako 1994). Because of the importance of the stock market and the lack of a banking-industry partnership as in Germany, R&D costs for smaller firms have run about 60 per cent higher in the UK than in Germany (Crafts 1991: 81–98).

However, the pressures of the financial markets, plus a corporate govern-ance system that gives the CEO great autonomy within the firm, has enabled fast-paced corporate restructuring to take advantage of growing markets. This is apparent in the experience of UK banks, whose radical restructuring enabled them to shift quickly to investment banking, ensuring them high profits, and in the experience of the chemical-pharmaceuticals industry, which was able to move rapidly into new growth fields demanding radical innovation of new products and more rapid rationalization in the produc-tion of simpler products by spinning off pharmaceutical divisions and by cost-cutting on the chemicals side (Vitols 2001: 353–7). It is important to note, however, that although pharmaceuticals have been touted as the great success British story, in 1994 they had a smaller share of world pharma-ceuticals output—6 per cent—than German or French firms—7 per cent each—and they in any case have done little to outweigh the dismal experience of British manufacturing generally (Froud *et al.* 1998).

The greatest changes in the structure of business relations have been related to privatization and deregulation. Privatization of monopolistic public enterprises in particular has moved inter-firm relations generally much farther in the direction of market capitalism, while deregulation of the markets in which privatized firms operate has promoted greater competition. The sheer amount of privatization was alone enough to change the structure of inter-firm relations, given how many public enterprises found themselves private: by 1987, 40 per cent of the state-owned industrial sector, or 19 state firms, had been privatized, and therefore much more subject to pressures for corporate performance. This did not always mean an improvement in performance, however, since the problems of British management remained, whether public or private, thereby often leaving the privatized companies more vulnerable to foreign takeover.

Moreover, although corporate performance pressures increased for privatized firms, market pressures did not necessarily, since privatization did not always entail the creation of highly competitive markets. The early privatizations in particular, such as those of British Telecom or British Gas, hardly brought more competition, despite recommendations even at the time for the need to introduce real competition into those markets (Johnson 1993: 156–62). In the case of BT, we find a public monopoly that was privatized as a private near- monopoly with little serious competition—it retained close to 90 per cent of the market, its only rival being Mercury—although this national market dominance certainly prepared BT for the coming European competition that was to open all national markets. Later privatizations went much farther in the creation of competitive markets, in particular that of the railroads, which were divided into a number of markets that reflected horizontal and vertical divisions of the former British Rail monopoly, with freight and passenger services, rolling stock companies, companies in charge of the tracks—which remained a monopoly—and so on (Denkhaus 1998). But this did not do much for the rail system's efficiency, price competitiveness, or solvency.

The Greater Arms' Length Relationships of the British State

Deregulation and privatization by government, together with subsequent European-led deregulation, has not just ensured that the traditional arms' length relationship between business and government has become more even distant; it has at the same time changed the terms of that relationship. From the 'hands-off' state, Britain has become a more regulatory state in which the arms' length relationship has gone from one focused on leaving business alone to organize and police itself as much as possible to one in which independent agencies and laws regulate business activities. Paradoxically, therefore, one could argue that the liberal state has in fact become more interventionist, since the agents of the state, in the form of regulatory agencies and courts, are now involved in determining activities which in the past were more the purview of business through private governments and/or accommodation by civil servants. But this is not an entirely accurate interpretation of what has actually happened, since the independent agencies and courts are not so much interventionist agents of the state as arbiters of the rules of the game. As such, much as in the United States which has always been much more of a regulatory and legalistic state in its approach to business, the role of the independent agencies and the law comes closer to the ideal-typical role of the liberal state as arbiter and setter of the rules of the game.

The new government relationship with business, moreover, is more truly arms' length. Planning was all but destroyed through the elimination of labour, the marginalization of key business players such as the Confederation of British Industry, and the end of government's institutional support. The traditional subsidy programmes were largely reduced and in some cases eliminated, although this sometimes simply meant replacing these with new, more 'supply-side' programmes, such as enterprise zones; and it did not stop large subsidies to bail out firms with some kind of national symbolism, such as Rover—even if it meant a subsidy to the foreign acquirer, BMW—the naval shipyard of Gowan, or the coal mining industry. The general level of subsidies declined from 2.7 per cent of GDP in 1975-9 to 2.3 per cent in 1980-4, and down to 1.7 per cent in 1985-8, at a time when subsidies in state and managed capitalist European OECD countries rose from 2.5 per cent of GDP in the first period to 2.7 per cent through the rest of the 1980s. By contrast, restrictive pricing, which is one of the greatest impediments to free markets, was left largely untouched during the 1980s (Johnson 1993: 186, 191-5). It had to wait until the 1990s to be attacked.

Most importantly, however, the government sought to put an end to the cosy relationships between managers and civil servants in government departments which were hidden from public view. Self-regulation would continue to be supported wherever possible, although increasingly independent regulatory agencies were substituted where self-regulation could not be counted on to stem anti-competitive practices, while laws were increasingly substituted for voluntary agreements and codes. Although some of the increasing juridification and regulation was the result of external pressures from the EU, which has tended to codify the rules much more than the

British—for example, when the EU in 1997 proposed to make Britain's own voluntary City code on takeovers an EU directive, over the objections of the Major government—most was the result of internal dynamics. In the utilities industries, for example, deregulation and privatization in the 1980s was accompanied by an increase in the powers of the public sphere, even as the state as such had retreated, with regulators having become powerful actors with a central role in policy-making, high visibility, and independence from the government and industry, as well as a clear set of ideas about promoting competition and protecting consumer interests (Thatcher 1998). In the securities industry, moreover, new laws came in response to excesses and abuses— such as insider trading laws in the securities industry in the aftermath of scandal—pushed by the Office of Fair Trading, which undertook extensive investigations into the anti-competitive practices of the informal cartels governing the stock-market business (Moran 1991). Securities deregulation was not only focused on promoting the expansion of the financial markets but also on ending the gentlemanly ethic that had acted increasingly as a constraint to new market forces and caused a crisis in the domestic securities industry by the late 1970s (Moran 1990). Deregulation did not, however, entirely end the informal arrangements. The independent regulatory board, the Securities and Investment Board (SIB), which replaced the informal set of non-governmental arrangements of the past, nevertheless allowed a certain number of 'private interest governments' to continue under its aegis. It is in fact only very recently that these have been done away with entirely as a result of reforms by the Blair government centralizing oversight of the securities industry in one agency.

Deregulation in industry was complemented by deregulation in industrial relations. But here, too, deregulation in fact in many cases meant more, not less, regulation and law. The difference is that, whereas deregulation of industry eliminated many restrictions to business operation, deregulation of industrial relations increased statutory control of unions (Hyman 1994). More specifically, Thatcher sought to create a freer labour market with a greater degree of 'flexibility' in employers' ability to hire and fire and a higher degree of decentralization in bargaining in which employers individually negotiate wages with employees. The idea was to have workers with fewer job protections and weaker, more decentralized unions—if any—and management with fewer restrictions on hiring and firing in order to enable individual employers and employees to respond quickly and efficiently to changing market conditions. In order to have this, however, Thatcher first had to neutralize labour. This demanded the crushing of union power through successful confrontations, done most dramatically in the context of the coal-miners' strike, and then making certain that it would not rise again by instituting legal measures to change the management-labour power balance (see Chapter 2). Privatization of public enterprise also served to weaken union power, long much stronger in the public sector than in the private. What is more, by reserving a certain portion of shares for employees, privatization also contributed to a decline in worker militancy through the increase in worker share ownership. In fact, worker militancy more generally declined from the mid-1980s on, although probably less because of the labour laws or even share ownership in privatized companies than because of the growing unemployment in the early to mid-1980s and the failures of confrontation tactics, given that management no longer backed down as it had in the past, in particular in the public sector where government was willing to absorb the costs of long strikes (Howell 1995, 1999). Moreover, where management introduced new human resource management techniques following the Japanese model, the reasons for dispute diminished with better labour-management relations and improved productivity.

The Move to Market-Reliant Labour Relations

Ironically enough, then, it was under Thatcher that 'voluntarism' in wage bargaining ended, with the explosion of laws governing labour–management relations. Any semblance of 'corporatism' also ended, moreover, with the termination of incomes policies in the 1980s, as Thatcher no longer depended on wage restraint since the increase in North Sea oil revenues solved the balance of payments problems. She also benefited from the discovery that higher levels of unemployment were electorally acceptable and from the reduction in the power of organized labour (Brown 1994: 32–7). By the 1990s, any return to incomes policy became improbable, as pay coordination in the private sector became a matter for single-employer bargaining at the enterprise or establishment level. Only in the public sector did government still have a role to play.

The changes in the microeconomic environment have been striking. Wage bargaining, from having been largely characterized by fragmented collective bargaining, became increasingly market-reliant through individual employer-employee contracts. Collective bargaining in 1980 covered approximately 75 per cent of private sector employees and almost 100 per cent of public sector employees; in 1990, coverage had dropped to 47 per cent of private sector employees and 80 per cent of public sector employees (Brown 1994: 31–2). Moreover, multi-employer bargaining has declined precipitously: from 43 per cent of workplaces covered by multi-employer bargaining to 14 per cent by 1998, while workers covered by collective bargaining agreements has dropped from 70 per cent in 1984 to 41 per cent by 1998 (Cully *et al.* 1999: 228–9, 241–2). Union power as judged by membership has also sharply diminished, with union membership as a proportion of total dependent employees having declined from 56.4 per cent in 1980 to 43.1 per cent in 1991. Where collective bargaining persists, it tends to involve single-union agreements at the firm level, where unions agree to flexibility in the use of labour, arbitration to avoid strikes, and works councils in return for union recognition (Howell 1995: 153).

Labour now has job availability in place of the job security of the past and, therefore, low unemployment but also generally lower wages. At the same time, however, the more competitive wage market has meant that workers with highly prized skills are able to sell them at a premium, leading to much greater wage differentiation. For business, greater market reliance means having a readily available pool of workers to draw on and the ability to hire the most qualified and to fire the redundant, where necessary. It also means less danger of lost income from strikes and job protests—Britain in the 1990s had the fewest days lost to strikes or work stoppages since records began in the late nineteenth century (Howell 1996: 517). This may not remain true, however, since the unions remain strong enough to take negative action but not strong enough to take positive action, say, by coordinating their wage demands with business (*The Economist*, 28 July 1998). Positive action would require mutual trust between labour and management, something that is often in short supply in more market-reliant wage-negotiation systems generally, by contrast with the managed capitalist system.

Blair's reforms since 1997 have done little to alter the radically decentralized management-labour relations instituted by Thatcher. But they have ameliorated the environment for labour, with the reintroduction of some positive rights and job protections for workers along with a minimum wage for the first time ever in British labour history and the acceptance of the EU Social Chapter for which Major had gained an opt-out. New Labour has also begun to engage in somewhat greater interventionism not only through more workers' rights but also through state-paid training schemes for workers and state-paid consultants to enhance working-time flexibility. At the same time, however, it has continued to promote neo-liberal reforms. These include initiatives with regard not only to business, with the end of self-governing arrangements in the securities industry, but to labour, with Blair's second-term initiatives to introduce greater competition into the public services as well as to increase private sector provision of public services.

Germany: Managed Capitalism under Strain

In contrast to Britain, Germany, with its system of managed capitalism, seemingly has resisted longest in instituting market capitalist reforms. Germany's ability to maintain its system virtually intact until the early 1990s has much to do not only with the strength of its economy but also with the strength of its institutions. However, by the mid-1990s, in response to the growing economic crisis brought about by the economic costs of unification and by the competitive pressures of globalization and European-led deregulation, Germany had begun to introduce market capitalist elements into its managed capitalist system. But change has been slow and has been largely accomplished in traditional fashion, through negotiation with the social partners and the *Länder*, thereby diminishing the potentially disruptive impact. In consequence, the overall outlines of the German managed capitalist system remain the same, even though fissures have been appearing in the traditional structures of business relations, state relations with business and labour, and industrial relations. Whether the introduction of market capitalist elements ultimately will make German managed capitalism more resilient and competitive, or will destroy the system as a whole, remains an open question, although the evidence so far points to renewed competitiveness.

The Post-war Model

Although the major outlines of the German managed capitalist system were already present in the early post-war period, this model nevertheless developed slowly over time. By the 1950s, the big banks, broken up by the allies at the end of the war, had reconstituted themselves to become the mainstays of industrial investment and planning. By the 1960s and 1970s, the business structure, with its close inter-firm and business-banking relationships, had become solidified. Moreover, although the macroeconomic environment for business was steadily improving during this period, it was only in the 1970s that the Bundesbank, always concerned with price stability and inflation and never really Keynesian, became the clear leader in the macroeconomic sphere, once it had switched to non-accommodating monetary policies (see Chapter 2). Government relations with business and labour similarly fell into their optimal pattern by the late 1960s, at the same time as the federal government gained greater fiscal control over the economy as a whole and the *Länder* reinforced their vocation in industrial policy. Finally, industrial relations, which were quite disruptive in the 1950s, gained their fully coordinative and cooperative character in the 1960s and their emphasis on wage restraint in the 1970s.[6] Only in the 1970s, then, did the system as such exhibit all the characteristics we now attribute to it, with industrial adaptability and economic stability and growth in the face of international adjustment pressures ensured by an independent central bank focused on monetary stability, by mutually reinforcing firms and banks supported by an 'enabling' state, and by cooperative, neo-corporatist industrial relations.[7] This pattern remained stable at least until the early 1990s.

Within this overall business structure, however, one could actually identify two distinct patterns of industrial order. In addition to the classic model of large-scale, vertically integrated firms with close ties to universal banks which appeared in the late nineteenth century, and which has been the major focus of scholarly discussion (see Gerschenkron 1962; Shonfield 1965), there has also been a more decentralized industrial order, more present in some regions than in others, which built on an older tradition of small-scale enterprises focused on craftsmanship and artisanry (Herrigel 1996, Ch. 1). This other industrial order has been characterized by dense networks of small and medium-sized firms in sectors such as machine tools in regions in which smaller savings and cooperative banks together with supportive local public and private institutions and enabling *Länder* governments facilitate the same kind of flexibility and specialized production also found among larger firms, along with greater stability through protection from bankruptcy in times of economic downturn (Herrigel 1994). In the 1960s and 1970s, these two patterns largely merged as more modern systems of mass production took over. But by the 1980s, they had begun to differentiate themselves again, as the demands of international competition intensified, as the larger firms moved from mass production systems to more flexible specialization, and as the smaller firms found outlets on the international markets (Herrigel 1996; Kern and Schumann 1989).

The cooperative relations within business, whether big or small and medium-sized, were complemented by equally cooperative relations with government, which acted as an 'enabler', facilitating interactions and providing support where needed. Government has to be understood in a very general sense, however, since the German federal government itself has had little independent role in economic decision-making, given the autonomous powers of the Bundesbank with regard to monetary policy, of the federal

---

[6] See, for example, Riemer (1982); Knott (1981); Herrigel (1996: Ch. 7); Turner (1991).

[7] See, for example, Dyson (1984); Esser, Fach, and Dyson (1984); Markovits (1982).

cartel office with regard to competition policy, of the *Länder* with regard to industrial policy, and of the 'social partners' with regard to industrial relations. This, together with the constitutional limitations on government interventionism and the need for agreement within coalition governments and often also for compromises with the opposition—in the Bundesrat—on any proposed industrial policy, has kept the federal government from intervening much directly.[8] Instead, it has focused on creating a positive environment for business. This has included providing general infrastructural supports, such as for research and development, promoting social cohesion through a generous welfare system, and equitable living conditions throughout the country through a redistributive system of revenue sharing across the *Länder* (Streeck 1997: 38).

But while the federal government has remained somewhat in the background, the *Länder* have taken a more direct role in facilitating business activity. The *Länder* have sought to create a supportive economic development environment and knowledge infrastructure through subsidies, research and development aid, co-financing of vocational training, creation of polytechnic institutes with profiles that fit the needs of local industries, and the like, as well as through financial policy (Deeg 1999). In consequence, although Germany's federal state has sometimes projected the image of the more laissez-faire, 'liberal state' of market capitalism, such a liberal appearance is deceptive given the enabling activity carried on by the *Länder*, which has itself grown appreciably beginning in the 1980s (Benz 1989). The limited role of the German federal state in industrial policy has meant, however, that it has been less able to take effective action in moments of crisis than more unitary managed capitalist states, such as Sweden, as for example in the crisis in the shipping industry in the 1970s (see Stråth 1994). With the exception of such sector-wide crises, though, the lack of industrial policy leadership at the centre has been generally offset by the independent powers of the *Länder*.

What is more, in the macroeconomic policy realm the difficulties of leadership have been offset by the independent powers of the Bundesbank and its relationship with the *Länder* and with the social partners, business and labour—which have together promoted the Bundesbank's goals of price stability. First and foremost, the independent Bundesbank's rule-based approach to monetary policy discouraged the federal government from electorally driven, inflationary policies as it freed government from the blame for monetary policy outcomes (McNamara and Jones 1995)—although not for

---

[8] See Katzenstein (1989); Jeffery (1996). But this has left significant coordination problems, given the interlocking system of responsibilities (see Scharpf 1977).

unemployment. Potential political pressures were also reduced by the inter-regional transfer system, in which revenue sharing of value added tax and other receipts are automatically redistributed from the richer regions to the poorer—although not as significant prior to unification, worth no more than a few hundred Deutschmarks per capita. By serving to cushion adjustments from temporary economic shocks and to promote economic convergence, the system ensured *Länder* support for Bundesbank independence while discouraging partisan activity from *Land* delegates to the Bundesbank Council (Costello 1993; McNamara and Jones 1995). Finally, stability has also been related to the wage-bargaining relationship between business and labour, since Bundesbank monetary targets have figured in trade union calculations of wage demands since the mid-1970s, when the Bundesbank shifted to a non-accommodating monetary policy.

In Germany, collective bargaining between the social partners has increasingly approximated a prices and incomes policy, enabling the federal government to avoid making a trade-off between low inflation and high unemployment, and increasing the effectiveness of Bundesbank control over inflation (Scharpf 1991: 133–9; Streeck 1994). The system itself is highly complex, given that the regulation of wages and work conditions takes place in a separate sphere, outside of the public policy arena, according to the principle of *Tarifautonomie*, which ensures that organized employers and workers negotiate independently, without government involvement, and with no statutory incomes policy, albeit with attention paid to the targets set by the Bundesbank. Further complexity is added by the informally centralized wage-bargaining system, which consists of a regionally patterned process where other sectors follow the lead of the pace-setting union-employer negotiations in the metal industry.

Conflict also comes in, however, as a result of the fact that wage bargaining has always involved reasonably contentious and sometimes even confrontational interactions preliminary to the actual negotiations behind closed doors—which generally lead to consensus (Scharpf 1991). In the 1960s in particular, the confrontations prior to negotiation were highly conflictual, as they were intended to push for an increase in the 'social' agenda of the social market economy through higher wages and better social insurance benefits. In the 1980s, the major conflicts involved government legislative proposals aimed at weakening organized labour in terms of their ability both to pursue strike activity—by limiting compensation to workers indirectly affected by strikes—and to organize worker representation within companies—by limiting union control of works councils. In both cases, the legislation had little effect because it was watered down first in the formulation process as a result of labour opposition, employer concern, and political divisions, and then in the implementation by employer reluctance to use the resulting law (Silvia 1988; Wood 2001: 266–72).

In Germany, in addition to the regionally patterned, national level of collective bargaining on wages and work time by strong, responsible national unions, the system of industrial relations has provided for another level of coordination at the plant level consisting of works councils concerned with shop-floor organization. In this flexible, dual system of industrial relations, firms benefited both from the informally centralized bargaining system which provided for wage restraint and from the decentralized works councils which facilitated the institution of work reorganization and technological innovation without significant disruption (Streeck 1984; Turner 1991). This, together with the system of co-determination whereby workers sat on the board and were privy to all information on corporate strategy and accounts, served to solidify labour–management cooperation, as did management's commitment to long-term employment and to investment in training. Moreover, the dual system of apprenticeship and training made possible by business-led coordination and government labour-market regulation has the benefit of providing employers with a steady supply of young people with relevant, transferable skills willing to work for lower wages at the same time as it reduces youth unemployment and ensures a smooth transition to work (OECD 1994; Culpepper 2001).

Although all of this taken as a whole made for higher wages and benefits, less market flexibility, and less independence in management decision-making than in market capitalist Britain, it also guaranteed greater productivity from more highly skilled, longer-term employees in whom the costs of training would be more than paid for by the resulting higher quality, higher value-added products, and employee-led innovation. What is more, all of this, together with a stable monetary environment and the availability of state support, promoted the kinds of investment decisions that favoured research and development, continual innovation through flexible specialization, and steady upgrading of production facilities. In consequence, what German goods lost in price competitiveness in international markets, given higher German production costs, they more than made up for in quality competitiveness across a wide range of manufacturing sectors.

The German system of managed capitalism, in short, ensured high international competitiveness for its products at the same time as it guaranteed high wages, low inequality of incomes, and high living standards for its population. Moreover, it was able to do this at a time when other countries were suffering from decreasing product competitiveness, declining wages, rising income inequality, and decreasing living standards. Germany's particular business structure, with the close business-banking partnership that provided long-term, low-cost financing at the same time as it protected it from takeovers, together with industry's near-symbiotic relationship with subcontractors, suppliers, and customers, had made German business less vulnerable to outside pressures and more resilient. Moreover, Germany's social concertation system had made possible innovations in production systems, and in particular the move from Fordism to flexible specialization (Piore and Sabel 1984) that had spared it the radical restructurings that businesses of other nations went through from the late 1970s on. But although Germany's highly cooperative set of labour relations enabled it to weather the adjustment problems of the 1970s without the waves of strikes other European countries suffered, by the mid-1990s it had begun to suffer from its high wages and labour inflexibility, with its businesses increasingly feeling the need for readjustment.

Managing Change in Managed Capitalism

Until 1989, Germany's managed capitalist system seemed not only unshakeable but also certain to maintain German prosperity with stable economic growth well into the twenty-first century. At this time, West Germany was the most internationally successful of all major economies, having had a larger share in visible world exports than Japan and about the same as the United States, and a larger trade and current account surplus than Japan, let alone the deficit-ridden US. Moreover, this was the case despite higher wages than in either of these two countries and less wage inequality (Streeck 1997). German unification changed all of this, as did subsequent pressures resulting from global competition.

The Changing Profile of the German Economy

Unification involved the extension to East Germany of the German institutional model of 'socially circumscribed markets, negotiated firms, enabling state intervention, and market-regulating associations' in the attempt to recreate the West German high-wage economy in the East. Instead, it resulted in the immediate collapse of the East German command economy, due in large measure to the East's much lower productivity rates, low-quality and high-priced—after the one-to-one parity of the Deutschmark—goods, and the relatively slow rate of investment by West German and foreign firms alike, concerned by unresolved issues related to property rights and environmental hazards. And this in turn brought the inevitable transfer of wealth from West to East, to the tune of approximately $US100 billion a year (Streeck 1997). By 1993, Germany was in its largest recession in the post-war period, with the rise in unemployment, already a problem in the 1980s, now at crisis proportions in the German view, although still lower than in France but way above Britain (see Fig. 4.4).

By the mid- to late 1990s, moreover, with the added pressures from global competition, Germany as a whole was suffering from too expensive products, too high labour costs, and too high unemployment at the same time as in-country investment—foreign and domestic—had declined, productivity had slowed, and innovation had dropped. Its share of world exports had been steadily declining since the late 1980s, although it remained well above the levels of France and Britain (see Fig. 4.1). The labour productivity figures, moreover, had slipped, largely as a result of adding East German figures to the West German in 1995, and was below that of France by four points in the mid-1990s in terms of value added per hour worked, although it remained, as always, far above Britain's (see Table 4.1). German businesses themselves bemoaned the lack of venture capital that they saw as promoting the innovativeness and entrepreneurial success of firms in market capitalist countries—by which they generally meant the US rather than the UK. They decried the lack of flexibility in employment which made them unable to respond more quickly to changing market conditions, an advantage not only of market capitalist countries such as the US and the UK but also of some other managed capitalist countries such as the Netherlands and Denmark. And they complained about the too high payroll costs that discouraged foreign direct investment, which resulted from the fact that the welfare state was largely financed by taxes on employers and employees rather than out of general taxation, as in market capitalist Britain and managed capitalist Denmark. Inward investment flows remained negligible, especially when compared with France, let alone Britain, throughout the 1990s (see Fig. 4.2).

The deteriorating economic outlook also affected the internal institutional relationships upon which the solidity of the macroeconomic environment rested. To begin with, problems developed in the relationship between the federal government and the Bundesbank as a result of government policies related to the conversion of the East German Mark to the Western Mark at a one-to-one ratio—rather than the two-to-one preferred by the Bundesbank—and the large reconstruction programme funded by massive transfers of tax revenues and deficit spending. Fiscal solidarity also came into question as the West German *Länder* insisted that the federal government should assume the larger burden in bringing the revenue of the Eastern *Länder* up to West German standards (Jeffery 1995; McNamara and Jones 1995). Finally, the unions' insistence on rapid nominal wage convergence for East German workers added to the escalation of unemployment in the Eastern *Länder* (Thelen 1993; Boche 1993: 86–8; Soskice and Ronald Schettkat 1993).

The rise in the exchange rate caused by the restrictive monetary policy of the Bundesbank, and the rise of non-wage labour costs followed by the mid-1990s wage hikes in West Germany, became increasingly problematic for German businesses seeking ways to reduce wage costs in response to growing global competition in the product markets and decreasing international competitiveness. From the mid-1990s on, in fact, most German firms began seeking to rationalize operations, shed workers, and export core activities in the face of the pressures to internationalize production locations. This came in response to the development of regional trade associations—such as NAFTA, Mercosur, and so on—with higher tariffs for outsiders than insiders, as well as from efforts to increase international competitiveness. Moreover, especially in response to the global competitive pressures, many German firms have instituted more market capitalist management strategies that in some cases seem a direct challenge to the traditionally cooperative inter-firm and labour–management relationship.

Whereas firms in market capitalist countries such as the United States and Britain had been among the first to locate abroad in the search for lower production costs, German big businesses with few exceptions had been among the last to internationalize, held captive by the closely networked inter-firm relations, the social concertation system, and the need for high-skilled labour to produce high-quality goods. But when they internationalized, they did it in a big way. At the same time as inward foreign direct investment lagged, outward investment increased exponentially as of the mid-1990s, outpacing the French (see Fig. 4.3).

Recent moves to the United States can be seen primarily as a response to NAFTA as well as the result of the search for lower wage costs, the case of BMW's first-ever foreign implantation in Spartanburg, South Carolina, where there are no unions and wages are half those of German workers. Internationalization for most German firms, however, is mainly Europeanization. Within the EU, the wave of mergers and acquisitions which began in the late 1980s had everything to do with the completion of the Single Market and the perceived need to have wider European coverage in order to take advantage of the new business opportunities, and little to do with the search for lower costs per se. By contrast, the move of production facilities to Eastern Europe are directly related to the search for lower costs as well as for geographically contiguous and culturally related countries where the German model can be transplanted relatively easily but costs are lower. The pattern for British firms is different: they have more far-flung operations in which they tend to acquire foreign firms rather than set up new ones (Lane 1998: 474–9).

In addition to internationalizing their operations in response to the pressures from globalization of the product markets and the regionalization of tariff regimes, many firms have also adopted a consciously market capitalist management strategy in terms of their internal organization and requirements for competitiveness. Starting in the early 1990s, companies segmented their operations into business units, decentralized into profit centres, outsourced non-core activities, moved from functional to product- and process-oriented types of organization, sought to develop new businesses with higher growth potential, introduced stock options as management incentives, set financial targets for evaluating management performance, and established value-oriented controlling systems and international accounting standards (Lane 1998; Jürgens, Naumann, and Rupp 2000: 73–4). For example, Hoechst, the chemicals and drugs giant, which had traditionally been highly centralized and hierarchical, reorganized and restructured beginning in 1994, giving business units greater autonomy while demanding a given level of profitability within three years, with those that couldn't or didn't facing sale or closure. Daimler-Benz also restructured significantly, selling off Dornier (aircraft), dismantling AEG (engineering), and allowing Fokker, the Dutch aircraft manufacturer in which it had a stake, to go bankrupt in 1996, then merging with Chrysler in 1999. It incorporated under German law rather than American, however, largely on the argument that German tax and other rules were actually more beneficial to company profitability than American ones, and that co-determination was no impediment to following more market-oriented practices.

The changes in the larger firms have also affected the smaller firms with which they are linked. The internal demands for greater competitiveness and return on investment from subsidiaries and subdivisions are often replicated in relations with suppliers and subcontractors, which have felt increasing pressures for cutting costs while maintaining quality. Illustrative is the case of Volkswagen, which had hired a former top manager of General Motors (Opel) to introduce market capitalist strategies throughout the firm, including with suppliers and subcontractors, primarily by squeezing them on costs in order to generate higher firm profits. In another case, though, Ford found itself without door locks because a supplier with something of a monopoly on the part squeezed back, delaying delivery for a couple of weeks and effectively shutting down the assembly line. However, the firm's solution—to look for additional suppliers—cuts down on efficiency although it may ensure continued supply. Moreover, the changed relationship with suppliers and subcontractors, from close cooperation to more arm's length relations, lowers trust and diminishes the network-based economic stability of the small and medium-sized firms which serve as the larger firms' suppliers and subcontractors. This in turn further undermines the network-based inter-firm relationship and has the potential of generating the more individualized inter-firm relations of the type found in market capitalism. And all of this together necessarily damages the cooperative, network-based inter-firm relationship that has been one of the key elements in the success of the German post-war economic model.

As a corollary to internationalization and adoption of market capitalist practices, some of the bigger, more internationalized firms also began floating shares on foreign capital markets as of the mid-1990s. Daimler-Benz was the first to list its shares on the New York Stock Exchange (NYSE), Deutsche Telekom—as part of the global offering related to its partial privatization—the second, followed by Hoechst. In 1998, even Siemens, which had long been a defender of Standort Deutschland, listed its shares on the NYSE (Loewendahl 1999). In so doing, moreover, all these firms accepted something that German firms generally had resisted for years: meeting the more stringent US rules, including Security and Exchange Commission rules on company reports and accounting standards. This meant laying bare company accounts that top management had always kept confidential, and in particular the large, hidden reserves that serve as a cushion in bad times and a source of investment capital when needed.[9] And it also meant looking for higher profits. More generally, of the DAX 30—the top 30 companies on the German stock exchange—in 1997, 33.3 per cent had adopted a profitability goal, 43.3 per cent international accounting standards, 33.3 per cent employee share-ownership programmes, 60 per cent stock option plans for managers, and 66.7 per cent quarterly reporting (Jürgens, Naumann, and Rupp 2000: 69).

Moreover, while the largest businesses have been listing their shares on the stock markets, the banks have been buying up the investment houses responsible for the listings (Griffin 1995; Cioffi 2000). Deutsche Bank's acquisition of the British investment house Morgan Grenfell, and later of Bankers' Trust, was only one of many attempts by the big German banks to buy themselves instant investment expertise and entrée into the financial markets—although this did not necessarily bring with it the return on investment of the British banks, which were twice as profitable as German banks, since this would have demanded much greater rationalizations at home (Vitols 2001). Moreover, the 1995 deregulation of the formerly small and underdeveloped German stock markets has also entailed greater German bank focus on the

---

[9] For more detail, see Ziegler (2000).

financial markets, to the detriment of their post-war vocation as leaders and financiers of business. And the banks have started to behave like pension and investment funds when it comes to their ownership stakes in German industrial corporations, by spinning off those stakes into separately managed holdings run on the basis of shareholder value principles (Jürgens, Naumann, and Rupp 2000: 70–1).

The Moderate Loosening of Ties in Business Interrelations

Thus, the structure of the business-banking relationship has been changing, with a greater distance than in the past between the big banks, which have been internationalizing and focusing more on the financial markets, and big businesses, which have increasingly been going to the financial markets. The changes have been quite modest, however. Internal financing remains the primary source of investment capital, at an average of 60.8 per cent between 1991 and 1998 and long-term loans were steady at an average of 15.4 per cent, despite the fact that the equity markets rose significantly, up from 1.7 per cent in 1991 to 11.9 per cent in 1998 (Jürgens, Naumann, and Rupp 2000: 62).

Moreover, the smaller, regional banks have so far seemingly remained true to their traditional vocation of business lending and strategic support. They have generally maintained their close partnership with the small and medium-sized companies—the *Mittelstand*—many of which are privately held, and most of which have so far not turned to the newly dynamized German financial markets for capital. This suggests that a pattern of greater differentiation between the two industrial orders may be emerging where, even if the classic partnership between big businesses and universal banks is eroding along with the close network-based inter-firm relationship, the more decentralized industrial order of close, cooperative networks of regional banks and small and medium-sized enterprises (SMEs) remains largely intact (Deeg 1999). Whether this separate pattern will continue is doubtful, however, given that, even if the business-banking partnership continues to be strong for SMEs, the competitive pressures on the export-focused SMEs and on international market-conscious *Länder* banks may have the same effect as on their larger brethren, not only by undermining the network-based relationship but also by encouraging firms to look to the capital markets for ready cash—if only to fund acquisitions—and the banks to impose more stringent requirements on loans. Moreover, on top of these competitive challenges are the legal challenges to the public status of the *Landesbanken* and savings banks by EU competition policy and the structural ones likely from the growing concentration of small and middle-sized banks and the likelihood of private—including foreign—bank acquisition (Lütz 2000).

For all this, however, the German model has not succumbed yet, and even the big German firms which have internationalized their operations, changed their management strategies, and listed their shares on the international financial markets have not entirely become pockets of market capitalism in managed capitalist Germany. Although there is much talk by CEOs of these firms about shareholder value, about paying more attention to quarterly reports, profits, and dividends, and about greater transparency, management priorities have not changed radically. In a comparative study of the priorities of management boards in 1998, for example, German boards were way behind the British on meeting financial goals—53 per cent vs 72 per cent—and on favouring mergers, acquisitions, joint ventures, and divestment—28 per cent vs 46 per cent—whereas they were way ahead on reducing costs—36 per cent vs 15 per cent—and on improving productivity—36 per cent vs 15 per cent (Korn/Ferry International 1998: 35; Jürgens, Naumann, and Rupp 2000: 66). Thus, although there has no doubt been an increasing focus on profitability, the traditional German values focused on productivity remain.

Moreover, the pressures on German managed capitalist firms are not the same as for firms in market capitalist countries, which tend to be much more highly capitalized on the markets and therefore much more vulnerable to pressures from institutional investors and to takeover from hostile bidders. Ownership structure alone ensures the differences.

German firms continue to remain closely held. Most German firms are not stock-market listed. Among the 170 largest listed German companies, nearly 85 per cent had a single shareholder with an ownership stake of 25 per cent or higher in 1990—by contrast with 16 per cent in Britain (Franks and Mayer 1995). Moreover, a majority of listed firms' shares in the domestic stock markets are owned or controlled by other corporations or the banks. In 1997, German market capitalization was still quite minimal, at 31.4 per cent of GDP compared with France's 40.6 per cent and the UK's 100.9 per cent of GDP, while of the 700 listed firms, a mere 35—including all DAX 30 companies—accounted for close to three-quarters of total market capitalization (Jürgens, Naumann, and Rupp 2000: 56). The structure of ownership, moreover, continues to follow the traditional pattern of strategic shareholding by corporations and financial companies. In 1998, industrial companies alone controlled 30.5 per cent of all shares, followed by insurance companies at 13.7 per cent and banks at 10.3 per cent. By contrast, investment funds held only 12.9 per cent and private households 15 per cent (Jürgens, Naumann, and Rupp 2000: 57). By 2001, moreover, the strategic holdings actually showed an increase, with corporations owning approximately 40 per cent of the German equity market while financial companies 25 per cent (*Financial Times*, 12 June 2001).

That said, although institutional investors' holding remain comparatively modest, at 15 per cent of all German shares in 1998, they have significant effects because of their large shareholdings in some of the biggest companies: for example, 48 per cent of Daimler-Benz, 71 per cent of Lufthansa, and 50 per cent of Hoechst in 1997(Jürgens, Naumann, and Rupp 2000: 58). Moreover, German pension funds, although still at a very low rate—$US124 billion at 6.1 per cent of GNP in 1999—are likely to grow significantly as a result of the pension reforms that will enable Germans to invest 1 per cent of their gross wages in savings instruments as of 2002, to reach 4 per cent by 2004. Moreover, the 2002 end to the capital gains tax, with the likely coming on to the market of a sizeable amount of strategic investors' holdings, is certain to increase the weight of the institutional investors. But it is not likely to produce a massive overnight change in the concentration of ownership, given not only the limits of the markets' ability to absorb such capital but also the fact that many strategic investors will hesitate to reduce their holdings too precipitously for fear of fuelling takeover attempts. For example, the insurance companies Munich Re and Allianz have not planned to reduce their cross-shareholdings to below 20 per cent, in order to protect against takeover. Moreover, others see financial advantage in maintaining their holdings, as in the case of Deustchebank's 12 per cent stake in Daimler-Chrysler. The main pressure will be on firms that are not performing well to do better or face divestment (*Financial Times*, 23 October 2000).

So long as the structure of share ownership changes relatively slowly, moreover, German firms will remain protected from the kinds of takeover pressures to which British firms are highly vulnerable. Hostile takeover bids have been rare, and are likely to remain so. Of the 222 hostile bids in Europe between 1990 and 1999, only four of the bids involved German companies, by contrast with the 148 from British firms, and only one was successful (Gibbs 1999: 7; Jürgens, Naumann, and Rupp 2000: 72). On the odd occasion when hostile bids have occurred, they have generally ended in compromise, as for example in the case of the attempt by Krupp to take over Thyssen in March 1997, which ended in Krupp's capitulation to political pressures for a merger instead.[10] And it was not until the end of 1999 that a hostile foreign takeover—of Mannesmann by Vodafone—was launched which proved successful, but this only because the board of supervisors remained neutral rather than fight it.

---

[10] For more detail, see Ziegler (2000).

Corporate governance structures favouring stakeholder control also protect German firms from financial market pressures. There has been little progress in overhauling corporate governance structures, despite the need in the face of major scandals. This has been mainly because of continued division over reform among parties in power—previously between the Christian Democrats and the Free Democrats, now within the Social Democratic camp—of the complexities given the different shareholders' interest groups involved, and of resistance from trade unions to giving up seats on the supervisory boards of co-determined firms (Lütz 2000). As a result, company law reform has been minimal, coming in response to corporate scandals rather than the pressures of the financial markets, and has not touched the dual board system or the principle of employee board representation (Jürgens, Naumann, and Rupp 2000; Ziegler 2000; Vitols 2001). Only in November 2001 did Schröder announce the establishment of a committee—to report in February 2002—to recommend on corporate governance. But rather than scrapping the dual model in favour of the Anglo-Saxon, the committee is expected to suggest ways of ensuring the current system's proper functioning: for example, by limiting the number of directorships to five, forbidding directors to sit on competing firms' boards, and ensuring real separation between management and supervisory boards by no longer allowing the chairman of the management board to retire to become the head of the supervisory board. And in the interim, Germany continues to have almost no independent directors and hardly any specialized board committees (see Table 4.2). Moreover, in December 2000 the government proposed reinforcing the system of co-determination, especially in SMEs.

The corporate governance structure also has a significant influence over the slow pace of corporate restructuring and repositioning in German industry by comparison with Britain. The constraints on top management, given the need to satisfy company stakeholders on the board of supervisors, not only strategic investors but also labour, puts brakes on the kinds of radical restructuring in which British CEOs have engaged in recent years. The banks have had greater difficulty rationalizing operations, despite poor profit performance, given employee resistance to workforce lay-offs and branch closures (Vitols 2001: 352–5). The German chemical/pharmaceutical industry has found it more difficult to move aggressively into the new growth fields in pharmaceuticals which demand radical innovation other than through relocation to and/or acquisition in the US or by 'exiting' Germany entirely, by moving operations—as in the case of Aventis, formed from the merger of Hoechst and Rhône-Poulenc, which is now headquartered in Strasbourg—or divesting their pharmaceutical operations entirely—BASF, and under discussion at Bayer (Vitols 2001: 355–7). Finally, although the corporate governance structures have not stopped massive lay-offs by major firms, such as Siemens and Daimler-Chrysler, bespeaking a major change from the past, they have ensured guarantees from management that they would be negotiated with labour rather than simply imposed, which is the market capitalist model.

Thus, although the network-based inter-firm relations and the business-banking partnership have both been loosening as elements of market capitalist practice have been adopted by some of the larger businesses and banks, the structure of German business relations has not become market capitalist, even if managed capitalism is under strain. Whether business relations will ultimately move so far in the market capitalist direction as to break apart the cooperative network-based system—either for the bigger businesses and banks alone, leaving managed capitalism to the smaller firms and regional banks, or for all firms—or whether it will go only far enough to create a more competitive managed capitalism, remains open to speculation. For the moment, however, Germany remains managed capitalist, even if its managed capitalism is under strain.

The Ongoing 'Enabling' Role of the German State

The state has played mainly a secondary role to business with regard to the process of adjustment except, of course, with regard to privatization and deregulation. The most dramatic changes in industry have probably been in the formerly highly state-regulated industries subject to privatization and deregulation. Although privatization in Germany has had nowhere near the impact it had in Britain or France—given that there were comparatively few state-owned firms to privatize with the exception of East German firms, that it came much later, mainly in the 1990s, that it was minimally ideological, and that it was negotiated cooperatively among the social partners—it has nevertheless made a major difference. It has affected some of the biggest public service providers in the German economy, such as the railroads—the Bundesbahn, now Deutsche Bahn—telecommunications—Deutsche Telekom—postal services—Deustche Post—and air transport—Lufthansa.[11] These firms have transformed themselves from monopolistic public administrations with middling performance into much better-performing—at least for the latter two—private enterprises with more of an eye for the bottom line and readier for the increased competition spurred by EU-led deregulation.

---

[11] On the ways in which Lufthansa has managed to innovate organizationally to overcome decision-making bottlenecks of the traditional German corporate governance system, see Lehrer (1997).

Privatization of these firms was also tied in to financial liberalization, with the sale of shares in Deutsche Telekom in particular serving as a spur to the newly deregulated German financial markets. Even before this, though, the privatizations of East German firms acted as an impetus for liberalization, with the Treuhand, the agency in charge of organizing the privatization process, turning to the international financial markets for capital for restructuring instead of the banks, which acted in their newer roles as traders and consultants rather than as credit providers (Czada 1993; Deeg 1999: Ch. 6).

Deregulation and privatization, with the concomitant rise of the regulatory state, has naturally also had an impact on government relations with business. But it has had much less of an impact than in Britain, given the smaller number of nationalized industries, the larger space given to the public sphere and the law, and the fact that regulation has had a strong post-war tradition in Germany. The establishment of regulatory agencies has in fact not been as problematic for Germany, mainly because Germany has already had any number of such agencies, among which is the anti-trust agency, the BundesKartellamt. Moreover, business has been more used to being governed by laws and the court system rather than by informal arrangement (see Chapter 2). Nonetheless, the introduction of regulatory agencies in domains formerly ruled by more cartel-like relationships among firms and cosy interactions with government administrators, whether in the regional financial markets or in telecommunications, has substituted more arms' length relations in areas traditionally characterized by close business-government cooperation. The resulting regulatory process itself, moreover, tends to allow for less flexibility than in the US, where the rules are formulated by the regulatory agencies themselves, or in the UK, where the agencies are able to make deals with regulated firms, because in Germany the rules are embodied in public law and to be applied without exception (Dyson 1992).

The government relationship to business with regard to subsidies and bailouts has also been much less affected than the British. This is because the *Länder* continue to have the greatest responsibility in this domain, and there has been no neo-liberal turn among the *Länder* when it comes to aiding industry. If anything, government industrial action has increased at the regional level in West Germany in response to industrial slowdown (Glassmann and Voelzkow 2001). This has equally been true for the former East Germany, where the federal government has also continued to play a major role in industrial reconstruction. Government industrial action, however, has been somewhat curtailed by EU Commission action that frowns on anything that looks as if it interferes with market competition, as in the case of Saxony's aid to Volkswagen (see Chapter 2).

While the government's supportive relationship with business has changed a bit, the government's essentially hands-off relationship with regard to industrial relations has hardly changed at all. And the only time it did seek to interfere, when it passed a law regarding sick pay which lowered the compensation to 80 per cent of normal pay, it contributed to a major, albeit momentary, rift in the management–labour relationship. This was resolved when companies agreed not to apply the law and unions agreed to other concessions (see Chapter 6).

Cooperative Labour–Management Relations under Strain

It is in the labour–management relationship, in fact, that the strains of economic adjustment are most apparent. In Germany, the corporatist system remained largely unchallenged until the mid-1990s. Labour and business, having learned the painful lesson of the mid-1970s on the importance of wage restraint, managed the adjustment to changing economic conditions reasonably cooperatively under the watchful eye of the Bundesbank through the 1980s and into the 1990s, although there were disputes over flexibility in the 1980s, especially over work-time reductions. But as of the mid-1990s, subsequent to the pressures related to unification, when West Germany's employment relations system—and not just the welfare state—was imported to the East, along with escalating wage costs resulting from labour's commitment to parity in wages and work conditions between East and West, the cooperative relationship began to deteriorate. This is when businesses began feeling the pressures of greater competition from globalization, and began pressing for greater wage moderation and greater flexibility in wages and employment conditions. And this is also when labour unions felt increasing pressures to compromise, given the rise in unemployment and the decline in their membership as well as of their coverage of firms. The system of co-determination, for example, had been eroding as a result of economic restructuring and the move toward a service economy, with the size of the 'co-determination-free zone' at company and plant level having grown from 51 per cent to 61 per cent of employees in the private sector in the mid-1990s (Jürgens, Naumann, and Rupp 2000: 73).

In response to the pressures of business, labour has had little choice but to allow capital a larger share of the social product, given that pushing for higher wages simply means lower employment for its members. But labour has also had to decide whether to give up on equality in wages and conditions of employment, that is, whether to agree to more differentiated wages which would better reflect the differential competitiveness of different industrial sectors and whether to accept more flexible working time for full-time workers and more part-time work with fewer protections. Business, at the same time, has had to decide whether to continue within the traditional wage-bargaining relationship, to opt out—in the case of smaller businesses— or to strike special deals—in the case of the largest businesses. In working this out, both labour and business have been subject to increasing inter- and intra-associational conflicts.[12] Moreover, the relationship between business and labour has become more confrontational, in word as well as in deed, as German workers have engaged in more job actions and strikes (see Chapter 6). But conflicts over sick pay in 1996, over the East German steel industry in 1998, and during the 1999 wage round all led to compromises which left both sides more or less satisfied. Employers themselves have seemed intent on avoiding conflict through a 'new partnership' with labour, as the metal industry association (Gesamtmetall) insisted in 1999 (Thelen 2001: 85). Moreover, after pressing for greater decentralization in bargaining in the mid- to late 1990s, the employers appear to have backed away from calls for revision of the Works Councils Act that would have allowed wage negotiations by plant-level works' councils on the grounds that industry-level bargaining on wages facilitates cooperative relations between works councils and employers (Thelen 2001: 85). However, the 'Alliance for Jobs' talks—the *Bündnis für Arbeit*—that were intended to introduce greater flexibility in the labour market through pension reforms and the like have been very slow to produce anything substantial.

A great deal is at stake here. Successful compromise could indeed save the corporatist system and put the economy back on track. Failure, by contrast, would not necessarily usher in a new era of decentralized, market capitalist labour–management relations but would rather more likely simply result in failed corporatism. The strong unions, after all, are not going to go away overnight. And the German government, unlike the British, has neither the power nor the legal right to legislate away the post-war rights and powers of the unions. Failure to reach compromise in Germany, in other words, could end up looking not like Britain of the 1990s but rather like the Netherlands of the 1970s, where the breakdown of the social concertation system came with escalating wage demands, increasing labour unrest, and declining economic performance.

France: The Transformation of State Capitalism

Whereas both Britain and Germany have so far largely remained true to their traditional models of capitalism, the one moving farther in the direction of

---

[12] For more detail, see Streeck and Visser (1997); Heinisch (1999); Thelen (2001).

ideal-typical market capitalism from 1979 on, the other maintaining managed capitalism for the most part as it was until the 1990s, France transformed itself beginning in 1983 so radically that one can ask whether the most ideal-typically state capitalist of countries still conforms in any way to the model. Confronted much like Britain with major external economic pressures beginning in the mid-1970s to which it also had great difficulty responding, France at first sought, like Britain, to go back to its roots. But whereas for Britain this meant policies that sought to institute more market capitalism in an increasingly open, neo-liberal, and market-oriented world, for France, with the Socialist victory in 1981, this meant rejecting that neo-liberal, market-oriented world for a return to neo-Keynesian macroeconomic policy, *dirigiste* or interventionist industrial policies, and wholesale nationalization. By 1983, however, French leaders had realized that this attempted return to ideal-typical state capitalism only exacerbated the country's economic problems. In an abrupt about-face, they seemingly embraced market capitalism, with liberalization of the financial markets, privatization of state-owned firms, deregulation of the rules governing business and industrial relations, decentralization of wage-bargaining, and so on.

In reality, although France has gone very far in the direction of market capitalism, it has not become a market capitalist system. Rather, it has instituted a more market-oriented capitalism in which the state nevertheless remains much more important than in either market capitalist or managed capitalist systems, even if its interventionism is much more circumscribed and, where it occurs, is more market-oriented. Put another way, although the state has largely given up on market-making, it continues to try to be market-shaping, whether in the structure of business relations or of industrial relations. Moreover, in this role, it has sometimes sought to reshape the market in a managed capitalist direction in the structure of both business relations and labour relations, and failed. But it is no more a managed capitalist system than it is market capitalist. It remains state capitalist, albeit a pale shadow of its former self, as government relations with business and labour are no longer state-led but continue to be state-influenced.

The Post-war Model

French state capitalism in the post-war period focused first and foremost on promoting rapid economic growth through business expansion and modernization. But although one can detect the beginnings of such state capitalism during the Fourth Republic, given the role of elite civil servants in industrial development through planning, it is only with the advent of the

Fifth Republic that the classic model of state capitalism as such came into being. For this is when the ideal-typically strong state, able and willing to take clear leadership over the economy, makes its appearance.

The state exercised its leadership in all spheres. In the macroeconomic sphere, until the collapse of the Bretton Woods system in the early 1970s the state promoted growth through its use of lax monetary policies linked to the state-administered credit-rationing system. This which enabled companies to prosper despite a high level of indebtedness by allowing high rates of inflation that governments would periodically counter through aggressive devaluations against the dollar, which in turn would give French firms a temporary competitive advantage. Unlike Germany, then, where an independent central bank was above all else focused on keeping inflation down in order to ensure steady economic growth through price and monetary stability, in France the government-controlled central bank used inflation and devaluation to stimulate growth. Moreover, unlike in Britain, where government focus was on the value of the pound and all else other than full employment was sacrificed to it, leaving business in particular battling the disadvantages of the pound when it was strong and without the time needed to build up investment reserves when it was weak, in France the government focus was on the health of business, seeking to ensure not only that the value of the franc benefited business but also that business had sufficient investment support even if it had not built up the necessary investment reserves. Because business in France has traditionally been under-capitalized, it was the state that consistently sought to remedy this not only through monetary policy but also through industrial and labour policy.

Planning and industrial policy were the preferred tools of a *dirigiste* state that did not trust business to modernize on its own, while state-organized wage bargaining and industrial relations were the state's answer to a contentious management-labour relationship that could not be expected to come up on its own with agreements supportive of general economic development. Thus, by contrast with Britain, where the state tended to intervene little and ineffectively when it did intervene, or with Germany, where the central state 'enabled' effective action but intervened little itself, in France the state intervened a lot and did so effectively as often as not.

The state was able to lead because state-educated, technically trained, elite civil servants, after a high-flying state career, would as often as not move on to business in a top position (Birnbaum *et al.* 1978; Birnbaum 1982; Bauer and Mourot 1987; Schmidt 1996: Chs 10, 11). This dual-career pattern fostered a natural affinity between business and government that came from top state and firm officials having attended the same schools and followed similar career paths. This made for a generally cooperative leadership pattern and for trust by business of the state—at least the larger businesses—and respect by the state for business. And it reinforced the state's institutional leadership capacity.

But the French state led differently with regard to business, for which relations were close and accommodating, from how it led with regard to labour, for which relations were distant and confrontational. For obvious reasons, therefore, the state generally had better success with business than with labour.

In France, the traditional structure of business relations was one mediated by the state, whether directly or by way of state-owned enterprise. If one were to categorize this relationship without considering the role of the state, then one would have to place inter-firm relations somewhere between market and managed capitalism. As in market capitalism, firms tended to be individualistic and competitive with one another, without the kind of supportive, coordinated networks that have developed in more managed capitalist settings. And yet there were loose networks of firms that did business with one another, as suppliers, providers of financial services, and so forth. Moreover, for a number of the larger firms, there were cross-shareholdings and cross-directorships that made for cosy interrelationships among firms and their CEOs, contributing to what in France was characterized as 'protected capitalism' (Morin 1974). This was nothing like managed capitalism, however, not only because the network relationships were not as mutually supportive, close, or trusting, but also because the providers of finance did not perform the same role at all as those in managed capitalist countries, nor, with the exception of two *banques d'affaires*—the business banks Paribas and Suez—did they hold major equity stakes in industry.

Into this mix came the French state, which provided the kind of coordination among firms that firms could not do for themselves and the kind of guidance and financing that only the banks in Germany could offer. Coordination and guidance came through state-organized planning and industrial policy while financing came through state subsidies and low-cost loan programmes and through more general macroeconomic control over bank lending through the credit allocation system (see Schmidt 1996: Chs 3, 9). The nationalized enterprises, moreover, also played a major role as leaders in technological innovation—especially the public infrastructural services such as the railroads, electricity, and telecommunications—and in ameliorating work conditions, especially Renault. What is more, they often played a supportive role with their suppliers akin to that of large firms in managed capitalism, by setting up cartel-like relationships to ensure predictability in such firms' environment and a steady flow of supplies for themselves. Economic development was, thus, highly centralized, with the strategies formulated in Paris by closely connected business and government elites carried out by the large firms, or 'national champions', which led standardization and productivity improvements throughout the country.

The French state's relationship with labour was not of the same order as that with business. Labour was rarely accommodated, never managed to co-opt the state, and generally resorted to confrontation, or at least the threat of confrontation, to get its way. Labour-management relations were similarly adversarial, with strikes and job actions much the only interaction, especially because the ideology of class conflict dominated workers' views of their situation. French labour's problem was its relative weakness—at its highest level, it never had more than a 25 per cent unionization rate, while it was largely impotent at the plant level—and its great disorganization. This resulted from union fragmentation, ideological divisions, and state legislation that allowed any union representing 3 per cent of the workforce to sign binding agreements, even if larger, more representative unions were opposed, and forbade union organization at the plant level before 1968. In consequence, organized labour's only real power came through staging strikes or even merely threatening them, which forced the state to be more generous in wage settlements than it might normally have been with a less confrontational and more organized labour force (Mouriaux 1991; Kesselman and Groux 1984; Schmidt 1999a).

Labour, as a result, had little direct control over its own environment or influence over the decisions that most affected it other than to say 'no', whether it involved the state-led industrial policy-making process, state-controlled vocational training and apprenticeships, occupational safety and health programmes, or even wage bargaining (Howell 1992). The French state organized wage bargaining, set the targets for the weak, decentralized peak associations of management and labour, stepped in to impose a wage settlement when the two parties could not agree, which was often, and then extended the agreement to the region or even nationwide through the 'extension procedure'. Although this system was certainly more effective than the pre-1979 'voluntarist' process of the British, the French wage-bargaining process was nevertheless much less effective than the German one, where salaries were often more in line with what the industry wanted and could afford.

All in all, then, French labour played a secondary role in French state capitalism, to be dominated or pacified, but certainly not to be trusted or dealt with as an equal part of a concertation process, as in Germany. In fact, if we were to characterize the pre-1979 British model with regard to state involvement as 'capitalism without business', given how little attention the state paid to business by contrast with labour due to its obsession with the value of the pound and wage restraint, and the German model as 'capitalism with labour', given the high involvement of labour in all aspects of economic decision-making, then we would have to call the French variant 'capitalism without labour', given how little labour mattered in economic decision-making or in macroeconomic policies which were so much more focused on business.

Transforming State Capitalism

Crisis hit French state capitalism in the mid-1970s. This resulted from the government's increasing inability to deal with the changing international economic environment and with failures encompassing national plans with inaccurate economic forecasts, industrial policies with inadequate or inappropriate investments, and 'national champions' that had become lame ducks.[13] Many firms were vulnerable to takeover, and generally in the red. Moreover, industrial relations were highly conflictual, leading to many days of work lost to strikes and stoppages.

The expansionist neo-Keynesian monetary policies, highly *dirigiste* industrial policies, and generous social policies of 1981, which Mitterrand had promised would solve these problems, instead led the country to the brink of economic disaster. The great U-turn in monetary policy of 1983, along with subsequent changes in the nature of state interventionism with regard to industry, brought the country back from the brink. Almost overnight, the government austerity programme that focused on lowering inflation and stabilizing the currency improved the climate for business. Most importantly, though, the changes in monetary policies brought with them major industrial policy change as well, since the *dirigisme* of the indicative plans, national industrial policies, and *grands projets* could no longer work in a more open economy where the government no longer had the resources, given budgetary austerity, the freedom, given European competition policy and GATT agreements, or the will, given changes in elite and public opinion, to intervene as it had in the past (Schmidt 1997d). Liberalization of the financial markets, deregulation, and privatization necessarily followed, and with it the reduction of the role of the state in business.

[13] See Schmidt (1996: Ch. 3); P. Hall (1986).

The Changing Profile of the French Economy

Development of the financial markets, to begin with, enabled business to replace state funding and bank debt with equity financing. Beginning in the early 1980s under the left, the new financial instruments such as certificates of deposit, capital bills, and negotiable treasury bonds, together with the liberalization of the Premier Marché for the largest companies, the founding of the Second Marché for medium-sized companies in 1983, the opening of the financial futures market in 1986—the Marché à Terme des Instruments Financiers (MATIF)—and of the Nouveau Marché in 1996 for the high-growth companies, has provided companies with tremendous new sources of funding. The privatization programme was also a great boon to the financial markets. Full or partial sell-offs of industrial or banking enterprises raised a total of €70 billion in public share offerings between 1986 and 2002 (*Le Monde*, 9 April, 2002). This, combined with the cutbacks in state subsidies and loans, has encouraged firms to turn increasingly to the financial markets for capital. Market capitalization of the French equity markets as a percentage of GDP went from a low of 5.6 per cent in 1982 to 37.2 per cent in 1993 and up to 111.5 per cent by 1999, while the annual volume of transactions on the French equity markets went from a low of 1.8 per cent in 1982 to 13.7 per cent in 1993 and up to 54.6 per cent by 1999 (O'Sullivan 2001). Concomitantly, shareholders jumped from 1.5 million between 1978 and 1982 to 6.5 million in 1986, stabilizing at 5.6 million in 2000—10 per cent of the population—as against 22 per cent for the US and 15 per cent for the UK (*Le Monde*, 6 July 2000). Stock options are also increasingly available in major companies, and again of recent vintage, with almost nine in every ten companies having put the plans in place since 1987, although the most rapid increase has come since the mid-1990s (O'Sullivan 2001; Goyer 2001).

Since the 1980s, French firms have also transformed themselves into highly competitive, internationalized companies. The nationalizations of the early 1980s, to begin with, proved salutary. They not only saved French industry from foreign acquisition but their restructuring along core activity lines ensured a major increase in company size while their re-capitalization by the state facilitated a return to competitiveness and solvency. Privatization continued improvement in these same directions, whether the major privatizations by the right from 1986 to 1988 and 1993 to 1997 or the often more partial privatizations by the left that occurred between 1988 and 1993 and the full as well as partial privatizations after 1997, enabling firms greater freedom to form strategic alliances and joint ventures as well as to go to the financial markets for further capital infusions (Schmidt 1996, 1997d, 1999c). Beginning in the mid-1990s, moreover, companies have been concentrating more on their 'core business' and divesting themselves of operations in which they lacked a comparative advantage (Goyer 2001). The result is that by the late 1990s French business had grown tremendously in size, scope, competitiveness, and profitability, while public sector ownership went from a peak of 10 per cent of the economy in 1985 down to its pre-war level of 5 per cent by the late 1990s (Israelewicz 1999: 120). In addition, public sector employment as a percentage of all employment fell from 10.5 per cent in 1985 to 5.3 per cent in 2000 (*Le Monde*, 9 April, 2002).

Moreover, French firms have modernized, slimmed down, and streamlined their operations, increased investment in research and development, gained greater industrial productivity, and made large enough profits towards the end of the 1980s to finance ambitious international merger and acquisition programmes.[14] In the late 1980s, with the rush to consolidate in view of the Single Market, the number of mergers and acquisitions jumped dramatically, from 284 in 1986 to 1774 in 1990. In the 1990s, more impressive was the value of the deals, which went from $US85 billion in 1991 to $558 billion in 1998, with the average transaction size increasing from $21 million to $104 million (O'Sullivan 2001). Between 1999 and 2001 alone, French firms had acquired some of the better-known foreign companies, such as Seagrams by Vivendi, and the UK mobile operator Orange by France Télécom. But French companies have also been acquired, such as the banks CCF and Hervet by the British HBSC, they have consolidated internally through takeovers such as Totalfina of Elf and BNP of Paribas, and they have even moved their headquarters out of France. The Netherlands has proven most popular for incorporation purposes, whether because it provides a neutral territory with lower corporate tax rates— the case of aerospace giant EADS, born from the fusion of the German DASA, the French Aérospatiale, and the Spanish Casa—or protection from hostile takeover—the case of the alliance of auto manufacturers Renault and Nissan.

Having been more nationally focused, less internationally competitive, and smaller—with the exception of only a few sectors of industry—than either British big business, which has always been very big and highly internationalized, or German big business, which has long been export-oriented and highly competitive, French firms by the early 1990s came to rival the British and German in size, scope, and foreign direct investments. Although French firms could not outdo the Germans in shares in world exports, they remained ahead of the British (see Fig. 4.1). And many of the larger French firms became as export-oriented as German firms, with annual turnovers reflecting large percentages of international sales, including Alcatel (83

---

[14] For more detail, see Schmidt (1996: 359–63); Amable and Hancké (2001); Gordon and Meunier (2001).

per cent), Axa (75 per cent) Dassault (82 per cent), Michelin (85 per cent), and Rhône-Poulenc (82 per cent) (*Nouvel Économiste*, 31 May 2000).

In addition, foreign direct investment has increased exponentially. France was second only to the UK in Europe in the late 1980s in investment out-flows, although in the mid-1990s the French fell behind the Germans in total amounts invested abroad (see Fig. 4.3). In investment inflows, however, France has consistently outdistanced the Germans, with capital inflows growing to record levels, making France in 1999 second only to the UK in Europe and third in the world, after the US (OECD 2000; and see Fig. 4.2). Concomitantly, openness to trade—exports plus imports as a share of GDP— has risen steadily, having gone from 23.3 per cent in 1962 to 49 per cent in 1997, which was at the same level as Germany (49 per cent), less than the UK (57 per cent), but much higher than either the US (25 per cent) or Japan (21 per cent) (OECD 1999). Thus, all the economic indicators suggest that the French economy has improved remarkably over the past quarter-century, having done at least as well as Germany or Britain, and in many cases better.

The Enhanced Autonomy in Business Relations

How did this transformation come about? First and foremost, in France as in Britain the change was largely the result of market-oriented reforms involv-ing the restructuring of business relations through the liberalization of the financial markets, deregulation, and the privatization of major nationalized enterprises. French business did not feel the immediate impact of these reforms as brutally as did business in Britain, however, mainly because change was state-led and state-cushioned. The French government's involvement in the reform process, in particular through its active role in restructuring nationalized enterprises, by contrast with the British government's absten-tionist role, ensured that French firms ultimately came out stronger and more competitive, by contrast with British firms which as often as not were acquired by foreign competitors. A case in point is the electronics industry, where over a ten-year period—1977–87—while Britain lost every major British consumer electronics manufacturer, France's Thomson emerged as number two in Europe—the result of state strategy to promote its leading firm as a 'national champion' and then as an 'international' one (Cawson 1994).

But although market-oriented, the French government's reforms have not been as market capitalist as they might appear on the surface. Not only did they not reproduce anything like the market-driven inter-firm relations of British market capitalism but they also introduced managed capitalist elements into the market-oriented reforms. Privatization, for instance, was market capitalist neither in process nor in expected result. Instead of an open bidding system, as in Britain, the French state hand-picked a hard-core group of investors—typically 15 or 20 industrial or financial enterprises held between 15 per cent and 20 per cent of shares—while reserving a certain amount for employees—up to 10 per cent—and for foreign institutions—up to 20 per cent, but 0 per cent in defence-related firms (Schmidt 1996: Chs 5, 6, 13). The state's role was therefore not just market-making, by selling off state-owned enterprise as in Britain. It was also market-shaping, as the state determined the face of future competition by choosing the key acquirers—a pattern, by the way, also followed in other state capitalist countries such as Italy and Spain.

The state sought to shape the market along the lines of managed capital-ism, with banks and insurance companies for the first time brought into the ownership of equity capital in industrial enterprise, to provide the kind of stability and long-term view that the German financial companies provided for German firms while protecting them against takeover. Such protection was enhanced by the high degree of company self-investment through share buybacks subsequent to privatization—often bringing company share ownership up to 30 per cent or higher—as well as in many cases by continued state ownership through the 'golden share'. But the fact that French financial companies came nowhere near the Germans in size, solidity, or experience, and that industrial enterprises gained the bulk of their capital from self-financing rather than from bank borrowing, meant that the French finan-cial enterprises were to be at best junior partners of industrial enterprises (Schmidt 1996: Ch. 13). The subsequent crisis of the banks, moreover, faced with major losses as a result of over-extension and bad loans—in particular the Crédit Lyonnais—ensured their lesser status.

The heyday of this cross-shareholding pattern lasted only from the mid-1980s to the mid-1990s. The cross-shareholdings began unravelling thereafter as hard-core investors, increasingly concerned about bottom lines and core businesses, started selling their cross-shareholdings on the financial markets and as foreign institutional investors increasingly bought up those and other shares on the French *Bourse* (Morin 1998). The unravelling began in 1996 when the CEO of Axa, Claude Bébéar, decided not to intervene to protect from takeover one of the companies in which he was a hard-core shareholder and when he followed this by selling off most of his cross-shareholdings. By 1997, CEOs such as André Lévy-Lang, head of Paribas, were selling off their cross-shareholdings, insisting that the cross-shareholding-based networks were a thing of the past, given the pressures of investors and the need to go back to basics instead of remaining conglomerates.[15] Most

---

[15] Interview with author, Paris, June 1997.

CEOs by this time, according to Jean Gandois, head of the CNPF, the employ-ers' association, had found that the cross-shareholdings engendered too many conflicts of interest while tying up too much capital.[16] Since 1998, moreover, capital market-related activities such as takeovers, mergers, and acquisitions have accelerated, as companies have used the 'immobile capital' tied up in the hard cores to invest and to expand. As a result, firms have no longer been able to count on the stability provided by hard-core sharehold-ers' longer-term investments, on the loyalty of those shareholders, who in the event of a hostile bid would be likely to sell to the highest bidder—for example, BNP in its hostile bid for Société Générale and Paribas—or on the protection of the state; the exception that makes the rule being the BNP hos-tile bid, when the Bank of France intervened to allow Société Générale to remain free once BNP had not acquired a majority of its shares.

But if France is no longer characterized by state capitalism or a weak managed capitalism, then what? Has there been a 'revolution' in French cap-italism, with the move from a system akin to 'Rhineland' network capitalism to one more closely approximating 'Anglo-Saxon' financial capitalism, as some commentators argue (Orléan 1999; Morin 2000)? They point in particu-lar to the tremendous increase in foreign share ownership, a large portion of which consists of North American institutional investors, which went from 10 per cent in 1985 to 35 per cent by 1997 (Morin 2000), up to 44 per cent by 1998 (Goyer 2001), and then by most accounts up to or above 50 per cent by 2001. And this, they argue, has driven the unravelling of the hard-core share-ownerships, the heightened takeover activity, and the new emphasis on shareholder value among CEOs.

This finance-driven view of French capitalism, however, overlooks a number of important factors that suggest that, although significant changes have indeed been under way, they fall short of a market capitalist revolution. First of all, foreign institutional investors, for all their potential threat, do not have significant stakes in most firms: only in six of the top 40 firms of the *Bourse*—the CAC 40—do the combined holdings of the three top institu-tional investors go above 5 per cent; for six others the holdings are between 2 per cent and 5 per cent, and for the remaining 25, below 2 per cent (Parrat 1999; Goyer 2001). Moreover, despite the increasing vulnerability to takeover related to the breakdown of the hard cores *qua* hard cores, there is still a lot of cross-shareholding left which reduces the liquidity of the markets: for example, the 20.5 per cent average equity stake of core shareholders in the CAC 40 in 1998, although down from 28 per cent in 1995 (Morin 1998).

---

[16] Interview with author, Paris, June 1997.

Other elements in the structure of ownership of French firms also diminish the threat of takeover. Many of the largest firms remain under family control—nine of which are among the CAC 40—while a majority of French firms are family owned: 50 per cent of the capital of all French firms, 12 per cent for quoted companies. Moreover, some of the highest performers continue to be state-held in full or in part: for example, in telecommunications, transport, and electricity, two of which are in the CAC 40. Of the remaining French firms on the CAC 40 index, many retain 'auto-control' through high levels of self-investment at around 50 per cent, in particular firms where founding entrepreneurs hold controlling interests—for example, Axa, LMVH, Cap Gemini. In short, even though hard-core shareholdings have been dropping, the bulk of French shares nevertheless remain more closely held than in market capitalist Britain.

In addition, the financial markets are not the main source of financing for corporate investment, which would be the expected role of the markets in a system allegedly moving toward market capitalism. Instead, the primary markets have been used mostly for financial restructuring by private firms and well as the state—through privatization—and for mergers and acquisitions. This is evident from the fact that the primary markets have not shown any dramatic upward surge in stock issues since the step increases in issues in the mid-1980s and that the largest increases in volume resulted from the privatizations, the proceeds of which went to reducing the public debt, financing current state expenses, and subsidizing state enterprises rather than to the privatized firms for investment purposes (Juvin 1995; O'Sullivan 2001). Where the financing of internal investment has been concerned, most of the larger firms have tended to look to retained earnings rather than the primary markets or to indebtedness—the pattern of the past. Between 1980 and 1996, self-financing rose by over 28 points, from 48.18 per cent to 76.39 per cent, while market financing grew by under 14 points, from 17.97 per cent to 31.1 per cent, and indebtedness as a source of financing plummeted by close to 40 points, from 38.28 per cent to minus 1.57 per cent (Insee 1998; Cieply 2001: 161).[17] Since 1999 with the advent of the euro, however, companies have increasing turned to the euro bond markets for financing. The number of bonds priced on the market rose from fewer than ten a year in the mid-1990s to 273 in 1999, the year of the introduction of the euro, and up

[17] Banking indebtedness in general has decreased, with the largest firms—over 2000 employees—having shown the greatest decrease, from around 75 per cent in 1985 to under 50 per cent in 1995, the larger of the medium-sized firms—between 500 and 2000—have dropped less, from around 85 per cent to under 70 per cent, while smaller firms—mainly the smallest firms with 0 to 20 employees—have remained relatively steady or gone up moderately (Cieply 2001: 164).

to 315 in 2001, with corporate issues of euro-denominated bonds in 2000 at 21 per cent—the second largest after the US, at 22 per cent, and well above Germany at 12 per cent (*Financial Times*, 22 October 2001).

With regard to merger and acquisition activity specifically, moreover, the driving force has not necessarily been the desire to please foreign investors. Some of the more avid acquiring firms have controlling interests still held by the state—for example, France Télécom—or held by individual entrepreneurs—for example, Axa under Claude Bébéar, LVMH under Bernard Arnault, Cap Gemini under Serge Kampf—whose expansionist tendencies may best be explained through the psychology of dominant personalities (O'Sullivan 2001). Even more importantly, the drivers of mergers and acquisitions are the competing pressures for productive capabilities, and are located squarely in the strategies of firms with regard to the product markets rather than the financial markets (Hancké 2001; Amable and Hancké 2001; O'Sullivan 2001).

Finally, although the discourse of CEOs certainly suggests that the financial markets, and in particular the foreign institutional investors, are the drivers of their new corporate strategies, this can be seen as a discursive strategy to keep institutional and other investors happy while holding other interests who might lay claim to corporate returns at bay (O'Sullivan 2001; Hancké 2001). It is significant that one of the main articles—and associated book (cf. Morin 1998)—announcing the victory of finance-led Anglo-Saxon capitalism focuses mainly on CEOs' discursive interaction with institutional investors, which is all about communicating continuously through road-shows and one-on-one meetings to explain that company strategy conforms to the dominant strategic model and that they 'submit to the imperative of profitability' (Morin 2001: 45–50). But at the same time as CEOs use the discourse of 'shareholder value' to seek to convince fund managers of their firms' prospects and of their own credibility, they use it to avoid demands on the company not only by workers, suppliers, and customers, but also the state—to forestall government intervention, most notably in those companies where it still holds shares (see Chapter 6).

This is not to suggest, however, that the discourse of 'shareholder value' is merely 'cheap talk'. 'Shareholder value' is certainly *a* driver of CEOs' strategies, but it is not *the* driver. CEOs do need to pay attention to foreign institutional investors' concerns since once their companies are listed on the stock exchange they are in fact more vulnerable to fluctuations in share price: something which hit Alcatel very hard in 1998 with a precipitous 38 per cent drop in its share price, the result of US pension funds' nearly overnight divestment in response to the CEO's failure to warn of unanticipated lower profits. They have begun to increase transparency through more complete annual reports and greater adherence to Anglo-Saxon accountancy standards[18]—although they remain behind even Germany on this—while they have added outside directors on their boards—up from 3 per cent in 1988 to 28 per cent in 1998 among CAC 40 firms—and set up specialized board committees (Goyer 2001: 138–41; and see Table 4.2). But transparency with regard to executive pay has remained minimal until recently, instituted by law only in 2001, while small shareholders have relatively few protections, a large majority of the directors remain more inside than outside, and only the hard cores of investors or members of the boards of directors have much power, which they rarely exercise. Moreover, CEOs have been happy to implement foreign institutional investors' recommendations when it comes to executive pay and stock options: French senior executives are now second only to the Americans with regard to stock options, which in 1999 were valued at FF 83.7 billion, amounting to 40 times the potential capital gains of the stock option plans of the Germans (*L'Expansion*, 14 September 2000: 48–9). And CEOs do want institutional investors' money—to fund acquisitions as well as to enhance their firms' standing by listing on the stock exchanges, in particular the US exchange (Morin 2000; O'Sullivan 2001). Thus, one could argue that the dialogue between CEOs and institutional investors privileges a 'capitalism of voice' that allows the institutional investors their say without, however, diminishing French firms' autonomy (Loriaux 2002).

Autonomy, in fact, is one of the keys to understanding the continuing differences between evolving French capitalism and British market capitalism, in which CEOs are much more subject to the dictates of the financial markets, and German managed capitalism, where CEOs are much more constrained by the network-based relationship and their boards of supervisors (see Chapter 3). The other key is the continuing greater capacity of the French state to intervene when it deems necessary and its importance as an indirect coordinator of business activity.

To begin with, many of the most salient elements of state capitalism remain in French capitalism even without state leadership, especially in terms of business interrelationships. These continue to look a lot like the traditional state capitalist pattern in terms of the circulation of elites at the top, even though the state is no longer the leader and strategist for business that it once was. The retreat of the state by way of privatization and cross-shareholdings led to the further colonization of business by state-trained,

---

[18] Much more significant for the increase in transparency, however, is the change in corporate strategy that has led to the dismantling of industrial conglomerates and the greater focus on core competencies (see Goyer 2002).

former civil servants in an extension of the old pattern of dominance of business by the interpenetrating political-financial-industrial elite (Schmidt 1996: Chs 10, 14; Bauer and Bertin-Mourot 1995). The shared state educational and career backgrounds that breed trust and mutual respect reinforced the system of cross-shareholdings, generating the high-level advice and even coordination on corporate strategies which have given the French elite network system an advantage over the more separate, individualistic, and competitive British firms (Hancké and Soskice 1996). Moreover, this elite coordination pattern has had the benefit of providing business heads with a large sphere of autonomy from the state while imbuing participants with the same high set of performance standards (Hancké 2001). The down side to this is that elite corporate dominance can cause managerial problems with regard to promotion from within (Schmidt 1996: Ch. 15). And it lends itself to abuses, whether because of the lack of oversight that permitted Crédit Lyonnais to over-extend itself dangerously and, ultimately, to require a massive government bail-out to avoid bankruptcy or because of the closeness of business-government ties that facilitate influence-peddling and bribery, most notably in the case of Elf, which brought down not only former foreign minister, Roland Dumas, but also the former Chancellor of Germany, Helmut Kohl.

At the same time, however, the interpersonal competitiveness of the elite, which also has it roots in the state-based elite educational system, provides for more individualism, inter-firm competition, and potential takeover fights than in managed capitalist Germany, where the emphasis on achieving consensus and cooperation has been much greater. This competitive pattern may help explain the gradual breakdown of the hard-core shareholdings, once French CEOs no longer needed one another as much, given increases in the size and strength of French firms through mergers and acquisitions as well as the development of internal capabilities for sustained profitability related to changes in relations with suppliers and improvements in worker training and company integration (Hancké 2001). A new pattern of French capitalism may in fact be emerging as a result of the consolidation of French industry and banking into a few very large players—two poles in banking, with Crédit Agricole likely to take over Crédit Lyonnais, and BNP Paribas to get its hands finally on Société Générale (*Financial Times*, 22 October 2001), along with the companies that have already grown into leaders in France, Europe, and/or the world, such as the insurer Axa; state-controlled telecommunications giant France Télécom; state-owned electricity giant EDF; the two car companies Renault and Peugeot; and the French-dominated European defence firm EADS.

The result is a French CEO who now has even more autonomy than before: more than in the post-war years, given the end of state strategic and financial leadership; more than in the nationalization period of intensified state capitalism beginning in 1981, given the end of state ownership; and more than in the privatization period of quasi-managed capitalism beginning in 1986, given the dissolution of the hard cores. In short, the end of the state's dream of German managed capitalism does not necessarily bring market capitalism but rather enhanced autonomy, with little constraint from the financial markets, business networks, or even the state, albeit with continued informal elite coordination.

This informal coordination at the top, moreover, is supplemented by coordination between large and small firms in a vertically integrated relationship. The relations between large firms and smaller firms continue to exhibit patterns of support established in earlier years—and reinforced for the nationalized companies in the early 1980s—although the content of that support has changed greatly. Large firms tend to dominate regional economies even more than in the past by integrating suppliers organizationally and technologically into their production systems, while being themselves subordinate to the strategies developed at firm headquarters, normally in Paris (Amable and Hancké 2001). But with the adoption of new production processes in the 1980s, in particular collaboration on design and 'just in time' delivery systems, the largest French firms have modernized their relations with suppliers in ways that brings them into a much closer collaboration or 'partenariat'. The relationship itself enables the large firms to ensure continued improvement of the quality of their suppliers' products and the efficiency of their operations while the suppliers gain more easy access to financing and stable demand (Hancké and Soskice 1996; Hancké 2001).

The production system, as a result, is dominated by large firms vertically integrated with their suppliers, which in most sectors combine mass production and low production costs with rapid model changes and a positioning in certain protected, highly profitable market niches. In the automotive industry, for example, Renault now combines mass production with innovative design; the steel industry dominated by Usinor is a highly integrated conglomerate of large-volume and small specialty producers; and the household equipment industry led by Moulinex and SEB has moved from one-function products into complex equipment.[19] Another pattern is typified in the ideal-typically state capitalist sectors of telecommunications, electricity, rail transport, and aerospace, however, where, competitive advantage has come

---

[19] See, for example, Freyssennet (1998); Smith (1998); Hancké (2001); Amable and Hancké (2001).

from the close coordination between high-flying top managers and the state engaged in a 'mission-oriented' approach to the development of specific technologies through high-profile *grand projets* which lead to radical innovation.[20] In other areas, however, such as pharmaceuticals, radical innovation came from the outside, from French firms' mergers and acquisitions, mainly in the US.[21] But however much French firms may have improved their competitiveness, they cannot rival the Germans for incremental innovation nor the Americans for radical innovation because of the differences in institutional framework (see Amable, Barré, and Boyer 1997: 145–50; Goyer 2002; and Chapter 3).

The restructuring of French industry from the mid-1980s on, in short, was the work of autonomous, mostly state-trained, informally coordinated business elites who followed a variety of different strategies. But this does not mean that the state has bowed out entirely from seeking to influence business. Much the contrary.

The State's More Indirect but Still Active Role

The state also provides coordination mechanisms that complement the horizontally integrated relationship among elites and the vertically integrated relationship among firms and their suppliers. Planning, already a mere vestige of its former self by the early 1980s, continues to be an exercise in which businesses participate because of its usefulness in what remains a state-organized exchange of information that helps provide a sense of direction to the firms, although it offers none of the subsidies of the past. Regional planning, along with other regional economic development programmes—promoted by the state mainly through, or in tandem with, the regions which had gained power, functions, and resources through the decentralization reforms of the early 1980s (Schmidt 1990)—has also been a significant source of coordination and support. Large firms, which have tended to dominate the regional production networks in France, have managed to take advantage of the wide range of regional economic development programmes and funds to modernize their suppliers' networks (Levy 1999; Amable and Hancké 2001).

Moreover, for small and medium-sized companies that are not directly tied in to large firms as suppliers or distributors, the state provides support through various ministerial departments—for example, ANVAR in the high-tech area—charged with promoting management capacity, worker skills, and

[20] See, for example, Cohen (1992); Suleiman and Courty (1996); Ziegler (1997); Finon and Staropoli (2001); Amable and Hancké (2001).

[21] See Sally (1995); Cantwell and Kotecha (1997); Goyer (2001).

even financing through regional development agencies as well as through public-private venture capital funds and other programmes designed to bridge the capital gap for SMEs (Cieply 2001). Although many of these initiatives proved costly and ineffective (Levy 1999), there is some evidence to suggest that efforts in the latter part of the 1990s have proven more successful, relayed by emerging business networks (Le Galès, Aniello, and Tirmarche 2001).

The state has also had a major impact on business through its social policies as well as through education and training programmes. In the 1980s, for example, the state's provision of early retirement programmes greatly facilitated the restructuring of industrial firms and the renewal of their workforce, with over 85 per cent of large mass producing companies—but only 33 per cent of smaller firms—having used such funds to move out of mass production into more diversified markets.[22] The renewal of the workforce in turn succeeded mainly because of the state's education policy, which set the ambitious target of increasing the number of young people completing the secondary school exit exam—the *baccalaureat*—from 40 per cent in 1984 to 80 per cent by the mid-1990s—and which reached 75 per cent by 1995 (Courtois 1995). This upgrading of generalist skills has been key to the reorganization of work, contributing to higher productivity by a reduction in the administrative costs of a whole range of lower-level management tasks, for example, administration, supervision, and maintenance (Lane 1989; Hancké 2001). Workers' jobs nonetheless remain more 'Taylorist'—that is, repetitive—given that centralized state programmes cannot provide the deep technological training that the German regional system produces (Soskice 1997*b*; Hancké 2001). But it serves the purposes of the larger French firms' flexible Fordist production model in which the education system provides general skills and firms add firm-specific skills (Boyer 1995; Culpepper forthcoming).

Finally, the state has not given up on state interventionism entirely, although it is more market-oriented than in the past and also much more circumscribed. Most importantly, while traditional industrial policy for the most part ended in 1988, it continued in a more market-oriented form for certain strategic industries in the high-tech and defence sectors, for failing industries of major size and importance, and for the 'monopolistic' public sector enterprises that were generally spared the often radical restructuring of the early to mid-1980s. In defence, for example, the state continually intervened in—often futile—efforts to shape the future of the French and European armaments industry and, thereby, the character of international competition: for

---

[22] See Salais and Tessier (1992). See also Guillmard (1991); Amable and Hancké (2001).

example, the marriage of Aérospatiale and Dassault which after much effort was finally consummated and which was subsequently complemented by the merger with Dasa. Increasingly, though, the state has given up attempts at national-level firm restructuring in favour of more coordinated European efforts at shaping the future of defence armaments development through the pressures available through defence spending (Serfati 2001).

For companies in severe financial straits, moreover, the state has continued to provide subsidies and bail-outs. But under the watchful eye of the EU Commission, which frowns on anything that looks like interference with market competition, the state has been much more rigorous in the conditions for aid than in the past by making it a one-shot deal contingent on a restructuring plan, a timetable for return to profitability, and privatization—although some firms did go back for aid repeatedly, such as Bull, Air France, and, most egregiously, Crédit Lyonnais. Moreover, in the whole area of the still-nationalized firms, in particular with the *service public* sectors, including transport, telecommunications, and electricity, the state continues to play a major role in influencing the shape and practice of the market, even though the EU has also been a significant force in setting the direction of reform (see Chapter 2).

Deregulation, however, has added to the loosening of ties between business and government by substituting a more arms' length relationship by way of regulatory agency and incontrovertible law for the closer, more accommodating relationships between ministry and industry of the past, much as it has in Britain and Germany. This means that businesses in certain deregulated sectors such as telecommunications, electricity, the financial markets, and communications—TV, radio—find themselves in a completely new set of relations with the state. In place of the cosy relationships of the past, these businesses are confronted with regulators in independent agencies who follow the rules without exception. The problem for the French here is not so much the increasing juridification, as it is for the British, since the French have always legislated a lot. It is the obligation of the state to apply the laws without exception and for business to accept that they will not gain any derogations. The loss of flexibility, then, is as much a problem for the French as for the British; but it means something very different. For the French, it means fewer laws but greater arms' length enforcement, by contrast with the British, for whom it means more laws and more arms' length enforcement (Schmidt 1999*b*).

Toward Market Reliance in Labour Relations plus State Action

Deregulation in industry was complemented by deregulation in industrial relations. The reforms of industrial relations that began in the 1980s have produced a radically changed environment for labour that is much more

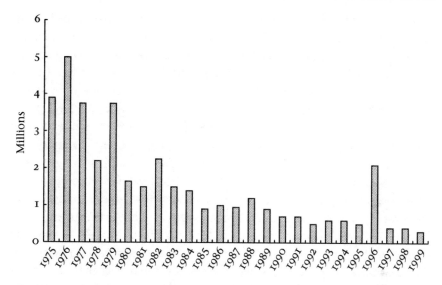

Fig. 4.5 Number of days of strikes in France, excluding the public sector, 1975–1999
Sources: DARES, Ministère de l'Emploi et de la Solidarité, *Le Monde* 12 October 1999.

market capitalist and much less unionized. The labour market has become much more flexible and wage bargaining much more market-reliant; the ideology of class conflict has largely disappeared and labour–management relations are generally good; strikes and job actions in all but a small but strategic part of the public sector are almost unknown; and union membership has declined drastically, from 18.7 per cent in 1980 to around 9 per cent by the mid-1990s (Boyer 1996: 47). Most telling is the precipitous drop in working days lost to strikes, with a high in 1976 of over 5 million days declining in the 1980s to an average of around 1 million a year, and then declining to half of that for most of the 1990s—although public sector strikes in the 1990s brought the number up closer to 1 million (see Fig. 4.5).

Ironically enough, the erosion of union power began with the measures in the early 1980s that were intended to increase workplace democracy through direct management-worker dialogue and to lead to a German-style coordination system in which employers and unions would bargain as equals without the heavy hand of the state fixing wages and work conditions. Instead, the measures weakened the unions unable to take control of the dialogues and began the process of radical decentralization of wage bargaining that culminated by the end of the decade in the state's abandonment of the entire system of government-organized, centralized wage negotiation.[23] Union

---

[23] See Kesselman (1989); W. R. Smith (1988); Howell (1992).

power also diminished in the wake of measures designed to promote flexibility in the conditions of employment, as well as with privatization, since workers in privatized firms tended not to reorganize themselves in unions once they had lost their public sector union status and membership. Labour militancy also declined because rising unemployment made workers generally fear for their jobs (Howell 1992), while the unemployed were bought off through generous unemployment compensation and easy routes to early retirement, especially in economically depressed zones hit by industrial restructuring. Workers also became more difficult to organize, given the decentralization of wage bargaining to the firm level, the introduction of greater variation in pay related to individual performance, and an increase in employee profit-sharing through stock options and other instruments (Schmidt 1999c). Finally, the renewal of the workforce related to the modernization of the shop-floor, with the presence of better-trained, more highly skilled workers for the new production processes, also weakened unions traditionally dependent on lower-skilled workers for support.[24] By the 1990s, in fact, only public sector employees were engaged in major walk-outs, generally in response to fears of privatization plans and the likely lay-offs that would follow from it.

France's industrial relations system, in consequence, has come to look a lot like market capitalism, although it is not quite as close to it as one might assume, whether in the profile of the workers, the relative flexibility of employers, or the role of the state in easing adjustment pains. First of all, workers are generally more highly skilled, better-paid, and better-trained, while products are generally of higher quality and less mass-produced than those found in market capitalist Britain. Whereas in 1982 close to 60 per cent of workers were semi-skilled or unskilled performing narrow tasks (d'Iribarne 1989), by the late 1990s, workers' skills had vastly improved and they mostly worked in polyvalent teams rather than individually (Duval 1998; Hancké 2001). The improvements can be seen in the steady increase in labour productivity in manufacturing which, below Britain's and Germany's in the 1960s, went above Britain's in the 1970s and 1980s and above Germany's in the 1990s (see Table 4.1). Moreover, productivity improved not only as a result of re-skilling but also of down-sizing, with many large firms having taken advantage of state-financed early retirement programmes—as noted above—to renew their workforces. Firms also kept their numbers of employees down and their flexibility up by an increase in subcontracting through the outsourcing of production and services. Finally, firms also took

---

[24] See Hancké and Soskice (1996); Hancké (1996); Amable and Hancké (2001).

advantage of the Auroux laws to promote better employee relations and worker integration into firm activities through quality circles, in which France leads Europe (Hyman 1994).

Second, reliance on the market is only partial. This is because of laws that continue to restrict business flexibility, whether on hiring and firing or on working hours, and because of the still-large public sector with special status and protections and which can still suffer from crippling strikes. Moreover, although the state has given up much of its interventionist capacity, it has nevertheless found new ways of intervening at the intersection of the management-labour relationship that are reminiscent of old-style state capitalism, as in the case of labour laws intended to moralize the market (see Chapter 2). It is important to note that in such cases, as with the 35-hour work week, although management was able to gain the advantage by renegotiating work conditions and hours without having as yet produced much in the way of new employment, the state had taken the initiative.

In industrial relations, then, the French state has moved much more towards market reliance without the mediating effects of the elements of managed capitalism that it introduced when reforming the structure of business relations. In bargaining, instead of getting pre-1995 Germany, France got post-1979 Britain. But its level of union membership is lower than in Britain as well as Germany; its workers' skills and training are much higher than in Britain but still lower than in Germany; its relative unit labour costs in the manufacturing sector only slightly above those in Germany but much lower than those in Britain; its productivity is higher; and its labour–management-relations are generally better than in Britain although not necessarily than in Germany (see Tables 3.4 and 3.5). In the case of the automotive sector, for instance, these factors translate into higher productivity rates and higher-quality products than in Britain, but still behind Germany. This is because of unions as weak and fragmented as those of Britain, although less confrontational, and 'enterprise committees' that have some potential, although so far they are less effective than the German works councils; a traditionally weak vocational training system—especially by contrast with the elite higher education system—which leaves the sector with a shortage of skilled workers; assembly-supplier relations characterized by vehicle manufacturer control over suppliers and subcontractors rather than the German relations of trust; and government intervention that, although neither cheap nor perhaps efficient, has at least had a positive impact (Dankbaar 1994).

Even without the cooperative labour relations of the managed capitalist system or the full flexibility of the market capitalist system, in brief, France has managed its transition reasonably well. It remains somewhere between the two other models, with the state having engineered the transition and waiting in the wings, ready to act wherever it deems it necessary now to influence industrial relations, but not any more to control.

Conclusion

In France, then, although state interventionism is much more circumscribed and more market-oriented where it occurs than in the past, the state nevertheless remains more important than in either market capitalist or managed capitalist systems. Even if the state has largely given up on market making, it has continued to try to be market shaping, despite the fact that its field of influence has become more and more restricted as a result of privatization, deregulation, and labour market decentralization. Moreover, it has sometimes sought to reshape the market in a managed capitalist direction while inadvertently creating the conditions for the move to market capitalism, as in the structure of industrial relations and firm ownership. But France is no more market capitalist than it is managed capitalist. And yet it cannot really still be called state capitalist, since the state is but a pale shadow of its former self with regard to business and labour, which are no longer state-led but continue to be indirectly state-influenced. As such, one might do best to see France's current economic practices as having moved from its post-war model of state-led capitalism to 'state-enhanced' capitalism, as the state has reduced its ability to act in its traditional areas of intervention in the macroeconomic and microeconomic arenas, even as it continues to seek to reform the socioeconomic, and as business has gained great autonomy while labour–management relations have lost their adversarial character.

Germany, by contrast, is in the midst of a reform process. For labour-management relations the central issue is whether the unions and management will achieve productive compromises on increasing flexibility and differentiation in wages and work conditions. For business relations, the main question is whether businesses and banks will be able to liberalize their interrelationships without destroying the overall cooperative, network-based structure of business relations. So far, Germany has managed to maintain its business structure and social concertation system intact, despite signs of strain and the pressures of unification with East Germany and globalization. But to what extent the tensions between internationalizing firms and banks, or between them and still domestically embedded firms and banks, let alone between increasingly profit-focused firms and wage- and/or job-focused employees will be resolved enough to ensure the transition to a more competitive managed capitalism remains uncertain. But one thing is clear: if

Germany does not succeed in the move to a more 'competitive' managed capitalism, the result will not be market capitalism. It will be failed managed capitalism.

In market capitalist Britain, finally, the deepening of market capitalism, together with the shedding of state capitalist and managed capitalist borrowings which began with Margaret Thatcher and continued with her Conservative party successor, John Major, has been extended by New Labour under Tony Blair as well, albeit with certain changes at the margins. A few of these changes have reversed Thatcherite policies, but most have moved Britain even farther toward the ideal-typical market capitalism. What is more, in Europe, Britain remains the market capitalist beacon, with Blair seeking to do in a more cooperative way what Major and Thatcher did in a more confrontational way.

The economic practices of all three countries, thus, show varying degrees of change in response to the pressures of globalization and Europeanization and to the policy responses. To understand fully why this was the case, just as to understand the differential policy responses to the pressures of globalization and Europeanization, we need to understand the political dynamics of adjustment, and the role of discourse in generating and legitimating ideas for change.

PART III

The Politics of Economic Adjustment

5

Discourse as Framework for Analysis: Policy Construction and Legitimization for Changing Policies and Practices

In the study of countries' economic adjustment to the pressures of globalization and Europeanization, scholars have tended to focus primarily on the changes in policies and practices, and to explain these in terms of actors' interest-based responses, of institutional path dependencies, and, less frequently, of culture and identity. The politics of adjustment and, within this, the role of discourse as an ideational and interactive component of change has received surprisingly little attention by comparison. But, without attending to the politics, we cannot understand how governments managed to gain agreement for change in policies and practices and, thereby, to overcome entrenched interests, institutional obstacles, or cultural blinkers to change. After all, we are talking about reforms that in many cases radically altered long-established policy legacies and went against long-standing policy preferences, challenging not only the narrow self-interests of large parts of the population but also commonly held national values and conceptions of identity. Economic vulnerability alone is not sufficient to explain change, although it is clearly an impetus to it; nor is political institutional capacity, since even if governments had the ability to impose change—for example, in systems with power concentrated in the executive—they still had to win elections and weather protests. And where governments did not have that capacity—for example, in systems with power dispersed among different institutions and collective actors—winning elections was only the half of it.

None of the three types of 'institutionalisms' (Hall and Taylor 1996), whether rational choice, historical, or sociological institutionalism, on its own can do enough to explain the often radical changes affecting European countries. These approaches tend to be largely static, and are better able to account for continuity rather than change. Rational choice institutionalism elucidates the interests and incentives for or against change, but has difficulty accounting for how policy actors overcome entrenched interests or alter their perceptions of interest. Historical institutionalists describe the historically dependent paths of development that represent institutional constraints to or opportunities for change, but have difficulty explaining how policy actors overcome institutional blockages or establish new institutional patterns. Sociological institutionalists illuminate the cultural rules and norms which frame policy actors' understandings of their interests and set imaginable avenues for change, but do little to shed light on how policy actors overcome cultural blinkers to change or create new cultural rules. For the dynamics of change, we must be able to go beyond 'politics as usual', that is, beyond an understanding of the interplay of interests, institutions, and cultures that represent the background conditions to change, to explain how policy actors create an interactive consensus for change, which necessarily can only come about through communication.

Discourse, as defined herein, consists of whatever policy actors say to one another and to the public in their efforts to generate and legitimize a policy programme. As such, discourse encompasses both a set of policy ideas and values and an interactive process of policy construction and communication.

In its ideational dimension, discourse performs both a cognitive function, by elaborating on the logic and necessity of a policy programme, and a normative function, by demonstrating the policy programme's appropriateness through appeal to national values. This part of my definition of discourse has much in common with studies of the ideas used in policy change, whether ideas are seen as representing the necessary conditions for collective action that serve to redefine economic interest and to reconfigure interest-based political coalitions;[1] as constituting the policy narratives, discourses, and frames of reference that serve to (re)construct actors' understandings of interests and redirect their actions within institutions;[2] or as reflecting the national identities, values, norms, and collective memories that serve to shape the incentive-based push of interests or the path-dependent pull of institutions.[3]

In its interactive dimension, discourse performs a coordinative function by providing a common language and framework for the construction of a policy programme and a communicative function through the public presentation and deliberation of the policy programme. This aspect of my definition

---

[1] See Hall (1989); Blyth (1997); Parsons (2000).

[2] See Larat (1999); Gottweis (1999); Radaelli (2002); Doty (1996); Milliken (1999); Jobert (1992); Muller (1995); Muller and Surel (1998).

[3] See Risse *et al.* (1999), Schmidt (2000b), Finnemore and Sikkink (1998), and Rothstein (forthcoming).

fits with two other distinct literatures. First, it parallels studies of the groups at the center of policy construction who generate the ideas that form the bases for collective action and identity, whether they are seen as 'epistemic communities', 'advocacy coalitions', 'discourse coalitions', policy mediators, or 'norm entrepreneurs'.[4] But second, it also builds on studies of the use of ideas in the process of public persuasion, whether those focused on electoral politics and mass opinion, on 'policy forums', on the discourse of democratic governance, on 'national political discourses', on the 'norm cascade' of the 'norm life cycle', or on 'communicative action'.[5]

In the economic adjustment process, then, discourse serves not only to generate the ideas for change in policies and practices in response to the pressures of globalization and Europeanization but also to legitimize them. Such a legitimizing discourse is especially important because the push for change comes not from the bottom up, that is, from popularly expressed support for global and European induced change, but rather from the top down, from modernizing governmental as well as business elites intent on promoting changes in national political-economic policies and practices as the only solution to domestic as well as European and global problems. The task for principal policy actors, therefore, is to convince the public that such change is not just necessary but also appropriate. This is facilitated by the construction of a discourse that projects a coherent vision of how the nation fits into an integrating Europe and a globalizing world that also taps into deeper structures of national values and identity.

Any such discourse will naturally be quite different in substantive content from one European member state to the next, given that member states not only started from very different political-economic specificities—in ideas and values as well as in policies and practices—but also have, as we have seen, responded differently to global and European pressures. However, they also differ in discursive process, largely due to differences in political institutions. The institutional context, in fact, tends to frame the discourse. Countries where power is concentrated in the executive are more likely to privilege the communicative discourse to the public than the coordinative discourse

---

[4] On epistemic communities, see Haas (1992); Mazey and Richardson (1996); Kohler-Koch (1997: 99–101); on advocacy coalitions, Sabatier (1998); on discourse coalitions, Lehmbruch (1999); on the policy mediators, Muller (1995) and Jobert (2001); and on norm entrepreneurs, Finnemore and Sikkink (1998).

[5] On electoral politics and mass opinion, see Mutz, Sniderman, and Brody (1996); on policy forums, Rein and Schön (1991); on democratic governance discourse, March and Olsen (1995); on national political discourses, Hall (1989: 383 f.), on norms, Finnemore and Sikkink (1998), and on communicative action, Habermas (1996).

among key policy actors, which tends to be emphasized more in countries where power is dispersed and where the larger number of policy actors involved in the construction of the policy programme concentrate more on reaching agreement among themselves than in communicating their agreements to the wider public. Complicating these discursive processes within the national context, moreover, is the growing importance of the European context, with trans-European coordinative discourses among policy actors adding to the national ones in increasing numbers of policy sectors while leaving to national actors the communicative discourse to the public.

These questions about the substantive content of discourse, or *how* discourse matters, and the institutional context of discourse, or *where* discourse matters, are joined by a final question: *when* does discourse matter, that is, when does it exert a causal influence over and above the push and pull of interests, institutions, or culture? Part of the reason why many scholars' accounts of economic adjustment tend to avoid discourse is that it is difficult to separate it from these other variables, to identify it as *the* independent variable. But instead of ignoring discourse because of the difficulties, because it cannot be *the* cause, it is much better to ask when is discourse *a* cause, that is, when does discourse serve to reconceptualize interests rather than just reflect them, to chart new institutional paths instead of simply following old ones, and to reframe cultural norms rather than only reify them.

The contrasting experiences of Britain, France, and Germany are illustrative of the differing causal influence of discourse. France and Britain constitute examples of most similar cases, having both been affected early by economic crisis, having both begun quite early to impose radical change in policies and practices, and having both had similar institutional contexts which privilege the communicative discourse. The main difference between the two has been in the impact of the discourse, with Britain proving more successful in changing policies and practices than France in large measure because of a communicative discourse that spoke early on to both the necessity and the appropriateness of change, as opposed to only the necessity, as in France until relatively late. By comparison with both France and Britain, Germany represents an example of a most different case, given that it was affected much later by economic crisis, began quite late to negotiate moderate change at best in policies and practices, and has a different institutional context that privileges the coordinative discourse. The institutional context alone ensures that the causal influence of discourse is more immediately apparent, in whether agreements are successfully negotiated, as opposed to after reforms are imposed, which is evident only through more indirect measures of opinion change and policy continuity. Leaving institutional context aside, the main difference between Germany and the other two countries is that discourse has seemingly had the least impact until very late, given governments' difficulties in persuading policy actors as much as the general public of either the necessity or the appropriateness of change in policies and practices.

I begin with the ideational dimension of discourse, by defining the parameters of both the cognitive and the normative aspects of discourse, elucidating the standards by which it can be evaluated, and exploring the factors that drive change in both the discourse and the policy programme. I next develop the interactive dimension of discourse, by defining the parameters of both coordinative and communicative stages of the discourses, differentiating their institutional contexts in different kinds of political systems and at different levels, national and European, and, finally, discussing the causal influence of discourse. Throughout, I use the cases of France, Britain, and Germany in illustration of how, where, and when discourse matters in political economic change. These cases are elaborated in much greater detail in the following chapter, to elucidate the political dynamics of adjustment in each of the three countries in question.

The Ideational Dimension of Policy Discourse

As the conveyer of a set of ideas and values, discourse represents the policy concepts and norms, methods and instruments, objectives and ideals contained in a policy programme. As such, it performs two functions. As part of its cognitive function, it serves to justify a policy programme by demonstrating its superiority in providing effective solutions to current problems and in anticipating, and thereby avoiding, future problems. As part of its normative function, it serves to legitimize the policy programme by demonstrating its appropriateness in terms of national values, whether long-standing or newly emerging (see Table 5.1).

Although these two functions of the discourse are analytically distinguishable, they are not easily separable empirically, since 'what is' often is also represented as 'what ought to be' and 'what ought to be' as 'what is.' The inseparability of the cognitive and normative aspects of discourse is also evident in the scholarly literature, both in the work of those most interested in how discourse represents the ideas and values of a policy programme and those more focused on how it ensures the success of a policy programme through sound arguments that resonate with national values. This account of the ideational dimension of discourse draws on both literatures.

Table 5.1 The ideational dimension of discourse

Function	Form	Ideational core	Representation
Cognitive	Define policy programme's technical purposes and objectives, offer solutions to problems, define policy instruments and methods	Principles and norms of (social) scientific discipline	Narratives, technical/ scientific arguments, paradigms, frames of reference, guidelines, techniques, recipes,
Normative	Define policy programme's political goals and ideals, appeal to long-standing or newly emerging values	Principles and norms of public life	metaphors, slogans, foundational myths, evocative phrases, images, etc.

In this section, I first define discourse, consider the ways in which the policy discourse taps into the deeper core of ideas and values of the polity, whether simply to reflect those ideas and values or also to affect them, and explore the possible disconnections between the discourse about a proposed policy programme and about the policy programme once implemented. Then, I discuss the different criteria for the success of discourse, both the cognitive arguments that justify a policy programme in terms of its problem-solving potential and the normative arguments that legitimize the programme by appealing to long-standing values and/or re-conceptualizing them. Finally, I examine the ideational processes and sources of change in discourse and policy programme, which may be revolutionary or evolutionary in processes and may be precipitated by external events or internal contradictions.

Policy Discourse and Policy Programme

Policy discourse is the sum of policy and political actors' accounts of a policy programme's purposes, objectives, and ideals which serve as a guide to action by defining the concepts and norms to be applied, identifying the problems to be solved, explaining the methods to be followed, developing the policy instruments to be used, and, all in all, framing the national policy discussion within a given policy arena—here political economy, but one could do the same for defence, citizenship, environment, and so on.[6] The policy discourse

---

[6] This draws on the definition of March and Olsen (1995: 45, 66), but it is more narrowly focused on discourse providing accounts of policy rather than of the polity as a whole).

itself represents the policy programme in myriad ways. It may introduce not only technical or scientific arguments but also more generally accessible narratives about the causes of current problems and what needs to be done to remedy them.[7] Thatcher's neo-liberal policy discourse, for example, took specialist arguments about the disastrous economic effects of neo-Keynesianism, which she claimed remediable only by monetarism, and combined them into a narrative about the benefits of thrift and hard work, which she illustrated, among other ways, through the experience of her grocer father. The policy discourse may also depict 'paradigms'[8] and frames of reference—*référentiels*[9]—that define causal ideas about reality as well as guidelines, techniques, or recipes for operating in reality, such as the 'social market economy' for the Germans (Streeck 1997), *'dirigisme'* for the French (Schmidt 1996), or neo-Keynesian 'pump-priming' and 'steering' for a range of countries (Hall 1989, 1993). In addition, the discourse may reduce policy complexities through evocative phrases, such as Prime Minister Blair's evocation of welfare as 'Not a hammock but a trampoline', through slogans such as that for Thatcher's first election campaign 'Labour's not working'—with pictures of long lines at the employment office—and foundational myths such as when Helmut Kohl at the time of German unification evoked an idealized version of the social market economy of the 1950s that would produce 'flowering landscapes' in East Germany in the 1990s as it had earlier in the West (see Chapter 6).

Finally, the discourse tends also to appeal to a deeper core of organizing principles and norms, tying its narratives and arguments to a more general body of knowledge and approach to reality. That deeper core encompasses not only the principles and norms of public life—on the normative side—but also the principles and norms of a relevant scientific discipline—on the cognitive side. For example, the political economic discourse will not only refer to formal political and economic concepts and norms, say, monetarism for Thatcher in 1979, neo-Keynesianism for the French Socialists in 1981, or ordo-liberalism for the Germans in the early post-war period. It will also invoke the ideas and values of the polity. In Germany, for example, the post-war discourse of the social market economy has drawn on the core principles and norms of cooperation and consensus-building that are at the foundations of the country's post-war federal democracy. In Britain, Thatcher's discourse situated its radical neo-liberal policy programme in terms of Britain's liberal state tradition and values of individualism. In France, the post-1983

---

[7] See, for example, Roe (1994); Hajer (1995); Radaelli (1999; 2001).

[8] See, for example, Hall (1993); Surel (1995).

[9] See Jobert (1992; 2001); Muller (1995); Surel (1995).

political economic policy discourse was careful to claim not to violate the polity's principles of social solidarity even as it described the neo-liberal policy programme that was to alter the role of the state in the economy. A policy discourse, after all, may appeal to some underlying ideas and values in the polity while promoting changes in others.

It is important to note, in fact, that, although the policy discourse makes appeal to the more general ideas and values in the polity, this does not mean, as some sociological institutionalists argue, that the discourse is inseparable from the 'underlying structure of belief, perception, and appreciation' on which policy positions rest (Rein and Schön 1991: 263, 289; Schön and Rein 1994: 22). On the contrary, the policy discourse is separable at least analytically from the underlying ideas and values of the polity, which are in the policy discourse but not of it. Such a separation underscores the ability of policy discourse to affect values rather than simply reflect them, to change the underlying structures of perception and belief as it influences the course of events through words as well as through the actions those words promote. This dynamic aspect of discourse is essential to understanding change. How this occurs will be explored below. Here, I only wish to underline the point that the policy discourse, along with the policy programme it promotes, can be an impetus to change in the ideas and values of the polity. Otherwise, how could we explain France's radical reversal of traditional state *dirigisme*, let alone Britain's revolutionary shift from the post-war consensus to Thatcher's radical neo-liberalism?

Policy discourse and the underlying ideas and values of the polity are not the only things that need to be separated analytically in order to explain the dynamics of change, however. For similar reasons, one needs also to differentiate the discourse about a proposed policy programme from the discourse about that policy programme once it is implemented. It is essential to differentiate between words, that is, between the discourse as it represents a policy program, and actions, that is, the policy programme as it is put into practice. For only in so doing can one take account of the ways in which the policy discourse connects with or, more importantly, is disconnected from a policy programme.

Such disconnections occur, for example, when a policy programme develops in ways that differ from its originating discourse. This was the case of post-war Britain, where neither the discourses of the Tories nor those of Labour when in power fitted the 'Butskellite' moderate liberal policy programme they both implemented. One must, in other words, consider not only what policy-makers say but also what they do. But what they do may not only be different from what they say, it also may simply not be said, with the policy programmes carried out without a policy discourse. A case in point is

Schröder's tax reform of December 1999 that eliminated capital gains tax for holders of large equity stakes in private enterprises, which not only was not discussed in the government before it was put into the budget but was also passed over in silence in the initial legislative debates, despite the fact that—or perhaps because—it more than any other single measure so far stands to alter the social market economy. Another example is the range of more redistributive welfare measures by the Blair government, which have been implemented 'by stealth' mainly because they clash with the neo-liberal discourse of self-reliance (see Chapter 6).

There are cases, however, where the absence of discourse occurs not because the policies do not fit with an ongoing policy programme but because the policy programme itself needs no discourse. This is generally the case when the ideas and values embodied by a policy programme are so generally agreed upon and accepted that they are part of the background assumptions that people operate under, and need not be articulated. This could easily be argued was the case in Germany in much of the post-war period until the early 1990s, where, whatever the disagreements over policy instruments among parties, whether in coalitions or with the opposition, among unions and employers' associations, or between the federal government and the *Länder*, none challenged the objectives or underlying principles of the policy programme of the 'social market economy' and therefore did not need to articulate a discourse. Only in 1990, with the challenge of unification, was the originating post-war discourse re-invoked by Helmut Kohl, as he sought to promote acceptance for the implementation of the social market policy programme in East Germany.

Ideational Criteria of Success for Policy Discourse and Programme

But if sometimes a policy discourse is not necessary and other times it does not reflect reality, how can one know when a discourse successfully promotes a policy programme? For this, we do best to turn to the cognitive and normative criteria for discourse derived from the philosophy of science and social science. The representational approach on its own does little to help explain why a policy discourse and programme gain acceptance or not. That the narrative tells a good story or that the metaphors are evocative is not sufficient. The story the discourse tells and the information it provides must also appear sound, the actions it recommends doable, the solutions to the problems its identifies workable, and the overall outcomes appropriate.

With regard to the cognitive criteria for success, the philosophy of science first tells us that the policy programme sketched out by the discourse need

Table 5.2 Ideational criteria for success of discourse about policy programme

Aspect	Logic of argument	Standards of argument
Cognitive	Justifies through logic of necessity	Provides core idea with great potential; demonstrates relevance, applicability, coherence, and greater problem-solving capacity of programme
Normative	Legitimizes through logic of appropriateness	Shows that responds to problems of polity; reflects/ affects national values

not initially be an elaborated structure (see Table 5.2). Rather, much like the classical definition of a paradigm in science (Kuhn 1970), the policy programme may consist of a central or basic idea that has great potential for further elaboration. That further elaboration, however, may look more like Lakatos's (1970) research programmes than a Kuhnian paradigm, with a 'core'—made up of the most basic principles, goals, assumptions about appropriate courses of action, and methods of translating general principles into action—which is likely to change very slowly compared with its 'periphery' of policy applications (see Majone 1989). The periphery itself can be conceived of as representing policy sectors for which the paradigm for a particular policy arena serves as a guide to action and which develop their own sectoral discourses for which the paradigmatic discourse serves as a template. In addition, while in some instances the paradigm's application in a given policy arena may be anticipated in the initial discourse and be applied across all sectors at the same time, in others the application may proceed sector by sector, as the ideas, problems, or solutions developed in the first serve as a 'paradigm' for another sector and in turn for yet others. This was the case, for example, with Thatcher's radical neo-liberal programme, which proceeded sector by sector, with the first term concerned primarily with monetary policy and industrial relations while the industrial policy of privatization that was later to become emblematic of her neo-liberal programme was barely even sketched out in the first election manifesto, and came only in the second term along with, even later, welfare and education policy. In Germany in the 1950s, by contrast, the various sectoral programmes that made up the social market economy developed together, growing by the late 1950s into a tightly coupled policy programme encompassing monetary policy, industrial policy, industrial relations, and social policy.

Thus, the originating policy discourse articulates a central idea for a policy programme that is generally rich enough in content to provide the basis for policy-makers to come up with solutions to a wide variety of policy problems, many of which may not have been anticipated in the initial policy programme. In addition to such 'heuristic' content,[10] however, we can also specify certain cognitive standards of success derived from the philosophy of science through which the discourse could be expected to justify the policy programme: relevance, applicability, and coherence.[11]

A discourse should offer arguments able to demonstrate, first, the policy programme's relevance, by accurately identifying the problems the polity needs or expects to be solved; second, the policy programme's applicability, by showing how it will solve the problems it identifies; and third, the policy programme's coherence, by making the concepts, norms, methods, and instruments of the programme appear reasonably consistent and able to apply without major contradiction to a wide range of problems.[12] Finally, the discourse must also situate the policy programme in relation to other such programmes, by showing how it can solve problems its predecessor or rival could not while anticipating, and avoiding, future problems.[13] Thatcher's originating discourse, for example, took care to spell out the policy programme's relevance, as it claimed to solve the monetary problems and labour strife that had virtually brought the country to a standstill; its applicability, by discussing how tightening monetary policy and clamping down on the unions would solve those problems; and its coherence, by linking the neoliberalism of its monetary policy, with the notion that the state should no longer directly manage the economy, to its industrial relations policy focused on destroying the unions' ability to disrupt the smooth operation of the economy. Moreover, it contrasted its monetarist policy solution with the failures

---

[10] This sense of 'heuristic' content is borrowed from the philosopher of science, Imre Lakatos (1970), who has this as a requirement for research programmes, although others also expect it without using the word, whether Kuhn (1970) for paradigms or Karl Popper (1961) for falsifiable explanations.

[11] These standards are not far from the basic standards that logical empiricists originally identified as necessary for explanation: logical consistency, empirical verifiability, and explanatory relevance (cf. Hempel 1965). The main difference here is that, in place of empirical verifiability, I have put applicability, in keeping with subsequent approaches in the philosophy of science—for example, Kuhn (1970), Lakatos (1970)—which substituted a success standard for a truth standard. I have also substituted the word 'coherence' for 'consistency', to emphasize the importance of the policy argument appearing to form a whole while allowing, nevertheless, for some contradiction even in the discourse. For further discussion of the standards in the philosophy of science, see Schmidt (1986).

[12] The emphasis here is on appearance because, while the discourse paints a coherent picture, the actual concepts, norms, policy instruments, and methods may in fact be logically or practically contradictory, as discussed below.

[13] This is the success standard typically used by Lakatos ((1970) as part of 'methodological falsification).'

of neo-Keynesianism and its harsh industrial relations policy with the previous laxness of both Labour and its own Tory predecessors.

Much of the political science literature that uses the philosophy of science language of 'paradigm' or 'research programmes' tends to concentrate on these cognitive aspects of policy ideas and discourse.[14] But in gaining or retaining acceptance for a policy programme, the discourse cannot rely on its cognitive function alone, and thereby justify the policy programme only in terms of the logic of necessity. A discourse that successfully promotes the ideas of a policy programme also needs to legitimize them in terms of their logic of appropriateness through appeal to values (see Table 5.2). The ideational success of Thatcher's policy programme, for example, was at least in part due to a discourse that emphasized not only the necessity of change through 'TINA—there is no alternative' but also its appropriateness, by legitimizing its policy prescriptions in terms of the country's long-standing adherence to liberal economic principles and their basis in deep-seated British values favouring individualism (Schmidt 2000b). By contrast, the policy programme of French governments of the left and the right from the mid-1980s to the late 1990s encountered problems related to the fact that, while they consistently emphasized the necessity of neo-liberal reform in their discourse, they barely spoke of its appropriateness other than to reiterate time and again without much conviction that they were defending traditional values of social solidarity. German Prime Minister Schröder's discourse in the late 1990s had even greater ideational problems, however, because he could convince of neither the necessity nor the appropriateness of neo-liberal reform. Instead of engaging in a discourse that sought to build from German values, he first adopted British Prime Minister Blair's discourse of the 'third way' in June 1999, then French Prime Minister Jospin's Socialist discourse in October 1999, before landing back in the traditional discourse of the social market economy in December 1999 with pledges to rescue Holzmann from bankruptcy and to protect Mannesman from takeover— which finally worked, but did nothing to promote his neo-liberal policy programme (see Chapter 6).

The ideational success of a policy programme, in other words, also depends upon the ability of the discourse to perform a normative function by providing arguments that show how the policy programme serves to build on long-standing values and identity while creating something new, better suited to the new realities and more appropriate than the old 'public philosophy' (Campbell 1998). Unlike in science, where the problems stem almost

---

[14] See, for example, Hall (1993); Surel (1995); Majone (1989).

entirely from the science-related concerns of scientists and the solutions are certified as such by scientists alone, in society, as Kuhn himself acknowledges (1970: 163–4), the problems stem from the societal concerns of the citizens while the solutions are recognized as solutions only if they are accepted as such by the citizens as well as by policy-makers (Schmidt 1988a). In society, in consequence, as opposed to science, the ideational task of a policy discourse is dual: (1) to provide cognitive arguments capable of satisfying policy-makers as to the robustness of the solutions provided by the policy programme, and (2) to provide normative arguments capable of satisfying policy-makers and citizens alike that those solutions respond to the real problems of the polity in ways that serve its underlying values, as elaborated in the polity discourse.

Normative legitimization, however, as noted earlier, does not entail that the policy programme promoted by a discourse simply conform to pre-existing national values. Much the contrary, since any new discourse that proffers a real shift in policy ideas may also promote the transformation of national values. National values, after all, are themselves generally 'contested and contingent', changing over time as conditions and attitudes change (Katzenstein 1996b: 2–3). Any society, moreover, has a large repertoire of values, some of which may be the subject of greater societal agreement than others, depending upon the degree of normative integration or fragmentation of the society itself. All countries have their own particular mix of values, with some newly emerging and others fading as needs and desires, mores and morals slowly change (see Schmidt 2000b). The role of discourse is to give expression to those value changes as its promotes them, whether the appeal is in the name of long-established values or newly emerging ones. As a result, although the policy discourse may reflect national values, it may also change them.

Change depends on whether the policy discourse reinforces as it reinterprets values central to the polity or challenges them through appeal to other values in the societal repertoire. And where a new policy discourse challenges values central to the polity, it may precipitate a crisis not only in the existing policy programme but also in the polity. The relationship is a complex one.[15] For our purposes, it is important to bear in mind only that, where a policy discourse appeals to values other than the predominating ones, it may bring about transformation not only in the policy paradigm but also in the polity. Thatcher's neo-liberal policy discourse, for example, brought about just such a transformation, as she challenged the interventionist principles and 'collectivist' values of post-war governments—whether the Tories'

---

[15] See the discussions of Wolin (1968); Dryzek and Leonard (1988).

'paternalism' or Labour's 'socialism'—in the name of the liberal economic principles and individualist values of the past. By contrast, Jospin's discourse about balancing 'efficiency' with 'equity' expected no such transformation as he sought to reconcile traditional social values of solidarity with economic values tied to neo-liberalism—although those economic values had themselves been transformed by previous governments' discourses in the move from *dirigiste* economic values to more neo-liberal ones with regard to the role of the state in the economy.

The policy discourse may prove transformative not only because of its prospective role, in showing the appropriateness of a proposed policy programme, but also in its retrospective role, by speaking to the appropriateness of the new practices generated by the policy programme as it is implemented.[16] For once a new policy programme is put into place, the policy discourse provides the public with a new frame within which to make sense of the new realities by which they live their lives—although an opposition discourse could do the same, with a negative spin rather than a positive one. After all, although Thatcher's policy discourse and programme did help get her elected, both remained highly contested for quite a while. Only as her policies began to take hold, altering people's experiences of work and welfare, did the discourse really permeate the polity, along with the liberal values it promoted, by providing the public with a positive way of thinking and talking about their new experiences—despite the best efforts of Labour to provide an alternative discourse promoting values of equality and principles of state interventionism while railing against the capitalist system of exploitation and bemoaning the social injustices resulting from growing inequalities and rising unemployment. Thatcher's discourse did have its limits, though. Although British ideas and values with regard to the economy did appear to change quite radically in a neo-liberal direction, the results were much more mixed with regard to the welfare state (see Schmidt 2000*b*).

Ideational Processes of Change in Policy Discourse and Programme

Any major shift in policy discourse, then, reflects something of a revolution in world view, since it comes not only with a radical shift in policy programme but also sometimes in the ideas and values of the polity as a whole. Such 'third-order' change can be seen as revolutionary in the sense that it alters all aspects of the policy programme: the policy objectives, instruments,

---

[16] For the contexts in which the prospective or the retrospective role is more predominant, see below in the discussions of the institutional contexts of coordinative and communicative discourses, and of the causal influence of discourse.

and ideals (Kuhn 1970; Hall 1993). Instead of revolutionary change in policy programme and an entirely new discourse, however, change can appear more evolutionary, whether through a renewal of the policy discourse and programme with new policy instruments but the same policy objectives and ideals—first-order change—or through its recasting with new policy instruments and objectives but the same core ideals—second-order change (see Table 5.3).

Revolutionary change in policy programme is not the same as a Kuhnian 'revolution' in scientific 'paradigm', which assumes the incommensurability of paradigms, thereby eliminating the possibility of understanding the previous paradigm or even of comparing 'facts' across paradigms (Schmidt 1987). This is not the case in society, even if it may be the—unlikely—case in science, since understanding of past ideas and values is always possible even if those ideas and values are not shared in the present, because they can be set into the ideational context of the past (Skinner 1988) or their progressive changes traced into the present (Pocock 1964). And although the 'facts' they evoke may be different, the data cited in evidence can be compared.

Even this picture of revolutionary change in policy programmes may be misleading, however. Change in policy programmes need not look like Kuhn's picture of science, in which one hegemonic paradigm is entirely abandoned in favour of its hegemonic successor—although this certainly fits the advent of Thatcherism in Britain or the great U-turn in economic policy in 1983 in Mitterrand's France. Instead, policy change may often look more like Lakatos's picture of overlapping research programmes, which are to some extent commensurable as they vie for recognition and acceptance. Here, although there is still likely to be one dominant policy programme in a given arena, there may be other minority discourses waiting in the wings,

Table 5.3 Evolutionary and revolutionary change in policy discourse and programme

Change in policy discourse and policy programme	Evolutionary		Revolutionary
	Renewed (first-order change)	Recast (second-order change)	New (third-order change)
Policy instruments	Changed	Changed	Changed
Policy objectives	Same	Changed	Changed
Policy core	Same	Same	Changed
Examples	Blair 1997	Schröder 1998	Thatcher 1979
	Jospin 1997	Mitterrand 1981	Mitterrand 1983

proposing alternative policy programmes and appealing to alternative sets of values in the polity, hoping one day to become dominant. Most often, the dominant policy discourse and programme is that of the government while the rival discourses and programmes are those of the opposition party, as, for example, with the Socialists in France from 1958 to 1981, or Labour in Britain between 1979 and 1997. But even a dominant programme need not be monolithic in discourse: the different parties in a government coalition and/or the different currents in a majority party may have separate discourses which are most often—but certainly not always—complementary in their descriptions of the joint policy programme. This was the case, for example, with the French neo-liberal coalition government of 1986 to 1988 as well as of successive German coalition governments led by Chancellor Kohl from 1981 to 1998 and by Schröder after.

Not all change in discourse and policy programme need be revolutionary, however. Instead, change can appear more evolutionary where a discourse and programme are supple enough over time to respond to changing needs and concerns in the polity. Here, rather than thinking of Kuhn's scientific paradigms or Lakatos's research programmes, we might do better to think of Stephen Toulmin's (1972) 'disciplinary enterprises' or Larry Laudan's (1977) 'research traditions', where certain elements in a policy programme change while others continue, whether the goals, problems, procedures, concepts, or even the ideals (see Schmidt 1986; 1988b). Thus, although Britain in 1979 and France in 1983 may still best be explained in 'revolutionary' terms, Britain under Prime Minister Blair, Germany under Chancellor Schröder, France under President Mitterrand from 1981 to 1983, and France under Prime Minister Jospin between 1997 and 2002 can all better be explained in 'evolutionary' terms. Even here, however, distinctions need to be made in terms of how significant the evolutionary change in policy discourse and programme.

Evolutionary change can be seen as entailing a renewal of the policy discourse and programme when the discourse claims to solve old concerns or new problems using new policy instruments without radically changing the policy objectives or ideals of the original policy paradigm. This can be likened to 'first-order' change in Kuhnian terms, where the policy instruments may change but not the objectives of a policy programme (see Kuhn 1970; Hall 1993). A case in point is Blair's policy programme, in which he maintained Thatcher's neo-liberal policy objectives while altering the policy instruments, for example, through social policies that emphasized improving opportunity through workfare rather than reducing dependency through lower benefits. Moreover, the discourse of the 'third way' justified the programme in terms of the 'risk society' created by globalization rather than economic crisis and legitimized it through appeal to values of responsibility and self-reliance, not, as did Thatcher, in the name of the past but rather in the name of the present and future, while at the same time tapping into deep-seated collectivist values about compassion, equality—at least of opportunity—and social justice (Schmidt 2000b). Similarly, the transition from the Juppé government to the Jospin government represented a renewal of the policy discourse and program. It added normative legitimization to the cognitive argument with its talk of balancing equity and efficiency, and changed the modalities but not the nature of the policies, by benefiting different socio-economic groups with the reforms—for example, with tax policies that benefited consumers instead of producers and lower rather than higher income groups (see Chapters 2, 6).

However, evolutionary change can instead take the form of a recasting of the policy discourse and programme, where new policies make seemingly radical change in the policy orientation and policy instruments without, however, disrupting the core ideas and/or values of the policy paradigm. This can be likened to 'second-order' change in Kuhnian terms, where the policy objectives change along with the instruments (see Kuhn 1970; Hall 1993). This better describes Schröder in Germany, who has sought to recast the discourse and programme of the social market economy by emphasizing the market and de-emphasizing the social in policy objectives and instruments without, however, rejecting core ideas about the social construction of the market and its consensus-oriented values. But it also fits France under Mitterrand 1981–3, where the core elements of the policy programme of *dirigisme* were enhanced through greater state interventionism, even as the Socialist discourse differed greatly from the Gaullist, by legitimizing the programme in terms of socialist values of equality and the break with capitalism (Schmidt 1996).

Sources of Change in Policy Discourse and Programme

But whether new, renewed, or recast, change comes as a result of crisis in the policy discourse and/or programme. This may come from outside events which the policy programme cannot solve and the discourse explain or from contradictions within and/or between policy discourse and programme as well as within and/or between master and sectoral discourses and programmes (see Fig. 5.1).

Most often, changes in policy discourse and programme occur in times of political, economic, and/or social crisis and are generated by the perceived

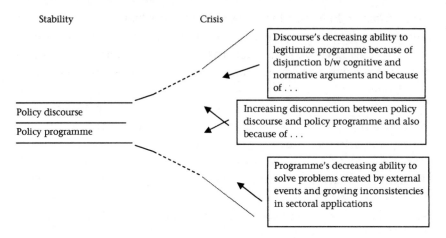

Fig. 5.1 Trajectory of policy discourse and programme in ideational crisis

inability of the old policy programme to solve the problems of the moment. Events, in other words, are key to creating a receptive environment for a new set of ideas (Hirschman 1989) or at least a reconsideration of the old ones. The economic crisis in the mid- to late 1970s following upon the two oil shocks was one such set of events, and led to the introduction of new policy programmes in a number of countries. This was most notably the case for Britain, with the move to neo-liberalism subsequent to Thatcher's election. In France, by contrast, the faded Gaullist policy discourse and programme of *dirigisme* were recast by the Socialists and, thereby, reinvigorated for a short time.

Crisis need not always bring in a new, renewed, or even recast discourse and policy programme, however. If a policy discourse and programme is supple enough, it can respond to a crisis in the polity without itself suffering from crisis. But this depends upon whether the programme can generate policy responses that are consistent with its overall policy programme and justifiable by the discourse. In Germany, the post-war discourse of the social market economy survived the economic crises of the 1970s intact, in large measure because its stability-based philosophy was supple enough to rally support for policies that promoted austerity, with the long-standing policy programme of the social market economy able to accommodate—in ideas and practice—the shift to monetarism by the Bundesbank. This was something that the fading Gaullist discourse of *dirigisme*, under Giscard d'Estaing, could not sufficiently justify, given a growth-oriented economic philosophy and political commitments to fighting unemployment, and that the Socialist discourse of *dirigisme*—under Mitterrand from 1981 to 1983—which proposed neo-Keynesian expansionism, chose to reject. For Germany, unification proved the more important crisis. But even here, instead of a rejection, recasting, or even renewal of the discourse and paradigm, the crisis provoked a restatement of the old policy programme of the social market economy by Chancellor Kohl and its establishment in East Germany.

Events become significant, in fact, when they prove anomalous—in Kuhn's words—in terms of the policy paradigm, that is, when the policies that normally follow from the policy programme fail to solve the problems created by those events and/or the discourse is unable to explain why the policies are not working. This is the period of 'policy delegitimation' (Goldstein and Keohane 1993: 12), 'third-order change' (Hall 1993), 'critical juncture' (Gourevitch 1986), 'ideational shift' (Marcussen 1998), 'organic crisis' (Gill 1995: 400), or 'creedal period (Blyth 1997: 245), when a 'window of opportunity' (Kingdon 1984) opens and the search for a new policy programme begins. In Britain, such a crisis period was clearly in evidence in the 1970s, as it was in France, whereas in Germany it began in the mid- to late 1990s.

External events are not the only impetus to change, however. Internal contradictions are also important, whether because of disjunctions between cognitive and/or normative aspects of the discourse, disconnections between the policy discourse and the policy programme, or inconsistencies in the application of the policy discourse and programme in related policy sectors.

One of the problems for the policy discourse is when the general cognitive arguments seem logically to contradict one another or to conflict with the normative. Most typical is when macroeconomic programmes that institute budgetary austerity collide with pledges to maintain expansive socio-economic programmes, or when cutbacks in the socio-economic arena offend deep-seated values of social solidarity. This has largely been the problem for France, where cognitive arguments that served to convince the public of the economic necessity of a neo-liberal policy programme did comparatively little to persuade the public of the appropriateness of change, with normative arguments finding little play other than in appeals to sacrifice in the face of crisis or in promises to honour long-standing values of social solidarity—even as unemployment continued to mount and the problems of 'exclusion' grew. The constant switching back and forth between governments of the left and the right between 1983 and 1997 is testimony to the problems of discourses that were essentially about the same neo-liberal policy programme. This is in contrast to discourses where the cognitive and normative mutually reinforce one another, as when a discourse that promotes both neo-liberal macroeconomics and social welfare cuts can appeal for legitimization to values of individualism. This was the case with Thatcher in Britain, who lasted in power close to twelve years, and her party 17.

The more tightly linked the various aspects of the policy programme, in fact, the greater the power of the discourse, but the greater the difficulties if problems develop in the policy application. Thus, for example, where the concepts and norms of the policy programme are grounded in ideology, the discourse can be particularly powerful as long as it has accurately predicted the potential impact of its policy prescriptions and has sufficiently legit-imized them in terms of renewed national norms and values—as was the case with Thatcher's ideologically grounded neo-liberalism. If, however, the ideo-logically based discourse becomes disconnected from the policy programme, because it fails to predict accurately the effects of its policy programme and/or cannot justify the different outcome in terms of the discourse, then the very coherence of the discourse is likely to cause it major trouble, and possibly spell its demise. Mitterrand's ideologically grounded socialism of 1981 to 1983, with its neo-Keynesian macroeconomic policies, its expansion-ist microeconomic policies, and its generous socio-economic policies, was abandoned because within the context of the ideology it could not cognit-ively account for the failure of the policies to promote growth or normatively legitimize the subsequent turn to budgetary austerity in terms of its social commitments—to say nothing, for the moment, about interests, that is, the government's worries about losing power given the severe economic crisis brought on by its policy programme.

Policy discourse, however, need not be based on ideology. In its absence, the discourse can evoke the future, as the French socialists' emphasis on modernization in their successful 1988 election campaign, or on maintaining past accomplishments, as the Kohl government did in its failed 1998 election campaign. What such discourse loses in the power of its ideological coher-ence, it gains in greater flexibility to use a wider range of policy concepts, norms, instruments and methods, even if they may be somewhat contradic-tory, as long as the discourse can maintain enough appearance of coherence to satisfy the public, even if not the pundits. A case in point is the 'third way' discourse of Tony Blair. In some cases, the very incoherence of a policy programme in practice may be an indicator of the political system's efficiency at maintaining compromise, as long as the discourse itself paints a coherent picture of the policy programme (Fouilleux 2001).

Coherence is also an issue with regard to the interrelationship between the policy discourse and the sectoral applications of the policy programme. For while the 'master' discourse tends to set out a wide and often vague set of principles,[17] its elaboration in a variety of different sectoral discourses

---

[17] My thanks to Wolfgang Streeck for suggesting the idea of master as opposed to sectoral discourses.

may lead to problems where the sectoral applications of the policy pro-gramme do not take. Where the difficulties in the application of the policy programme are minor, as when residues of earlier policies affect the imp-lementation of the policy programme or earlier sectoral discourses contami-nate the new one, the 'anomalies' do not tend to undermine the master discourse, which generally manages to pass over the differences in silence. The danger is that, as anomalies accumulate in the sectoral applications, the master discourse becomes less convincing and the overall policy programme less viable.

More problematic, however, is when a sector as a whole remains anom-alous. This has typically been the case for the agricultural sector. But this sec-tor has not posed serious coherence problems for most EU member states' political economic discourses. This is because agriculture fits perfectly within the context of most countries' post-war social welfare discourses and policy programmes[18] and has enjoyed a separate status not only because of its long-standing Europeanization through the Common Agricultural Policy but also because of its close connection to deep-seated values in the polity connected to the land, especially in France.

Social policy reform has posed much more of a coherence problem for neo-liberal policy programmes. In France, the long delay in the extension of the moderate neo-liberal policy programme to the welfare state can be explained by governments' unwillingness to challenge core social values of the polity. In Britain, it stemmed from Thatcher's inability to affect those core values, in particular with regard to the universal services of the National Health Service and the state education system, although Thatcher did introduce some competition in these sectors. It took Blair to complete the Thatcher revolution in the welfare arena, with a discourse that mixes neo-liberal and collectivist values, as noted earlier.

Finally, EU member states generally have been finding it increasingly difficult to maintain the coherence of their national discourses and policy programmes in the face of the growing number of policies, let alone ideas, coming from above, mainly European but also global, as well as from below, from sectors that change in response to the ideas as well as policies coming from above. It may very well be that these increasing complications demand a master discourse that is even vaguer than in the past in terms of its policy ambitions, given the increasing Europeanization of political economic policy-making, but also more flexible in its appeal to values, made easier since the end of major left-right divides. The ability of any policy discourse to succeed depends not only on the cognitive and normative merits of the

---

[18] My thanks to Beate Kohler-Koch for this caveat.

policy programme, however, but also on the discourse's ability to gain and maintain a constituency for its policy programme first among policy elites and then among the public at large. Neither sound arguments based on a reasonable representation of the policy programme's solutions to the polity's problems nor strong legitimization for those arguments based on resonance with national values—whether reinterpreted old values or newly emerging ones—are enough to explain the ideational success of a policy programme. Policy actors must be able to use the discourse effectively not only to build a coalition for reform but also to enable political actors to inform and orient the public by giving it a clear vision of where the policy programme is taking the country and making clear not only why it is necessary but also why it is appropriate. The interactive process involved in articulating a discourse, in other words, is as important as the discourse's ideational content.

The Interactive Dimension of Policy Discourse

As an interactive process, discourse involves not only the groups responsible for generating the policy ideas but also those responsible for taking those ideas from construction to communication to the public. As such, discourse performs two functions. As part of its coordinative function, it serves to provide policy actors with a common language and ideational framework through which they can together construct a policy programme, debate its merits, refine it, and come to agreement on its implementation. As part of its communicative function, the discourse serves political actors as the means for persuading the public, through discussion and deliberation, that the policies developed at the coordinative phase are necessary—cognitive function—and appropriate—normative function (see Table 5.4).

These coordinative and communicative stages of discourse are generally both analytically and empirically separable, even though they are not always distinguishable from one another at the margins. The separation of the coordinative and communicative stages of discourse is also evident in the scholarly literature, which tends to divide between those interested in the communities responsible for the generation and implementation of policy ideas and those more concerned with the communication of those ideas to the larger public. This account of discourse, again, draws on both literatures.

To this, I add an emphasis on the institutional context that sets the locus of discourse in different European member states as well as in the EU. For

Table 5.4 The interactive dimension of discourse

Function	Actors	Interlocutors	Generator of ideas	Purpose	Form
Coordinative	Policy actors	One another	Epistemic community, discourse coalition, advocacy coalition, policy entrepreneur	Construct policy programme, come to agreement	Provide language and framework for policy actors' discussion and deliberation
Communicative	Political actors	Public	Policy actors, political entrepreneur	Communicate to public, provide orienting and legitimizing information	Translate programme into accessible language for public discussion and deliberation

although all countries along with the EU have both coordinative and communicative discourses, some emphasize the one and some the other, largely due to how their electoral systems, governance structures, and policy-making processes influence the configuration of power and authority. In 'single-actor' countries such as France and Britain, which are characterized by a strong concentration of power and authority in the executive, the communicative discourse tends to be more elaborate, as governments which have the political institutional capacity to impose reform seek to convince the public of the necessity and appropriateness of their policy programmes. In 'multi-actor' systems such as Germany and the EU, which are characterized instead by a dispersion of power, the coordinative discourse tends to be more elaborate, as key policy actors which have the political institutional capacity at most to negotiate reform seek to reach agreement on a policy programme. This in turn determines where we look for the causal influence of discourse: at the communicative stage of discourse for single-actor systems, in the reactions of the public as well as the most affected interests; and at the coordinative stage for multi-actor systems, in whether policy actors reach any agreement at all. The EU, moreover, adds to the national level of discourse another level, intensifying the coordinative discourse but doing little to affect the communicative discourse.

How Discourse Functions: The Two Stages of Interaction

The coordinative and communicative stages of discourse are interdependent, with the coordinative discourse constructing the policy programme which the communicative discourse then conveys to the public, the responses of which then feed back into the coordinative discourse. The key actors in these two stages are distinct, even though some may operate in both spheres, and others may operate outside of them but have significant impact on both. In the coordinative stage of discourse, the principal interlocutors are the policy actors, governmental and others, who construct a proposed policy programme often using policy ideas developed by discursive policy communities and conveyed by policy entrepreneurs. In the communicative stage, the key interlocutors are the political actors, politicians and others, who present the programme developed in the context of the coordinative discourse to the general public as well as more informed publics for discussion, deliberation and, ideally, modification of the policy programme (see Fig. 5.2).

The Coordinative Stage of Discourse

Any discourse, whether new or ongoing, performs a coordinating function by providing the frame within which policies can be elaborated by the key policy actors involved in the construction of the policy programme. The frame provided by the discourse generally offers a common language through which the different groups central to the policy process can talk to

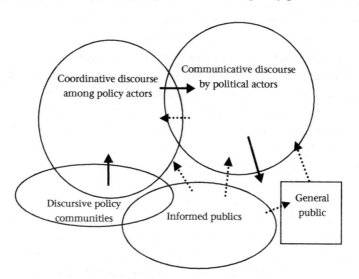

Fig. 5.2 The flow of ideas and discourse among actors in the policy process

Solid arrows show direction of ideas and discourse, dotted arrows show feedback, overlap shows where some actors may operate in both spheres.

one another and a common vision in terms of which they can iron out their differences. These policy actors normally consist of national governmental actors, both politicians and civil servants, along with, depending upon the institutional context, leaders of major interest groups, the heads of business associations and unions, sub-national government officials, and other significant actors such as government-appointed experts or publicly notable personalities. Their discussions serve as the forum in which a policy programme is constructed, that is, where policy ideas are articulated, developed, and deliberated; where the cognitive arguments about the programme's necessity are hammered out and the normative arguments about the programme's appropriateness evoked; where the policy instruments, objectives, and ideals are sketched out; where deals are negotiated, bargains struck, and conflicts worked out; and where implementation plans are laid out.

Although government officials and other key policy actors tend to be central to the construction of a discourse, they need not be the originators of the ideas informing the discourse, which may instead be the product of policy experts, scientists, university professors, think tanks, research institutes, the press, interest group leaders, electoral candidates, and even social movements. The interconnections between the actors central to policy construction and those central to the generation of the policy ideas are many and varied, since ideas 'do not float freely' (Risse-Kappen 1994) but are carried and conveyed by individuals with differing degrees of closeness to the policy process. These 'generators of ideas' may be loosely connected individuals united by a common set of ideas in 'epistemic communities' (Ruggie 1975; Haas 1992) such as the Europe-wide epistemic community focused on EMU (McNamara 1998; Verdun 1999; Marcussen 1998), the British epistemic community consisting of neo-liberal converts in the financial press, banking, economics, and the Conservative Party in the mid-1970s (Hall 1993), or the French epistemic community of the 'new' economists and philosophers on the right in the mid-1970s (Jobert and Thérèt 1994) which was joined on the left in the mid-1980s by proponents of the great U-turn in economic policy (Jabko 1999; see also Chapter 6). However, the ideas may be promoted by more closely connected individuals united by the attempt to put those ideas into action through 'advocacy coalitions' (Sabatier 1998; Sabatier and Jenkins-Smith 1993) or 'discourse coalitions' (Wittrock, Wagner, and Wollmann 1991), as in Germany in the early post-war period with the idea of the social market economy (see Lehmbruch 1999). But they may also be individuals who, as 'entrepreneurs' (DiMaggio 1986; Fligstein and Mara-Drita 1996; Finnemore and Sikkink 1998) or 'mediators' (Muller 1995), draw on and articulate the policy ideas of discursive communities and coalitions. This was the case of Jacques Delors with regard to the great U-turn in France and the Single

Market as well as EMU in the EU (Ross 1995; Fligstein and Mara-Drita 1996; Jabko 1999), and in early post-war Germany, of Alfred Müller-Armack, the man responsible for leading the discourse coalition centred on the social market economy (see Chapter 6).

Whatever the source of the ideas, however, policy actors are the key players in the coordinative discourse. It is they who, when confronted with crisis and/or made aware of it by new discursive communities or coalitions, bring to the table policy ideas promoted by those very communities or coalitions, of which they may be members. It is in this context that they engage in both arguing and bargaining (see Risse 2000) in their efforts to work together to build a common programme or to battle to impose their own. The parties to the coordinative discourse, after all, need not share all the same ideas, beliefs, and goals in order to promote a common policy programme. Instead, they may be united by agreement on certain policy objectives or the use of certain policy instruments, despite differing core ideals. They may agree on the cognitive justification for the policy programme but disagree over the normative arguments to use in legitimization. They may agree on an overall policy programme but disagree over the nature and range of its sectoral applications. Their interests may naturally be different, but they may nevertheless agree on the institutional arrangements to be set up to arbitrate among those interests (see Jobert 2001). The balance of power among key policy actors, moreover, may entail that, even where disagreement exists on a wide range of questions, the least powerful will agree to the majority's preference on policy programme in exchange for certain concessions.

However, whatever the initial disagreements, once a new policy programme is agreed, it is likely to become the framework for the future coordinative discourse among policy actors. But this is possible only if the communicative discourse is also successful. Although discursive communities and entrepreneurs along with the policy actors in the coordinative discourse tell us a lot about the discursive construction of policy programmes, to stop here is to assume that elite interactions alone explain policy outcomes. This is only one piece in a larger puzzle.

The Communicative Stage of Discourse

It is one thing to coordinate the construction of a discourse by building agreement on a policy programme among key policy actors central to the policy-making process, another to communicate it successfully to the public at large, which is the essential criterion for a shift in policy programme. And for this one needs political actors, politicians as well as those tied to them as spokespersons, spin doctors, handlers, campaign managers, speech writers, and others in the political process, who win elections in democracies primarily on the basis of their communicative skills and who are in the business of marketing the policy programme that will guarantee them not just election but re-election.[19] It is often in the electoral process that key political actors present the central ideas and underlying values of the policy programme in a manner accessible to the larger public, providing it with a new frame of reference within which they can understand and interpret events, and a clear picture of what can be done.[20] From the point of view of the public, this communicative aspect of the discourse responds to its need for a sense of orientation with regard to the country's present and future and for a sense of legitimacy with regard to government policy.

This public communication by political actors is where the overall outlines of the policy programme may be most clearly articulated. This is where the ideas developed in the coordinative realm by key policy actors, among them many of these self-same political actors, are translated into the communicative realm. The overall outlines of the policy programme are given expression in a 'master' discourse by a 'master' politician, generally the president or prime minister once elected, while the sectoral applications are presented in sectoral discourses by the other members of government. Ludwig Erhard was clearly the key political actor who gave expression to the master discourse of the social market economic programme in Germany in the 1950s; De Gaulle, for the *dirigiste* discourse and programme in France in the 1960s; and Thatcher, for the neo-liberal discourse and programme in Britain in the 1980s (see Chapter 6). Their ministers were the ones to give expression to the sectoral discourses that followed from the master discourse and which were often developed in conjunction with them, if not dictated by them.

This is also where the coherence of a discourse may be most clearly seen, since key political actors' pronouncements can enhance or diminish the appearance of coherence. And the more coherent the government's communicative discourse as well as the clearer the picture it provides the public, the more likely the public will see events from that point of view (Zaller 1992: 8–9). However, whether the party or coalition in power can present a single image to the public depends upon many things, not only on the quality and coherence of the ideas developed at the coordinative stage of the discourse

[19] Because of the law of anticipated reaction or the notion of the 'fleet in being', politicians adopt discourses that are constructed in such a way as to be normatively and not just cognitively acceptable, and therefore to be potential national discourses rather than simply the ideas of a technocratic or academic elite (Scharpf 1997*b*).

[20] On how political elites influence the public, see, for example, Zaller (1992); Mutz, Sniderman, and Brody (1996).

but also, equally importantly, on the leadership's control over its own members, whether in government or in parliament. This is something Blair in Britain has been past master at, as he has insisted on vetting everything that comes out of key ministers' offices, and Jospin in France has also been rather good at, as he has orchestrated his ministers' public pronouncements on significant topics while leaving them free on a range of other issues. Both are in great contrast to Schröder in Germany, at least in his first year in office, when he had little control over his ministers, not only over coalition members but even those in his own party, in particular over his Minister of Finance Oskar Lafontaine (see Chapter 6).

The success of a new policy discourse, then, is predicated upon its ability to offer arguments that convince not only policy-makers but also the public. But this is not always possible, since, however good the arguments, the public may weary of the discourse while waiting for the policy programme to deliver the promised pay-offs. In this case, the success of a policy programme may be ensured by public attention being distracted for a time by other kinds of discourse that focus on other kinds of issues of popular import—for example, military, moral, cultural. Sometimes, these come up conveniently to save a politico-economic discourse and policy programme in trouble, ensuring re-election for a government that might have lost on the basis of public perceptions of its performance at that particular juncture. In Britain, for example, Thatcher's neo-liberal economic discourse was eclipsed for a while in the aftermath of the Falklands War by her more militaristic incantations of past British military glory and memories of Empire, which helped usher the Tories back into office—although a divided opposition was the main factor—despite public disenchantment at the time with the policies linked to the politico-economic discourse. The relationship between a discourse and elections, in other words, is contingent. Such a wide range of factors could explain winning—or losing—elections that politicians' discourse can naturally only be one piece in a very large and complex puzzle.

The need to communicate with the public is nonetheless central to the survival not only of the policy programme supported by the discourse but also of the political actors who depend for re-election at least in part on the public acceptance of that programme. Although policy change can be imposed even without a communicative discourse—for example, where the coordinative discourse substitutes for it (see below) or where a policy is instituted without any discussion whatsoever (see above)—the legitimizing aspects of the communicative discourse are generally necessary for the policy programme's long-term acceptance and survival.

At this communicative stage, moreover, there is also a deliberative element. Policy elites do not just tell the public what the policy programme is all about; they also listen, and adjust the programme where necessary in response to public opinion. To ensure public acceptance, the policy programme promoted by government through its communicative discourse tends to become the subject of a broader policy discussion in society generally engaged in by the 'policy forums' that serve as the institutional vehicles for debates on public policy issues (Rein and Schön 1991). This informed public consists of opinion leaders such as newspaper editorialists, television commentators, corporate executives, opposition party members, labour leaders, policy experts in universities and think-tanks, heads of major interest groups, party activists, members of public interest organizations, civic action groups, social movements, churches, and so forth. And it is also made publicly accessible through open meetings, newspaper articles, election campaigns, the Internet, and so on. This is where policy programmes and/or their sectoral applications developed generally outside of public view in the 'closed debates' among policy elites, experts, and 'attentive publics' are put to the test in the 'open debates' that take place in the public sphere when an issue has gained public attention (Guiraudon 1997). This is where the discursive policy communities that may or may not have had an influence on policy construction at the coordinative stage of discourse get another chance to have an impact, this time by influencing the general public and, thereby, key policy and political actors—as members of the informed public (see Fig. 5.2). And here, too, therefore, the policy programme as much as the discourse may be modified in response to the reactions of this 'public of organized private persons' or the 'bourgeois public sphere' (Habermas 1989).

Public discussion within the context of the communicative discourse ensures not just the widest possible dissemination of information about the policy programme but, even more importantly, the widest possible debate about it. Any monopolistic control or monolithic approach can be problematic, since critical stances are often helpful in clarifying the issues and even modifying positions (March and Olsen 1995: 82–3). Criticism, as long as it brings reasoned responses from the policy elites involved in policy construction and implementation, may be vital to ensuring the legitimacy and viability of the policy paradigm. Moreover, the lack of criticism does not necessarily signal acceptance or agreement; it may merely hide disagreement and make it more difficult for government to gain a sense of the fault lines. Moreover, it can undermine democracy since it may leave the public vulnerable to the political extremes on the right as much as the left able to take advantage of the silence for populist or demagogic purposes. In France, for example, the taboo on criticism of EMU enforced by mainstream parties of the left and the right from the end of the Maastricht debates to the 1997 election campaign left the field entirely open to the only voices talking about the dangers of European integration, in particular on the extreme right.

The quality of the deliberation and the quantity of participation also matters. On quality—if we leave aside such imponderables as speakers' persuasive powers based on rhetorical eloquence or psychological 'interactivity' with other interlocutors—much depends upon how much the interlocutors plumb the depths of the cognitive and normative arguments developed at the coordinative stage of discourse. On quantity, as Habermas (1992a,b) argues, the more general the discussion, the more likely that what starts out as government commitment can become a national conviction and even be accepted as part of 'public truth'. 'Public truth' is one of the normative requirements of a non-coercive public discourse in Habermas' definition of discursive democracy, as a necessary component of the ideal democratic state which underlies the 'interpretive communities' within which mutual understanding is to emerge (Habermas 1992a: 449). Adopting this concept is admittedly problematic for our purposes, since it is more prescriptive than descriptive of the empirical role of discourse in contemporary democracy, which is my focus here. It also tends to idealize public participation by assuming that a communicative discourse characterized by wide-ranging public deliberation will always lead to more progressive outcomes. There are in fact cases where issues have been better left to the coordinative realm than the communicative. In immigration policy, for example, in countries where the discussion went beyond the closed debates or coordinative discourses of policy-makers into the open and highly politicized debates of the more general public, no amount of communicative discourse by the government could succeed in convincing the public of the value of more progressive immigration policy (Guiraudon 1997, 2000). Moreover, politicians have time and again not made public all the potential problems of a policy programme for fear that what was necessary would not be done. But the concept is nonetheless part of the basic values of democratic polities and useful as one of the measures by which the public judges communicative discourse, despite the fact that it is not always truthful—if policy-makers don't tell the truth, or at least the whole truth—not always generally accepted—which often takes time—and not always a good thing—since it may go against unpopular but progressive measures.

Communication of a truth-oriented nature is key not simply to the marketing of a discourse, in short, but to the maintenance of democracy. Discourse is one of the essential elements of democratic politics, helping to hold a democracy together by giving the population a sense of joint purpose and meaning, to counter narrow self-interest in favour of a more common interest, to support long-standing interests, institutions, and culture, or to alter them. Moreover, politicians' pursuit of public acceptance of a policy programme through discourse is at the very foundations of representative democracy, with elections most often the way to consecrate a discourse or bury it. Whatever the cognitive and normative commitments of the policy elite, in a democracy they must be able successfully to communicate these to the larger public as they coordinate the elaboration and implementation of the policies with relevant policy players. But there is nothing inevitable about discourse. Although there is always discourse, nations at any given time may have better or worse discourses, meaning that some may be better able than others to generate and legitimize policies promoting change or continuity. Moreover, although there are always both coordinative and communicative discourses, most countries tend to emphasize one or the other, depending on institutional context, with the concomitant benefits from the strength of the one and the problems from the weakness of the other.

Where Discourse Matters: The Institutional Context of Policy Discourse

Although all countries have both coordinative and communicative discourses, the balance in favour of one or the other tends to depend largely on the institutional context which frames the discursive process, determining who articulates the discourse, how it is articulated, and towards whom it is primarily directed. Generally speaking, the degree of concentration or dispersion of power and authority affects how restricted or extensive is the set of policy actors involved in coordinating the construction of the policy programme and whether the focus of policy actors is more on communicating with the public than with one another (see Table 5.5). Simply stated, where the concentration of power is high, as in single-actor systems such as France and Britain, the coordinative discourse tends to be thin and the communicative discourse more elaborate than where power is dispersed, as in multi-actor systems such as Germany and the EU, in which the coordinative discourse tends to be more elaborate than the communicative. Complicating this even further, however, is that where the EU level of policy-making intermingles with the national, the coordinative discourse becomes more elaborate for both national single-actor and multi-actor systems, even as the communicative discourse remains largely what it was, given the absence of a significant EU-level communicative discourse.

Table 5.5 Coordinative and communicative discourse in single- and multi-actor systems

Discourse	Institutional context	
	Single-actor system	Multi-actor system
Coordinative discourse	Thin	Elaborate
Communicative discourse	Elaborate	Thin

National Single-Actor Governance Systems

In countries where power and authority are concentrated in the executive, with majoritarian electoral systems, statist policy-making processes, and unitary states, the coordinative discourse tends to be quite thin. Policy construction tends to be the product of a restricted, government-centred set of policy actors—whether a governmental-technocratic elite as in France or a governing party elite as in Britain—who tend to formulate policies largely absent outside input—whether of the larger party, the opposition, the social partners, subnational governments, or other societal interests. Here, although the ideas may originate in an epistemic community and be promoted by a discourse coalition or advocacy coalition, the policy mediator is most often a government-related actor who coordinates the construction of the policy programme and has the greatest resources with regard to expertise. In the modernization of the French economy, for example, the policy mediators were the sectoral governmental actors who translated the more general modernizing ideas expressed in the master discourse into sectoral policies, aided by the higher level civil servants of the *grands corps de l'État* who have a monopoly on expertise (Jobert and Muller 1987; Jobert 2001).

By the same token, however, the communicative discourse tends to be quite elaborate, since this is the principal way in which governments with the political institutional capacity to impose their policy initiatives seek to convince the public that their policy programmes are not only necessary but also appropriate, in order to win them over to their initiatives. In such 'single-actor' systems, debate and deliberation over major policy initiatives tends to go on in the wider public sphere, if at all, as policies formulated unilaterally by a small elite face public scrutiny (see Fig. 5.3).

In this context, governments generally try to speak in one voice and, thereby, to project a sense of coherence and vision in policy programme as

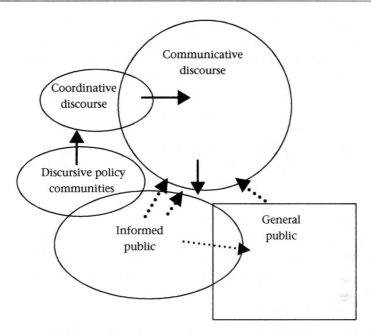

Fig. 5.3 The flow of ideas and discourse in single-actor systems

Solid arrows show direction of ideas and discourse, dotted arrows show feedback, overlap shows where some actors may operate in both spheres.

well as to promote the public impression of a government that knows what it is doing and doing what it promised. In Britain, given a single-party system elected on the basis of first-past-the-post majoritarian elections, this is easier than in France, given a two-round majoritarian election system that always produces coalition governments and often even different majorities for president and prime minister, in cases of *cohabitation*. Thus, the main 'communicator' in Britain is the prime minister, although Thatcher and Blair were better able to project a sense of coherence than Major, with his thin majority and his difficulties in maintaining party discipline in particular with regard to the Eurosceptics. In France, by contrast, although the main communicator was originally expected to be the president alone—de Gaulle, given that the Constitution of the Fifth Republic was written with him in mind—it inadvertently allowed for the communicative discourse to be split into two voices where the prime minister was of a different party—for example, between President Mitterrand and Prime Minister Chirac in the mid-1980s and beginning in the late 1990s between President Chirac and Prime Minister Jospin—or even more, given government coalition members' separate, although generally complementary, discourses.

But whether the government speaks in many voices or few, the public itself has very little voice in debate and deliberation in anything other than an adversarial manner. Because there is typically relatively little consultation with the most affected interests or open discussion at the coordinative stage of the discourse, the only course of action left at the communicative stage if the public and/or interest groups are opposed to a policy is protest. This may be in words—by way of polemics by the informed public consisting of the press, interest group leaders, experts, and/or the opposition—or in action, most immediately through demonstrations and strikes—mainly France—or more delayed, through sanctions imposed by the general public at election times—in Britain, given its less confrontational tradition. It is this public reaction, moreover, which leads governments to decide whether to persist with the policy or withdraw it, whether to accommodate the concerns of the most affected interests or to risk electoral defeat and/or confrontation in the streets. Where the societal opposition to the policy is low, the government's policy ideas are implemented with little change, as in the case of monetary policy under Thatcher or private pension reforms under Balladur; where it is high, the ideas are not likely to be implemented, as in Thatcher's plans to partially privatize health care financing or Juppé's plans to reduce public pension benefits.[21]

In certain policy sectors, though, this overall pattern of thin coordinative and thick communicative discourse led mainly by the government no longer characterizes discursive interactions. Liberalization, deregulation, Europeanization, and labour market decentralization have all reduced the government's central communicative role as it has reduced the scope of its powers. In its place, in France in particular, business has gained a clearer communicative voice in its adversarial stance against the governments' welfare and employment measures—replacing the opposition—while the Jospin government's attempts to encourage greater concertation among the social partners in labour policy and pension policy has increased the importance of the coordinative discourse, although not necessarily its success rate. In Britain, by contrast, the liberalizing reforms have shifted the locus of the coordinative discourse from government to privatized firms which now talk more to independent regulators and to decentralized labour, which has also largely lost its communicative voice. In both countries, therefore, reforms have brought the countries closer to multi-actor systems; but the differences remain ones in kind rather than degree, since where the government retains power and authority the communicative discourse remains predominant.

---

[21] On Britain, see Walsh (2000a); on France, see Levy (2000).

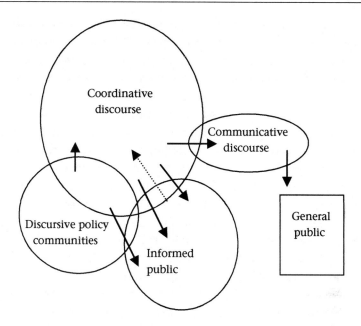

Fig. 5.4 The flow of ideas and discourse in multi-actor systems

Solid arrows show direction of ideas and discourse, dotted arrows show feedback, overlap shows where some actors may operate in both spheres.

National Multi-Actor Governance Systems

In countries where power and authority is more dispersed, with proportional representation systems, corporatist policy-making processes, and/or federal states, the coordinative discourse tends to be more elaborate and the communicative discourse quite thin, since the coordinative discourse is the principal way in which governments which lack the institutional capacity to impose reform manage to negotiate change with the wide range of actors involved through a process of mutual persuasion about the policy programme's necessity and appropriateness.[22] In such multi-actor systems, therefore, debate and deliberation over major policy initiatives tends to go on mainly behind closed doors, among the very policy actors involved in the elaboration of the policy programme, who are focused on agreeing among themselves and then on persuading their constituencies—as members of the informed public—that the agreement is acceptable according to those constituencies' own particular cognitive and normative criteria (see Fig. 5.4).

---

[22] The one exception is Switzerland in cases of referendums, where the decisions taken in the context of coordinative discussions must then be legitimized in public, through communicative discourses (Bonoli and Mach 2000; Schmidt 2000*b*).

Policy construction tends to be the product of a wide cross-section of policy actors encompassing not only governmental political and technocratic elites but also the social partners—as in Germany and the smaller consociational democracies like Denmark, Austria, and the Netherlands—sub-national governments—as in federal systems such as Germany, Belgium to an even greater extent, and Austria to a lesser extent—and even opposition parties—as in Germany. Here, the originators and promoters of the ideas, whether as part of epistemic communities, discourse coalitions, or advocacy coalitions, may incorporate the policy mediator, who in turn may be connected to any one of the numbers of policy actors involved in policy construction, governmental or non-governmental, each of which may have its own sources of expertise through research institutes, networks of experts, and so on. In Germany, the coordinative discourse is generally the product of the government in conjunction with coalition partners, the opposition—especially if it holds the majority in the Bundesrat, the upper house—sub-national governments—via the Bundesrat or directly—the social partners, and other relevant organized interests. In wage-bargaining, however, the coordinative discourse has been loosely coordinated between the Bundesbank, which before the euro set targets, and the regionally patterned bargaining of the social partners in the *Tarifautonomie* system, leaving government-related actors on the sidelines.

Within this context, therefore, the bulk of debate and deliberation with the citizenry comes through the 'sub-discourses' of policy elites discussing with their own constituencies the results of the negotiations while leaving to the government the task of communicating the results of the compromise in more vague terms to the general public. As a result, the communicative discourse is necessarily thin, since the compromises reached in private may not withstand public scrutiny. They risk being unravelled if made public because they are likely to violate to some extent the ideas and/or values contained in the different groups' sub-discourses. Such a discourse is therefore unlikely to provide the public with significant orienting or legitimizing information beyond what it may have obtained as members of constituent groups, let alone to develop into some kind of 'public truth' in the Habermasian sense.[23]

But however open or closed to the public, the coordinative discourse is generally cooperative.[24] In Germany, in fact, although the outcome of the discussions is typically consensus, the process itself may entail a great deal of conflict, especially at the outset, as each of the parties to the discussion sets

[23] On the range of problems stemming from a lack of inclusiveness or transparency in the coordinative discourse, see Schmidt (2000*b*).

[24] But see Schmidt (2000*b*) for the many different ways in which such cooperation is manifest.

out its position. Such conflict may remain private, as it sometimes does in the case of policy agendas worked out among government coalition partners, or it may spill out into the public sphere, as it often does in particular in the case of government and opposition or business and labour at the preliminary stages of wage bargaining. Among the social partners, in fact, tremendous verbal conflict and public posturing and threats characterize what happens outside the meetings—which is also a way for policy elites to gauge public attitudes and factor these into their negotiating positions—but cooperation characterizes the closed meetings, especially as compromise draws near—such that the whole process has been termed 'antagonistic cooperation' (Scharpf 1991: 117; Lehmbruch 1978). The resulting consensus between the social partners, moreover, is upheld by a rigid legal framework to ensure that the consensus holds, and to preserve order and stability in the labour relations system as a whole (Heinisch 1999). In the case of coalition governments, the consensus is ensured by the threat of government collapse, whereas, in the case of agreements between government and opposition, it is more often the fear of electoral sanction that guarantees continued cooperation, given a public which expects cooperation to produce effective action.

In multi-actor systems, in short, the coordinative discourse tends to be the more elaborate and important stage of discourse than the communicative, which tends to be much thinner. Only in election periods is the communicative discourse significant. Here, it often is used to persuade the public of the necessity and appropriateness of the policy programme generated within the context of the coordinative discourse—however open or closed—and implemented by government. But rather than serving to legitimize the policy programme after the fact, it may instead work at cross-purposes with any continued coordinative discourse, since the adversarial pronouncements of the political parties in the heat of the election campaign are likely to hinder cooperation in the coordinative discussions behind closed doors among government coalition partners and/or with the opposition. This was certainly the case in Germany in the year running up to the September 1998 federal elections for the Bundestag, when the Social Democrats were unwilling to compromise in expectation of electoral victory, and in the succession of *Land* elections for the Bundesrat following the federal elections, when the Christian Democrats were unwilling to compromise in the expectation of gaining the majority in the Bundesrat.

At critical moments, however, when the coordinative discourse breaks down, the communicative discourse can play a key, positive role by providing a new frame within which policy actors can reconstruct the coordinative discourse and, thereby, re-conceptualize their interests and reassess their values.

Under such circumstances, governments in multi-actor systems may use the communicative discourse in a manner similar to that in single-actor systems, in an effort to persuade the public and the most affected interests of a better course of action. But, unlike in single-actor systems, the government may not have the power to impose that course of action, but just to exhort all parties to the debate to come to the table. In Germany, Schröder has so far been unsuccessful in coming up with such a new frame, as noted earlier, try as he might through borrowing from British and French discourses, leaving key groups of policy actors closed in their separate sub-discourses without a renewed common language and framework within which to re-conceptualize their interests or reassess their values. Other multi-actor systems, by contrast, have been much more successful, such as the Netherlands with regard to the reform of work in the early 1980s and of welfare in the early 1990s,[25] or Italy with regard to industrial relations and pension reform after 1992.[26]

The Supranational Multi-Actor Governance System of the European Union

The European Union, as a supranational, multi-actor governance system, shares many characteristics with national multi-actor systems. As at the national level, so at the EU level, a wide range of policy actors, governmental as well as non-governmental, negotiate the construction of policy programmes through an elaborate coordinative discourse. In most political economic sectors, the negotiations involve a complex system of Commission-organized discussions among experts, interest groups, governmental representatives, lobbyists, and the like—'comitology'—together with deliberations in the Council of Ministers and debates in the European Parliament, and thus are best described as 'supranational governance' (Sandholz and Zysman 1989). Only in treaty negotiations and in a few sectors such as security and defence could one argue that the coordinative discourse is more akin to that of single-actor systems, where governments are the primary policy actors able to impose decisions—and where intergovernmentalism still rules (Moravcsik 1993a). But even in the security and defence domain, the governmental actors are many rather than one, and must negotiate agreements with one another in such a way that, at least since the great breakthrough in St Malo in 1998, the coordinative discourse can be termed not so much intergovernmentalism any more but rather 'supranational intergovernmentalism' (Howorth 2000).

---

[25] See Visser and Hemerijck (1997); Cox (2001); Schmidt (2000b).
[26] See Ferrera and Gualmini (2000); Schmidt (2000b; 2002a).

The ideas informing these EU coordinative discourses also come from sources similar to those found in national multi-actor systems. The EU benefits from epistemic communities or advocacy coalitions in ever-growing numbers of sectors, such as in central banking and monetary policy, as noted above, where the ties between European and national policy-makers are particularly close, and where the national-level policies are tightly linked to the European.[27] The Commission not only benefits from the ideas of existing Europe-wide epistemic communities, however; it also seeks to create such discursive communities. This has been the case, for example, of the recently proposed decentralization of certain aspects of competition authority to national courts, where one highly placed official described the Competition Directorate as seeking to establish something like an epistemic community of judges with a view to building a common competition policy culture and set of practices across Europe even without a central set of European Court of Justice (ECJ) or Competition Directorate decisions in the area.[28] Similarly, moreover, one could argue that in employment policy the open coordination model represents a way of creating a kind of discursive community which, instead of recommending actual policy programmes, promotes the kind of 'social learning' or apprenticeship that had been going on in monetary policy since the 1980s, as evidenced by the process of mimesis in practices and, as we have already seen, in language (Palier 2000).

In social policy, however, the Commission has not only sought to build the networks of experts necessary for an epistemic community, it has also acted as a policy entrepreneur (Cram 1993), most recently by seeking to articulate the ideas for a 'European Social Model'. With regard to women's issues as well, it has been a policy entrepreneur in creating the very interest groups with which to develop the ideas on equality it then conveyed to the other EU policy actors, including the ECJ for enforcement (Mazey 1995). In agriculture, moreover, the Commission has even been described as a 'constrained political entrepreneur' because of its role not simply in representing a range of policy ideas to other actors involved in the coordinative realm but also in negotiating agreements with member states as well as foreign governments, in the context of the GATT (Fouilleux 2001).

The European Union's coordinative discourse, however, is complicated by the fact that it is multi-level (see Kohler-Koch 1996; Marks, Hooghe, and Blank 1996) as well as multi-actor. Many of its policy actors are also engaged in national coordinative discourses and many of its ideas come from experts

---

[27] Mazey and Richardson (1996); Kohler-Koch (1997: 99–101); Verdun (1999); Sabatier (1998); Marcussen (1998).   [28] Interview with author, Brussels, June 2000.

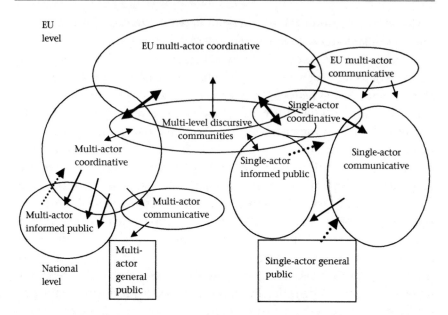

Fig. 5.5 The flow of ideas and discourse in EU supranational multi-actor system

Solid arrows show direction of ideas and discourse, dotted arrows show feedback, overlap shows where some actors may operate in both spheres.

in EU-level discursive communities who also operate in national ones. More-over, the patterns of interaction with national level actors differ depending upon whether the national institutional context is single- or multi-actor, complicating national-level discourse, but in different ways—too complicated to elaborate here except through illustration (see Fig. 5.5). To take just one example, in single-actor systems the coordinative discourse may continue to exclude policy actors at the national level who participate in coordinative discussions at the EU level.[29] In France, for example, business has become a major partner of government at the EU level even though at the national-level government still maintains its traditional distance (Schmidt 1996; 1999c).

But while the EU multi-actor, multi-level discourse is highly elaborate and complicated, given the two-level or even three-level—in the case of regional policy—game it involves, the EU-level communicative discourse is very thin—even thinner than that of national multi-actor systems. The problems are obvious: without a single language, a Europe-wide system for European Parliament elections, strong European parties, a European president, a European identity and culture, let alone a European polity, the EU-level

[29] On the implications of this for national governance practices and democracy, see Schmidt (2002b).

discourse simply cannot have the same kind of legitimizing power as the national discourse. Although the president of the Commission ordinarily speaks for the EU, it is one among many voices—and a parallel voice rather than a stronger or louder one at that when it comes to the Council of Ministers. In fact, it is from national leaders that much of the EU-level discourse is heard, whether they speak as members of the EU for all member states—especially when President of the European Council—or for themselves and their own national publics. But here again, there are significant differences in impact on single-actor and multi-actor national systems, with single-actor systems again the most affected (see Schmidt 2002*b*). This is because whereas most legitimization in multi-actor systems comes through deliberations within the context of the coordinative discourse, in single-actor systems most legitimization comes through the communicative discourse, which is made especially difficult when EU policies do not fit well with national policy legacies and preferences. In telecommunications and electricity, for example, the EU-led reforms in Germany needed little communicative discourse, since all parties to the negotiations in both sectors had already convinced one another of the appropriateness of liberalizations that went much farther than EU demands. By contrast, the French government has had a hard time with its communicative discourse in both sectors, whether to persuade the public that extensive liberalization was appropriate in telecommunications or to convince it that it was protecting the public service mission in electricity despite partial liberalization (see Chapter 2).

The absence of a Europe-wide communicative discourse also adds confusion to the national-level communicative discourse. This is because national political actors are the primary interlocutors at one and the same time for the EU to the country and for the country to the EU. As such, at the same time as they mostly speak positively about European integration in their very different communicative discourses on the EU, they also may use the EU to push through policies they would not otherwise have been able to. This has been especially the case with regard to monetary integration for a number of countries—for example, Italy, Belgium, and Greece—mainly as a function of the 'paradox of weakness' (Grande 1996), where they used the EU in the discourse as the '*vincolo esterno*', or compelling external constraint, to overcome resistance to reform (Featherstone 2001*b*). But it has also been true for a number of public service sectors—as we have seen for France with regard to telecommunications, Germany for electricity, and Britain and Germany for rail transport. Although in many cases reform has been facilitated by this blame-shifting approach, it can backfire if the public begins to perceive the

EU as bringing unwelcome change—as in Denmark in the recent referendum on the euro or Ireland with regard to the Treaty of Nice.

In short, as the EU increases the spread of ideas and the span of its coordinative discourse, it expands member states' coordinative discourse and increases the pressures on the communicative. But again, this differs according to country, a function of institutional context as well as, of course, of national ideas and values. The impact of such discourse, however, also varies.

When Discourse Matters: The Causal Influence of Policy Discourse

In what has come before, we have seen *how* discourse matters to changing economic policies and practices, by exploring the ways in which discourse has promoted continuity and/or change in policy programmes, and *where* it matters, that is, at what point in the discursive process it is most developed in different institutional contexts. But can we know *when* it truly matters, that is, when it is more than simply a reflection of interests, path dependence, or cultural norms; when it goes beyond these to alter perceptions of interest, to chart new institutional paths, and to create new cultural norms?

Discourse vs. Culture, Institutions, and Interests as Causes

Showing that policy discourse exerts causal influence is not simple. First of all, the ideas articulated by a discourse cannot easily be separated from the interests which find expression through them, from the institutional interactions which shape their expression, or from the cultural norms that frame them. Culturally specific conceptions colour the manner in which new ways of doing and thinking develop, are articulated, and are adopted in any given country; and they set the limits to the transferability of new ideas (Katzenstein 1996*b*). Thatcher's neo-liberalism worked in Britain because it resonated in a culture that has traditionally valued a limited state and liberal economic principles. But this could not be transposed 'as is' to France, despite the best efforts of neo-liberal ideologues beginning in the early 1980s, given the continuing importance of the role of the state in the political imagination (Schmidt 1996: Ch. 5).

Institutions, however, also matter. While cultures may make policy elites blind to the possibilities of new ideas, institutions may limit their receptivity (see Héritier, Knill, and Mingers 1996) or their 'administrative viability' (Hall 1989: 373–5), affecting whether they will be adopted and how they will be adapted. Together, culture and institutions help explain, for example, why the development of the national railway system was state-led in France, where policy elites not only had the capacity to intervene but also believed state intervention was necessary and appropriate, while in the United States the railway system was developed by private actors, where only limited state action was possible and assumed appropriate (Dobbin 1994).

Interests, of course, matter too, since these can derail the most strongly supported sets of ideas even if the institutions are receptive and the culture compatible. And no amount of discourse will succeed in promoting a new policy programme where it does not address the interests of societal groups, in particular powerful groups. This could simply mean giving voice to such interests. But more likely it also means attempting to overcome entrenched interests by altering perceptions of interest not only cognitively, by arguing that change is necessary and in the best—material—interests of all, but also normatively, by arguing that change is in the public interest—or common good—and therefore the appropriate thing to do. This—ultimately—worked in the case of Thatcher's neo-liberal programme and initially for the Socialists' neo-Keynesian expansionism in France. But, as noted above, when in France the policy programme did not deliver what it promised, proving to be neither in the best economic interests of the country nor in the political interests of the governing party, the Socialists abandoned the discourse along with the policy programme.

For discourse to have a significant influence in the adoption of a policy programme, in short, it must be able to help policy actors overcome entrenched interests, institutional obstacles, and cultural blinkers to change. But while this may help explain why and how a given policy programme is adopted, it does not explain why an opening to a new discourse and policy programme occurs in the first place. For this, we need to set the new policy discourse and programme against a background that takes into account, first, the precipitating events that create enough uncertainty to leave an opening to ideas and values that challenge the predominant ones; second, the eroding interest coalitions in response to crisis that increase receptivity to the discursive re-conceptualization and reconfiguration of interests; third, the loosening institutional constraints to change in the face of crisis and interest realignments that allow new institutional paths to be considered; and fourth, the questioning of cultural norms in the midst of crisis, interest realignment, and institutional redefinition that lead to new rules of action.

Finally, the precipitating events, eroding interest coalitions, loosening institutional constraints, and cultural questioning that create the background conditions for change cannot on their own explain it. For this, we also need to consider such mediating factors (outlined in Chapter 2) as a country's degree of economic vulnerability to external economic forces, its political institutional capacity to impose or negotiate reform, its long-established policy legacies, and its long-standing policy preferences in addition to the discourse that enhances the capacity to reform by convincing the public of the necessity and appropriateness of reversing policy legacies and policy preferences in the face of economic vulnerability.

As a consequence of the great variety of factors that come into play, discourse should be seen as one among a number of variables that affect change. But because it rests, as it were, on top of the other variables, enhancing political institutional capacity for change by affecting perceptions and preferences, it at the very least serves to 'enable' change (Diez 1999)—although it may even be the very variable or added influence that makes the difference. This it is likely to do through the re-conceptualization of long-standing notions of self-interest, the reframing of institutional rules and cultural norms, and the appeal to general interests over narrow self-interest.

However, discourse may just as easily be a mere accompaniment to policies that result from strategic bargaining among interests, as a mere epiphenomenon of the strategic interactions of policy elites intent on promoting their own self-interest and that of their constituencies. It may do little more than serve as a reinforcement of policies that follow long-established institutional paths, or as a reiteration or even reification of long-accepted cultural rules and norms. After all, policy elites are always talking. The question is: when is policy discourse more than just 'cheap talk'? When does it do more than simply express the negotiating positions of different parties to policy construction or the debating positions of different publics in policy forums? When is it, in the terms of the international relations negotiation literature, more 'arguing' than 'bargaining', where arguing is seen as a distinct mode of interaction to be differentiated from either the strategic bargaining of rational choice or the rule-guided behaviour of sociological institutionalism (see Risse 2000). When could one call policy discourse transformative rather than merely instrumental? In short, when is it more than the simple expression of interests by rational actors, of the path-dependent institutional interactions among collective actors, or of the cultural norms and values embedded in actors' everyday actions and identity?

The Causal Influence of Discourse in Institutional Context

To establish the causal influence of discourse, it is first necessary to establish where the discourse might exert its influence. This depends upon institutional context. In single-actor systems, where governments engage in a restricted coordinative discourse and a more elaborate communicative discourse in order to convince the public of the necessity and appropriateness of the reforms they have the capacity to impose, the causal influence of discourse is ascertainable subsequent to reform, in the responses of the public. This may be gauged through protests that derail a policy reform—even if this may sometimes merely show the power of entrenched interests, as has often been the case in France—or public quiescence—even if this may instead mean that the population was distracted by an overriding discourse in another arena, as in the case of Thatcher's election following upon the Falklands war. It may be established through elections that consecrate a discourse and policy programme by bringing a party to power or that bury one or both through the party's defeat—even though there are many other possible reasons for electoral success or failure, such as a divided opposition, unexpected events, or newly-breaking scandals. And it may be seen through shifts in public opinion and attitudes over time—even if this may be contingent on a variety of other factors, such as public views of a government's performance generally—or shifts in party positions and discourse, as opposition parties find themselves unable to win elections except after they have taken on board key elements of the previous government's discourse and/or policy programme—in particular the case of Blair.

In multi-actor systems, by contrast, where key policy actors engage in an elaborate coordinative discourse and a thinner communicative discourse in order to reach agreement on the necessity and appropriateness of the reforms they have the capacity at best to negotiate, the causal influence of discourse is ascertainable before reform in whether key policy actors actually reach agreement or not. Here, therefore, instead of looking for evidence of the causal influence of discourse in protests, elections, opinion polls, and attitude surveys of the public, one does better to delve into the negotiations among policy actors coordinating policy construction, their communications with their constituent members, and the opinions of policy elites and their constituents. Thus, the influence of discourse could be gauged by how fast or slowly all parties come to agreement—even though negotiations can be slowed up for a wide range of reasons, not the least of which are institutional arrangements that make for lengthy negotiations, as in Germany's complex federal structure and its sequenced wage bargaining system, or the communicative discourses during election periods that work at cross-purposes with the coordinative, as in Germany in the late 1990s. Its relative influence can even be established in the event of a failure of agreement, however, depending upon whether the impediments to agreement were many or few—for example, whether there is one deal-breaking issue or many, with almost total understanding or a complete lack of it among bargaining parties. The agreement's continuation over time, however, also attests to the discourse's causal influence, that is, whether subsequent elections result in the

victory or defeat of the negotiating political parties or, even without elections, whether the agreement unravels because of protest by the negotiating
parties' constituents or by the more general public.

After determining the locus of the potential influence of a discourse, it is
useful to try to control for as many variables as possible in order to establish
when discourse is a major factor without which we cannot understand
change. For this, we do well to compare reasonably matched sets of cases in
either single- or multi-actor systems, whether two countries with similar
background conditions in terms of events, interests, institutions, and/or
culture, or one country at different times where little other than the policy
discourse changes. France and Britain constitute the matched pairs of cases
in this study on the basis of similarities in many of the background conditions.[30] Although there were only superficial similarities in ideas, given
differences in national understandings of what neo-liberalism was and what
it entailed in terms of reform, there were significant similarities in events
because both countries suffered from severe economic crisis in the late 1970s
and early 1980s; in interests, since both were politically polarized between
right and left and economically divided between capitalists focused on neo-
liberal reform and labour pulling for more socialist and collectivist values; and
in institutions, with majoritarian electoral systems, a unitary state, and statist
policy-making processes, even if in Britain power is more concentrated than
in France. Germany is an example of a most different case at the same time as
it is illustrative of the different way in which discourse may exert a causal
influence. It has differed from both France and Britain in ideas through the
1980s and much of the 1990s, with the minimal influence of neo-liberalism;
in events, since economic crisis came only in the 1990s; in interests, because
there was much less polarization between right and left or division between
capitalist and labour interests; and in institutions, with proportional electoral
system, a federal state, and corporatist policy-making processes.

Britain under Thatcher provides the best case for the causal influence of
communicative discourse, while France prior to Jospin demonstrates the
effects of the lack of a sufficiently legitimizing communicative discourse.
Thatcher's neo-liberal discourse proved transformative, successfully justify-
ing her radically neo-liberal policy programme not only by elaborating on
the necessity of change due to the failures of past policies but also on their
appropriateness in terms of a new way of promoting traditional British liberal
values of individualism and a limited state. The success of the discourse
resulted not only from its cognitive and normative merits, however, but also

---

[30] For a similar approach to socioeconomic change in six countries, see Schmidt (2001b).

because it was based on a re-conceptualization of middle-class interests, along with policies that reinforced such interests. Its success was evident in the growing public acceptance of neo-liberal values with regard to the changing structure of the economy and work, although this was more mixed with regard to welfare. It was also clear from the continuation of the discourse and policy programme not just by the Conservatives under Thatcher's successor, John Major, but by 'New Labour' under Tony Blair, which was unable to win power until it had adopted major elements of the neo-liberal discourse along with the policy programme.

In France under governments of the left and the right between 1983 and 1997, the discourse was much less of a factor in explaining policy change. While governments' communicative discourses provided convincing cognitive arguments about the necessity of a moderate neo-liberal policy programme, with Europeanization to protect the country against the incursions of globalization, the normative arguments claiming to honour values of social solidarity were not persuasive. The expansion of the welfare state through the 1980s can be seen more as providing the interest-based incentives to ensure acquiescence from the most affected interests, that is, to buy off the workers through the expansion of unemployment and early-retirement programmes, than as the fulfilment of the socialists' normative commitments to social solidarity. The lack of a normatively legitimizing discourse able to reconcile neo-liberal policies with traditional social values became increasingly problematic beginning in the early 1990s, as recession and the Maastricht criteria reduced governments' capacity to use interest-based incentives to ensure social peace, and as the economic adjustments related to the neo-liberal policy programme and European monetary integration were seen increasingly to conflict with social solidarity, whether because of proposed cuts in social programmes or in the 'service public'. This was dramatically brought home with the 1995 strikes in response to reforms the Juppé government sought to impose without any communicative discourse at all. It was only with the Jospin government beginning in 1997 that a normatively legitimizing discourse focused on a balance between efficiency and equity seems to have been persuasive to the public, as is evident from the greater success at instituting welfare reform in a climate of greater social peace and government popularity.

Germany had none of the problems of France or Britain in the 1970s or 1980s, given a coordinative discourse that served cognitively and normatively to legitimize the policy programme of the social market economy. Only in the 1990s, as a result of the pressures of unification and globalization, has it encountered problems. However, the breakdown of the coordinative discourse beginning in the mid- to late 1990s has meant that, despite the need, there was been little movement on pension reform throughout the decade, in fact, not until 2001, or on increasing flexibility in labour relations. This is when a communicative discourse capable of reframing the coordinative could have exerted a causal influence on policy change in this multi-actor system. But it has not been forthcoming, since the Schröder government has not as yet managed to recast the traditional discourse of the social market economy in such a way as to reframe the coordinative discourse among the social partners, the *Länder*, and the opposition.

Conclusion

Discourse, in sum, has mattered to the adjustment process in all three countries, with its presence in many cases easing adjustment while its absence in many cases stymieing reform. Discourse has proven important to policy adjustment both ideationally, by representing a policy programme as conceptually sound—cognitive function—and resonating with national values—normative function; and interactively, by serving policy actors as the basis for constructing a policy programme—coordinative function—and political actors as the basis for persuading the larger public as to its merits—communicative function. Discourse encounters ideational problems when the policy programme it promotes can no longer solve the problems of the polity and/or when it can itself no longer coherently explain the necessity of the policy programme or convince of its appropriateness. And it generates interactive difficulties when it does not help key policy actors build towards agreement on a policy programme at the coordinative stage of the discourse or when it does not help key political actors satisfactorily legitimize the policy programme to the general public at the communicative stage. Institutional context also matters, however, since in single-actor systems the communicative discourse is the more important stage of the discourse, and therefore where it may exert a causal influence, whereas in multi-actor systems it is at the coordinative stage. In all of this, finally, Europeanization and to a lesser extent globalization are also significant: on the ideational dimension, they may challenge not only the ideas and values of a given policy arena but even those of the polity as a whole; on the interactive dimension, they alter who is involved in the coordinative discourse at the same time as they complicate the legitimizing function of the communicative discourse. In the following chapter, this will be illustrated through a more detailed account of the discursive trajectories of Britain, Germany, and France.

6

The Role of Discourse in the Political Dynamics of Adjustment in Britain, France, and Germany

Britain, France, and Germany have followed very different trajectories in their adjustment to globalization and Europeanization, both in policies and practices. This can be explained not only by reference to differences in levels of economic vulnerability to external forces, political institutional capacity to reform, policy legacies, and policy preferences, but also to the relative successes and failures of their policy discourses. Britain's early, radical move to neo-liberalism in its policies and to even greater market capitalism in its practices had much to do with a transformative discourse that convinced the public that change was both necessary and appropriate. France's somewhat later, more moderate neo-liberal reform of its state-led policies, along with the market-oriented transformation of its state-capitalist practices, owes much to a discourse that convinced the public of the necessity of such changes. But general public concern, in particular with regard to the social spillovers of the changes, ensured that further reforms long foundered on the lack a discourse capable of persuading the public of their appropriateness. Germany's very late neo-liberal reform of its 'enabling' policies and even later market-oriented regeneration of its managed capitalist practices are in part the result of the absence of a discourse capable of generating a consensus among policy actors and the general public that change was not only necessary but also appropriate.

Britain: Constructing a Transformative Discourse

British governments, starting with Thatcher, have been remarkably successful in constructing a legitimizing discourse that projects a convincing vision of Britain in and out of an integrating Europe while thoroughly in a globalizing world. Their pro-global stance, which has roots in the country's more open economic history, in conjunction with their moderately anti-European stance—until the Blair government—which enabled them to gain opt-outs from the Social Chapter of the Maastricht Treaty and from EMU, fitted in well with a neo-liberal discourse that propounded the roll-back of the state in all policy arenas—monetary, industrial, labour, and social. With regard to Europeanization, in fact, Britain's resistance to monetary integration finds as much justification in the discourse as its opposition to EU rules in industrial, labour, or social policies. With the May 1997 change in government, however, the discourse has been in the process of renewal, not only because the Blair government has largely abandoned the Conservatives' anti-Europe stance but also because it has sought to convince the public that 'New Labour' has taken a 'third way' between the left and the right, and is fulfilling many old Labour aspirations through new Thatcherite policy means.

The Post-war Paradigm and Discourse

In Britain, the early post-war period was characterized by a set of policy prescriptions from the Conservatives and Labour that were so close that they were seen as tweedledum and tweedledee, or 'Butskellism'—under Tory Prime Minister Macmillan, to refer to the fact that the policies of his Chancellor of the Exchequer, Robert Butler, were the same as those of the previous Labour Chancellor Hugh Gaitskell—that lasted from the 1950s to the 1970s. Whether the Conservatives or Labour were in power, a quasi-liberal political-economic policy programme held, where liberalism was apparent in the openness of the economy, the generally hands-off policies toward business, and the emphasis on voluntarism in management-labour relations. But it was only quasi-liberal given a more interventionist state which retained a large nationalized sector, engaged in experiments with French planning and Swedish-type social concertation, and periodically attempted to establish incomes policies or imposed wage controls.

The two political parties' policies were in fact quite close in both content and style, even if not in discourse. The Tory paternalists in control of the Conservative party until Thatcher's takeover in the mid-1970s conceived of conservatism as non-ideological, neither an 'ism' nor even an idea (Gilmour 1977: 121). They were imbued with a pre-capitalist ethic and the 'gentlemanly culture' where 'the pursuit of consensus acted as a brake on radical change and as a catalyst to accommodation'. They shared with the Labour 'gentlemen' not only a consensual policy style but also a disdain for business—despite the fact that the Conservatives were seen as the 'party of business' and that there was a faction of the Conservatives who were pro-capitalist—and a sense of mutual obligation to provide for community welfare (Hetzner 1999: 37–9). Moreover, their policy programme was little different from that of Labour in its neo-Keynesian macroeconomics and in its support for continuing public ownership and social welfare measures, although their discourse differed in emphasis and in imagery, given the paternalism of the Tory view versus the class-based, egalitarian language of Labour (Hetzner 1999: Ch. 1).

The differences in policy paradigms and discourse had crystallized by the 1970s, however. While Labour had moved to the left, with a more clearly socialist ideology and a policy programme promoting greater government intervention, corporatist industrial relations, and neo-Keynesian monetary policies, the Tories had moved to the right with a neo-liberal ideology that rejected socialism and corporatism in favour of monetarism and laissez-faire capitalism. But as the economic crisis of the mid-1970s progressed—once the Labour government's monetary policies proved so disastrous that it had to turn to the IMF to bail out the country and the experiment in corporatism failed, as the union's initial wage moderation in response to the government's appeal to the self-sacrificing 'spirit of Dunkirk' and 'to give a year to Britain' gave way to wide-scale strikes in the 'winter of discontent' of 1978–9—neo-liberalism increasingly gained ground. In many cases, influential supporters of planning and Keynesianism who came to believe in the importance of market forces and a more limited state developed the neo-liberal ideas which were then popularized through the publications of think tanks such as the Institute of Economic Affairs and the Centre for Policy Studies (Hayward and Klein 1994: 96–9), while the financial press played a major role in focusing dissatisfaction with the economic policies of the day and promoting monetarism (Hall 1993). Although the ideas developed by this 'epistemic community' were clearly not new, given the long history of economic liberalism in Britain going back to Adam Smith and the Scottish economists and more recently to those influenced by the work of Hayek, Friedman, and others, they came back renewed and reinvigorated in the New Right around Thatcher—who became party leader in 1975—and a number of her closest advisers, and in a form not seen before. With the election of Margaret Thatcher in 1979, Britain acquired a brand new discourse and programme that broke with the past.

The Radical Neo-Liberal Paradigm and Thatcherite Discourse

Thatcher quite consciously chose to articulate a neo-liberal ideology as a counter to Labour's 'socialist' and 'corporatist' ideology, which she abhorred, and to the Tory paternalists' wishy-washy approach to economics and govern-ance, which she disdained. With her confrontational style and its explicit rejection of consensus politics, her espousal of monetarism against previous governments' neo-Keynesian interventionism in the economy, and her emphasis on competitive capitalism as a counter to the cooperative capital-ism of Labour and the Tory paternalists, Thatcher sought to produce a revo-lution in her own party as much as in the polity. Thus, Thatcher, together with a few other conservative converts to neo-liberalism who saw themselves as 'outsiders', sought to impose their ideology on the party while ridding it of its consensual tendencies. Policy construction, in consequence, was a confid-ential affair, with the ideas coming from close allies in the Cabinet and hand-picked advisers in the 'Policy Unit' in the Prime Minister's office at 10 Downing Street. In battles internal to the Cabinet once in power, Thatcher was constantly fighting the 'wets', whom she saw as soft on state interven-tionism, on Europe, and on all those things about which she felt it was only appropriate to be 'dry'. In government, moreover, she was also waging war against the powerful civil service, which she held responsible for the wrong-headed economic policies of the post-war period. And although she did not succeed in politicizing the civil service or destroying its vaunted neutrality, as some have argued, Whitehall did change, with the rewards going to the more dynamic and efficient implementers of government efforts to roll back the state (Hennessey 1989).

In Britain, then, a paradigm change came about through the construction of a discourse and policy programme by a small political party elite that man-aged to capture first the party leadership and next the election, and then to impose its pro-market, anti-state programme via the strong state apparatus. But although Thatcher had the political institutional capacity simply to impose her pro-market, anti-state programme via the strong state apparatus, and little to fear from elections once the Social Democrats had seceded from the Labour Party, she nevertheless engaged in an elaborate communicative discourse with which she sought to persuade the general public that her neo-liberal programme was not only necessary to put the economy back on its feet but also appropriate. Thus, Thatcher sought to redefine core social and political values while revitalizing the economy, reforming the state, and forg-ing a broad cross-class coalition of support for such economic and political change (see S. Hall 1988).

Thatcher herself had a keen sense of the importance of communicating her policy programme to the public, and took every opportunity to do so. Thatcher's cognitive arguments were focused on convincing the public that 'there is no alternative' (TINA) to her economic policies, as she talked in her first electoral mandate in particular of the 'Revival of Britain'—the title of a collection of speeches—and the need to reverse the decline which had been the focus of much of the economic discourse of the 1960s and 1970s, contrasting her own monetarist paradigm with Ted Heath's earlier failed return to Keynesianism (Hall 1993: 290). In the campaign itself, she used a top advertising agency, Saatchi and Saatchi, to come up with a highly effective campaign slogan to get her ideas across, 'Labour isn't working', on a poster which showed a long, snaking queue at the labour office. Moreover, she presented her programme as revolutionary, not only as a break with past Tory and Labour practice but also as a way of 'breaking the consensus and tackling traditionally immune targets' such as the trade unions, local government, and nationalized industries (speech to the press 18 January 1984, cited in Hedetoft and Niss (1991).

Thatcher's normative arguments complemented the cognitive, and concentrated on persuading the public that her economic policies were appropriate because based on deep-seated values favouring a limited state and liberal economic principles (Marquand 1988), with their basis in deep-seated British values—even if these were more Methodist than Church of England, and more from the Midlands than central London. Thatcher also talked of the need to return to 'Victorian' values, which for her included the importance of hard work, self-reliance, living within one's income, helping one's neighbour, pride in country (interview with the BBC, 1983, cited in Hedetoft and Niss 1991). In addition, Thatcher defended the people's right 'to be unequal' and sought to convince the public that inequalities were necessary to encourage the 'spirit of entrepreneurship' and raise British economic performance, while government attempts to reduce inequalities were not only costly and ineffective but also dangerous because they created a dependency culture.[1] She was particularly insistent on the need for 'rolling back the frontiers of the Welfare State' and promoting an 'enterprise culture' in order 'to change Britain from a dependent to a self-reliant society. From a give-it-to-me to a do-it-yourself nation; to a get-up-and-go instead of a sit-back-and-wait-for-it Britain' (London Times, 9 February 1984). In keeping with this emphasis on self-reliance, instead of government being responsible for solving Britain's problems, she sought to shift the onus to the people (Riddell 1989: 1). And with regard to welfare recipients in particular, she insisted on distinguishing between the 'deserving' and the 'undeserving' poor when providing assistance (Thatcher 1993).

---

[1] See Evans and Taylor (1996); Wilding (1994); Leydier (1998).

Thatcher's policy paradigm, as with the Kuhnian notion of paradigm, was only vaguely sketched out initially. The discourse presented a set of neo-liberal ideas about what was to be done, which then were developed, sector by sector, largely on an experimental basis, with success in one area encouraging the move to the next. While certain policies were implemented in full, moreover, others were barely put into force, depending upon the centrality of the policy to the government's political-economic paradigm as well as the government's view of its potential electoral repercussions.

During her first mandate, Thatcher held true to the monetarist approach to economic management announced in the Conservative election manifesto of late 1977, titled *The Right Approach to the Economy*, which called for a 'virtuous circle' of low inflation resulting from sterling appreciation and income from North Sea oil—despite the fact that it did not turn the economy around nearly as quickly as she had forecast. Moreover, she paid little regard to business protests that the monetary policies, together with the concomitant major appreciation of the pound sterling, were sending them into bankruptcy—complaints which she dismissed as 'rubbish', claiming the problem instead to be firms' 'patchy' management and their having 'found it convenient to be regulated by government and saved by subsidies' (Holmes 1985: 155–6). Support for a quick lowering of inflation came instead from representatives of the City as well as the Institute of Directors (Walsh 2000*a*: 52–6).

Fortunately for Thatcher, continued poor economic performance was overshadowed by her great popularity in the aftermath of the Falklands War, with her militaristic incantations of past British military glory and nostalgia for the Empire as well as her claims that 'We have ceased to be a nation in retreat', given not only military victory but also the economic renewal to come from her economic policies, despite 'enemies within', that is, striking trade unions (cited in Lynch 1999: 57). This helped usher the Tories back into office—although the main electoral factor was the divided, unelectable opposition—despite public disenchantment with her neo-liberal politico-economic paradigm.

Thatcher's discourse proved more convincing during her second mandate. Not only did the macroeconomic programme finally appear to be bearing fruit but the privatization of major enterprises along with the sale of council housing also proved popular, even if it did not quite produce a people's capitalism in the stock market or turn new home owners into budding capitalists—and it proceeded with hardly a peep from the now divided Labour Party or the unions. With regard to labour policy, moreover, Thatcher's hard-nosed approach to the unions turned out to be generally popular to citizens weary of constant crisis and work stoppages and no longer sympathetic since the 'winter of discontent' of 1978–9 (Middlemas 1991). Moreover, as unemployment mounted and poverty rose as a by-product of monetarism and privatization, Thatcher blamed the victim and sought to cut social expenditures and to crush the unions further. Rather than buy off the workers through generous social policies, as in France, she sought to get the 'middle classes'—with the definition now including 'workers', or at least those with jobs—to buy into neo-liberal ideas and values not just through a discourse that appealed to the general interest and focused on economic revival but also through policies that catered to their more narrow self-interests such as lower taxes, higher levels of public spending, and privatization (see King and Wood 1999: 382–4). Thatcher also enlisted business in her crusade against the unions. Initially divided on how far to go in reducing union power, employers increasingly rallied to the cause: the Confederation of British Industry (CBI) went from scepticism to enthusiasm by 1981, while the Institute of Directors, always supportive of the most radical reform, ended up providing the template for the 1988 Employment Act (Auerbach 1990; Wood 2001: 260–6), suggesting that a successful coordinative discourse had developed between employers and the government.

Social welfare reform, however, was another matter. In the end, Thatcher did not go nearly as far as her rhetorical attacks on the 'culture of dependency' promised, mainly because of her concerns about public opposition. In areas where the notion of rights was universalistic and the middle classes benefited, such as the National Health Service (NHS), Thatcher found herself repeatedly defending her record. By contrast, where Thatcher could distinguish between the 'worthy poor' and the feckless and the idle, she had much less difficulty in legitimizing reductions, for example, in social assistance, unemployment, and housing programmes. However, even in those area of universalistic provision where Thatcher was unable to diminish state spending she did put neo-liberal ideas into effect. For example, with the partial privatization of pensions above the basic pension, she reinforced individual responsibility and exposure to market risks. And even though Thatcher did not interfere in principle with universal provision of health or education, the institution of competition in the NHS and in tertiary education was a way of encouraging 'capitalist' values of entrepreneurialism in place of—in Thatcher's view—'socialism'.

Thatcher's more moderated approach to social policy by contrast with monetary or industrial policy reflects the fact that, while the discourse could be seen as transformative with regard to public attitudes to the structure of the economy and of work, it was not with regard to the structure of the welfare state (see Schmidt 2000b). Whereas opinion polls of the mid- to late

1980s suggest that Thatcher moved the British toward more 'capitalist' values through acceptance of greater inequalities in wealth and rewards based on performance, more individual responsibility, and entrepreneurialism, they show that she did not by any means eradicate 'socialist' values with regard to health and welfare (Crewe 1991; Hetzner 1999: 124; Schmidt 2000b: 240–1). Other polls confirm that, while the electorate showed little change in its strong support for government responsibility with regard to the NHS and social security, they seemed to accept other Thatcherite values about individual responsibility, to wit, that the government not be responsible for maintaining full employment or for equalizing incomes (Taylor-Gooby 1991).

Thatcher's policies and discourse on Europe were another matter again. Whereas her neo-liberal paradigm was by its very nature pro-global, given the commitment to open markets and open borders, it was not necessarily pro- or anti-European; by contrast with the politico-economic issues, the political institutional issues related to sovereignty, which were the main complication in the British relationship with the European Community throughout the post-war period, were much more clearly anti-European (see Larsen 1997). For Thatcher, Europe represented as much an opportunity—to extend laissez-faire capitalism to the Continent—as a threat—with the extension of Continental-style state interventionism to Britain. And whereas the opportunity presented itself with the Single Market Act of 1986, with Thatcher using accommodating, 'communautaire' language as she sought to lead Europe toward a greater market liberalism, the threat appeared with the proposed Maastricht Treaty beginning in 1988, with its promise of integration in both monetary and social policies.

The threat was perceived as greatest with regard to the Social Chapter, about which Thatcher was in perfect agreement with her closest advisers and Cabinet ministers. For Thatcher and advisers, this constituted an unacceptable violation of neo-liberalism because, as she insisted in her famous Bruges speech on 20 September 1988, 'we certainly do not need regulations which raise the cost of employment and make Europe's labour market less flexible and less competitive with overseas suppliers . . . And certainly we in Britain would fight attempts to introduce collectivism and corporatism at the European level . . .' (Thatcher 1989). With monetary union, however, the issue was not as clear-cut. Where Thatcher, along with some advisers, perceived threat, mainly on grounds of loss of national sovereignty and control if the central bank were to become independent and monetary policy were administered by a central European bank (Busch 1994), others saw opportunity, on the grounds that this would institute sound neo-liberal macroeconomic policy throughout Europe; and they split publicly with her on the issue

(Larsen 1997: 66–8). Moreover, there was also strong support for the EMU among the Tories' business constituency, which saw it as ensuring a stable currency and encouraging the generalization of market principles to fiscal and social policies, as well as among British monetary authorities, who wanted to participate in its construction to avoid the problems of the 1970s, when they took on board policies that they had had no part in constructing (Verdun 1996). Thatcher's increasingly confrontational stance toward the European Community, which threatened to isolate the country, together with growing dissension among the party leadership on her position—and not to forget the highly unpopular poll tax—ultimately led to her forced resignation as head of the party and Prime Minister. This suggests that Thatcher's problems were with the coordinative discourse rather than in the communicative, in her increasing unwillingness to listen to the growing number of dissenting voices among her own closest allies, let alone in the rest of the party leadership.

For John Major, Thatcher's anointed successor as Prime Minister, therefore, the course was clear: negotiate in a more accommodating manner, but don't give in on the Social Chapter, and be cautious on EMU. The opt-outs on both Social Chapter and EMU accomplished these purposes. After the negotiation of the Maastricht Treaty and the controversy over its ratification, moreover, the government shifted from discussing the big issues to criticizing details of environmental and social legislation and of poor financial control and overzealous bureaucracy (Wallace 1996: 69). The discourse for a long time, therefore, was something of a low-pitched, moderately anti-European rhetoric, conveying the image of an ever-watchful British government, quick to protest against anti-liberal incursions. By the mid-1990s, however, the discourse began to get more strident, as it had during Thatcher's last couple of years in office, in this case because the Eurosceptics were growing ever stronger and Major's majority ever thinner. Add to this the disaster of the mad cow disease (BSE), where Major was valiantly trying to save British cows from slaughter, or what were seen as even more egregious regulatory encroachments by the EU Commission, such as the extension of the 48-hour work week to Britain on grounds of occupational safety and health, despite the British opt-out from the Social Chapter, and it is understandable that the Major government found it increasingly convenient to point out the dangers of Europeanization without mentioning its other merits, whether in playing to the Eurosceptics in Parliament in order to retain their allegiance or to the Eurocrats in Brussels to broker the best deal.

By now, criticism of the EMU and even the EU had become almost a sine qua non of British political life, whether by the government, Parliament, or the newspapers. While Tory backbenchers in particular were increasingly vocal in their criticism of Major's 'softness' on Europe, Fleet Street had a field day with EC regulations, with specious headlines, for example, on EU banning of curved bananas and square gin bottles. The danger for Britain was that, as the anti-European rhetoric escalated, the rational discourse that with Thatcher had consistently put European integration squarely within the neo-liberal vision of Britain's future, as part of a larger, neo-liberal Europe and world, was being forgotten—not so much by the elite, and in particular the business elite, which was well aware of the benefits of continued integration for the country's global competitiveness, as by the population, making it more open to demagogic manipulation from the anti-European Union forces. And all of this represented a major challenge for the newly elected Blair government—as the Labour Party found already in the 1997 election campaign, having time and again had to qualify its statements about how much and where Britain would opt back in. And to the extent that the Conservatives have now become largely an anti-European party, it will continue to promote divisions that Blair might find difficult to overcome.

But although the Conservative legacy on Europe may have left the Blair government in some difficulty, this is much less the case on other policy issues, mainly because Major did little to depart from Thatcher's legacy—nor has Blair. The real proof of the transformative power of Thatcher's discourse and policy programme comes from the fact that the Labour Party was not to win another election until it had thoroughly altered its policy programme and discourse to come close to the Thatcherite.

The Neo-Liberal Transformation of Labour's Post-war Paradigm and Discourse

While Thatcher, with the Conservative Party firmly in hand, was 'selling' her neo-liberal political-economic paradigm to the public, the Labour Party was going through its own transformation. When Thatcher first came into office, the Labour party presented a radically opposing political-economic paradigm to Thatcherite neo-liberalism. Much like the Socialists in France, Labour's 'Alternative Economic Strategy' proposed socialism in one country, with a mix of protectionism, assistance to nationalized industry, renationalization, and reflationary neo-Keynesian spending programmes with the express purpose of insulating the country from global economic pressures. This went hand in hand with Labour's 1983 manifesto commitment to withdraw from the EC, given that its policies were in clear opposition to Labour's proposed economic programme. Labour's position was thus in opposition not only to globalization but also to European integration, with an anti-global rhetoric to counter Thatcher's pro-global one, and an even more anti-European rhetoric than that of Thatcher. From the 1950s to the 1980s, in fact, the Labour party was concerned that the EEC was something of a capitalist club for the rich and, especially in the 1950s and 1960s, when parties of the right predominated, worried that it would frustrate socialist policy initiatives in Britain. Moreover, its opposition to EEC entry on 'Tory terms' reflected its hostility to the Heath government's economic and industrial relations policies (Daniels 1998).

The transformation of Labour was gradual across the 1980s. By the mid-1980s, with the failure of the French Socialist experiment in 1983 which cast doubts on the viability of their programme, many in the Labour Party, in particular the leadership and the 'soft' left, had shifted away from their earlier domestic economic strategies based on reflationary policies toward a focus on the EC as the arena for attainment of Labour economic objectives. In fact, in the Labour Party's coordinative discourse, European integration was used by modernizers as a rhetorical strategy in support of changes in party structure and policy (Geyer 1998: 90). This had not only to do with an acceptance of the inevitability of more neo-liberal monetary policy and the benefits of greater economic coordination across countries but also the hope that social policies ruled out at the national level would find greater support at the EC level, with Delors' concept of a 'social Europe'. This also provided a European cause to use with the electorate against Thatcher (Daniels 1998: 87–8).

By the late 1980s, much of the Labour Party, along with the unions, had come to have a more positive attitude toward the EC. By 1989, the Labour Party had committed itself to support the pound's entry into the ERM—even though divisions remained within the party—and in 1993 it supported ratification of the Maastricht Treaty. And when Blair took over the party, he not only supported the macroeconomic orthodoxy of price stability, abandoning once and for all Keynesian demand management policies; he also got rid of one of the last vestiges of 'socialism' in 1995 by eliminating Clause IV from the Labour Party Constitution, which committed the party to nationalization. Most telling is that, once elected, he immediately gave the Bank of England de facto independence, at the same time as he 'opted in' to the Social Charter of 1989—and the Social Chapter of the Maastricht Treaty—which had so appalled Thatcher and out of which Major had opted. Moreover, he also adopted a minimum wage—in great contrast to Old Labour's earlier voluntarism. On the euro, however, Blair exercised caution, in part because the lack of preparation prior to his arrival in power necessitated a delay in order to bring the economy and institutions in line, in part because of the legacy of John Major's increasingly anti-European discourse and the Eurosceptic press which has had a great influence on the public.

The gradual shift in the Labour Party's view of capitalism as well can be seen not only in the policies but also in the discourse, as the Labour Party moved from clear hostility to the market to general scepticism, then to general acceptance and, by 1992, to open embrace, with the 1992 election manifesto claiming 'not to replace the market but to ensure the market works properly'. The changing communicative discourse, however, rather than using a pro-Europe discourse as the cognitive justification for the neo-liberal turn, as had the Socialists in France, instead used globalization. This is understandable, not only given the charged political atmosphere with regard to Europe, in particular with the opposition's increasingly anti-European rhetoric and the popular polemics of the press, but also because of the traditional pro-global discourse. Unlike Thatcher's pro-global discourse, though, where opening up to global forces followed from her ideologically grounded, neo-liberal justification for change, Blair's pro-global discourse has presented globalization as the primary rationale for neo-liberal reform.

Necessity, rather than ideology, was the key to Blair's discourse on globalization, with globalization presented as an economic constraint and an opportunity (Hay and Rosamund 2000). Blair's stated commitment to 'work with the grain of global change' and to have his administration 'accept, and indeed embrace, the global market' (speech to the Singapore Business Community, 8 January 1996, cited in Hay and Watson 1998) was geared to reassuring the international financial markets, just as was its granting of de facto independence to the Bank of England to set interest rates or its 'golden rule' of borrowing only for investment and not consumption, as well as the 'sound money' paradigm. All of this sent a signal to the financial markets that, by depoliticizing monetary policy decisions, the government would be sure to be 'tough on inflation, tough on the causes of inflation'—although this was also a signal of the government's commitment to joining EMU sometime in the future. Globalization, as the 'necessity' of satisfying the inflation demands of the global foreign exchange markets was also cited as the reason for government policies to keep wages and social benefits down (Chancellor's budget speeches, July and November 1997, cited in Hay and Watson 1998), while globalization as the challenge to the competitiveness of business was the rationale for promoting greater flexibility in the labour markets.

In the context of the globalization discourse, moreover, the cognitive justification was not, as one might have expected, focused on rejecting the Thatcherite paradigm but, rather, on differentiating the policy programme of New Labour from that of Old Labour. In fact, the promoters of New Labour seemed mostly intent on suggesting continuity with the Thatcherite programme and distancing themselves from the 'failed world of Old Labour' by making clear that 'good government' was 'minimal government' and that it was important to recognize that 'choices are constrained; there are no panaceas, and the solutions adopted by left and right may often overlap' (Tony Blair, speech to the BDI, Bonn, Germany, 18 June 1996, cited in Hay and Watson 1998). With his 'third way', however, Blair sought to convince the electorate that his was an approach which was somewhere between the neo-liberal right and the old socialist left, embracing the 'risk society' resulting from globalization while promoting an active, inclusive civil society and reconstructing, rather than shrinking or enlarging, the state (Featherstone 1999). With this came a new vocabulary as well, which *The Economist* (19 December 1998: 40) encapsulated perfectly in a very funny table on the differences in language employed by the right, the left—Old Labour—and the 'third way'—New Labour. In the economic realm, where the right speaks of 'bosses' and the left of 'workers', the third way speaks of 'consumers'. In welfare, where the right talks of the 'feckless' and the left 'the oppressed', the third way talks of 'the excluded'. Other comparisons are, respectively, small government, big government, clever government; competition, planning, teamwork; silent majorities, vocal minorities, focus groups; market, state, community; and colleague, comrade, contact.

But what then of the normative aspects of the discourse? The 'third way' has been Blair's attempt to differentiate himself from both Thatcher's ideological appeal to the values of individualism and laissez-faire capitalism and old Labour's appeal to values of equality, community, and socialism. With the third way, as set out in a speech to the Labour Party Congress in Bournemouth on 28 September 1999, Blair claims through 'patience, prudence, and modernization' not to set a new course 'between conservatism and progressivism' but rather to take a progressive course which distinguishes itself 'from all conservatisms, whether of the left or the right' and which ensures that 'after a century of antagonism, economic efficiency and social justice finally work together'. As such, Blair's third way represents something of a reversal of Old Labour's desire to move to a more social-democratic vision in favour of a return to the original Beveridge vision of the welfare state, with liberal notions of individualism and responsibility while promoting universalism in health and education.

With the third way, Blair has essentially provided a theory of why the welfare state should not be developed further, why it should not be socially supportive but only enabling, as a 'trampoline' rather than a 'hammock', to provide 'not a handout' but a 'hand up'. On pensions, for example, Blair introduced reforms that go neither the route of Major—who in the 1997 Conservative campaign manifesto proposed an ill-conceived full privatization of pensions, 'Basic Pensions Plus'—nor that of Old Labour, with its ill-fated 1992 campaign promise to re-link pensions to earnings, which may have lost Labour the election because it was seen as fiscally irresponsible. In fact, instead of increasing the basic pension to promote Old Labour concerns about equality and redistribution, New Labour has provided more funding for education, training, and welfare-to-work programmes in order to 'promote opportunity instead of dependence', to foster social mobility, and to reverse 'social exclusion': a term Blair mainly uses as synonymous with poverty, which he himself defined as 'a short-hand label for what can happen when individuals or areas suffer from a combination of linked problems such as unemployment, poor skills, low incomes, poor housing, high crime environments, bad health and family breakdown' (Opportunity for All 1999: 23). Even in higher education, tuition fees need not be seen as an attack on principles of equality, since in breaching traditional universalism they are mainly reducing middle class entitlements—even though they could also adversely affect some of the working poor or middle-income students who do not qualify for scholarships. But this interpretation of the reform has not been the focus of Blair's discourse, nor have his more 'socialist' or redistributive policies, such as increases in the level of social assistance and the minimum wage, which have seemingly been instituted 'by stealth' since they have had much less attention in the discourse (Rhodes 2000).

With Blair, then, as with Thatcher, there is a clear recognition that a fully developed communicative discourse is of the essence, and that the prime minister's primary business is one of public persuasion. The coordinative discourse, by comparison, is almost non-existent, with the elaboration of the policy programme the product of a small group of close advisers and key Cabinet ministers. Even more than with Thatcher, party discipline is a major concern of New Labour—so much so that there are those who have jokingly referred to Blair's approach as akin to Lenin's democratic centralism, so much has he sought to muzzle backbench party members. Blair's control of public communication, moreover, is much greater than Thatcher's ever was. His press office, overseen by Alasdair Campbell, with its units of strategic communication and of refutation, vets all major public statements by all members of government except for the most powerful—such as the Chancellor of the Exchequer and the Minister of Foreign Affairs—before their pronouncement and responds to all political attacks, whether from the press, the Commons, or Old Labour.

France: In Search of a Legitimizing Discourse

Since 1983, with the adoption of a moderate neo-liberal political-economic policy programme, French governments have been markedly unsuccessful in constructing a legitimizing discourse capable of projecting to the public a convincing vision of how France fits within an integrating Europe and a globalizing world. Ever since the Mitterrand government abandoned its socialist discourse in the early 1980s when it converted to a neo-liberal policy programme and the right failed to sustain its radical neo-liberal discourse of the mid-1980s in the face of electoral defeat, French policy elites have been in search of a new discourse that would serve to legitimize the country's liberalizing economic transformation in terms of national values and identity. In its absence, successive governments have more often than not justified neo-liberal policy change by reference to the challenges of Europeanization and globalization, generally by presenting the changes related to European integration as necessary to protect the country against the incursions of globalization while enhancing France's economic power in Europe and the world. In consequence, the public has had to settle for successive communicative discourses that, whether from governments of the right or the left, have all provided the same justification for why change has been economically necessary but insufficient legitimization of its appropriateness in terms of social values. Over the course of the 1990s in particular, this became more and more problematic as the economic adjustments related to the neo-liberal policy programme and European monetary integration were seen increasingly to conflict with long-standing values related to social solidarity, given continuing high unemployment and cuts in social programmes, and to undermine the *service public*, given rationalization, deregulation, and even privatization in public sector infrastructural services and utilities.

The Post-war Paradigm and Discourse

During the post-war period up until 1983, the dominant political-economic paradigm was *'dirigisme'*, or state interventionism, in which the state was to lead economic growth and industrial development by whatever means it saw fit. Although the paradigm began in the early post-war period, with the planning process directed by the technocratic elite of the state, it did not gain a fully legitimizing discourse until Charles de Gaulle became President at the inception of the Fifth Republic in 1958. It was de Gaulle who put the political-economic programme at the centre of his vision of France becoming a major world power and a leader in Europe. In the discourse, he made appeal to national pride with his talk of French *'grandeur'* and independence, and sought to build on a sense of France's exceptionalism as well as its history of state interventionism that goes all the way back to Louis XIV and his minister Colbert. The industrial policies that created and promoted the 'national champions', the public sector enterprises which were to provide a high level of infrastructural services and perform a public service mission—electricity, air transport, later the railroads and the telephone—and the *'grands projets'* were all presented as symbols for a France which was to be strong and sufficiently industrialized that it would never again suffer defeat at the hands of Germany or any other power—including the United States. Even after de Gaulle's departure from the scene, his successors used much the same discourse, despite the fact that by the mid-1970s the policy programme was no longer accomplishing what the discourse proclaimed, as the national champions were coming to be seen as 'lame ducks' and the *grands projets* white elephants.

All the while, however, there were rival discourses, in particular those of the opposition Communists and Socialists which increasingly overlapped by the 1970s, as the two parties of the left made a common front. Their policy programme was less a rejection of the ideas contained in the old Gaullist policy paradigm, however, than a re-invigoration of them, as they called for more state interventionism in response to the economic crisis beginning in the mid-1970s through the full-scale nationalization of industry, the return to neo-Keynesianism, and generous social policies. The policy programme's normative legitimization, however, was completely different from the Gaullist. Although the appeal to traditional political values and national pride remained with regard to the role of the state in restoring French economic prowess, there was also a post-war Marxian ideology which infused the discourse, insisting on the necessity of increased state interventionism to solve the economic crisis through 'socialism in one nation' and talking of the capitalist 'wall of money', of CEOs of major firms as exploiters, of the 'break with capitalism' through the nationalization of the means of production, and of the need to break the class bias of French society and to promote equality (Schmidt 1996: Ch. 4).

Thus, when the Socialists swept into power in 1981, although the discourse changed, the basic political-economic paradigm did not. In fact, Mitterrand promised a return to state capitalism's roots, to the fundamentals of the *dirigiste* paradigm, muddied by the preceding few years when France had joined the European Monetary System and the Conservative government had instituted a moderate budgetary austerity programme and more liberal industrial policy. The problem for the Socialists, however, was that neither their renewed *dirigiste* policy programme nor their ideologically grounded discourse could stand up to events. Not only was the policy programme unsustainable economically, but the discourse itself could neither cognitively account for the failure of the policies to promote growth nor normatively justify the subsequent turn to budgetary austerity in terms of its political and social commitments. And therefore, when the Socialists abandoned their policy programme in 1983, they also dropped the discourse.

The 1983 change in policy programme and discourse appeared so abrupt, in fact, that it could be characterized as a Kuhnian revolution in paradigm. But even with Kuhnian-like revolutions the ground has to be prepared ideationally—and was, in the coordinative discourses within political parties, among experts, and even in the state apparatus. The policy programme itself had increasingly come under attack, and not only in its 1981 socialist incarnation, for its growing failure to deliver on its promises. The second half of the 1970s saw the rise of a new epistemic community made up of the 'new' economists who questioned the continuing validity of the economics of the *dirigiste* paradigm and the 'new' political philosophers who questioned the all-important role of the state. Moreover, the ranks of the upper-level civil service were slowly being filled with graduates of elite state schools—the *grands écoles*, and particularly the École Nationale d'Administration and the Institut d'Études Politiques—imbued with pro-market notions while more and more politicians on the right, in particular in the political clubs around the Union pour la Démocratie Française (UDF), were becoming converts to neo-liberalism (Jobert and Théret 1994; Lordon 1999: 179). What is more, beginning in 1981 with the victory of the Socialists, the number of right-wing politicians who embraced neo-liberalism increased exponentially, not only among the UDF but also among the Rassemblement pour la République (RPR), the Gaullists who until then had with few exceptions continued to have faith in the powers of the strong French state. Once the Socialists took control of government, the 'retreat of the state' became the new, radical neo-liberal ideology of the right as a whole (Baudoin 1990; Godin 1996; Schmidt 1996: Ch. 5).

Even among the Socialists after their accession to power, however, neo-liberalism was gaining ground—although they never called it that. Already between 1981 and 1983, the policy programme and its discourse were undergoing subtle changes, as the Socialist government began to liberalize the financial markets, dropped many of its more radical policy promises—for example, to institute a National Investment Bank or worker self-management—and, while continuing to talk about it, quickly gave up the attempt to institute neo-corporatist concertation with the social partners, labour and business (Jobert and Théret 1994: 40–3). Moreover, it increasingly justified nationalization in nationalistic terms—that is, to save firms from foreign takeover—as opposed to Marxian terms, and soon rehabilitated business by calling CEOs no longer 'exploiters' but 'creators of riches' and by treating 'profit' no longer as a dirty word (Schmidt 1996: Ch. 4). As one Socialist put it, 'We went from the idea of a break with capitalism to the very different idea of a break with the failures of capitalism' (Zinsou 1985: 61). Economic interest, of course, had everything to do with these changes, given the Socialists' growing concern with deepening economic crisis and double-digit inflation. The Socialists' own political interests, however, also played a large role, since the Socialists increasingly recognized that, if they did not do something to turn the economy around, they would lose the next election. As one insider explained it, the Socialists were already faced with a major dilemma after one year in power: if they accepted reality, they had to renounce their socialist doctrine, and thus be plunged into ideological crisis; if they rejected reality and stayed with their ideology, they would lose politically.[2]

The Moderate Neo-Liberal Paradigm in Search of a Discourse

In 1983, in the face of major economic crisis, the socialists accepted that their policy programme was unsustainable economically, and jettisoned the discourse along with the policy programme. The turning point came in March, as a small group of Socialist Party leaders conferred with President Mitterrand on the choice of policy: whether to institute budgetary austerity and stay in the EMS—the argument of Jacques Delors as policy mediator for the pro-European discourse coalition—or to pull out, put up protective economic barriers, and seek to maintain French 'exceptionalism'. The coordinative discourse here was extremely restricted: neither Communist coalition partners nor the larger party was consulted (Bauchard 1986); and Mitterrand himself was alone to decide. The change itself involved the conversion of a small governmental elite of the Socialist Party in power rather than, as in Britain, the takeover of a party and the conquest of power by a small 'discourse coalition' of neo-liberal converts in the Conservative Party.

Ultimately, Mitterrand's decision was based on the belief that there was no alternative to a U-turn in economic policy, with monetarist monetary policies to be followed by more supply-side industrial policies, and with the

---

[2] Interview with author, Paris, 13 March 1991, cited in Schmidt (1996: Ch. 4).

retreat of the state (see Chapter 2). But how to formulate a communicative discourse that would justify such a neo-liberal policy programme without a neo-liberal discourse? The neo-liberal discourse was not an option, not only because it had already been taken up by the right since the 1981 elections but also because it so clearly contradicted the Socialists' own 1981–3 discourse— even though Michel Rocard and supporters had a similar discourse prior to 1981. Unlike Thatcher, whose neo-liberalism was a matter of ideology and normatively as well as cognitively presented as the only thing to do, for which there was no alternative, for Mitterrand and the Socialists it was a matter of necessity, cognitively right but normatively difficult—and for many disillusioned Socialists impossible—to legitimize. And certainly, they could not demonstrate its appropriateness in terms of the socialist values they had espoused throughout the post-war period.

The communicative discourse which followed was all about economic necessity and the need to relaunch growth and fight unemployment. The Socialists talked about the *'contrainte extérieure'* or the external constraints imposed by globalization and the need to remain in the European Monetary System, which would act as a shield against globalization. Modernization and competitiveness became the new imperatives, with 'competitive disinflation,' the *'franc fort'*, and the 'fight against inflation' the new catchwords in the monetary policy arena, with bringing inflation down below that of Germany, in order to ensure that French workers were getting the jobs going to Germany, the new exhortatory goal. Industrial dynamism, profits, and the disengagement of the state became the catchwords in the industrial policy arena, as Laurent Fabius, first as Minister of Industry and then Prime Minister, exhorted French firms to 'get out of the red', warning that 'heads would roll' in companies that failed to return to profitability and that 'lame ducks' would no longer be rescued from bankruptcy (*Le Monde*, 31 March 1985).

This discourse on the need to restructure the economy was effective, if we judge from the opinion polls. These showed public confidence in CEOs along with the entrepreneurial spirit on the rise and the public's view of business as exploiter on the decline along with a new realism in the population (Schmidt 1996: Ch. 4). By 1986, private entrepreneurs even credited the Socialists with 'renewing the capitalist spirit in France' (*Financial Times*, 26 June 1986). Although there can be no doubt that the economic improvement had a lot to do with the new neo-liberal policies, there can also be little doubt that changing attitudes resulting from the discourse that legitimized those policies also had an important influence, especially since the attitudinal changes for the most part came prior to the economic improvement, by 1983 and 1984, whereas the clear signs of improvement began only in 1985.

But while the Socialists' discourse was quite successful in persuading the public as to the cognitive merits of the policy programme, it did little with regard to its normative merits. When the Socialists did refer to values in their efforts to legitimize the policy programme, they mainly appealed to French national pride and spoke of the economic combat for national survival and of national revival. And although the Socialists did speak some of social justice—Mitterrand especially—the discourse had changed from one focused on equality and the effort to equalize income disparities to one of social solidarity, which represented the tacit acceptance of the inequalities of income and social insurance provisions necessitated by a more neo-liberal approach to economic management (Jobert and Théret 1994: 72–8). Solidarity itself, however, came increasingly to have two meanings: one connoting acceptance of inequalities in income and social insurance, the other evoking societal solidarity as part of the combat against social exclusion (Spicker 1997).

By 1984, moreover, Mitterrand himself had begun to differentiate his presidential discourse from that of the government, increasingly elaborating a discourse about the ideas and values of the polity as a whole by contrast with the government's policy discourse. Thus, he insisted that his role was not to talk of 'rigueur', or austerity, but rather to identify the 'grands objectifs', the 'projet de civilisation', and to act as the 'guarantor of national unity and social justice' (Labbé 1990: 155–8) even as the government continued to decentralize and restructure the economy; and later, once Chirac was in office from 1986 to 1988, Mitterrand increasingly sought to emphasize his role as statesman—or 'Dieu', as the French jokingly began to call him—as above the fray of party politics, like de Gaulle before him, even though his communicative discourse was as much focused on maintaining his own power vis-à-vis the opposition in government as it was in providing a unifying vision for the country. Thus, while Mitterrand left to the government the cognitive task of explaining the necessity of change, he himself was focused on the normative. But instead of arguing for the appropriateness of the neo-liberal policy programme, he seemingly implied that it was inappropriate by proclaiming to defend the long-standing values of social solidarity.

The problem with the discourse was that, even as Mitterrand pledged to defend social solidarity, the reality of increasing unemployment and 'exclusion' as a by-product of industrial rationalizations and restructurings resulting from the neo-liberal policies seemed to belie this. The discussion of social solidarity itself was more focused on providing interest-based incentives for those most affected by the neo-liberal restructuring of the economy than on redefining interests, individual obligations, and state responsibility with regard to social policy, as it had with Thatcher in Britain. Thus, the generous unemployment compensation programmes, extensive use of early retirement, and increases in social spending throughout the 1980s can be seen as much as a way of buying off the most affected interests as the defence of traditional values. And in the interim, the Socialists did not in any way address the seemingly logical contradiction between belt-tightening neo-liberal economic policies and expansive social policies.

Moreover, although one might have expected the right-wing government that came to power in 1986 on the basis of a radical neo-liberal programme to be better able to reconcile this contradiction, it did not. For although it adopted something of a Thatcherite, ideological discourse on the reasons for restructuring the economy—for example, to increase individual responsibility, innovativeness, and independence while engineering a retreat of the state—their discourse when it came to social policy issues remained very much the same as that of the Socialists, with social solidarity still the watchword (see Schmidt 1996: Ch. 5), as Prime Minister Chirac himself repeatedly made clear that his policies would not challenge the 'republican consensus'. The right, in fact, was not nearly as ideologically neo-liberal as its discourse suggested (Leterre 2000).

In its time in office, however, the problems of the right were less with the communicative discourse than with the coordinative discourse within the government coalition. Prime Minister Chirac seemed to spend less of his time trying to communicate to the public about the appropriateness of the retreat of the state through privatization and deregulation than attempting to coordinate a government riven by divisions between ministers who sought to institute radical neo-liberal reform—such as shutting down the Ministry of Industry—generally members of the UDF, and others, mostly RPR, who were wedded to much more moderate reform. When the right lost the elections in 1988, mainly because it was perceived as more radical and less stable than the Socialists, it also largely abandoned the discourse.

But the moderate neo-liberal programme continued under subsequent governments, whether of the left or the right, without providing any better reconciliation of the cognitive and normative aspects of the discourse. This was as true under the Socialists until 1993—even if Prime Minister Rocard placed greater emphasis on not abandoning the victims and addressing the problems of 'exclusion'—as it was under succeeding right-wing governments until 1997, when Prime Minister Jospin did come up with a legitimizing discourse that appeared to resonate with the public.

The Problems of Normative Legitimization in the 1990s Discourse

Whereas the failures of the discourse were not terribly problematic in the mid- to late 1980s as the economy picked up and social spending continued to rise, they became increasingly so by the early 1990s as the country slid into recession and pressures built to lower budget deficits and public debt in the run-up to EMU. In place of a fully legitimizing discourse to support continuing reform, the leadership of both right and left spoke of the importance of European integration as a shield against globalization. In the monetary policy arena, it was to protect the country against the vagaries of the international financial markets while promoting economic stability and growth. In the industrial policy arena, deregulation and privatization were presented as necessary to meet the competitive challenges of European integration and globalization. Even in the social policy sphere, once welfare reform began in earnest under the right starting in 1993, the discourse related to Europe was initially invoked in justification. But it was just as quickly dropped when it was seen to be leading to anti-European sentiment, with references instead focused on internal factors—demographic in particular—pushing change. It is telling that, at the time of the strikes and public demonstrations in 1995 against Juppé's welfare reform, globalization, and not Europeanization, was blamed—despite the fact that the latter was the more proximate cause—with a *Le Monde* (7 December 1995) headline reading 'La Premiére Révolte contre la Mondialisation' (see Hay and Rosamund 2000).

Although their pro-European and anti-global discourse worked for a while, with a permissive consensus assured by the growing economic prosperity, by the mid-1990s the lack of a fully legitimizing discourse began to take its toll in the face of economic recession, the 1992 run on the franc, continued high unemployment, and the increasing incursions on the welfare state. The problems did not really come to a head with the debates surrounding the 1992 Maastricht referendum, since these were primarily focused on the political-institutional impact of European Monetary Union. They came soon thereafter, however, as successive governments began to institute cuts in welfare and social security in the mid-1990s and to deregulate and privatize in the *service public* arena, as European pressures for deregulation intensified.

The problems related to the discourse on Europe had to do with the fact that in the 1990s up until the 1997 elections there was very little public deliberation about the economic consequences of EMU. In fact, the mainstream parties maintained something of a taboo on criticism of it. '*La pensée unique*', or the 'single-minded thought' that enjoined against criticizing the EMU, as it was termed by the few who did criticize it (for example, Todd 1998), stymied any thoroughgoing, open discussion of the potential problems involved, and especially any linkages between the restrictive budgetary policies related to meeting the Maastricht criteria and cuts in the social policy arena.

The taboo, or dominant conviction, itself stemmed in large measure from the fact that perseverance with monetary integration had become not only a point of honour for most mainstream politicians of the left and the right, given the sacrifices since the mid-1980s that included suffering high unemployment and too-high interest rates, but also a source of national pride, given France's economic leadership role in the EU that accompanied its perseverance (Schmidt 1997*b*). Equally importantly, a majority of policy elites, not just politicians but also central bankers, business and labour leaders, saw EMU almost entirely in positive light, although their reasons for support differed. For French monetary authorities, EMU would institutionalize 'German' monetary policies—that is, policies focused on stability—within a European framework in which France would have a voice. For business leaders, a stable single currency would ensure more attention to market principles and was likely have a spillover effect on fiscal and welfare areas. Finally, for labour leaders, EMU would promote economic growth along with the further development of the EU, which would provide greater opportunities for them to put non-monetary issues, such as the Social Chapter, on the agenda (Verdun 1996). But all this did was to leave the public with little more than exhortations to continued sacrifice and incantations on the future benefits of EMU, and therefore more vulnerable to demagoguery from the extreme right (Schmidt 1997*a*).

Only with the 1997 election campaign was the taboo against criticism of the EMU lifted, allowing public debate to flourish. On the right, the divisions ran very deep, primarily in the RPR, where a number of powerful politicians broke with the official pro-EMU line. On the left, Jospin espoused a tolerance for pluralism in the coalition of the left as an 'exercise in the democratic confrontation of ideas' (Cole 1999) and necessarily so, given criticism from within the coalition government, in particular from the Communists.

For mainstream parties of both the left and the right, the problem has been less European integration per se than how to legitimize a neo-liberal political-economic programme which has increasingly impinged on the social policy arena. This represented both a cognitive problem, because of the seeming logical contradiction between economic belt-tightening and generous social services, and a normative one, given continued underlying French conceptions of the obligations of '*l'état républicain*', of the Republican state, to guarantee citizens' social justice through the provision not just of traditional social services but also public infrastructural services.

Opinion polls show a growing sense of dissatisfaction among the general population: for example, that 'people like them' lived less well than before—from 50 per cent in 1981 to 62 per cent in 1994—and that there needed to be a complete change in society—which went from 35 per cent in 1989 to 53 per cent in 1994 (Sofres 1996). The acceptance of neo-liberal economic values, moreover, indicated by positive attitudes to profits, business, or capitalism, after rising appreciably in the 1980s plummeted in the early 1990s: for example, profit, with 37 per cent for and 39 per cent against in 1980, switched to 54 per cent for and 32 per cent against in 1988, only to return to negative values in 1994, with 43 per cent for and 49 per cent against (Sofres 1996). Finally, large majorities of the French continued to be very attached to their public system of social security, thinking that most services worked well, and supported a continued state role in the provision of such services (Sofres 1995, 1998; discussed in Schmidt 2000b). On the list of things in 1996 that worried people the most for the next few years, attacks on their social rights came in second, at 43 per cent—after racism, at 56 per cent—by contrast with the disappearance of the French nation in the European Union, in fifth place with 25 per cent worried (Sofres 1996). It is also important to note here that the public protests related to cutbacks in the welfare state have generally not been focused on EMU, which people seemed to have largely accepted. Opinion polls have found that 58 per cent of the French accept that monetary integration justifies sacrifices such as the reduction of public spending and public debt, with 34 per cent against (Schwok 1999: 63).

For the French public, therefore, cuts in social services and rationalization and privatization in public services were bound to be problematic. And it was even more problematic for the highly unionized public sector workers who would be most affected by the reforms, who also had great capacity for mobilization and protest. In this context, a discourse would have helped that sought to coordinate policy construction with the unions through 'concertation' or, failing this, to legitimize the reforms to the more general public through discussion not only of the necessity of reform, given the growing deficits of the social security system, but also of its appropriateness, through an appeal, for example, to intergenerational solidarity. But it was not forthcoming. Instead, the public's experience of monetary, industrial, and labour policy reform since the early 1980s—where government promises that just one liberalizing measure more would solve the problems of unemployment proved to be pipe dreams, whether it was reducing the inflation rate to bring jobs to France, allowing wages to give way to profits in order for investment and jobs to follow, or enabling employers to fire so that they would be more inclined to hire—left the public distrustful of further reform in the social policy arena (Levy 2000). Moreover, the lack of real consultation or coordination with the social partners made labour especially wary of government initiatives in this area.

Under both Prime Ministers Edouard Balladur (1993–5) and Alain Juppé (1995–7), protests and strikes were the natural outcome. Balladur's approach was to float policies like trial balloons, with little coordinative or communicative discourse, waiting to see the reaction and withdrawing the policies in the event of significant protest (see Levy 2000). This meant that many initiatives focused on the rationalization or privatization of public infrastructural services were withdrawn in response to strikes by public sector unions, but that private sector pension reform held, given the near impossibility of organizing protest in an environment of low unionization and high job insecurity, given high unemployment. But when Juppé tried a similar reform for public sector pensions at the same time as rationalization plans for the national railway, public sector strikes paralysed the country. The strikes themselves gained widespread sympathy from the public not so much because of the content of reform—a majority of French, 51 to 40 per cent (Sofres 1996: 29), at the time had accepted that the government had to put into place drastic social security reforms[3]—as because of the style. This was mainly because Prime Minister Juppé not only ignored the social partners in a reform which he proudly declared was of his construction alone, with perhaps a handful of advisers, but also failed to communicate about the reform to the public at large—assuming, possibly, that the reform of public sector pensions would pass as unnoticed as the similar reform of private sector pensions had in 1993 with Balladur. Juppé's rationale, summarized in his legitimizing principle of 'equality of sacrifice' for policies that spared no one, which was a direct response to Balladur's method in which legitimacy was assumed if there was no public protest, ended up generating much more protest and pleasing even fewer people than Balladur (Levy 2001).

It is telling that, in his 1996 New Year's speech to the nation right after the strikes, President Chirac emphasized that the lesson to be learned from the strikes was that one would not change France without the French: more dialogue and concertation was the only means to reform (Schmidt 1997b). But this is no easy task for French governmental elites who have rarely achieved much dialogue or concertation in the social policy arena with French citizens, and have generally sought more to impose or to pacify, in the face of protest, than to listen. Moreover, even if the government were truly eager to listen, the intermediary bodies necessary to such concertation are either

---

[3] On the method of the reform, see Bonoli (1997) and Vail (1999).

weak or missing, by contrast with Germany, and Parliament has never acted as an effective voice for citizen concerns, by contrast with Britain.

The Socialist Discourse of Legitimization of the Moderate Neo-Liberal Paradigm

The Socialists in government between 1997 and 2002, however, did better in terms of both dialogue and concertation, as well as in softening the impact of the neo-liberal policy programme. Their ideas about how to proceed with political economic reform in the first place differentiated them from previous right-wing governments. As then Finance Minister Dominique Strauss-Kahn explained it, whereas the right—much like Thatcher—said that it had first to engage in structural reform in order to get growth, regardless of the pain, the Socialist government felt that it needed to generate growth first by other means—for example, through consumer confidence—and then it could restructure without the pain.[4] Moreover, the government sought to link its ideas of reform to its socialist heritage. Thus, for example, in a speech for the debate on 'Can We Regulate the Economy' organized by the journal *Alternatives Économiques*, Jospin explained that, by focusing on the conditions of production, the government was going back to socialism's intellectual roots in Saint-Simon, Proudhon, and Marx: that is, in its search for 'the most just and efficient way to create riches'. Although it was also concerned with redistribution, which came historically much later, with Keynes and Beveridge, it would accomplish this by creating jobs and thereby 'promote the solidarity that is at the heart of the concept of redistribution'. This approach, Jospin continued, would create a new alliance between working and middle classes by having the first 'admit that high-skilled work and innovation should be recompensed' while persuading the second that 'economic success can only be collective' since 'we must at the same time rely on the dynamic forces of society and respond to the problems of the excluded' (November 15, 2000). These ideas translated into a policy programme in which, the government explained, it would pursue moderate change with 'neither pause nor acceleration' in the pace of reform, neither slashing benefits to the poor nor doing nothing while the social security system goes into deficit; neither declaring class warfare on the rich nor allowing the privileged not to pay their share; and neither dismantling the welfare state nor failing to address its dysfunctions (Levy 2000).

---

[4] Interview with author, Paris, October 1999.

In promoting its ideas, the government's coordinative discourse was much more accommodating than previous governments'. The government opened up policy construction to a less restricted group of policy elites, including not only government coalition members but also the social partners in the case of reforms in social security or industrial relations—for example, the 35-hour work week; and it convened experts in advisory commissions in the case of controversial issues. What is more, its communicative discourse directly focused on the problems of the fit between neo-liberal policy programme and social values by seeking to persuade the public that it is possible to have reforms that can be economically efficient and at the same time promote social equity as well as, in the oft-repeated phrases of governments of right and left, to combat social exclusion and heal the 'social fracture'. This was echoed in the government's refrain on globalization—and tacitly Europeanization: 'yes to the market economy but no to the market society'. And it was also reflected in the government's legitimization of all of its specific policy initiatives.

With its discussion of how its privatizations respected rules of efficiency and equity, for example, the Jospin government ensured them greater success than the previous government. By securing investment and guaranteeing jobs, for example, by selling companies in defence, aeronautics, and financial sectors to companies with complementary lines of business, while involving the unions in the negotiations—in contrast to the right's focus on state disinvestment, regardless of its impact on jobs or on industrial strategy, and lack of worker consultation—the Jospin government by 2000 had managed to sell more public enterprises than five of the previous French governments combined. It succeeded in particular in a number of high-profile cases in which the Juppé government failed because of either worker protest or technical mistakes: for example, Thomson Multimedia, CIC, GAN, Aérospatiale (see discussion in Levy 2001). Its more redistributive fiscal policies, by taxing and eliminating benefits for the rich while reducing the burdens on the poor and by raising taxes on business and lowering them on consumers—rather than the other way around, which had been Juppé's solution— served to increase public confidence and consumer spending. The government has also been more successful in social security reforms not only because of the legitimizing content of the discourse but also because of the coordinative process, through more 'corporatist' negotiation of reform including the creation of private pensions funds administered by the social partners—rather than private companies, as the right had sought to do (see Chapter 2).

The government had a more difficult time in its direct relations with business. When the Socialists first came into office in June 1997, espousing what to some appeared to be a return to a more left-wing agenda, CEOs of publicly held firms were concerned about an end to continued privatization and a renewal of interventionism. In response, CEOs used arguments about the logic of the market to forestall government intervention. In June 1997, just as the Socialists had pledged to stop France Télécom's partial—20 per cent—privatization, the company's CEO, Michel Bon, insisted that one needed to talk of the 'sale of shares on the market', and not even use the word 'privatization', because it was the 'logic of the market' according to which the firm needed to operate. By this he meant that the firm needed to proceed to the rationalizations and restructurings necessary to ensure its place as a global player rather than operate as a state enterprise, subject to the logic of a *service public* enterprise.[5] The 20 per cent stock flotation, though delayed, did subsequently follow. At this same time, when Louis Schweitzer, head of Renault, in which the state still held a large stake—(33 per cent—was under fire for closing the Vilvoorde plant in Belgium to move to Spain, his argument with the government was that it could indeed dismiss him for the decision but it still could not go against the will of the Board of Directors, which had voted on that decision.[6] And the government did not.

The Socialists, in fact, essentially bought into the CEOs' discourse on the 'logic of the market' and continued with an active programme of privatization and a hands-off approach to business, although they had moments of great discomfort as a result. One such moment was when Michelin in September 1999 announced large profits and at the same time major lay-offs of workers. Jospin's initial response, stating that there was nothing that he could do, that this was globalization, created a firestorm of protest, with one commentator noting that most people in France 'find it hard to accept that the triumph of a pure shareholder logic means that retired Americans, many living under the Florida sun, should decide the professional and personal fate of much younger French workers, through the decisive power wielded by pension funds' (Dominique Moisi, *Financial Times*, 27 September 1999: 2). This led Jospin to try to recoup the following week by proposing government measures on part-time employment—which was essentially a way to distract the media from the initial gaffe, since part-time employment had nothing to do with Michelin. But this and other labour and social policy measures did not make business happy.

Business was for the most part less than enthusiastic with regard to employment policy, and in particular the 35-hour work week. Business held major protest rallies, despite the fact that it had for the most part

---

[5] Interview with author, Paris, June 1997.   [6] Interview with author, Paris, June 1997.

negotiated cooperatively with labour and even had the upper hand in instituting greater flexibility in the workplace as a result. Through its main professional association, the MEDEF, business was also developing more of a clear
communicative voice, with the president, Ernest-Antoine Sellière, fulminat-
ing against the government 'which brakes' and 'puts sticks in the wheels' of
those who work the wheels (*Le Monde*, 25 January 2001) while his number
two, Denis Kessler, acted as the policy mediator responsible for articulating
the employers' demands for a *refondation sociale*—social overhaul—in welfare
policy and institutions. The employers' association took the lead in place of
the opposition party in voicing its own recommendations with regard to
social policy, proposing a *refondation sociale* in which labour and social
policy would be completely revamped; and it even opted out of the
system of co-management of the social security system with the unions—
as of June 2001—until such a time as the *refondation sociale* occured.
Government in this context sought to be a moderating force between
business and labour, insisting that business had to take its responsibilities
seriously by creating new jobs as it reduced working hours, but that it also
had to be protected from excessive requirements urged by labour and its
Communist coalition partner.

On Europe, too, the Socialists sought to project an image of moderation
and consistency in words and action by seeking to balance the commitment
to the EMU with the defence of the 'European social model' against
the excesses of 'Anglo-Saxon liberalism' and United States-led globalization,
as noted above. This also meant seeking to limit the impact of Europe-led
deregulation on the *service public*, something the French government felt it
had managed to some extent during its presidency in 2000 by gaining
European partners' acceptance of a 'certain conception of public service that
is French' which 'talks not of the preservation but of the evolution and
enrichment of universal service'—in the words of Christian Pierret, Secretary
of State for Industry, in speech to the delegation of the National Assembly on
the EU on 1 February 2001. Europeanization also figured in the discourse on
globalization, as a shield against it. And it was clearly effective, if we judge
from the fact that 73 per cent of the public saw European integration as the
means to fight its detrimental effects (Meunier 2000: 114).

Globalization itself became an increasing focus of Jospin's discourse.
Within the context of its impact on France, the discourse was increasingly
split between the cognitive, with globalization described as a competitive
challenge France is able to meet so long as it continues with privatization and
deregulation, and the normative, with globalization decried as a destructive
force when firms lay off workers even though they are making profits—as in

the cases of the restructuring of Danone and Marks and Spencer, which announced closure of all of its French outlets in March 2001. On top of this, Jospin also tapped into the more basic ideas and values of the polity by deploring the impact on French culture and identity of globalization, now understood as homogenization resulting from American cultural imperialism (see Meunier 2000; Hay and Rosamund 2000). In this, he followed the lead of José Bové, the man who put the torch to a McDonald's restaurant railing against globalization's imposition of 'la malbouffe', or bad foods, and thereby became an instant cultural hero because 'resistance to the hegemonic pretences of hamburgers is, above all, a cultural imperative' while 'McDonald's red and yellow ensign is the new version of America's star-spangled banner, whose commercial hegemony threatens agriculture and whose cultural hegemony insidiously ruins alimentary behaviour—sacred reflections of French identity' (editorial in Le Monde, cited in Meunier 2000: 107). To solve these problems and others at the international level, Jospin's policy recommendations involved remaining open to competition in global finance and trade without, however, leaving everything up to the markets, by creating a regulatory framework or set of rules which could frame firm action and protect against pressures for a race to the bottom. As Jospin explained it,

We fully recognize globalization, but we do not see it as inevitable. We seek to create a regulatory system for the world capitalist economy . . . so that we can influence the process of globalization and control its pace for the benefit of society . . . This need to take control in adapting to reality places a special responsibility on the state . . . Often it is the only agent that can clear away or navigate around the archaic forces standing in the way of what society wants. (*Guardian*, 16 November 1999, cited in Clift 2000)

Jospin's speech in Rio in April 2001 echoed these same themes.

The construction of the discourse across policy areas and themes itself remained the work of a restricted governmental elite: Jospin himself plus Ministers such as Dominique Strauss-Kahn (Finance) on globalization and economic policy, Martine Aubry (Social Affairs) on social policy, and others, working in multiple, bilateral conversations rather than in a large group. According to Strauss-Kahn, the policy programme and discourse went in tandem—and worked because they were coherent.[7] Moreover, while the Prime Minister articulated the general government discourse, the various ministers were responsible for their own sectoral discourse—once, of course, it was cleared with the Prime Minister. This was made apparent in the

---

[7] Interview with author, Paris, 4 October 1999.

Wednesday parliamentary question periods—which Jospin was one of the first Prime Ministers actually to attend regularly—where Jospin had his ministers respond to the questions concerning their sectors, even when he was the one asked the question, unless, of course, the issue was so controversial that the Prime Minister had to speak to it.

The Jospin government, then, managed to construct a discourse which was sufficiently legitimizing to allow for a wide range of reforms that under earlier governments had been stymied or generated social conflict. Jospin's success was evident from his unprecedented popularity during his first three years in office, despite economic problems which improved only towards the end of those three years. Having started with a 47 per cent approval rating at the time of his election, he reached a high of 63 per cent right after the Soccer World Cup in July 1998, and settled at a comfortable 55 per cent by May 2000 according to the IFOP opinion survey, with other surveys placing him even higher (*Le Monde*, 3 June 2000: 6). Subsequent slippage in popularity owed much to problems with Jospin's discourse, which increasingly lost its persuasiveness once the two ministers most responsible for its balanced construction—Aubry and Strauss-Kahn—had left the government. The presidential election fiasco of April 2002, moreover, when Jospin came in third behind the extreme right candidate Le Pen and the incumbent president Chirac, had much to do with his lacklustre campaign discourse, and the splintering of the left's vote among a number of minor parties. Most importantly, however, the discourse of security had crowded out any discussion of economy policy, which had been Jospin's trump card.

The communicative discourse was not Jospin's only problem in his last two years in office, however. The government still confronted great difficulties not only because of the institutional context that made productive coordinative discourse with the social partners difficult, and thus hindered reform efforts. Social policy reform, although at least making some headway, unlike under Juppé, nevertheless still had a long way to go before it would have resolved the problems of the social security system or joblessness. Moreover, the government no longer had a monopoly on the communicative discourse in this sphere, given business's new voice.

Germany: Recasting the Traditional Discourse

Since the late 1950s up until the 1990s, German governments were successful in sustaining a legitimizing national discourse that projected a convincing vision of Germany securely ensconced within an integrating

Europe and a globalizing world. As long as the German economy flourished and Germany managed to dominate European monetary policy and delay adjusting its industrial policy, German governments found it relatively easy to reconcile their pro-European and pro-global stance with a discourse that infused liberal market notions with social commitments in the political-economic paradigm of the 'social market economy'. But in the 1990s they found it much harder to maintain that discourse unchanged, let alone the policy programme it supported, following the economic problems and costs related to unification, the competitive pressures from globalization, and the deregulatory policies promoted by Europeanization. Rather than abandoning the discourse, however, they attempted to recast it to fit the changing realities by emphasizing the market and de-emphasizing the social in the discourse of the social market economy. The task has in some ways been more difficult than in France or Britain because of the institutional context which privileges the coordinative over the communicative discourse, and includes a much wider range of policy elites in the negotiation of change.

The Post-war Policy Paradigm and Discourse

In Germany, the post-war political-economic paradigm of the 'social market economy', essentially set by the late 1950s, lasted largely unquestioned up until the 1990s, as did the discourse which served to legitimize it. The social market economy meant essentially the same thing to the major parties throughout this period, Christian Democrats and Social Democrats alike: a market system which, although competitive, was accepted as politically instituted and socially regulated rather than assumed to be ideally free but constrained by government; firms which were seen as social institutions rather than as networks of private contracts or the property of shareholders; a state which was expected to act in an 'enabling' rather than in either a laissez-faire or an *étatiste* manner; an economic governance system which was to be managed primarily by publicly enabled associations engaging in widespread, organized cooperation and bargaining rather than by civil servants as administrators or regulators; and a welfare system which was to provide a protective net against the pitfalls of the market (Streeck 1997). The core of the discourse about the social market economy also differed little, even though the party discourses differed somewhat across time. The market side of the discourse emphasized the liberal nature of the economy, the federal state's hands-off approach to industry and its limited powers with regard to the economy—passing over the *Länder's* larger involvement in local industrial policy—and the Bundesbank's role as the independent guardian of the stability of the currency and, by extension, of the economy. The social side focused on the cooperation of business and labour in the setting of wages and work conditions in their separate sphere of activity, and on the generous welfare state (Schmidt 2000*b*: 275).

The discourse and the paradigm were developed between the late 1940s and the late 1950s, and represented the compromise between liberal capitalist and social democratic/Christian democratic ideas; between traditionalist and modernist practices, whether liberal or socialist; and between capital and labour social groupings. The compromises meant that the market economy contained traditionalist status protections for farmers, civil servants, and small and medium-sized businesses—the *Mittelstand*—a large welfare state component, and strong unions which were nevertheless willing to coexist with more traditional forms of social organization and to compromise with capital (Streeck 1996).

The paradigm of the social market economy was largely the invention of academic economists at the end of the Second World War, led in particular by Alfred Müller-Armack, at the head of the economic policy section of the federal Ministry of Economics, who came up with an eclectic brand of liberalism which he named the 'social market economy' as a middle way between collectivist socialism and laissez-faire capitalism (Nicholls 1994). The concept of the social market economy essentially brought together the 'ordo-liberal' concepts of the pre-war years with social policy postulates from the social-Catholic tradition, mixing a liberal view of minimal state action in the market with an acceptance of interventionism with regard to government promotion of full employment, government regulation of utilities, transport, agriculture, and the credit system, and government provision of social welfare—as long as it was 'market-conforming' (Lehmbruch 1999; Nicholls 1994). But while the ideas came from this 'discourse coalition' of academic economists (Lehmbruch 1999), led by Müller-Armack who acted as policy entrepreneur, the 'marketing' of the paradigm must be credited to Ludwig Erhard—also an economist, but better known for his government roles. His communicative discourse was largely responsible for the social market economy's public acceptance (Nicholls 1994, 1997; Giersch, Paqué, and Schmieding 1992).

The political-economic paradigm of the social market economy was the perfect formula for Adenauer in the Christian Democratic Union (CDU), since it promoted party unity by serving to reconcile the left wing made up of social Catholics and Protestants sympathetic to the idea of 'Christian socialism' to the neo-liberal restoration of a capitalist market economy. For the Social Democratic Party (SPD), the paradigm was a harder sell. But although it rejected the social market economy at first, claiming that it had nothing 'social' about it, by 1952 it had already shifted positions, having introduced the formula 'competition as far as possible, planning as far as necessary'; and by 1959, with the Bad Godesberg programme in which it abandoned socialism for social democracy, it essentially reconciled itself to the social market economy and began talking about it increasingly in much the same basic ways as the CDU (Lehmbruch 1999). The trade unions also bought in to the paradigm and the discourse in the 1950s, mainly because of the system of co-determination instituted at that time and the *Tarifautonomie* system which gave them major responsibility, along with employers, for the social aspects of the social market economy in terms of wage levels, work conditions, and welfare—that is, the unemployment system and pensions.

From the 1950s until the 1990s, little was to change in the policy paradigm or the discourse, even though there were moments when other elements were grafted onto the paradigm or entered into the discourse, making it appear as if the paradigm were evolving into something greater than it had been in the beginning. In the mid- to late 1960s, neo-Keynesianism took hold for a time as the 'Grand Coalition' government engaged in greater market interventionism than the paradigm was originally assumed to allow, with 'global steering' the term for the demand management and counter-cyclical measures such as public investment and tax cuts which served to stimulate growth. This enabled Karl Schiller, Social Democratic minister of the economy from 1967 to 1971, to proclaim that he had achieved a synthesis of the 'Keynesian message' and the *'Freiburger Imperativ'* of ordo-liberalism (Lehmbruch 1999). In the early 1970s, moreover, there was an unsuccessful movement to take this interventionism much farther, with a short-lived discourse and a thwarted attempt at policy change from the Chancellor's office, that challenged the liberal view of the federal state by proposing a more coordinated approach to development through state planning in such areas as research and technology, industrial investment, education, and urban renewal. By the mid-1970s with the turn to monetarism, however, even any pretence to neo-Keynesianism or coordinated planning was gone.

When the CDU came to power in the early 1980s, in coalition with the now radically neo-liberal Free Democrat Party (FDP), the swing in the direction of greater liberalism and even less interventionism seemed assured. Chancellor Helmut Kohl's discourse propounding the retreat of the state and the importance of the free market echoed the neo-liberal themes of Thatcher and Reagan. But Kohl's discourse was not followed up by significant neo-liberal policy change in terms of either privatization or deregulation. The budgetary consolidation that did ensue represented more of a return to the traditional conservative, stability-oriented approach to macroeconomic policy than any new move toward neo-liberalism. In addition, although the FDP and a few others in the CDU did call for a return to individual responsibility and independence through cuts in social programmes, this had little effect on government policy. What cuts in welfare programmes there were resulted from the need to balance the budget, not from ideology, and were in any case offset by an expansion in redistributive programmes focused in particular on the family (Lehmbruch 1994: 206–7; Manow and Seils 2000). And the basic political-economic paradigm of the social market economy essentially remained intact.

Thus, whereas in the aftermath of the economic crises of the mid- and late 1970s France and Britain changed their discourses and policy paradigms, in Germany the post-war discourse about the political-economic paradigm of the social market economy survived the crisis intact. This was in large measure because both Germany's policy programme and discourse were supple enough to support policies that promoted austerity. But it was also because Kohl lacked not only the ideology of a Thatcher in Britain but also the capacity to impose more radically neo-liberal policies, given the political institutional context. The high level of autonomy of government ministries, together with the strength of organized interests as well as the *Länder* in the policy process, meant that, even had there been the will, which there was not, there was little way to institute any coordinated neo-liberal reform. There was also relatively little electoral support for change, given that the only party proposing serious neo-liberal reform was the FDP, whose electoral support never rose above the single digits. The public on the whole did not seem to support any changes to the structure of welfare and work, and did not seem to favour the kinds of policies that are normally associated with neo-liberal reform. In a wide variety of ISSP surveys, the German public proved largely opposed to liberal notions that assumed that business profits would improve everyone's standard of living, that large differences in income were necessary for a country's prosperity, or that financial incentives were necessary for people to take extra responsibility (see Schmidt 2000b: 276–7). And finally, there was also less need for such radical change in Germany in the 1980s since the currency remained sound and the economy highly competitive.

Moreover, as a corollary to this, neither globalization nor European integration was perceived as a threat to Germany. As the lead economy in Europe and long a global competitor, given its strong export sector, global competitive pressure did not represent the kind of challenge for Germany that it did for France. Rather, globalization was seen by Germany in as positive a light as it was seen by Britain, although not so much for reasons of neo-liberal economic ideology, as was true for Thatcher, as for reasons of economic interest, given that it ensured the opening of foreign markets to German goods and helped promote German competitiveness. What is more, unlike Britain and more like France, European integration was also perceived in a positive light, although not so much because it represented a shield against global pressures, as it did for the French, as because it was a further guarantee of German competitiveness in European markets. In consequence, the discourse tended to be both pro-global and pro-European. And this was only reinforced by political interests and commitments from the beginning of the post-war period that saw economic integration as a guarantee for peace as well as prosperity.

The Neo-Liberal Challenges to the Post-war Paradigm and Discourse

In the 1990s, the post-war paradigm of the social market economy along with its legitimizing discourse came under increasing strain. First unification, which extended the paradigm and the discourse to East Germany, then recession in the mid-1990s, followed by increasing competitive pressures from globalization and deregulatory pressures from European integration, all raised a growing number of questions about the viability of the German system.

Unification in 1990 represented a major challenge with regard not only to the construction of a new policy programme for the East but also to the discourse. In confronting the crisis, the Kohl government chose to re-emphasize the liberalism of its early-1980s discourse and to reinvigorate the paradigm of the social market economy of the early post-war years. The interactive dimension of the discourse, however, represented a departure from the traditional pattern. Instead of the usual emphasis on the coordinative construction of the discourse and policy programme among a wide number of policy actors, the discourse was the construction of a restricted governmental elite, communicating directly with the public. The communicative discourse substituted itself for the usual coordinative not only because the crisis situation demanded quicker decision-making than the normal consensus-building process but also because there was little chance of building consensus among the usual policy actors. On the one-to-one conversion of the currency, while government leaders and the East German public were convinced that German monetary union together with the introduction of a market economy would solve all problems, the Bundesbank and independent economic experts considered it an economic disaster—and preferred maintaining a separate currency—whereas the Ministry of Economics and other government experts saw it as a political necessity. Moreover, although the opposition found it hard to object to monetary union, and may have lost the election on the basis of SPD candidates' initial questioning of it, they were not likely to agree with the government on the wide range of matters to be decided, given the intense electoral competition for new voters in the run-up to the 1990 elections (Lehmbruch 1994: 222–5).

The government's electoral success had a lot to do with a communicative discourse that evoked traditional values related to the social solidarity and the economic liberalism contained in the initial concept of the social market economy. The discourse not only emphasized the need to equalize conditions between West and East as quickly as possible but also evoked parallels with the early post-war period, by presenting a mythical reconstruction of Ludwig Erhard's construction of the social market economy as a rupture with both the authoritarian economy of the National Socialists and the planned economy proposed by the Socialists under the allied occupation, with the 1948 monetary reform and abolition of price controls as essential elements in the return to economic health (Lehmbruch 1994). Thus, it argued that there would be no sacrifice, just 'flowering landscapes', and represented monetary union, the abolition of price controls, and privatization in East Germany as a contemporary panacea capable of reproducing the earlier success, without any pain for the East or any new taxes for the West. Neither promise, of course, could the government fulfil, although the appeal to pure self-interest instead of the willingness to sacrifice did win it the elections—and made it impossible for Prime Ministerial candidate Lafontaine to make such an argument. The danger in providing such an unrealistic picture of the future, appealing to pure self-interest instead of to the willingness to sacrifice, was that it ultimately only increased the East's disappointment when the anticipated economic miracle did not come about, contributing to the subsequent malaise and the increase in support for the extreme right.

Subsequently, as unemployment continued to rise and privatization proved problematic, the government moderated its more radical neo-liberal faith in the market and returned to more corporatist concertation and cooperation with the opposition. This was especially true at the *Land* level, as 'grand coalition' and Social Democratic governments in the East engaged in more active labour market policy and even acquired shares in privatized firms in order to maintain their viability. Moreover, a growing Social Democratic majority in the *Länder*, which in turn produced an SPD majority in the Bundesrat, forced the CDU-led government to compromise increasingly with the opposition on issues such as social policy and tax reform.

Despite the increasing difficulties faced by the economy in consequence of unification, however, there was essentially a taboo against blaming unification for the necessary belt-tightening and economic adjustments. Notwithstanding tacit acknowledgment of the impact of unification on German economic, political, and social life, the most any major politician was willing to say publicly was that mistakes were made in the unification process, especially with regard to the exchange value of the mark. Controversy did erupt, however, with regard to how to allocate the costs, with the federal government having been forced to shoulder a larger burden since some *Länder* were unwilling to extend the system of fiscal solidarity to the East.

European integration was similarly passed over mainly in silence in the early and mid-1990s, not, so much because of any taboo, as there was in France, but because there was general agreement among all parties to the discourse about its appropriateness. As Theo Waigel put it in 1992, one of the advantages of EMU for Germany was that 'we are exporting our model of stability to Europe' (cited in Hedetoft 1998). Subsequently, though, EMU faced increasing opposition in the run-up to the introduction of the euro—not, however, because of fears of loss of sovereignty, as was true for Britain and even France, but because of fears that the euro would not be as hard a currency as the Deutschmark. Although the government and the opposition were in favour—despite the fact that at one point the CSU leader in Bavaria favoured postponement, as did Schröder in the SPD—along with employers' associations, focused on the savings allowed by a single currency and on the generalization of market principles to other areas, such as fiscal policy and social security (Verdun 1996), the Bundesbank and numerous economic experts were increasingly resistant. They were concerned about the ability of other member states to meet the Maastricht criteria—in particular Italy—and then stick to them in order to ensure a strong currency equal to the Deutschmark, and about the ability of the new European Central Bank (ECB) to institute monetary policies that would be as successful in maintaining price stability as the Bundesbank. Germany lost the moral and fiscal high ground, however, when its difficulties in reducing the budget deficit led it to engage in financial juggling of a kind similar to that of other countries, when Minister of Finance Waigel sought to improve the 1997 accounts through a revaluation of the Bundesbank's gold reserves. Such difficulties, together with concerns about the consolidation of public budgets in France and Italy as well as Germany, in turn sparked a call for postponement from German economists in a letter which appeared in the *Financial Times* and the *Frankfurter Allgemeine* on 9 February 1998 (Paterson 1998: 31-3). All of this, in turn, had largely turned the public against the euro. Public opinion was generally averse to the loss of the Deutschmark, with a February 1998 poll finding 58 per cent of respondents against the introduction of the euro, with 30 per cent in favour, and 52 per cent assuming a delay in its introduction, with 40 per cent expecting a start on time (Camerra-Rowe 1999). But the public was never consulted via referendum, unlike the French; and the introduction of the euro fell far enough between election periods not to have much of an effect. The single currency went forward nonetheless, as a political decision by the government.

In any event, whatever the discussions of the euro later in the decade, in the early and mid-1990s there was little focus in the discourse on the impact of either unification or European integration. Instead, discussion of the problems confronting Germany primarily focused on globalization. But this is not to say that the traditionally pro-global stance turned anti-global, only that globalization was increasingly used in Germany in the way Europeanization was used in France in the 1980s as an incitement to change and an excuse for it, and in Britain in the late 1990s as a economic constraint and an opportunity. Chancellor Kohl, for example, legitimized the welfare reforms between 1996 and 1998 in terms of globalization, arguing that Germany must 'balance anew and secure for the future the relationship between social services and economic productivity under changed global economic and demographic conditions' (speech on 26 April 1996, cited in Banchoff 1999: 20).

By using globalization as the reason for change, Germany managed to avoid some of the worst problems of France, with its pro-European rhetoric, and of Britain, with its anti-European rhetoric, since both rhetorics risked jeopardizing their countries' commitment to further integration. The danger for Germany, however, was that globalization alone would not be enough to convince the public of the need for neo-liberal belt-tightening, and that it could be seen more as an external menace to be resisted than as only one of a set of forces—internal ones related to unification and changing demographics as well as external ones related also to Europeanization—that demanded reform of the social security and the jobs system if the country was to remain competitive. In fact, during this period the rise of the extreme right, in particular in the East, was linked to the malaise provoked by global pressures as well as to the fallout from unification, even if this was not stated aloud. Moreover, it also provoked a response on the left of the Social Democratic Party, with party leader Oskar Lafontaine denying any 'imperative [*Zwang*] that required the subordination of social security and social justice to globalization' (speech on 28 June 1996, cited in Banchoff 1999: 21).

The government, interestingly enough, was not the main purveyor of the discourse of globalization—although it did use it. Rather, as the economy deteriorated in the mid-1990s, big businesses were the ones to take up globalization as a rallying cry. Led by Hans-Olaf Henkel, the head of the main employers' association, the BDI, big businesses became increasingly confrontational in their public expression of dissatisfaction with wage bargains they felt were excessively high and employment conditions they insisted were much too rigid. Henkel himself attacked the unions for undermining the spirit of individualism and self-determination he felt Germany required (*Financial Times*, 24 June 1996) and argued that his own confrontational style was necessary to make a dent in the system and to unmask the unions.[8] This is when the wage-bargaining system itself looked as if it was falling apart, as smaller employers began leaving the employers' associations such as Gesamtmetall that made up the BDA—the business peak association involved in bargaining—in response to what in their view were excessive wage increases. Even the business structure seemed to be succumbing to neoliberalism, as the heads of big businesses which went public by listing their stocks on the US and the newly deregulated stock exchange became more vociferous in their use of the language of shareholder value and in extolling the benefits of profitability, competitive capitalism, and flexibility. Despite the discourse, however, hostile takeover attempts remained rare (see Chapter 4) and confrontations with labour generally led to compromise.

The sick-pay controversy was a case in point. The unions were infuriated not only because the cuts from full salary to 80 per cent would have cost the average sick worker over $US300 a month but also because of the principle of the thing, since the law purported to take sick pay out of the autonomous collective bargaining sphere. When Daimler-Benz announced it would cut sick leave to match the lower standards, 100,000 workers protested, and Daimler backed off in the face of strikes. In the end, the sick-pay controversy was resolved more or less to the satisfaction of both sides: while the unions could claim a symbolic victory, since no large employers ultimately used the law, the employers were nonetheless able to save money, mainly because the unions made other concessions in exchange for the restoration through collective bargaining agreements of 100 per cent of sick pay—although now calculated solely on base pay, without overtime.

Moreover, subsequent to this and other highly explosive confrontations in the mid-1990s, which had led the unions to abandon the *Bündnis für Arbeit*—'Alliance for Jobs'—talks, the conflictual character of management-labour relations moderated greatly—and labour and management returned to more cooperative, coordinative discussions. In those areas where

---

[8] Interview with author, Bonn, January 1997.

labour-management relations were largely autonomous from government, the social partners went ahead with liberalizing compromises related to combating unemployment and increasing productivity, balancing management's desires for greater flexibility and lower wage rises with labour's concerns about job security. The discourse itself became less divisive: by 2000, 'sustainability' had become the new concept around which the head of the BDI, Henkel, sought to centre reform.

But while the social partners moved forward, government became increasingly paralysed in the run-up to the September 1998 elections, unable to reach a compromise with the opposition on its tax and welfare reform initiatives. The election campaign, in which the communicative discourse of government and opposition was of necessity more elaborate, worked at cross-purposes with the coordinative discussions behind closed doors, which were particularly non-cooperative as each side accused the other in their election campaigns of responsibility for the lack of reform. Beyond this, while Kohl ran on his record, and focused on the importance of maintaining past accomplishments, Schröder offered only vague promises rather than a fully developed policy programme, and sought to appeal to business by advocating liberalizing and modernizing policies and to labour by pledging to preserve Germany's generous welfare state through the roll-back of the government's modest cuts in pensions and sick pay. During the ensuing policy paralysis, which was decried by the President of Germany himself, it was assumed that significant reform would not occur until after the elections, once a new government was in place.

From the time of his election to the end of 1999, however, Schröder had yet to institute major reform in either tax policy or welfare policy, although he kept some of his electoral promises to the unions with regard to reversing certain CDU reforms and passed some initiatives on employment and social security that proved so impractical that they too had to be reversed. In the early months after the elections, Schröder deliberately stayed in the background, expecting that the coordinative discussions behind closed doors organized by the government in conjunction with the social partners in the Alliance for Jobs would lead to a wide range of liberalizing reforms on welfare and work. But these dragged on without producing substantial movement. The problem was a growing split within and between management and labour camps. Among employers, while some had been pushing hard for greater wage differentiation and a reduced role for central bargaining agreements, claiming that the rigid structure of the labour market was to blame for high unemployment and declining competitiveness, others preached caution and had begun harking back to the benefits of corporatism and the need to maintain consensus. A similar split between those for and against compromise appeared within labour. The strongest of the unions, the metal workers' union, had been hardening its stance, returning to a neo-Keynesian view by blaming mistaken monetary policy rather than labour market structure for the country's problems, and asking for larger wage rises, including a 6 per cent pay rise in 1998, which led to an agreed 3.5 per cent increase. Others, however, such as the chemical workers' union, which had been more concerned about rising unemployment and declining competitiveness in their sectors, had been seeking more moderate wage rises and were willing to allow for greater differentiation in wages. In between were the government and reformers on both sides, who hoped for greater accommodation by both labour and management, convinced that increased flexibility and differentiation in wages and work were the only way to save the corporatist system as well as the economy.

Tax reform as well as welfare reform was also stymied in consequence of the successive elections in the *Länder*, which quickly reversed the SPD's majority in the Bundesrat. The constant electioneering here too ensured that a communicative discourse focused on the voters worked at cross-purposes with any compromise on tax or welfare reform between government and opposition. In fact, even minor reform proposals generated protest from the Christian Democrats in opposition, who accused the Social Democrat-led government of seeking to destroy the security of the pension system, with reform initiatives they themselves had proposed while in office—in much the same way as the Social Democrats in opposition had accused the Christian Democrat-led government of dismantling the welfare state, although the SPD's opposition had been substantive, the CDU's tactical.

Finally, the government also confronted difficulties within its own ranks. In the first months in office, the government often seemed to speak with two voices: that of Chancellor Schröder, who appealed to business with his espousal of market liberalization, and that of party chairman and Minister of Finance Oskar Lafontaine, who appealed to the left of the party and the unions and appeared to reject market liberalization with his espousal of neo-Keynesian stimulation of demand through the lowering of interest rates, redistribution of income, and greater government management of the economy. His calls for the European Central Bank to reduce interest rates, moreover, caused discomfort not only for Schröder but also for EU member governments, in particular because this seemed to have the opposite effect on the ECB—which softened its position only once Lafontaine had left office, lowering interest rates in April 1999. Although Lafontaine's precipitous resignation as Minister of Finance and party chairman in March 1999 left

Schröder, who took over as party chairman and appointed someone more attuned to his own liberalizing views to the Ministry of Finance, as the principal voice of government, it also meant that the left was without a champion in the government and therefore initially at least harder to control. Moreover, as the SPD has moved toward the centre, it has found itself with greater competition from the left, in particular the Democratic Socialist Party (PDS) made up of former East German Communists in the former East German *Länder*, as well as sometimes in conflict with its coalition partner, the Greens (Camerra-Rowe 1999).

In response to electoral successes of the opposition in the *Länder* as much as in the face of stalemate in the social partners' discussions and the growing challenge from the left, Schröder finally began to take his message public with a clear communicative discourse—in great contrast to the first months in office, when he had been curiously silent, seemingly waiting for the coordinative discussions among the social partners in the Alliance for Jobs to point the way to reform. In the summer and into the autumn, Schröder began to articulate a more clearly neo-liberal policy programme and discourse. This was most apparent in Schröder's ill-conceived and ill-received espousal of the '*neue Mitte*' or 'third way' in a joint policy paper co-authored with Tony Blair, in which he insisted that 'for the new politics to succeed, it must promote a go-ahead mentality and a new entrepreneurial spirit at all levels of society' and must be more in tune with the challenges of globalization since 'In a world of ever more rapid globalization . . . we need to create the conditions in which existing business can prosper and adapt, and new business can be set up and grow' (Blair and Schröder 1999).

However, the neo-liberal message was also delivered in somewhat different fashion in the report around that same time by Schröder's Minister of the Economy, Werner Müller, which called for a radical reduction in state intervention and greater individual responsibility. Here, instead of Blair's 'third way', the report invoked more home-grown values by extolling the ideas of private initiative and self-provision as envisaged by Ludwig Erhard. Schröder himself seemed to warm to his communicative task on this, given that by 16 September 1999, in a speech to the Reichstag, he had abandoned his usual low-key approach to deliver an impassioned appeal for budget cuts—of $16 billion, which included slashing ministerial budgets by an average of 7 per cent, freezing pensions in real terms until 2001, and holding down welfare payments—on the grounds that Germany could no longer 'devour the resources that should nourish our children'. Moreover, he legitimized his actions in terms of a higher interest, insisting that although the harsh criticism from the labour unions claiming he was reneging on traditional

SPD values of social fairness pained him, 'even with close friends, the public good must sometimes take precedence over individual interests' (*New York Times*, 17 September 1999).

By late October 1999, however, in the face of continued electoral defeat, Schröder seemed to have reversed himself yet again, moving to a discourse which had much more in common with that of the French socialists, with an appeal to social justice. But, regardless of the changes in substance, the discourse did not resonate. And it was his own supporters and the trade unionists who engaged in mass protests that same month against his proposed austerity package and plans to limit rises in state pensions to the rate of inflation for the next two years. Only in December, once Schröder had spoken out against the hostile takeover attempt of Mannesmann by Vodafone and intervened to avoid bankruptcy for Holzmann did he regain credibility, by making clear through actions as well as words that he was intent on protecting the traditional social market economy even as he sought to liberalize it.[9] Tellingly, however, the late-December tax reform that stood to have the greatest impact on the traditional German social market economy, by eliminating the capital gains tax on shales of shares, was instituted without much discourse at all, let alone any regarding its potential effects.

Schröder's problems suggest that a forceful communicative discourse can be of the essence in a country such as Germany, where the complexity of the institutions and rules of interaction lead to a 'joint-decision trap' when the coordinative consensus breaks down (Scharpf 1988). Given Germany's current problems, for which what is required is nothing less than a recasting of the traditional post-war discourse to legitimize a more liberal turn in the social market economy, only a coherent communicative discourse will do. But for this, Schröder would have needed to construct a discourse that convinced the public not only of the necessity of neo-liberal reform but also of its appropriateness. And here, he would have done better to leave aside the Blairite values of the 'third way' and the Jospinian values of French socialism to come up with ones that resonated better with the Germans, drawing on the country's own symbols and values. His appeal to inter-generational values was in fact a step in that direction. But even this would not have been enough since, unlike in more single-actor systems, where a persuasive communicative discourse accompanying the imposition of reform may be sufficient, since a public that is persuaded of the necessity and appropriateness of reform is most likely to vote the reform party back into office, in

---

[9] He was also helped by the discrediting of Kohl and the CDU as a result of undeclared slush funds controlled by the former Chancellor.

multi-actor Germany such a discourse can be only the first step in the process of reform. For in a system of joint decision-making where the government does not have the capacity to impose, a communicative discourse is not sufficient. Here, reform also depends upon the further ability of the communicative discourse to frame the coordinative discourse among the social partners, the opposition, the *Länder* governments, and the federal government. Schröder, in other words, would have to construct a discourse capable of appealing to the general public while at the same time providing key policy actors with the language and set of concepts that would enable them to reconstruct their coordinative discourse and, with it, to create a new basis for consensus. By 2002, Schröder had not managed to construct such a discourse. And yet Germany has nevertheless slowly muddled through to reform, suggesting that even shards of a communicative discourse can promote change in the coordinative discourse once policy actors become convinced of the necessity of policy change in the face of economic crisis.

Conclusion

In Britain, one policy paradigm, the neo-liberal, and one discourse, the Thatcherite, has predominated since 1979. Although it may have taken Thatcher some time to convince the public and the politicians of the necessity, let alone the appropriateness, of neo-liberal reform, she largely succeeded, as evidenced by the fact that her Tory successor Major continued her neo-liberal programme with a somewhat kinder and gentler manner and discourse, and that New Labour under Blair has picked up the neo-liberal baton, renewing the Thatcherite discourse while giving the policy programme new *élan* rather than rejecting it. Blair's approach may be neo-liberalism with a human face, given the greater—at least verbal—attention to the poor and dispossessed, but it is still neo-liberalism in its support of a more liberal, open, and market-oriented economy and its acceptance of a more restricted welfare state. With such a legitimizing discourse, successive governments have for better or worse managed to convert the country without the kind of disruption faced by France in the 1990s and, arguably, with less public dissatisfaction.

In France, the problem since the early 1980s has been French governments' inability to fashion a coherent discourse to legitimize the conversion to a more liberal, open, and market-oriented economy and to a more restricted welfare state in the face of globalization and Europeanization. The absence of a fully legitimizing discourse, capable of speaking to the value of reform and not just to the need for it, led to public malaise and protest, stymied necessary welfare reform efforts, and contributed to the rise of the extreme right. These are problems which Germany also began to experience in the mid- to late 1990s.

Germany under Schröder only just started the process of trying to recast its post-war social market paradigm and discourse. Success in such an effort is not at all certain, however, given an institutional context in which government cannot impose reform or even speak in a single voice, and which requires major policy actors together to recast the old policy paradigm and discourse or to forge new ones. In this way, countries such as Britain and France have it easier, given that discourse and policy programme are the product of more restricted, government-centred elites. However, as we have seen, even in these countries it has not been so easy. Britain seems to have been the more successful not only because of an institutional context which allowed the government to speak in a single voice and thereby to deliver a strong communicative message but also because it had a leader who had the courage of her convictions and was able to persuade the public of the value as much as of the necessity of the reforms as she imposed them. France has had greater difficulty not only because of an institutional context which left government with a less unified voice but also because its leaders have had fewer clear convictions and thus have long been less able to deliver a strong communicative message capable of persuading the public of the value of the reforms which they imposed.

Conclusion: The Futures of European Capitalism

Although globalization at a very general level and Europeanization on a much more concrete level have promoted convergence in national policies through greater market liberalization, in national practices through greater market orientation, and in national politics through more neo-liberal ideas and discourse, great divergence remains. European countries have not only followed different pathways to adjustment, they are likely to maintain these differences into the future. National policies are not the same even when they are patterned on EU rules and regulations; national practices remain differentiable into at least three varieties of capitalism despite similar policies and common economic challenges; and national discourses remain distinct even when they seemingly use the same language. With all this said, there can nonetheless be little doubt that globalization has been a potent force for change in national economies, promoting market liberalism through the internationalization of financial markets and trade, pushing the rationalizing of governments and the diminution in their welfare state functions, and loosening the traditional ties of business with government and labour. But for EU member states, European integration has been an even more potent force for change, given jointly agreed policies that created an opening to global forces even as they protected against them. Such policies have brought convergence in monetary policy, liberalization in industrial policy, decentralization in labour policy, and rationalization in social policy. They have ensured that EU member state governments are much less able to make decisions autonomously, without regard to external economic forces and actors, or even to control economic forces and actors in the national economy. But in exchange for the loss in national autonomy and control, governments have gained greater shared supranational authority and control. Such gains, however, have created additional losses in autonomy, although these are minimal when governments, alone or in tandem with other collective actors, make the decisions jointly at the supranational level, greater when delegated bodies make the decisions, and maximal when supranational collective actors or bodies take decisions without member states' direct or indirect involvement.

Behind these generalized effects of globalization and Europeanization lies a highly complicated and differentiated set of national experiences of adjustment. For although European countries have all experienced losses of autonomy and control in exchange for gains in supranational authority and control, the extent of these losses differs depending on countries' vulnerabilities to global or European economic forces, their political institutional capacity to impose or negotiate change, the degree of 'fit' with their long-standing policy legacies or long-held policy preferences, and the ideas and discourse that may serve to increase capacity to reform by changing perceptions of vulnerabilities and legacies and, thereby, preferences. These mediating factors help explain why countries vary not only in the timing but also in the manner of their adjustment to global and European economic pressures, with greater or lesser losses of national autonomy and control.

Within the EU, moreover, the differential kinds of compliance constraints imposed by EU decisions in any given policy sector are added factors in explaining variation in adjustment—that is, whether countries respond with inertia, absorption, or transformation to EU decisions that proffer highly specified rules that are potentially highly coercive; less specified rules that are therefore potentially coercive to a lesser degree; suggested rules that potentially promote mimesis; or no rules at all that may nonetheless engender regulatory competition. Thus, for example, even a highly specified rule will not be experienced as coercive if a country can easily absorb the changes because of a 'fit' with policy legacies and preferences. By contrast, when a more or less specified compliance rule goes against policy legacies and preferences, the response may be inertia even in the face of high economic vulnerability if a country cannot muster the political institutional capacity to change. Transformation may instead be the outcome when, in the face of high economic vulnerability, a country can muster the capacity to reverse policy legacies and preferences, but this occurs mostly only when aided by a sufficiently legitimizing discourse. In cases of a suggested rule or none at all, by comparison, the lack of fit with policy legacies and preferences is even more likely to lead to inertia unless high economic vulnerability and strong political institutional capacity together with a persuasive discourse promote transformation.

The differential policy responses to the external pressures of globalization and Europeanization up until now suggest that countries will continue to respond in their different ways long into the future. However much farther globalization will go, which is anybody's guess since 11 September 2001, one thing we already know: countries have internationalized at different rates to varying degrees in different ways, and will continue to do so. I use the term 'internationalize' rather than 'globalize' deliberately here. While the international economy may be seen as increasingly 'global', given the differences in kind and not just degree from the past in economic interdependence, countries' economies remain decidedly national even as they internationalize. Thus, the global and the national can be seen as two different albeit interpenetrating levels of activity, with national governments and businesses in particular moving in and out of both levels.

Europeanization is another story, however, since the interpenetration has gone much father. Common EU policies with regard to the single currency and the single market, along with open methods of coordination for labour markets and the welfare state, are moving EU member states toward an integrated European economy much less distinguishable from the national economies that constitute it. Some time in the not too distant future, if monetary and market integration continue at the pace they have until now, we are more likely to speak of the European economy than the French, the German, or the British, much as in the US we speak of the American economy even though there is underneath it a New England economy, a Midwestern economy, and a Californian, as well as Wall Street. But even with an increasingly European economy, significant differences among European countries will remain—not only in policies but also in practices.

The economic, institutional, and ideational pressures related to globalization and Europeanization, together with the policies instituted in response to those pressures, have no doubt had a tremendous impact on the configuration of European countries' capitalisms by altering the defining structural interrelationships of business, government, and labour at the core of their economies. Generally speaking, although big business has not become 'stateless', the internationalization of the financial markets and trade has nevertheless promoted change in the structure of business relations, with business having become more autonomous as it has grown bigger in size, more international in scope, and more dependent for capital on the financial markets than on the banks or the state. This, together with government deregulation and privatization, has in turn helped loosen the traditional ties between business and government. Business experiences less direct governmental interference or constraint as governments have eased the rules governing business, substituted more formal, arms' length relations through regulatory agencies in place of the closer administrative relationships or self-regulation of the past, and moved countless state-owned firms into the private sector. Finally, the increasing mobility, autonomy, and independence of business, together with governments' liberalizing tendencies, have also shifted the balance in industrial relations. Business has become stronger in bargaining power while labour has weakened as it has mostly lost its traditional protective support from government. And this in turn has incited labour to become at the very least less adversarial if not more cooperative, and has made wage bargaining generally more market-reliant and decentralized.

But although all European countries' political-economic practices have changed considerably in consequence of their liberalizing political-economic policies, this has not led to a convergence toward market capitalism, as most of the globalization literature assumes. Neither has it resulted in a binary division of capitalism into market capitalism or managed capitalism, with the concomitant demise of state capitalism, as much of the contemporary political economy literature on the varieties of capitalism seems to imply. Rather, European countries continue to be differentiable along the lines of the three post-war models, even if the degree of differentiation has diminished as they have all moved in a more market-oriented direction. By the beginning of the 2000s, whereas Britain's market capitalism had only intensified, Germany's managed capitalism was under great strain but nevertheless moving towards greater competitiveness, while France's state capitalism had been transformed from 'state-led' capitalism to a kind of 'state-enhanced' capitalism. These three countries' capitalisms remain divergent because of the path-dependence of their economic and political institutions and the cultural and historical framing of their approaches to change.

Still today, then, capitalism remains nationally based and distinguishable according to three main varieties. But over time, as European monetary and market integration proceed, with the single currency helping to consolidate the Single Market and fuelling greater cross-European financial market integration and business concentration, the national varieties of capitalism that have been the focus of this book may become less salient than sectoral or regional differences.

Sectoral differences are already important in Europe, as corporate strategies have increasingly concentrated on core activities within sectors while moving from the national to the European and even global level; as labour unions bargain increasingly with an eye to Europe-wide competition rather than to purely national factors; and as companies attempt to copy the production and innovation systems of the most successful firms in the sector and/or acquire what they cannot copy. But because firms' ingredients for success are generally nationally embedded—in the particular kinds of business inter-relationships, financing arrangements, labour skills, and state support within a given variety of capitalism—it may very well be that in the future sectors will increasingly be dominated by firms patterned according to the national variety of capitalism that is most internationally competitive for that sector. This could mean an increasingly geographical division of sectors within Europe, where the dominant firms in a given sector would come from those countries which provide it with certain comparative advantages. But it need not, given the mergers and acquisitions movement that has increasingly obscured firms' 'nationality'.

However, it is likely to ensure that firms in financial services, biotechnology, and the 'new economy' more generally will increasingly operate along market capitalist lines, regardless of the variety of capitalism to which their home country conforms overall—with more arms' length relations between firms, more contractual relations between management and labour, and a more 'hands-off' state together promoting radical innovation, high profits, and a short-term investment focus. By contrast, firms in high-precision engineering and manufacturing are likely to increasingly adopt the techniques of 'competitive' managed capitalism, with closer inter-firm relations, more cooperative management-labour relationship, and an 'enabling' state ensuring incremental innovation and strong profits over the longer term. Finally, firms in sectors such as defence, which are influenced by the priorities set by national governments and the EU, or the railroads, which require heavy investments with low rates of return over long periods of time, are likely to follow the patterns of 'state-enhanced' capitalism, with more state involvement regardless of the nature of business and labour interrelationships, levels of profit, or patterns of innovation.

For the moment, such sectoral differentiations appear in the EU as sub-patterns within overall patterns that continue to be largely identifiable in national terms. But at some point soon, the European political economy as a whole rather than national political economies may become the more appropriate level of analysis, and sectors across Europe the most appropriate focus. But national differences will nevertheless continue to matter. This is because, whatever the sector, countries that developed from post-war market capitalism will continue to have more individualistic and competitive inter-firm relations, those that developed from managed capitalism will seek greater cooperation and consensus in labour-management relations, and those from post-war state capitalism will almost always have a state that seeks to influence both business and labour where it sees the need.[1]

---

[1] Studies engaged in sectoral analyses already bear this out (see Hollingsworth, Schmitter, and Streeck 1994).

Regional economies, moreover, are likely to become increasingly significant as added sources of differentiation. Here, too, the differences are already apparent within countries, as regions dominated by large firms exhibit more hierarchical patterns of business interrelationships than those in which small and medium-sized businesses prevail, especially in Italy and Germany.[2] Regional governments' activities are likely also to become greater sources of divergence as devolutionary and decentralizing reforms along with subsidiarity afford regions greater freedom and resources in their relationships with business. Finally, in border regions, cross-border relationships are also leading to distinctive business-government-labour interrelationships and productive activities, as on the French-German, French-Italian, and French-Spanish borders.

In short, although for the moment national varieties of capitalism still represent the optimal unit of analysis, studies of sectors and regions are increasingly likely to provide the clues as to how countries' economic governance systems are evolving, along with the varieties of capitalism which best approximate them.

Most studies of the changes in national political economies would have stopped here. But they would therefore have missed out on the politics of economic adjustment, that is, not only on how policy actors managed to reach agreement on the construction of the policy programmes that changed political-economic practices but also on how political actors sought to gain acceptance for these policies and practices through legitimizing discourses capable of convincing the public that change was both necessary and appropriate. Discourse matters because it contributes to the adjustment process as a way both of coordinating policy construction and of communicating it to the general public, although in single-actor countries the communicative discourse is the more privileged and in multi-actor countries it is the coordinative.

In the realm of discourse, just as in the realms of policy and practice, the pressures of globalization and European integration have not produced convergence. National discourses remain distinct not only because of who constructs them and to whom they may be directed but also because they are informed by national culture and values, so much so that even the use of the same words, whether related to neo-liberal globalizing ideas or common European policies, generally carry subtle and sometimes even not-so-subtle differences in meanings.

Moreover, countries have had very different levels of success with their discourses in the process of adjustment. On the ideational dimension, this has

---

[2] See, for example, Locke (1995); Herrigel (1996); Crouch *et al.* (2001).

depended upon how convincing the arguments about the necessity of the new policy programme were, by demonstrating its relevance, applicability, coherence, and greater problem-solving capacity, as well as about its appropriateness by showing how it responded to the problems of the polity while resonating with national values. Success, however, also depended on the interactive dimension, that is, on whether the discourse exerted a causal influence before the fact, enabling policy actors in multi-actor systems to gain agreement on a policy programme, or after the fact, enabling political actors in single-actor systems to change opinions and win elections.

Discourse itself matters most in moments of crisis, when the accepted ideas and discourse no longer sufficiently explain, by way of justification or legitimization, the policies, the policies no longer appear to solve the problems of the day, and/or the practices they facilitate no longer work. The crisis itself is mostly the result of external events, although it may also come from internal contradictions in and/or between the discourse, the policies, and the practices. But it will affect countries differently, given differences in economic vulnerability, in the political institutional capacity to reform, in the 'fit' with policy legacies and policy preferences, and in the ability of the discourse not only to generate the ideas that are used to produce the policies that lead to changes in practices but also to legitimize the changes in policies and practices (see Fig. 7.1).

How, then, does one characterize the future of European capitalism? Not as one future but as several, with European countries pursuing different pathways to adjustment in response to the pressures of globalization and European

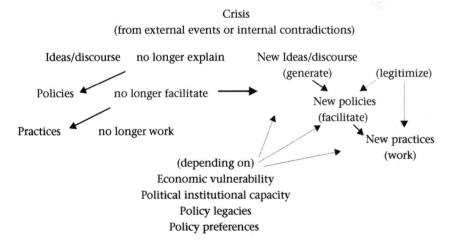

Crisis
(from external events or internal contradictions)

Fig. 7.1 The flow of ideas/discourse, policies, and practices

integration. Instead of convergence, we do better to talk of European countries going in the same liberalizing direction, but making different policy choices within the more restricted range available; of moving towards greater market orientation while continuing to conform to three national varieties of capitalism, even if sectors and regions may become more salient in an increasingly integrated European economy; and of persisting with different culturally and historically rooted discourses that serve for better or for worse to generate and legitimize the liberalizing changes in policies and market-oriented changes in practices.

References

Abélès, Marc and Bellier, Irène (1996). 'La Commission Européenne, du Compromis Culturel à la Culture Politique du Compromis'. *Revue Française de Science Politique*, 46: 431–56.

Adams, M. (1999). 'Cross holdings in Germany'. *Journal of Institutional and Theoretical Economics*, 1/155: 80–109.

Allen, Chris, Gasiorek, Michael, and Smith, Alasdair (1998). 'The Competition Effects of the Single Market in Europe'. *Economic Policy*, 27: 441–86.

Alter, Karen (1998). 'Who Are the "Masters of the Treaty"? European Governments and the European Court of Justice'. *International Organization*, 52/1: 121–47.

Amable, Bruno, Barré, Rémi, and Boyer, Robert (1997). *Les Systèmes d'Innovation à l'Ère de la Globalisation*. Paris: Economica.

—— and Hancké, Bob (2001). 'Innovation and Industrial Renewal in France in Comparative Perspective'. *Industry and Innovation*, 8/2: 113–33.

Andrews, David M. (1994). 'Capital Mobility and State Autonomy'. *International Studies Quarterly*, 38: 193–218.

Ansell, Christopher K. and Weber, Steven (1999). 'Organizing International Politics: Sovereignty and Open Systems'. *International Political Science Review*, 20/1: 73–93.

Artis, M. J. (1998). 'The United Kingdom', in James Forder and Anand Menon (eds), *The European Union and National Macroeconomic Policy*. London: Routledge.

Aspinwall, Mark (1999). 'Trains, Planes, and Automobiles: Transport Governance in the European Union', in Beate Kohler-Koch and Rainer Eising (eds), *The Transformation of Governance in the European Union*. London: Routledge.

Atkinson, Rob and Davoudi, Simin (2000). 'The Concept of Social Exclusion in the European Union: Context, Development and Possibilities'. *Journal of Common Market Studies*, 38: 427–48.

Auerbach, Simon (1990). *Legislating for Conflict*. Oxford: Clarendon.

Bairoch, Paul (1996). 'Globalization Myths and Realities: One Century of External Trade and Foreign Investment', in Robert Boyer and Daniel Drache (eds), *States against Markets: The Limits of Globalization*. London and New York: Routledge.

—— and Kozul-Wright, Richard (1996). *Globalization Myths: Some Historical Reflections on Integration, Industrialization, and Growth in the World Economy*. Geneva: UNCTAD.

Baldwin, Richard E. and Krugman, Paul (2001). 'Agglomeration, Integration and Tax Harmonization'. *Bulletin of the Centre for Economic Policy Research*, 76/Spring <http:www.cepr.org/pubs/dsp/dp2630>

Ball, George W. (1967). 'The Promise of the Multinational Corporation'. *Fortune*, 75/6: 1 June.

Banchoff, Thomas (1999). 'The Force of an Idea: Globalization and the German Social Market Economy'. Paper presented to the Annual Meeting of the American Political Science Association Atlanta, GA, August–September.

Barbier, J. C. (1998). 'Aspects Cognitifs et Normatifs de la Construction des Politiques de l'Emploi entre Niveaux Nationaux et Communautaire'. Paper presented at the workshop Les Outils Analytiques de l'Apprentissage Institutionnel, Association Française de Science Politique, RECO-ARASSH Program, Grenoble, 14–15 December.

Barnet, Richard J. and Cavanagh, John (1994). *Global Dreams*. New York: Simon and Schuster.

Bartlett, Christopher A. and Hideki, Yoshihara (1988). 'New Challenges for Japanese Multinationals: Is Organizational Adaptation their Achilles Heel?' *Human Resource Management*, 27/1: 19–43.

Bauchard, Philippe (1986). *La Guerre des Deux Roses: Du Rêve à la Réalité, 1981–1985*. Paris: Grasset.

Baudouin, J. (1990). 'Le "moment" néo-libéral du RPR'. *Revue Française de Science Politique*, 40/6: 830–44.

Bauer, Michel and Bertin-Mourot, Bénédictine (1987). *Les 200*. Paris: Seuil.

—— —— (1995). *L'Accès au Sommet des Grandes Entreprises Françaises 1985–1994*. Paris: Le Seuil.

Baums, T. and Fraune, C. (1995). 'Institutionelle Anleger und Publikumsgesellschaft: Eine Empirische Untersuchung'. *Die Aktiengesellschaft*, 3: 97–112.

Benner, Mats and Vad, Torben (2000). 'Sweden and Denmark: Defendong the Welfare State', in Fritz W. Scharpf and Vivien A. Schmidt (eds), *Welfare and Work in the Open Economy. Vol. II: Diverse Responses to Common Challenges*. Oxford: Oxford University Press.

Benz, Arthur (1989). 'Intergovernmental Relations in the 1980s'. *Publius*, 19/4: 203–20.

—— and Goetz, K. H. (1996). *A New German Public Sector? Reform, Adaptation and Stability*. Aldershot: Dartmouth.

Best, Michael (1990). *The New Competition: Institutions of Industrial Restructuring*. Cambridge, MA: Harvard University Press.

Birnbaum, Pierre (1982). *The Heights of Power*. Chicago: University of Chicago Press.

—— Barucq, Charles, Bellaiche, Michel, and Marie, Alain (1978). *La Classse Dirigeante*. Paris: Presses Universitaires Françaises.

Blair, Tony and Schröder, Gerhard (1999). 'Europe: The Third Way/Die Neue Mitte' <http://www.labour.org.uk/views/index.html>

Blank, Stephen (1978). 'Britain: The Politics of Foreign Economic Policy, the Domestic Economy, and the Problem of Pluralistic Stagnation', in P. Katzenstein (ed.), *Between Power and Plenty*. Madison: University of Wisconsin Press.

Blyth, Mark M. (1997). '"Any More Bright Ideas?" The Ideational Turn in Comparative Political Economy'. *Comparative Politics*, 29/2: 229–50.

Boche, Jörg (1993). 'Franco-German Economic Relations', in Patrick McCarthy (ed.), *France-Germany, 1983–1993: The Struggle to Cooperate*. New York: St Martin's Press.

Boix, Charles (1998). 'The Size of Government, Economic Development, Trade, and Democratic Institutions'. Paper prepared for delivery at the Annual Meeting of the American Political Science Association, Boston, MA, August–September.

Boltanski, Luc and Chiapello, Eve (1999). *Le Nouvel Esprit du Capitalisme*. Paris: Gallimard.

Boltho, Andrea (ed.) (1982). *The European Economy: Growth and Crisis*. Oxford: Oxford University Press.

—— (1996). 'Has France Converged on Germany? Policies and Institutions since 1958', in Suzanne Berger and Ronald Dore (eds), *National Diversity and Global Capitalism*. Ithaca, NY: Cornell University Press.

Bonoli, Giuliano (1997). 'Pension Politics in France: Patterns of Co-operation and Conflict in Two Recent Reforms'. *West European Politics*, 20: 111–24.

—— and Mach, André (2000). 'Switzerland: Adjustment Politics within Institutional Constraints', in Fritz W. Scharpf and Vivien A. Schmidt (eds.), *Welfare and Work in the Open Economy. Vol. II: Diverse Responses to Common Challenges*. Oxford: Oxford University Press.

—— and Palier, Bruno (1997). 'Reclaiming Welfare: The Politics of French Social Protection Reform', in Martin Rhodes (ed.), *Southern European Welfare States*. London: Cass.

Börzel, Tanja (1999). 'Toward Convergence in Europe? Institutional Adaptation to Europeanization in Germany and Spain'. *Journal of Common Market Studies*, 39: 573–96.

—— and Risse, Thomas (2000). 'When Europe Hits Home: Europeanization and Domestic Change'. *European Integration Online Papers* (EIOP), 4/15 <http://eiop.or.at/eiop/texte/2001-006a.htm>

Bowles, P. and Wagman, B. (1997). 'Globalization and the Welfare State: Four Hypotheses and Some Empirical Evidence.' Paper presented at the 38th Annual Convention of the International Studies Association, Toronto, 18–22 March.

Boyer, Robert (1995). 'Wage Austerity and/or an Education Push: The French Dilemma'. *Labor* (Special Issue): 19–66.

—— (1996). 'L'Étatisme Français', in Colin Crouch and Wolfgang Streeck (eds), *Les Capitalismes en Europe*. Paris: La Découverte.

—— and Drache, Daniel (eds) (1996). *States against Markets: The Limits of Globalization*. London and New York: Routledge.

Broadberry, S. and Crafts, N. (1996). *British Economic Policy and Industrial Performance in the Early Postwar Period* (Discussion Paper 292). London: Centre for Economic Performance, London School of Economics.

Brown, William (1994). 'Incomes Policy in Britain: Lessons from Experience', in Ronald Dore, Robert Boyer, and Zoe Mars (eds), *Return to Incomes Policy*. London: Pinter.

Busch, Andreas (1994). 'Central Bank Independence and the Westminster Model'. *West European Politics*, 17/1: 53–72.

—— (2000). 'Unpacking the Globalization Debate: Approaches, Evidence and Data', David Marsh and Colin Hay (eds), *Demystifying Globalization*. London: Macmillan.

Cairncross, Alec (1985). *The Years of Recovery: British Economic Policy 1945–1951*. London: Methuen.

Cameron, David (1996). 'Exchange Rate Politics in France, 1981–1983: The Regime-Defining Choices of the Mitterrand Presidency', in Anthony Daley (ed.), *The Mitterrand Era: Policy Alternatives and Political Mobilization in France*. London: Macmillan.

—— (1998).'Creating Supranational Authority in Monetary and Exchange-Rate Policy: The Sources and Effects of EMU', in Wayne Sandholtz and Alec Stone Sweet (eds), *European Integration and Supranational Governance*. Oxford: Oxford University Press.

—— Kim, Soo Yeon, and McDermott, Kathryn A. (2000). 'Openness, Political Institutions, and the Size of Government'. Paper prepared for delivery at the

Annual Meeting of the American Political Science Association Washington, DC, August–September.

Camerra-Rowe, Pamela (1999). 'Charting a New Course? German Social Democracy between European Integration and Party Politics'. Paper prepared for the Sixth Biennial European Community Studies Association Meeting, Pittsburgh, PA, 2–6 June.

Campbell, David (1993). *Politics without Principles: Sovereignty, Ethics, and the Narratives of the Gulf War*. Boulder, CO: Lynne Rienner.

Campbell, John L. (1998). 'Institutional Analysis and the Role of Ideas in Political Economy'. *Theory and Society*, 27: 377–409.

Cantwell, John and Kotecha, Usha (1997). 'The Internationalization of Technological Activity: The French Evidence in a Comparative Setting', in Jeremy Howells and Jonathan Mithie (eds), *Technology, Innovation and Competitiveness*. Cheltenham: Edward Elgar.

Caporaso, James (1987).'Labor in the Global Political Economy', in James A. Caporaso (ed.), *A Changing International Division of Labor*. Boulder, CO: Lynne Reiner.

—— (1996). 'The European Union and Forms of State: Westphalian, Regulatory or Post-Modern?' *Journal of Common Market Studies*, 34: 29–52.

Casper, Steven, Lehrer, Mark, and Soskice, David (1999). 'Can High-Technology Industries Prosper in Germany? Institutional Frameworks and the Evolution of the German Software and Biotechnology Industries'. *Industry and Innovation*, 6: 5–26.

Castells, M. (1996). *The Rise of the Network Society*. Oxford: Blackwell.

Caves, M. (1996). *Multinational Enterprise and Economic Analysis*. Cambridge: Cambridge University Press.

Cawson, Alan (1994). 'Sectoral Governance in Consumer Electronics in Britain and France', in Roger Hollingsworth, Philippe Schmitter, and Wolfgang Streeck (eds), *Governing Capitalist Economies*. Oxford: Oxford University Press.

CEPII (1998). *Compétitivité des Nations*. Paris: Economica.

Cerny, Philip (1994). 'The Dynamics of Financial Globalization'. *Policy Sciences*, 27: 319–42.

—— (1995). 'Globalization and the Changing Logic of Collective Action'. *International Organization*, 49: 595–625.

Chester, N. (1975). *The Nationalization of British Industry 1945–1951*. London: HMSO.

Cieply, Sylvie (2001). 'Bridging Capital Gaps to Promote Innovation in France'. *Industry and Innovation*, 8/2: 159–78.

Cioffi, John (2000). 'Comparative Capitalisms and Corporate Governance Regimes: A Comparative Analysis of Legal Change and Institutional Structure'. Paper prepared for presentation at the Annual Meeting of the American Political Science Association, Washington DC, 30 August–3 September.

Clayton, R. and Pontusson, Jonas (1997). 'Welfare State Retrenchment and Public Sector Restructuring in Advanced Capitalist Societies'. Paper presented to the annual meeting of the American Political Science Association, Washington DC, 28–31 August.

Clift, B. (2000). 'Third Way of *Realisme de Gauche*? The New Social Democracy in France'. *Radical Philosophy*, 201: 2–4.

Coates, David (1994). *The Question of UK Decline: The Economy, State and Society*. Hertfordshire: Harvester Wheatshaft.

—— (1999). 'Models of Capitalism in the New World Order: The UK Case'. *Political Studies*, 47: 643–60.

—— (2000). *Models of Capitalism: Growth and Stagnation in the Modern Era*. Cambridge: Polity Press.

Coen, David (1997). 'The Evolution of Large Firm Political Action in the European Union'. *Journal of European Public Policy*, 4/1: 91–108.

—— (1998). 'The European Business Interest and the Nation State: Large-Firm Lobbying in the European Union and Member-States', *Journal of European Public Policy* 18/1: 75–100.

Cohen, Elie (1992). *Le Colbertisme Hi-Tech. Économie des Télécom et du Grand Projet*. Paris: Hachette.

Cole, Alistair (1999). 'Europeanization, Social-Democracy and the French Polity: Lessons from the Jospin Government.' Paper presented to the Sixth ECSA Conference, Pittsburgh, PA, 2–5 June.

Coleman, William D. (1996). *Financial Services, Globalization and Domestic Policy Change: A Comparison of North America and the European Union*. London: Macmillan.

Confederation of British Industry (1999). *Economic and Business Outlook*. London: CBI.

Cooper, Richard N. (1968). *The Economics of Interdependence*. New York: McGraw-Hill.

Costello, Declan (1993). 'The Redistributive Effects of Interregional Transfers: A Comparison of the European Community and Germany', in *European Economy: The Economics of Community Public Finance* Reports and Studies 5. Luxembourg: EC.

Courtois, Gérard (1995). 'Education et Formation: Grandes Tendances', in *L'État de la France 95–96*. Paris: La Découverte.

Cowles, Maria Green (2001). 'The TransAtlantic Business Dialogue', in Maria Green Cowles, James Caporaso, and Thomas Risse (eds), *Europeanization and Domestic Change*. Ithaca, NY: Cornell University Press.

—— Caporaso, James, and Risse, Thomas (2001). *Europeanization and Domestic Change*. Ithaca, NY: Cornell University Press.

Cox, Robert Henry (2001). 'The Social Construction of an Imperative: Why Welfare Reform Happened in Denmark and the Netherlands but not in Germany'. *World Politics*, 53: 463–98.

Crafts, N. (1991). 'Reversing Relative Economic Decline? The 1980s in Historical Perspective'. *Oxford Review of Economic Policy*, 7: 81–98, 94.

Cram, Laura (1993). 'Calling the Tune without Paying the Piper? Social Policy Regulation: The Role of the Commission in European Community Social Policy'. *Policy and Politics*, 21: 135–43.

Crewe, Ivor (1988). 'Has the Electorate become Thatcherite?', in Robert Skidelsky (ed.), *Thatcherism*. Oxford: Basil Blackwell.

—— (1991). 'Values: The Crusade that Failed', in Dennis Kavanagh and Anthony Seldon (eds), *The Thatcher Effect*. Oxford: Oxford University Press.

Crouch, Colin (1994). 'Incomes Policies, Institutions and Markets: An Overview of Recent Developments', in Ronald Dore, Robert Boyer, and Zoe Mars (eds), *The Return to Incomes Policy*. London: Pinter.

—— (2001). 'Italie et Royaume-Uni: Les Surprises d'une Comparaison'. *Critique Internationale*, 8: 121–32.

Crouch, Colin and Streeck, Wolfgang (eds) (1997). *Political Economy of Modern Capitalism: Mapping Convergence and Diversity*. London: Sage.

—— Trigilia, Carlo, LeGalès, Patrick, and Voelzkow, Helmut (eds) (2001). *Local Production Systems in Europe: Rise or Demise?* Cambridge: Cambridge University Press.

Cully, Mark, Woodland, Stephen, O'Reilly, Andrew, and Dix, Gill (1999). *Britain at Work: As Depicted by the 1998 Employee Relations Survey*. London: Routledge.

Culpepper, Pepper (2001). 'Employers, Public Policy, and the Politics of Decentralized Cooperation in Germany and France', in Peter A. Hall and David Soskice (eds), *Varieties of Capitalism: The Institutional Foundations of Comparative Advantage*. Oxford: Oxford University Press.

—— and Finegold, David (eds) (1999). *The German Skills Machine*. Oxford: Berghahn.

—— (forthcoming). *Rethinking Reform: The Politics of Decentralized Cooperation in the Advanced Industrialized Countries*.

Czada, Roland (1993). 'Die Treuhandanstalt im Umfeld von Politik under Berbänden', in Wolfram Fischer, Herbert Hax, and Hans-Karl Schneider (eds), *Treuhandanstalt. Das Unmögliche Wagen*. Berlin: Akademie Verlag.

—— (1998). 'Vereinigungskrise und Standortdebatte. Der Beitrag der Wiedervereinigung zur Krise des westdeutschen Modells'. *Leviathan*: 24–59.

Daly, Mary (2000). 'A Fine Balance: Women's Labour Market Participation in International Comparison', in Fritz W. Scharpf and Vivien A. Schmidt (eds), *Welfare and Work in the Open Economy. Vol. II: Diverse Responses to Common Challenges*. Oxford: Oxford University Press.

Daniels, Philip (1998). 'From Hostility to "Constructive Engagement": The Europeanization of the Labor Party'. *West European Politics*, 21/1: 72–96.

Dankbaar, Ben (1994). 'Sectoral Governance in the Automobile Industries of Germany, Great Britain, and France', in Roger Hollingsworth, Philippe Schmitter, and Wolfgang Streeck (eds), *Governing Capitalist Economies*. Oxford: Oxford University Press.

Davies, Paul and Freedland, Mark (1993). *Labor Legislation and Public Policy: A Contemporary History*. Oxford: Clarendon Press.

Deeg, Richard (1999). *Finance Capitalism Unveiled: Banks and the German Political Economy*. Ann Arbor: University of Michigan Press.

Dehousse, Renaud (1992). 'Integration v. Regulation?'. *Journal of Common Market Studies*, 30/4: 383–402.

de Jong, Henk Wouter (1997). 'The Governance Structure and Performance of Large European Corporations'. *Journal of Management and Governance*, 1: 5–97.

Denkhaus, Ira (1998). 'Railroads' (Ph.D. thesis). Cologne: Max Planck Institute for the Study of Societies.

Deutsche Bundesbank (1997). *Geschiftsbericht der Deutschen Bundesbank für das Jahr 1997*. Frankfurt: Deutsche Bundesbank.

Dezalay, Yves and Garth, Bryant (1995). 'Merchants of Law as Moral Entrepreneurs: Constructing International Justice from the Competition for Transnational Business Disputes'. *Law and Society Review*, 29/1: 27–64.

Dickens, Linda and Hall, Mark (1995). 'The State: Labour Law and Industrial Relations', in Paul Edwards (ed.), *Industrial Relations: Theory and Practice in Britain*. Oxford: Blackwell.

Diez, Thomas (1999) 'Speaking "Europe": The Politics of Integration Discourse'. *Journal of European Public Policy*, 6/4 (supplement): 598–613.

Dillingham, Alan J. (1996). 'The Costs of Convergence: The Case of France'. *ECSA Review*, 9/2: 10.

DiMaggio, Paul (1986). 'Structural Analysis of Organizational Fields', in Barry Staw and L.L. Cummings (eds), *Research in Organizational Behavior* 8. Greenwich, CT: JAI Press.

Dinan, Desmond (1994). *Ever Closer Union? An Introduction to the European Community*. London: Macmillan.

d'Iribarne, Philippe (1989). *La Logique de l'Honneur: Gestion des Entreprises et Traditions Nationales*. Paris: Seuil.

Dobbin, Frank (1994). *Forging Industrial Policy: The United States, Britain, and France in the Railway Age*. New York: Cambridge University Press.

Dore, Ronald (1994). 'Introduction: Incomes Policy: Why Now?', in Ronald Dore, Robert Boyer, and Zoe Mars (eds), *The Return to Incomes Policy*. London: Pinter.

—— (1997). 'The Distinctiveness of Japan', in Colin Crouch and Wolfgang Streeck (eds), *Political Economy of Modern Capitalism: Mapping Convergence and Diversity*. London: Sage.

—— Boyer, Robert and Mars, Zoe (eds) (1994). *The Return to Incomes Policy*. London: Pinter.

Doremus, Paul N., Keller, William W., Pauly, Louis W., and Reich, Simon (1998). *The Myth of the Global Corporation*. Princeton: Princeton University Press.

Döring, Herbert (1994). 'Public Perception of the Proper Role of the State', in Wolfgang C. Müller and Vincent Wright (eds), *The State in Western Europe: Retreat or Redefinition*. London: Frank Cass.

Doty, Roxanne (1996). *Imperial Encounters*. Minneapolis: University of Minnesota Press.

Drahos, Michaela (1999). 'Convergence of National Competition Laws: The Cases of Germany, Austria, and the Netherlands', paper prepared for the Sixth ECSA Biennial International Conference Pittsburgh, PA, 3–6 June.

Dryzek, John (1990). *Discursive Democracy: Politics, Policy, and Political Science*. Cambridge: Cambridge University Press.

—— and Leonard, Stephen T. (1988). 'History and Discipline in Political Science'. *American Political Science Review*, 82, 4: 1245–60.

Duina, Francesco (1999). *Harmonizing Europe: Nation-States within the Common Market*. New York: State University of New York Press.

—— and Blithe, Frank (1999). 'Nation-States and Common Markets: The Institutional Conditions for Acceptance'. *Review of International Political Economy*, 6: 494–530.

Dumez, Hervé and Jeunemaître, Alain (1996). 'The Convergence of Competition Policies in Europe: Internal Dynamics and External Imposition', in Suzanne Berger and Ronald Dore (eds), *National Diversity and Global Capitalism*. Ithaca, NY: Cornell University Press.

—— —— (forthcoming). 'Le Marché de la Défense: Quels Modèles de Relations Transatlantiques?' *Critique Internationale*.

Dunning, John (1988). 'Changes in the Level and Structure of International Production: The Last One Hundred Years', in J. Dunning (ed.), *Explaining International Production*. London: Unwin Hyman.

Dunning, John (1993). *The Globalization of Business*. London: Routledge.

—— (1997). *Alliance Capitalism and Global Business*. London: Routledge.

Duval, Guillaume (1998). *L'Entreprise Efficace à l'Heure de Swatch et McDonalds: La Seconde Vie du Taylorisme*. Paris: Syros.

Dylla, Bronwyn (1998). 'EU Constraints on Industrial Assistance: How Member-States Adapt to a Supranational Watchdog'. Paper prepared for delivery at the annual meeting of the American Political Science Association, Boston, 3–6 September.

Dyson, Kenneth (1984). 'The State, Banks and Industry: The West German Case', in Andrew Cox (ed.), *State, Finance, and Industry: A Comparative Analysis of Post War Trends in Six Advanced Industrial Economies*. New York: St Martin's.

—— (1992). 'Theories of Regulation and the Case of Germany: A Model of Regulatory Change', in Kenneth Dyson (ed.), *The Politics of German Regulation*. Dartmouth: Aldershot/Brookfield.

—— and Featherstone, Kevin (1999). *The Road to Maastricht: Negotiating Economic and Monetary Union*. Oxford: Oxford University Press.

Edwards, Jeremy and Nibler, Marcus (2000). 'Corporate Governance in Germany: The Role of Banks and Owner Concentration.' *Economic Policy*, 31: 239–67.

Egan, Michelle (1997). 'Modes of Business Governance: European Management Styles and Corporate Cultures.' *West European Politics*, 20/2: 1–21.

—— (2001). *Constructing a European Market: Trade Barriers, Regulatory Strategies and Corporate Responses*. Oxford: Oxford University Press.

Eichengreen, Barry and Ritschl, A. (1998). *Winning the War, Losing the Peace? Britain's Post-War Recovery in a West German Mirror* (Discussion Paper 1809). Washington, DC: Center for Economic Policy Research.

Eising, Rainer (2002). 'Policy Learning in Embedded Negotiations: Explaining EU Electricity Liberalization', *International Organization,* 56/1: 87–122.

—— and Jabko, Nicolas (2002). 'Moving Targets: Institutional Embeddedness and Domestic Politics in the Liberalization of EU Electricity Markets'. *Comparative Political Studies*.

Eltis, Walter and Higham, David (1995). 'Closing the UK Competitiveness Gap'. *National Institute Economic Review*, No. 154, November.

Enderlein, Henrik (2001). 'Wirtschaftspolitik in der Währungsunion. Die Auswirkungen der Europäischen Wirtschafts-und Währungsunion auf die finanz-und lohnpolitischen Institutionen in den Mitgliedsländern' (Dissertation). Cologne: Max Planck Institute for the Study of Societies.

Esping-Andersen, Gosta (1990). *Three Worlds of Welfare State Capitalism*. Cambridge: Polity Press.

—— (1999). *Social Foundations of Post-Industrial Economies*. Oxford: Oxford University Press.

Esser, Josef (1995). 'Germany: The Old Policy Style', in Jack Hayward (ed.), *Industrial Enterprise and European Integration: From National to International Champions in Western Europe*. Oxford: Oxford University Press.

—— Fach, Wolfgang and Dyson, Kenneth (1984). 'Social Market and Modernization Policy: West Germany', in Kenneth Dyson and Stephen Wilkes (eds), *Industrial Crisis: A Comparative Study of State and Industry*. New York: St Martin's Press.

Estevez-Abe, Margarita, Iversen, Torben, and Soskice, David (2001). 'Social Protection and the Formation of Skills: A Reinterpretation of the Welfare State', in Peter A. Hall and David Soskice (eds), *Varieties of Capitalism: The Institutional Foundations of Comparative Advantage*. Oxford: Oxford University Press.

Eurostat (various years). *Basic Statistics of the European Union*. Brussels: Commission of the European Communities.

Evans, B. and Taylor, A. (1996). *From Salisbury to Major: Continuity and Change in Conservative Politics*. Manchester: Manchester University Press.

Evans, M., Paugam. S., and Prélis, J. (1995). *Chunnel Vision: Poverty, Social Exclusion, and the Debate on Social Welfare in France and Britain* (Discussion Paper WSP/115). London: LSE-STICERD Welfare State Programme,.

Evans, Peter B. (1993). 'Building an Integrative Approach to International and Domestic Politics: Reflections and Projections', in Peter B. Evans, Harold K. Jacobsen, and Robert D. Putnam (eds), *Double-Edged Diplomacy: International Bargaining and Domestic Politics*. Berkeley: University of California Press.

Faure, Alain, Pollet, Gilles, and Warin, Philippe (1995). *La Construction du Sens dans les Politiques Publiques: Débats autour de la notion de Référentiel*. Paris: L'Harmattan.

Favier, Pierre and Martin-Rolland, Michel (1996). *La Décennie Mitterrand. 1: Les Ruptures 1981-1984*. Paris: Seuil.

Fawcett, Helen (1995). 'The Privatization of Welfare: The Impact of Parties on the Private/Public Mix in Pension Provision'. *West European Politics*, 18/4: 150–69.

Featherstone, Kevin (1998). '"Europeanization" and the Centre Periphery: The Case of Greece in the 1990s'. *South European Society and Politics*, 3/1: 23–39.

—— (1999). 'The British Labor Party from Kinnock to Blair: Europeanism and Europeanization'. Paper prepared for presentation at the ECSA Sixth Biennial International Conference, Pittsburgh, PA, 2–5 June.

—— (2001a). 'Three Dimensions of "Europeanization": Institutional, Strategic, and Cognitive'. Unpublished manuscript.

—— (2001b). 'The Political Dynamics of External Empowerment: The Emergence of EMU and the Challenge to the European Social Model.' Paper presented the ECSA Seventh Biennial International Conference Madison, Wisconsin, 31 May–2 June.

Ferrera, Maurizio and Gualmini, Elisabetta (1999). *Salvati dal'Europa?* Rome: Il Mulino.

—— (2000). 'Italy: Rescue from Without?', in Fritz W. Scharpf and Vivien A. Schmidt (eds), *Welfare and Work in the Open Economy. Vol. II: Diverse Responses to Common Challenges*. Oxford: Oxford University Press.

Finegold, David and Soskice, David (1988). 'The Failure of Training in Britain: Analysis and Prescription'. *Oxford Review of Economic Policy*, 4/3: 21–53.

—— and Wagner, Karin (1997). 'When Lean Production Meets the "German Model": Innovative Responses in the German and US Pump Industries'. *Industry and Innovation*, 4: 207–32.

Finnemore, Martha and Sikkink, Kathryn (1998). 'International Norm Dynamics and Political Change'. *International Organization*, 52: 887–917.

Finon, Dominique and Staropoli, Carine (2001). 'Institutional and Technological Co-Evolution in the French Electronuclear Industry'. *Industry and Innovation*, 8/2: 179–99.

Fioretos, Orfeo (2001). 'The Domestic Sources of Multilateral Preferences: Varieties of Capitalism in the European Community', in Peter A. Hall and David Soskice (eds), *Varieties of Capitalism: The Institutional Foundations of Comparative Advantage*. Oxford: Oxford University Press.

Fitoussi, Jean-Paul and Le Cachewx, Jacques (2002). *Rapport sur |'État de |'Union Européenne 2002*. Paris: Fayard and Sciences Po.

Fligstein, Neil (1997). 'Is Globalization the Cause of the Crises of the Welfare States?' Paper prepared for the Annual Meeting of the American Sociological Association, Toronto, August.

—— and Mara-Drita, Iona (1996). 'How to Make a Market: Reflections on the Attempt to Create a Single Market in the European Union'. *American Journal of Sociology*, 102: 1–32.

Forder, James and Menon, Anand (eds) (1998). *The European Union and National Macroeconomic Policy*. London: Routledge.

Foreman-Peck, James and Millward, Robert (1994). *Public and Private Ownership of British Industry 1820–1990*. Oxford: Clarendon Press.

Fouilleux, Eve (2001). 'The European Commission, A Constrained Political Entrepreneur'. Paper prepared for presentation at the conference on Ideas, Discourse, and European Integration, European Union Centre, Harvard University 11-12 May.

Franks, J. R. and Mayer, C. P. (1995). 'Ownership and Control', in H. Siebert (ed.), *Trends in Business Organization: Do Participation and Control Increase Competitiveness?*. Tübingen: JCB Mohr.

Freeman, R. B. (1995). 'Are Your Wages Set in Beijing?'. *Journal of Economic Perspectives*, 9/3: 15–32.

Freiden, Jeffrey and Rogowski, Ronald (1966). 'The Impact of the International Economy on National Policies: An Analytic Overview', in Robert Keohane and Helen Milner (eds), *Internationalization and Domestic Politics*. New York: Cambridge University Press.

Freyssenet, Michel (1998). 'Renault: From Diversified Mass Production to Innovative Flexible Specialization', in M. Freyssenet *et al.* (eds), *One Best Way? Trajectories and Industrial Models of the World's Automotive Producers*. Oxford: Oxford University Press.

Frieden, Jeffrey A. (1991). 'Invested Interests: The Politics of National Economic Policies in a World of Global Finance'. *International Organization*, 45: 425–51.

Froud, Julie, Haslam, Colin, Johla, Sukhdev, Williams, Karel, and Willis, Robert. (1998). 'British Pharmaceuticals: A Cautionary Tale'. *Economy and Society*, 27: 554–84.

—— —— —— —— —— (2000). 'Shareholder Value and Financialization: Consultancy Promises, Management Moves'. *Economy and Society*, 29: 80–110.

Galbraith, John K. (1969). *The New Industrial State*. Harmondsworth: Penguin.

Ganghoff, Steffen (2000). 'Adjusting National Tax Policy to Economic Internationalization: Strategies and Outcomes', in Fritz W. Scharpf and Vivien A. Schmidt (eds), *Welfare and Work in the Open Economy. Vol. II: Diverse Responses to Common Challenges*. Oxford: Oxford University Press.

Garrett, Geoffrey (1992). 'International Cooperation and Institutional Choice: The EC's Internal Market'. *International Organization*, 46: 533–60.

—— (1995). 'Capital Mobility, Trade, and the Domestic Politics of Economic Policy'. *International Organization*, 49: 657–87.

—— (1998a). *Partisan Politics in the Global Economy*. Cambridge: Cambridge University Press.

—— (1998b). 'Global Markets and National Politics: Collision Course or Virtuous Circle?'. *International Organization*, 52: 787–824.

—— (1999). 'Globalization and Government Spending around the World'. Paper prepared for presentation at the Annual Meeting of the American Political Science Association Atlanta, GA, August–September.

—— and Lange, Peter (1991). 'Political Responses to Interdependence: What's Left for the Left'. *International Organization*, 46: 539–64.

—— and Mitchell, Deborah (2001). 'Globalization and the Welfare State'. *European Journal of Political Research*, 39/2: 145–77.

—— and Weingast, Barry R. (1993). 'Ideas, Interests, and Institutions: Constructing the European Community's Internal Market', in Judith Goldstein and Robert O. Keohane (eds), *Ideas and Foreign Policy: Beliefs, Institutions, and Political Change*. Ithaca, NY: Cornell University Press.

Gereffi, G. and Korzeniewicz, M. (eds) (1994). *Commodity Chains and Global Capitalism*. Westport: Praeger.

Gerschenkron, Alexander (1962). *Economic Backwardness in Historical Perspective*. Cambridge, MA: Harvard University Press.

Geyer, Robert (1998). 'Globalization and the Non-Defence of the Welfare State'. *West European Politics*, 21/3: 77–102.

Gibbs, P. (1999). 'Mergers and Acquisition Research.' Unpublished report (15 April), JP Morgan Securities.

Giersch, Hans, Paqué, Karl-Heinz, and Schmieding, Holger (1992). *The Fading Miracle: Four Decades of Market Economy in Germany*. Cambridge: Cambridge University Press.

Gill, Stephen (1995). 'Globalisation, Market Civilisation, and Disciplinary Neoliberalism'. *Millennium*, 24: 399–424.

Gilmour, Sir Ian (1977). *Inside Right: A Study of Conservatism*. London: Hutchinson.

Gilpin, Robert (1975). *U.S. Power and the Multinational Corporation*. New York: Basic Books.

Glassmann, Ulrich and Voelzkow, Helmut (2001). 'The Governance of Local Economies in Germany', in Colin Crouch *et al.* (eds), *Local Production Systems in Europe: Rise or Demise?*. Cambridge: Cambridge University Press.

Godin, Emmanuel (1996). 'Le Néo-Libéralisme à la Française: Une exception?' *Modern and Contemporary France*, NS4, 1: 61–70.

Goldin, Miriam, Wallerstein, Michael, and Lange, Peter (1999). 'Postwar Trade-Union Organization and Industrial Relations in Twelve Countries', in Herbert Kitschelt *et al.* (eds), *Continuity and Change in Contemporary Capitalism*. New York: Cambridge University Press.

Goldstein, Judith and Keohane, Robert O. (eds) (1993). *Ideas and Foreign Policy: Beliefs, Institutions, and Political Change*. Ithaca, NY: Cornell University Press.

Goldthorpe, John (ed.) (1984). *Order and Conflict in Contemporary Capitalism: Studies in the Political Economy of Western European Nations*. Oxford: Oxford University Press.

Goodman, John B. (1992). *Monetary Sovereignty: The Politics of Central Banking in Western Europe*. Ithaca, NY: Cornell University Press.

—— and Pauly, Louis W. (1993). 'The Obsolescence of Capital Controls? Economic Management in an Age of Global Markets'. *World Politics*, 46/1: 50–82.

Gordon, Philip and Meunier, Sophie (2001). *The French Challenge: Adapting to Globalization*. Washington, DC: Brookings Institution.

Gottweis, Herbert (1999). *Regulating Genetic Engineering in the European Union: A Post-Structuralist Perspective*. London: Routledge.

Gough, Ian (1996). 'Social Welfare and Competitiveness'. *New Political Economy*, 1: 209–32.

Gourevitch, Peter (1986). *Politics in Hard Times: Comparative Responses to International Economic Crises*. Ithaca, NY: Cornell University Press.

Goyer, Michel (2001). 'Corporate Governance and the Innovation System in France, 1985–2000'. *Industry and Innovation*, 8: 135–58.

—— (2002). 'Corporate Governance, Employees and the Focus on Core Competencies in France and Germany', in Curtis Milhaupt (ed.), *Global Markets, Domestic Institutions: Corporate Law and Governance in a New Era of Cross-Border Deals*. New York: Columbia University Press.

Grande, Edgar (1996). 'Des Paradox der Schache, Forschungspolitik und die Einflusslogik europäischer Politikverflechtung', in M. Jachtenfuchs and Beate Kohler-Koch (eds), *Europäischer Integration*. Opladen: Leske und Budrich.

Grant, Wyn with Sargent, Jane (1987). *Business and Politics in Britain*. London: Macmillan.

—— (1995). 'Great Britain: The Spectator State', in Jack Hayward (ed.), *Industrial Enterprise and European Integration: From National to International Champions in Western Europe*. Oxford: Oxford University Press.

Greenspan, Alan (1998). 'The Globalization of Finance'. *Cato Journal*, 17: 243–50.

Greider, William (1997). *One World, Ready or Not: The Manic Logic of Global Capitalism*. New York: Simon and Schuster.

Griffin, John (1995). 'Institutional Change as a Collective Learning Process? A US–German Comparison of Corporate Governance Reform.' Paper prepared for delivery at the Annual Meeting of the American Political Science Association Chicago, 31 August–4 September.

—— (2000). 'Making Money Talk: A New Bank-Firm Relationship in German Banking?' Paper presented to the Annual Conference of the Society for the Advancement of Socio-Economics, London, July.

Gros, Daniel and Thygesen, Niels (1992). *European Monetary Integration*. London: Longman.

Guillmard, Anne-Marie (1991). 'France: Massive Exit through Unemployment Compensation', in Martin Kohli *et al.* (eds), *Time for Retirement: Comparative Studies of Early Exit from the Labor Force*. Cambridge: Cambridge University Press.

Guiraudon, Viriginie (1997). 'Policy Change Behind Gilded Doors: Explaining the Evolution of Aliens' Rights in Contemporary Western Europe 1974-1994' (Ph.D. thesis). Cambridge, MA: Department of Government, Harvard University.

—— (2000) 'European Integration and Migration Policy: Vertical Policy-Making as Venue Shopping'. *Journal of Common Market Studies*, 38: 249–69.

Haas, Ernst (1958). *The Uniting of Europe: Political, Social, and Economic Forces, 1950–1957*. Stanford: Stanford University Press.

—— (1964). *Beyond the Nation-State*. Stanford: Stanford University Press.

Haas, Peter M. (1992). 'Introduction: Epistemic Communities and International Policy Coordination'. *International Organization*, 46: 1–35.

—— and Adler, Emmanuel (1992). 'Conclusion: Epistemic Communities, World Order, and the Creation of a Reflective Program'. *International Organization*, 46 (Special Issue): 367–90.

Habermas, Jürgen (1989). *The Structural Transformation of the Public Sphere* (trans. T. Burger and F. Lawrence). Cambridge, MA: MIT Press.

—— (1992a). 'Further Reflections on the Public Sphere', in Craig Calhoun (ed.), *Habermas and the Public Sphere*. Cambridge, MA: MIT Press.

—— (1992b). *The Theory of Communicative Action*. Cambridge: Polity Press.

—— (1996). *Between Facts and Norms: Contributions to a Discourse Theory*. London: Polity Press.

Hajer, Maarten (1995). *The Politics of Environmental Discourse*. Oxford: Clarendon Press.

Hall, Peter (1986). *Governing the Economy: The Politics of State Intervention in Britain and France*. New York: Oxford University Press.

—— (1989). 'Conclusion', in Peter A. Hall (ed.), *The Political Power of Economic Ideas: Keynesianism across Nations*. Princeton: Princeton University Press.

—— (1993). 'Policy Paradigms, Social Learning and the State: The Case of Economic Policy-Making in Britain'. *Comparative Politics*, 25: 275–96.

—— (2000). 'Organized Market Economies and Unemployment in Europe: Is it Finally Time to Accept Liberal Orthodoxy?', in Nancy Bermeo (ed.), *Context and Consequence: The Effects of Unemployment in the New Europe*. New York: Cambridge University Press.

—— and Soskice, David (2001). 'Introduction', in Peter A. Hall and David Soskice (eds), *Varieties of Capitalism: The Institutional Foundations of Comparative Advantage*. Oxford: Oxford University Press.

—— and Taylor, Rosemary (1996). 'Political Science and the Three New Institutionalisms'. *Political Studies*, 44: 936–57.

Hall, Stuart (1983). 'The Great Moving Right Show', in S. Hall and M. Jacques London (eds), *The Politics of Thatcherism*. London: Lawrence and Wishart.

—— (1988). *The Hard Road to Renewal: Thatcherism and the Crisis of the Left*. London: Verso.

Hancké, Bob (1996). 'Labor Unions, Business Co-ordination and Economic Adjustment in Western Europe, 1980–1990' (Discussion Paper). *Wissenschaftszentrum Berlin* (August).

—— (2001). 'Revisiting the French Model: Coordination and Restructuring in French Industry', in Peter A. Hall and David Soskice (eds), *Varieties of Capitalism: The Institutional Foundations of Comparative Advantage*. Oxford: Oxford University Press.

—— and Soskice, David (1996). 'Coordination and Restructuring in Large French Firms: The Evolution of French Industry in the 1980s' (Discussion Paper). *Wissenschaftszentrum Berlin*.

Hantrais, Linda (1995a). 'French Social Policy in the European Context'. *Modern and Contemporary France*, NS 3, 4: 381–90.

—— (1995b). *Social Policy in the European Union*. London: Macmillan.

Harcourt, A. J. (2000). 'European Institutions and the Media Industry: European Regulatory Politics between Pressure and Pluralism' (Ph.D. thesis). Manchester: Department of Government, University of Manchester.

Harmsen, Robert (1999). 'The Europeanisation of National Administrations: A Comparative Study of France and the Netherlands'. *Governance*, 12/1: 81–114.

Haverland, Markus (1999). 'National Adaptation to European Integration: The Importance of Institutional Veto Points.' Paper prepared for presentation at the Sixth Biennial International Convergence of the European Community Studies Association Pittsburgh, PA, 2–5 June.

Hay, Colin and Marsh, David (2000). 'Introduction', in Colin Hay and David Marsh (eds), *Demystifying Globalization*. London: Macmillan.

—— and Rosamund, Ben (2000). 'Globalization, European Integration and the Discursive Construction of Economic Imperatives.' Paper prepared for presentation for the International Political Science Association's 18th World Congress of Political Science, Quebec City, 1–5 August.

—— and Watson, Matthew (1998). 'Rendering the Contingent Necessary: New Labour's Neo-Liberal Conversion and the Discourse of Globalisation.' Paper prepared for presentation to the annual conference of the American Political Science Association, Boston, 3–6 September.

Hayward, Jack (1973a). 'National Aptitudes for Planning in Britain, France, and Italy'. *Government and Opposition*, 9: 407.

—— (1973b). *The One and Indivisible French Republic*. New York: Norton.

—— (1982). 'France: The Strategic Management of Impending Impoverishment', in Andrew Cox (ed.), *Politics, Policy, and the European Recession*. New York: St Martin's.

—— and Klein, Rudolf (1994). 'Grande-Bretagne: De la Gestion Publique à la Gestion Privée du Déclin', in Bruno Jobert (ed.), *Le Tournant Néolibéral en Europe*. Paris: L'Harmattan.

Hedetoft, Ulf (1998). 'Germany's National and European Identity: Normalisation by other Means', in Carl Lankowski (ed.), *Break Out, Break Down or Break In? Germany and the European Union after Amsterdam* (Research Report 8). Washington: AICGS.

—— and Niss, Hanne (1991). 'Taking Stock of Thatcherism.' Aalborg: Department of Languages and Intercultural Studies, Aalborg University, 4.

Heidrun, Abromeit (1990). 'Government–Industry Relations in West Germany', in Martin Chick (ed.), *Governments, Industries, and Markets*. Aldershot: Edward Elgar.

Heinisch, Reinhard (1999). 'Coping with the Single Market: Corporatist Response Strategies in Germany and Austria.' Paper prepared for presentation for the Sixth Biennial Conference of the European Community Studies Association Pittsburgh, PA., 2–5 June.

Held, David, McGrew, Anthony, Goldblatt, David, and Jonathan Perraton (1999). *Global Transformations: Politics, Economics and Culture*. Stanford, CA: Stanford University Press.

Helleiner, Eric (1994). *States and the Reemergence of Global Finance*. Ithaca, NY: Cornell University Press.

—— (1999). 'Sovereignty, Territoriality, and the Globalization of Finance', in David A. Smith, Dorothy J. Solinger, and Steven C. Topick (eds), *States and Sovereignty in the Global Economy*. London: Routledge.

Hemerijck, Anton and Schludi, Martin (2000). 'Sequences of Policy Failures and Effective Policy Responses', in Fritz W. Scharpf and Vivien A. Schmidt (eds), *Welfare and Work in the Open Economy. Vol. I: From Vulnerability to Competitiveness*. Oxford: Oxford University Press.

Hempel, Carl (1965). *Aspects of Scientific Explanation*. New York: Free Press.

Hennessy, Peter (1989). *Whitehall*. London: Fontana.

Héritier, Adrienne (2000). 'Differential Europe: National Administrative Responses to Community Policy', in Maria Green Cowles, James Caporaso, and Thomas Risse (eds), *Europeanization and Domestic Change*. Ithaca, NY: Cornell University Press.

—— (2001*a*). 'Market Integration and Social Cohesion: The Politics of Public Services in European Regulation'. *Journal of European Public Policy*, 8: 825–52.

—— (2001*b*). 'Differential Europe: New Opportunities and Restrictions for Policy-Making in Member-States', in Adrienne Héritier *et al.* (eds), *Differential Europe: European Union Impact on National Policy-Making*. Boulder, CO: Rowman & Littlefield.

—— Knill, Christophe, and Mingers, Susanne (1996). *Ringing the Changes in Europe: Regulatory Competition and Redefinition of the State: Britain, France, Germany*. Berlin, New York: DeGruyter.

Herrigel, Gary (1994). 'Industry as a Form of Order: A Comparison of the Historical Development of the Machine Tool Industries in the United States and Germany', in Roger Hollingsworth, Philippe Schmitter, and Wolfgang Streeck (eds), *Governing Capitalist Economies*. Oxford: Oxford University Press.

—— (1996). *Industrial Constructions: The Sources of German Industrial Power*. New York: Cambridge University Press.

Hetzner, Candace (1999). *The Unfinished Business of Thatcherism*. New York: Peter Lang.

Hirschman, Albert O. (1989). *National Power and the Structure of Foreign Trade*. Berkeley: University of California Press.

—— (1989). 'How the Keynesian Revolution was Exported from the United States, and other Comments,' in Peter A. Hall (ed.), *The Political Power of Economic Ideas: Keynesianism across Nations*. Princeton: Princeton University Press.

Hirst, Paul and Thompson, Grahame (1996). *Globalization in Question: The International Economy and the Possibilities of Governance*. Cambridge: Polity Press.

—— —— (2000). 'Globalization in One Country? The Peculiarities of the British'. *Economy and Society*, 29: 335–56.

Hobson, John (2002). 'Disappearing Taxes or the "Race to the Middle"? Fiscal Policy in the OECD', in Linda Weiss (ed.), *States in the Global Economy: Bringing Domestic Institutions Back In*. Cambridge: Cambridge University Press.

Hoffmann, Stanley (1966). 'Obstinate or Obsolete? The Fate of the Nation State and the Case of Western Europe'. *Daedalus*, 95: 892–908.

—— (1982). 'Reflections on the Nation-State in Western Europe Today'. *Journal of Common Market Studies*, 21: 21–37.

Hollingsworth, Roger, Schmitter, Philippe, and Streeck, Wolfgang (eds) (1994). *Governing Capitalist Economies*. Oxford: Oxford University Press.

Holmes, Martin (1985). *The First Thatcher Government 1979–1983: Contemporary Conservatism and Economic Change*. Boulder, CO: Westview Press.

Holstein, William J. (1990). 'The Stateless Corporation'. *Business Week*, 14 May: 98–100.

Howarth, David (2001). 'The French State in the Euro Zone: "Modernization" and Legitimzing Dirigisme in the "Semi-Sovereignty" Game', in Kenneth Dyson (ed.), *The European State in the Euro-Zone*. Oxford: Oxford University Press.

Howe, Geoffrey (1994). *Conflict of Loyalty*. London: Macmillan.

Howell, Chris (1992). *Regulating Labor: The State and Industrial Relations Reform in Postwar France*. Princeton: Princeton University Press.

—— (1995). 'Trade Unions and the State: A Critique of British Industrial Relations'. *Politics and Society* 23/2: 149–83.

—— (1996). 'Women as the Paradigmatic Trade Unionists? New Work, New Workers, and New Trade Union Strategies in Conservative Britain'. *Economic and Industrial Democracy*, 17: 510–43.

—— (1999) 'Unforgiven: British Trade Unionism in Crisis', in Andrew Martin and George Ross (eds), *The Brave New World of European Labor: European Trade Unions at the Millennium*. New York: Berghahn.

Howorth, Jolyon (2000). 'European Integration and Defense: The Ultimate Challenge?' *Chaillot Papers*, 43. Paris: Institute for Security Studies of the WEU.

—— (2001). 'Ideas and Discourse in the Construction of a European Security and Defence Policy'. Paper prepared for presentation for the conference on Ideas and Discourse in European Integration at Harvard University, Cambridge, MA, 11–12 May.

Hu, Y. (1992) 'Global Corporations are National Firms with International Operations'. *California Management Review*, 34/2: 107–26.

Huber, Evelyn, Ragin, Charles, and Stephens, John (1993). 'Social Democracy, Christian Democracy, Constitutional Structure, and the Welfare State'. *American Journal of Sociology*, 99: 711–49.

Hyman, Richard (1994). 'Industrial Relations in Western Europe: An Era of Ambiguity?'. *Industrial Relations*, 33/1: 1–24.

Hymer, Stephen (1972). 'The Multinational Corporation and the Law of Uneven Development', in Jagdish Bhagwati (ed.), *Economics and the World Order—From the Nineteen Seventies to the Nineteen Nineties*. New York: Macmillan.

Insee (1998). *L'Économie Française: Rapport sur les Comptes de la Nation*. Paris: Insee.

Israelewicz, Eric (1999). *Le Capitalisme Zinzin*. Paris: Bernard Grasset.

Iversen, Torben, and Pontusson, Jonas (2000). 'Comparative Political Economy: A Northern European Perspective', in Torben Iversen, Jonas Pontusson, and David Soskice (eds), *Unions, Employers and Central Banks*. Cambridge: Cambridge University Press.

Jabko, Nicolas (1999). 'In the Name of the Market: How the European Commission Paved the Way for Monetary Union'. *Journal of European Public Policy*, 6: 475–95.

Jackson, Greg (2001). 'La Compétitivité et l'Égalitarisme Allemands et Japonais à l'Épreuve'. *Critique Internationale*, 8: 133–45.

Jacquemin, A. and Pench, L. (eds) (1997). *Europe Competing in the Global Economy: Reports of the Competitiveness Advisory Group*. Cheltenham: Edward Elgar.

Jacquet, Pierre and Pisani-Ferry, Jean (2001). 'Economic Policy Co-ordination in the Euro-Zone: What has been Achieved? What Should be Done?' *Centre for European Reform*. (January).

Jeffery, Charlie (1995). 'The Non-Reform of the German Federal System after Unification'. *West European Politics*, 18/2: 252–72.

—— (1996). 'The Territorial Dimension', in Gordon Smith, William E. Paterson, and Stephen Padgett (eds), *Developments in German Politics* (2nd edn). London: Macmillan.

Jobert, Bruno (1992). 'Représentations Sociales, Controverses et Débats dans la Conduite des Politiques Publiques'. *Revue Française de Science Politique*, 42: 219–34.

—— (2001). 'Europe and the Reshaping of National Forums: The French Case'. Paper prepared for presentation at the conference Ideas, Discourse and European Integration, European Union Center, Harvard University, Cambridge, MA, 11–12 May.

—— and Muller, Pierre (1987). *L'État en Action*. Paris: Presses Universitaires de France.

—— and Thérét, Bruno (1994). 'La Consécration Républicaine du Néolibéralisme', in Bruno Jobert (ed.), *Le Tournant Néolibéral en Europe*. Paris: L'Harmattan.

Johnson, Christopher (1993). *The Grand Experiment: Mrs Thatcher's Economy and How it Spread*. Boulder, CO: Westview Press.

Jones, Erik (2001). 'European Monetary Union as a Response to Globalization.' Paper prepared for presentation at the Seventh Biennial Conference of ECSA Madison, Wisconsin, 31 May–2 June.

Jupille, Joseph and Caporaso, James (1999). 'Institutionalism and the European Union: Beyond International Relations and Comparative Politics'. *Annual Review of Political Science*, 2: 429–44.

Jürgens, Ulrich, Naumann, Katrin, and Rupp, Joachim (2000). 'Shareholder Value in an Adverse Environment: The German Case'. *Economy and Society*, 29: 54–79.

Juvin, Hervé (1995). 'Les Répercussions Économiques et Financières', in F. Dion (ed.), *Les Privatisations en France*. Paris: Notes et Études Documentaires No. 5024.

Kapstein, Ethan (1994). *Governing the Global Economy*. Cambridge, MA: Harvard University Press.

Kassim, Hussein (1998). 'The European Union and National Policy Making: The Case of Air Transport.' Paper prepared for presentation at the annual meetings of American Political Science Association Boston, MA, 3–6 September.

Katzenstein, Peter (ed.) (1978). *Between Power and Plenty: Foreign Policies of Advanced Industrialized States*. Madison: University of Wisconsin Press.

—— (1985). *Small States in World Markets*. Ithaca, NY: Cornell University Press.

—— (1989) 'Conclusion', in Peter Katzenstein (ed.), *Industry and Politics in West Germany: Toward the Third Republic*. Ithaca, NY: Cornell University Press.

—— (1996a). 'Regionalism in Comparative Perspective'. *Cooperation and Conflict*, 3/2: 123–59.

—— (1996b). *Cultural Norms and National Security: Police and the Military in Postwar Japan*. Ithaca, NY: Cornell University Press.

Kayatekin, Serap A. and Ruccio, David F. (1998). 'Global Fragments: Subjectivity and Class Politics in Discourses of Globalization'. *Economy and Society*, 27/1: 74–96.

Keohane, Robert O. and Stanley Hoffmann (1991). 'Introduction', in Robert O. Keohane and Stanley Hoffmann (eds), *The New European Community: Decision-Making and Institutional Change*. Boulder, CO: Westview.

Kern, Horst and Schumann, Michael (1989). 'New Concepts of Production in German Plants', in Peter Katzenstein (ed.), *Industry and Politics in West Germany: Toward the Third Republic*. Ithaca, NY: Cornell University Press.

Kesselman, Mark (1989). 'The New Shape of French Industrial Relations: Ce n'est plus la même chose', in Paul Godt (ed.), *Policymaking in France: From de Gaulle to Mitterrand*. London: Pinter.

Kesselman, Mark and Groux, Guy (eds) (1984). *1968–1982: Le Mouvement Ouvrier Français*. Paris: Editions Ouvrières.

Kindleberger, Charles (ed.) (1970). *The International Corporation*. Cambridge, MA: MIT Press.

King, Desmond and Wood, Stewart (1999) 'The Political Economy of Neoliberalism: Britain and the United States in the 1980s', in Herbert Kitschelt *et al.* (eds), *Continuity and Change in Contemporary Capitalism*. New York: Cambridge University Press.

Kingdon, John W. (1984). *Agenda, Alternatives, and Public Policy*. Boston: Little, Brown.

Kitschelt, Herbert, Lange, Peter, Marks, Gary, and Stephens, John (eds) (1999). *Continuity and Change in Contemporary Capitalism*. New York: Cambridge University Press.

Klein, R. (1989). *The Politics of the NHS*. London: Longman.

Knill, Christophe (1998). 'European Policies: The Impact of National Administrative Traditions'. *Journal of Public Policy*, 18: 1–28.

—— and Lehmkuhl, D. (1999). 'How Europe Matters: Different Mechanisms of Europeanization'. *European Integration Online Papers* (EIOP), 3/7 <http://eiop.or.at/eiop/texte/1999>

—— and Lenschow, Andrea (1998). 'Coping with Europe: The Impact of British and German Administrations on the Implementation of EU Environmental Policy'. *Journal of European Public Policy*, 5: 595–614.

—— —— (2001). 'Adjusting to EU Regulatory Policy: Change and Persistence of Domestic Administrations', in Maria Green Cowles, James Caporaso, and Thomas Risse (eds), *Europeanization and Domestic Change*. Ithaca, NY: Cornell University Press.

Knott, Jack (1981). *Managing the German Economy: Budgetary Politics in West Germany*. Lexington, MA: Lexington Books.

Kobrin, Stephen (1997). 'The Architecture of Globalization: State Sovereignty in a Networked Global Economy', in John Dunning (ed.), *Globalization, Governments, and Competitiveness*. Oxford and New York: Oxford University Press.

Kogut, Bruce, Shan, Weijian, and Walker, Gordon (1993). 'Knowledge in the Network and the Network as Knowledge: The Structuring of New Industries', in Gernot Grabher (ed.), *The Embedded Firm: On the Socioeconomics of Industrial Networks*. New York: Routledge.

Kohler-Koch, Beate (1996). 'Catching up with Change: The Transformation of Governance in the European Union'. *Journal of European Public Policy*, 3: 359–80.

—— (1997). 'Organized Interests in European Integration: The Evolution of a New Type of Governance?', in A. Young and H. Wallace (eds), *Participation and Policymaking in the European Union*. Oxford: Oxford University Press.

—— and Eising, Rainer (eds) (1999). *The Transformation of Governance in the European Union*. London: Routledge.

Korn/Ferry International (eds) (1998). *European Boards of Directors Study*. New York: Korn/Ferry International.

Korpi, Walter (1995). 'Un État-Providence Contesté et Fragmenté. Le développement de la citoyenneté sociale en France. Comparaisons avec la belgique, l'Allemagne, l'Italie et la Suède'. *Revue Française de Science Politique*, 45: 632–67.

Krasner, Stephen (1999). 'Globalization and Sovereignty', in David A. Smith, Dorothy J. Solinger, and Steven C. Topick (eds), *States and Sovereignty in the Global Economy*. London: Routledge.

Krugman, Paul (1995). 'Growing World Trade: Causes and Consequences'. *Brookings Papers on Economic Activities*: 327–62.

—— and Venables, A. J. (1995). 'Globalization and the Inequality of Nations'. *Quarterly Journal of Economics*, 110: 857–80.

Kuhn, Thomas (1970). *The Structure of Scientific Revolutions* (2nd edn). Chicago: University of Chicago Press.

Kurzer, Paulette (1993). *Business and Banking: Political Change and Economic Integration in Western Europe*. Ithaca, NY and London: Cornell University Press.

Labbé, Dominique (1990). *Le Vocabulaire de François Mitterrand*. Paris: Presses de la Fondation Nationale des Sciences Politiques.

Ladrech, Robert (1994). 'The Europeanization of Domestic Politics: The Case of France'. *Journal of Common Market Studies*, 32: 69–88.

—— and Marlière, Philippe (eds) (1999). *Social Democratic Parties in the European Union: History, Organization, Policies*. London: Macmillan.

Laffan, Brigid (1998). 'The European Union: A Distinctive Model of Internationalization?'. *Journal of European Public Policy*, 5: 235–53.

Lakatos, Imre (1970). 'Methodology of Scientific Research Programmes', in Imre Lakatos and Alan Musgrave (eds), *Criticism and the Growth of Knowledge*. Cambridge: Cambridge University Press.

Lane, Christel. (1989). *Management and Labour in Europe: The Industrial Enterprise in Germany, Britain and France*. Aldershot: Edward Elgar.

—— (1995). *Industry and Society in Europe*. Aldershot: Edward Elgar.

—— (1998). 'European Companies between Globalization and Localization: A Comparison of Internationalization Strategies of British and German MNCs'. *Economy and Society*, 27: 462–85.

Lange, Peter and Regini, Marino (eds) (1989). *State, Market and Social Regulation: New Perspectives on Italy*. Cambridge: Cambridge University Press.

Larat, Fabrice (1999). 'The Political Dimensions of Narrative'. Paper prepared for delivery at the 27th Annual ECPR Joint Session of Workshops, Mannheim University, 26–31 March.

Larsen, Henrik (1997). *Foreign Policy and Discourse Analysis*. London: Routledge.

Laudan, Larry (1977). *Progress and Its Problems*. Berkeley: University of California Press.

Laurence, Henry (1996). 'Regulatory Competition and the Politics of Financial Market Reform in Britain and Japan'. *Governance*, 9: 311–41.

Lawrence, R. Z. (1997). 'Current Economic Policies: Social Implications over the Longer Term', in *Societal Cohesion and the Globalizing Economy*. Paris: OECD.

Lawson, Nigel (1993). *The View from Number 11: Memoirs of a Tory Radical*. London: Doubleday.

Lazonick, William and O'Sullivan, Mary (1997). 'Finance and Industrial Development. Part I: The United States and the United Kingdom'. *Finance History Review*, 4: 7–29.

Le Galès, Patrick, Aniello, Valeria, and Tirmarche, Olivier (2001). 'Between Large Firms and Marginal Local Economies: The Making of Systems of Local Governance in France', in Colin Crouch *et al.* (eds), *Local Production Systems in Europe: Rise or Demise?* Cambridge: Cambridge University Press.

Lehmbruch, Gerhard (1978). 'Party and Federation in Germany: A Developmental Dilemma'. *Government and Opposition*, 13: 151–77.

—— (1994). 'République Fédérale d'Allemagne: Le Cadre Institutionnel et les Incertitudes des Stratégies Néo-Libérales', in Bruno Jobert (ed.), *Le Tournant Néo-Libéral*. Paris: L'Harmattan.

—— (1995). 'From Authority State to Network State: The German State in Perspective', in F. Naschold and M. Muramatsu (eds), *State and Administration in Japan and Germany*. Berlin: De Gruyter.

—— (1999). 'The Rise and Change of Discourses on "Embedded Capitalism" in Germany and Japan and their Institutional Setting.' Paper prepared for presentation for the Workshop Project on Germany and Japan organized by Wolfgang Streeck and Ronald Dore, Max Planck Institute, Cologne, 24–6 June.

—— and Schmitter, Phillipe C. (eds) (1982). *Patterns of Corporatist Policy-Making*. Beverly Hills, CA: Sage Publications.

Lehrer, Mark (1997). 'German Industrial Strategy in Turbulence: Corporate Governance and Managerial Hierarchies in Lufthansa'. *Industry and Innovation*, 4: 115–40.

—— (2001). 'Macro-Varieties of Capitalism and Micro-Varieties of Strategic Management in European Airlines', in Peter A. Hall and David Soskice (eds), *Varieties of Capitalism: The Institutional Foundations of Comparative Advantage*. Oxford: Oxford University Press.

Leibfried, Stephan and Pierson, Paul (1995). 'Semisovereign Welfare States: Social Policy in a Multitiered Europe', in Stephan Leibfried and Paul Pierson (eds), *European Social Policy: Between Fragmentation and Integration*. Washington, DC: Brookings Institution.

Leterre, Thierry (2000). *La Gauche et la Peur Libérale*. Paris: Presses de Sciences Po.

Levy, Jonah (1999). *Tocqueville's Revenge: Dilemmas of Institutional Reform in Post-Dirigiste France*. Cambridge, MA: Harvard University Press.

—— (2000). 'France: Directing Adjustment?', in Fritz W. Scharpf and Vivien A. Schmidt (eds), *Welfare and Work In the Open Economy. Vol. I: From Vulnerability to Competitiveness*. Oxford: Oxford University Press.

—— (2001). 'Partisan Politics, and Welfare Adjustment: The Case of France'. *Journal of European Public Policy*, 8: 265–85.

Lewis, Jeffrey (1998). 'Is the "Hard Bargaining" Image of the Council Misleading? The Committee of Permanent Representatives and the Local Elections Directive'. *Journal of Common Market Studies*, 36: 479–504.

Leydier, Gilles (1998). 'Dimensions of Inequality in French and British Political Discourses since the Early 80s', in John Edwards and Jean-Paul Révauger (eds), *Discourses on Inequality in France and Britain*. Aldershot: Ashgate.

Locke, Richard M. (1995). *Remaking the Italian Economy*. Ithaca, NY and London: Cornell University Press.

—— and Baccaro, Lucio (1999). 'The Resurgence of Italian Unions?', in Andrew Martin and George Ross (eds), *The Brave New World of European Labor*. New York: Berghahn.

Loewendahl, Henry B. (1999). 'Siemens' "Anglo-Saxon" Strategy: Is Globalizing Business Enough?'. *German Politics*, 8/1: 89–105.

Lordon, Fréderic (1999). 'Croyances économiques et pouvoir symbolique'. *L'Année de la Régulation*, 3. Paris: La Découverte.

Lorenz, Detlev (1992). 'Economic Geography and the Political Economy of Regionalization: The Example of Western Europe'. *The American Economic Review*, 82:

Loriaux, Michael (1991). *France after Hegemony: International Change and Financial Reform*. Ithaca, NY: Cornell University Press.

—— (1989). 'Socialist Monetarism and Financial Liberalization in France', in Michael Loriaux *et al.*, *Capital Ungoverned: Liberalizing Finance in Interventionist States*. Ithaca, NY: Cornell University Press.

—— (2002, forthcoming). 'France: A New Capitalism of Voice?', in Linda Weiss (ed.), *States in the Global Economy: Bringing Domestic Institutions Back In*. Cambridge: Cambridge University Press.

Ludlow, Peter (1982). *The Making of the European Monetary System: A Case Study of the Politics of the European Community*. London: Butterworth.

Lütz, Susanne (1998). 'The Revival of the Nation-State? Stock Exchange Regulation in an Era of Internationalized Financial Markets'. *Journal of European Public Policy*, 5: 153–69.

—— (2000). 'From Managed to Market Capitalism? German Finance in Transition'. *German Politics*, 9/2: 149–70.

Lynch, Philip (1999). *The Politics of Nationhood*. Basingstoke: Macmillan.

McCarthy, Patrick (1990). 'France Faces Reality: Rigueur and the Germans', in Patrick McCarthy (ed.), *Recasting Europe's Economies: National Strategies in the 1980s*. Lanham: University Press of America.

McGee, A. and Weatherhill, S. (1990). 'The Evolution of the Single Market: Harmonization or Liberalization'. *Modern Law Review*, 53: 159–77.

McKeown, Timothy (1999). 'The Global Economy, Post-Fordism, and Trade Policy in Advanced Capitalist States', in Herbert Kitschelt *et al.* (eds), *Continuity and Change in Contemporary Capitalism*. New York: Cambridge University Press.

McNamara, Kathleen (1998). *The Currency of Ideas: Monetary Politics in the European Union*. Ithaca, NY: Cornell University Press.

—— and Jones, Erik (1995). 'A Defining Power? Germany in European Monetary Affairs'. Paper prepared for presentation at the Annual Meetings of the American Political Science Association Chicago, 31 August–4 September.

Majone, Giandomenico (1989). *Evidence, Argument and Persuasion in the Policy Process*. New Haven: Yale University Press.

—— (ed.) (1996). *Regulating Europe*. London and New York: Routledge.

Manow, Philip and Seils, Eric (2000). 'Adjusting Badly: The German Welfare State, Structural Change and the Open Economy', in Fritz W. Scharpf and Vivien A. Schmidt (eds), *Welfare and Work in the Open Economy. Vol. II: Diverse Responses to Common Challenges*. Oxford: Oxford University Press.

March, James G. and Olsen, Johan P. (1989). *Rediscovering Institutions*. New York: Free Press.

—— —— (1995). *Democratic Governance*. New York: Free Press.

Marcussen, Martin (1998). *Central Bankers, the Ideational Life-Cycle and the Social Construction of EMU* (EUI Working Papers, RSC No. 98/33). Florence: Robert Schuman Center.

Marginson, P. and Sisson, K. (1994). 'The Structure of Transnational Capital in Europe: The Emerging Euro-Company and its Implications for Industrial Relations', in R. Hyman and A. Ferner (eds), *Frontiers in European Industrial Relations*. Oxford: Basil Blackwell.

Markovits, Andrei (ed.) (1982). *Model Germany*. New York: Praeger.

Marks, Gary, Hooghe, Liesbet, and Blank, Kermit (1996). 'European Integration since the 1980s: State-Centric versus Multi-Level Governance'. *Journal of Common Market Studies*, 34: 341–78.

Marquand, David (1988). *The Unprincipled Society*. London: Fontana.

Martin, Andrew (1997). 'What Does Gobalization Have to Do With the Erosion of Welfare States? Sorting out the Issues' (ZeS-Arbeitspapier Nr.1). Bremen: Zentrum für Sozialpolitik, University of Bremen.

Mazey, Sonia (1995). 'The Development of EU Equality Policies: Bureaucratic Expansion on Behalf of Women?'. *Public Administration*, 73: 591–609.

—— and Richardson, Jeremy (1996). 'EU Policy-making: A Garbage Can or an Anticipatory and Consensual Policy Style?', in Yves Mény, Pierre Muller, and Jean-Louis Quermonne (eds), *Adjusting to Europe: The Impact of the European Union on National Institutions and Policies*. London: Routledge.

Mélitz, Jacques (1993). 'Monetary Policy in France', in Michele Fratianni and Dominick Salvatore (eds), *Handbook of Monetary Policy*. Westport, CT: Greenwood Press.

Mény, Yves, Muller, Pierre, and Quermonne, J. L. (eds) (1996). *Adjusting to Europe: The Impact of the European Union on National Institutions and Policies*. London: Routledge.

Meunier, Sophie (2000). 'The French Exception'. *Foreign Affairs*, 79/4: 104–16.

Middlemas, R. K. (1979). *Politics in Industrial Society: The Experience of the British System since 1911*. London: André Deutsch.

—— (1986). *Power, Competition, and the State. Vol. I Britain in Search of Balance 1940–1961*. Stanford: Hoover Institution Press.

—— (1991). *Power, Competition, and the State. Vol. III: The End of the Postwar Era: Britain since 1974*. Basingstoke: Macmillan.

Milliken, Jennifer (1999). 'The Study of Discourse in International Relations: A Critique of Research and Methods'. *European Journal of International Relations*, 5: 225–54.

Milward, Alan (1992). *The European Rescue of the Nation-State*. Berkeley: University of California Press.

Mishra, Ramesh (1996). 'The Welfare of Nations', in Robert Boyer and Daniel Drache (eds), *States against Markets: The Limits of Globalization*. London and New York: Routledge.

Moene, Karl Ove and Wallerstein, Michael (1993) 'What's Wrong with Social Democracy?', in Prana Bardhan and John Roemer (eds), *Market Socialism: the Current Debate*. Oxford: Oxford University Press.

Moran, Michael (1990). 'Regulating Britain, Regulating America: Corporatism and the Securities Industry', in Colin Crouch and Ronald Dore (eds), *Corporatism and Accountability: Organized Interests in British Public Life*. Oxford: Clarendon Press.

—— (1991). *The Politics of the Financial Services Revolution: The U.S.A, U.K., and Japan*. New York: St Martin's Press.

Moravscik, Andrew (1991). 'Negotiating the Single European Act: National Interests and Conventional Statecraft in the European Community'. *International Organization*, 45: 651–88.

—— (1993a). 'Preferences and Power in the European Community: National Interests and Conventional Statecraft in the European Community'. *International Organization*, 47: 473–524.

—— (1993b). 'Preferences and Power in the European Community: A Liberal Inter-governmentalist Approach'. *Journal of Common Market Studies*, 31: 611–28.

—— (1994). *Why the European Community Strengthens the State: Domestic Politics and International Cooperation* (Working Paper 52). Cambridge, MA: Center for European Studies, Harvard University.

—— (1998). *The Choice for Europe*. Ithaca, NY: Cornell University Press.

Morin, François (1974). *La Structure Financière du Capitalisme Français*. Paris: Calmann-Levy.

—— (1998). *Le Modèle Français de Détention et Gestion du Capital*. Paris: Les Éditions de Bercy.

—— (2000). 'A Transformation in the French Model of Shareholding and Management'. *Economy and Society*, 29/1: 36–53.

Morlino, Leonardo (1999). 'Europeanization and Representation in Two Europes. Local Institutions and National Parties'. Paper prepared for the workshop on Multi-level Party Systems: The Reshaping of National Political Representation, European University Institute, Florence, 16–18 December.

Mosley, H. and Schmid, G. (1993). 'Public Services and Competitiveness', in K. S. Hughes (ed.), *European Competitiveness*. Cambridge: Cambridge University Press.

Mouriaux, René (1991). 'Trade Unions, Unemployment, and Regulation: 1962–1989', in James F. Hollifield and George Ross (eds), *Searching for the New France*. New York: Routledge.

Muller, Pierre (1995). 'Les Politiques Publiques comme Construction d'un Rapport au Monde', in Alain Faure, Gielles Pollet, and Philippe Warin (eds), *La Construction du Sens dans les Politiques Publiques: Débats autour de la notion de Référentiel*. Paris: L'Harmattan.

—— and Surel, Yves (1998). *L'Analyse des Politiques Publiques*. Paris: Monchrestien.

Murray, Alasdair (2001). *The Future of European Stock Markets*. London: Centre for European Reform (May).

Mutz, Diana C., Sniderman, Paul M., and Brody, Richard A. (1996). *Political Persuasion and Attitude Change*. Ann Arbor: University of Michigan Press.

Newman, Michael (1996). *Democracy, Sovereignty and the European Union*. New York: St Martin's Press.

Nicholls, A. J . (1994). *Freedom with Responsibility: The Social Market Economy in Germany, 1918–1963*. Oxford: Oxford University Press.

—— (1997). *The Bonn Republic: West German Democracy, 1945–1990*. London: Longman.

Notermans, T. (1993). 'The Abdication of National Policy Autonomy: Why the Macroeconomic Policy Regime Has Become So Unfavorable to Labor'. *Politics and Society*, 21/2: 133–67.

OECD (Organization for Economic Cooperation and Development) (1994). *Apprenticeship: Which Way Forward?* Paris: OECD.

—— (1995). *The New Financial Landscape. Forces Shaping the Revolution in Banking, Risk Management and Capital Markets*. Paris: OECD.

—— (various years) *Economic Outlook*. Paris: OECD.

—— (various years) *Historical Statistics*. Paris: OECD.

—— (various years). *Labour Force Statistics*. Paris: OECD.

—— (various years) *National Accounts*. Paris: OECD.

OECD (various years). *Revenue Statistics*. Paris: OECD.

Ohmae, Kenichi (1990). *The Borderless World: Power and Strategy in the Interlinked Economy*. New York: Harper Business.

—— (1993). 'The Rise of the Regional State'. *Foreign Affairs*, 72: 78–87.

Oman, Charles (1994). *Globalisation and Regionalisation*. Paris: OECD Development Center.

Orléan, André (1999). *Le Pouvoir de la Finance*. Paris: Odile Jacob.

O'Sullivan, Mary (2001). 'Equity Markets and the Corporate Economy in France: Recent Developments and Their Implications for Corporate Governance'. Unpublished Manuscript.

Palier, Bruno (2000). 'Does Europe Matter? Europeanisation et Réforme des Politiques Sociales des Pays de l'Union Européenne'. *Politique Européenne*, 2/September.

Parrat, Frédéric (1999). *Le Gouvernement d'Entreprise: Ce qui a déjà changé, ce qui va changer*. Paris: Maxima.

Parsons, Craig (2000). 'Domestic Interests, Ideas and Integration: The French Case'. *Journal of Common Market Studies*, 38: 45–70.

Pastor, Manuel (1999). 'The Mexican Peso Crisis', in David A. Smith, Dorothy J. Solinger, and Steven C. Topick (eds), *States and Sovereignty in the Global Economy*. London: Routledge.

Patel, P. and Pavitt, K. (1991). 'Large Firms in the Production of the World's Technology: An Important Case of "Non-Globalization"'. *Journal of International Business Studies*, 22/1: 1–21.

Paterson, William E. (1998). 'EMU and Germany', in Carl Lankowski (ed.), *Break Out, Break Down or Break In? Germany and the European Union after Amsterdam* (Research Report 8). Washington: AICGS.

Pauly, Louis (1995). 'Capital Mobility, State Autonomy and Political Legitimacy'. *Journal of International Affairs*, 49: 369–88.

Perez, Sofia (2000). 'From Decentralization to Reorganization: Explaining the Return to National Bargaining in Italy and Spain'. *Comparative Politics*, 32: 437–58.

Pierson, Paul (1996). 'The New Politics of the Welfare State'. *World Politics*, 48: 143–79.

—— (1997). 'Skeptical Reflections on "Globalization" and the Welfare State'. Paper presented at the International Conference on Socio-Economics, Montreal, July.

—— (1998). 'Irresistible Forces, Immovable Objects: Post-Industrial Welfare States Confront Permanent Austerity'. *Journal of European Public Policy*, 5: 539–60.

—— and Smith, M. (1993). 'Bourgeois Revolutions?' *Comparative Political Studies*, 25: 487–520.

Piore, Michael and Sabel, Charles (1984). *The Second Industrial Divide: Possibilities for Prosperity*. New York: Basic Books.

Pocock, J. G. A. (1964). 'The History of Political Thought', in Peter Laslett and W. G. Runciman (eds), *Philosophy, Politics and Society* (second series). Oxford: Blackwell.

Pollard, Sidney (1992). *The Development of the British Economy 1914–1990*. London: Edward Arnold.

Pontusson, Jonas and Swenson, Peter (1996). 'Labor Markets, Production Strategies and Wage-Bargaining Institutions: The Swedish Employer Offensive and the Politics of Institutional Change in Sweden'. *Comparative Political Studies*, 28: 117–47.

Popper, Karl (1961). *Logic of Scientific Discovery*. New York: Basic Books.

Porter, Michael (1990). *The Competitive Advantage of Nations*. London: Macmillan.

Putnam, Robert (1993). *Making Democracy Work: Civic Traditions in Modern Italy*. Princeton: Princeton University Press.

Quinn, Dennis (1997). 'The Correlates of Change in International Financial Regulation'. *American Political Science Review*, 41: 771–813.

Radaelli, Claudio (1999). 'Harmful Tax Competition in the European Union: Policy Narratives and Advocacy Coalitions'. *Journal of Common Market Studies*, 37: 661–82.

—— (2000*a*). 'Whither Europeanization? Concept Stretching and Substantive Change'. Paper presented at Political Studies Annual Conference, London, 10–13 April.

—— (2000*b*). 'Policy Transfer in the European Union'. *Governance*, 13: 25–43.

—— (2002, forthcoming). 'The Power of Policy Narratives in the European Union: The Case of Tax Policy', in Dietmar Braun and Andreas Busch (eds), *The Power of Ideas: Policy Ideas and Policy Change*. Cheltenham: Edward Elgar.

Reder, Melvin and Ulman, Lloyd (1993). 'Unionism and Unification', in Lloyd Ulman, Barry Eichengreen, and William T. Dickens (eds), *Labor in an Integrated Europe*. Washington, DC: Brookings Institution.

Regini, Marino (1997). 'Still Engaging in Corporatism? Recent Italian Experience in Comparative Perspective'. *European Journal of Industrial Relations*, 2: 259–78.

—— (2000). 'Between Deregulation and Social Pacts: The Responses of European Economies to Globalization'. *Politics and Society* 28: 5–33.

—— and Regalia, Ida (1997). 'Employers, Unions and the State: The Resurgence of Concertation in Italy'. *West European Politics*, 20: 210–30.

Reich, R. B. (ed.) (1988). *The Power of Public Ideas*. Cambridge: Ballinger.

—— (1991). *The Work of Nations*. New York: Knopf.

Rein, M. and Schön, D. A. (1991). 'Frame-Reflective Policy Discourse', in P. Wagner *et al.* (eds), *Social Sciences, Modern States, National Experiences, and Theoretical Crossroads*. Cambridge: Cambridge University Press.

Reland, Jacques (1998). 'France', in James Forder and Anand Menon (eds), *The European Union and Macroeconomic Policy*. London: Routledge.

Rhodes, Martin (1995). '"Subversive Liberalism": Market Integration, Globalization and the European Welfare State'. *Journal of European Public Policy*, 2/3: 384–406.

—— (1996). 'Globalization and West European Welfare States: A Critical Review of Recent Debates'. *Journal of European Social Policy*, 6: 305–27.

—— (1997). 'Globalization, Labour Markets, and Welfare States: A Future of "Competitive Corporatism?"', in Martin Rhodes and Yves Meny (eds), *The Future of European Welfare*. London: Macmillan.

—— (2000). 'Restructuring the British Welfare State: Between Domestic Constraints and Global Imperatives', in Fritz W. Scharpf and Vivien A. Schmidt (eds), *Welfare and Work in the Open Economy. Vol. II: Diverse Responses to Common Challenges*. Oxford: Oxford University Press.

—— and Van Apeldoorn, Bastiaan (1997). 'Capitalism versus Capitalism in Western Europe', in Martin Rhodes, Paul Heywood, and Vincent Wright (eds), *Developments in West European Politics*. London: St Martin's Press.

Riddell, Peter (1989). *The Thatcher Decade*. Oxford: Blackwell.

Riemer, Jeremiah (1982). 'Alterations in the Design of Model Germany: Critical Innovations in the Policy Machinery for Economic Steering', in Andrei S. Markovits (ed.), *The Political Economy of West Germany: Modell Deutschland*. New York: Praeger.

Risse, Thomas (2000). '"Let's Argue!" Communicative Dialogue in World Politics'. *International Organization*, 54/1: 1–39.

—— (2001). 'Who Are We? A Europeanization of National Identities?', in Maria Green Cowles, James Caporaso, and Thomas Risse (eds), *Europeanization and Domestic Change*. Ithaca, NY: Cornell University Press.

—— Englemann-Martin, Daniela, Knopf, Hans-Joachim, and Roscher, Klaus (1999). 'To Euro or not to Euro? The EMU and Identity Politics in the European Union'. *European Journal of International Relations*, 2/2: 147–87.

Risse-Kappen, Thomas (1994). 'Ideas do not Float Freely: Transnational Coalitions, Domestic Structures, and International Institutions'. *International Organization*, 48/2: 185–214.

Rodrik, Dani (1997). *Has Globalization Gone too Far?* Washington, DC: Institute for International Economics.

—— (1998). 'Why do more Open Economies have Bigger Governments?'. *Journal of Political Economy*, 106: 997–1032.

Roe, Emery (1994). *Narrative Policy Analysis: Theory and Practice*. Durham, NC: Duke University Press.

Rometsch, Dietrich and Wessels, Wolfgang (eds) (1996). *The European Union and Member-States: Toward Institutional Fusion*. Manchester: Manchester University Press.

Rosamund, Ben (1999). 'Discources of Globalization and the Social Construction of European Identities'. *Journal of European Public Policy*, 6/4 (special issue): 652–68.

Rosenau, James (1990). *Turbulence in World Politics: A Theory of Change and Continuity*. Princeton: Princeton University Press.

—— (1995). 'Governance in the 21st Century'. *Global Governance*, 1: 13–43.

—— and Ernst-Otto Czempiel (eds) (1992). *Governance without Government: Order and Change in World Politics*. Cambridge: Cambridge University Press.

Rosenzweig, Phillip M. (1994). 'The New "American Challenge": Foreign Multi-nationals in the United States'. *California Management Review*, 36/3: 107–23.

Ross, George (1995). *Jacques Delors and European Integration*. Oxford: Oxford University Press.

—— (1998). 'European Integration and Globalization', in Roland Axtmann (ed.), *Globalization and Europe: Theoretical and Empirical Investigations*. London and Washington: Pinter.

—— (2000). 'Labor Versus Globalization'. *The Annals*, 570/July: 78–91.

—— (n.d.). 'EMU and the French Model of Society'. Unpublished manuscript.

Rothstein, Bo (2000). 'Trust, Social Dilemmas, and Collective Memories'. *Journal of Theoretical Politics*, 12: 477–501.

Ruggie, John (1975). 'International Responses to Technology'. *International Organization*, 29: 557–83.

—— (1982). 'International Regimes, Transactions, and Change: Embedded Liberalism in the Postwar Economic Order'. *International Organization*, 36: 379–415.

Sabatier, Paul A. (1998). 'The Advocacy Coalition Framework: Revisions and Relevance for Europe'. *Journal of European Public Policy*, 5/1: 98–130.

—— and Jenkins-Smith, H. C. (eds) (1993). *Policy Change and Learning: An Advocacy Coalition Approach*. Boulder, CO: Westview.

Sachwald, Frédérique (2001). 'Les fusion-acquisitions, instruments de la destruction créatrice', in *RAMSES*. Paris: Dunod.

Sako, Mari (1994). 'Neither Markets nor Hierarchies: A Comparative Study of the Printed Board Industry in Britain and Japan', in Roger Hollingsworth, Philippe Schmitter, and Wolfgang Streeck (eds), *Governing Capitalist Economies*. Oxford: Oxford University Press.

Salacuse, Jeswald (1991). *Making Global Deals: Negotiating in the International Marketplace*. Boston: Houghton Mifflin.

Salais, Robert and Tessier, L. (1992). 'Modernisation des Entreprises et Fonds National de l'Emploi: une Analyse en terme de Mondes de Production'. *Travail et Emploi*, No. 51: 49–69.

Sally, Razeen (1995). *States and Firms: Multinational Enterprises in Institutional Competition*. New York: Routledge.

Sandholz, Wayne and Zysman, John (1989). '1992: Recasting the European Bargain'. *World Politics*, 42/1: 95–128.

Sapir, André (2001). 'Who is Afraid of Globalization? The Challenge of Domestic Adjustment in Europe and America'. *Bulletin of the Centre for Economic Policy Research*, 76/Spring <http:www.cepr.org/pubs/dsp/dp2630>

Sassen, Saskia (1991). *The Global City: New York, London, Tokyo*. Princeton: Princeton University Press.

—— (1996). *Losing Control? Sovereignty in the Age of Globalization*. New York: Columbia University Press.

—— (1999). 'Embedding the Global in the National: Implications for the Role of the State', in David A. Smith, Dorothy J. Solinger, and Steven C. Topick (eds), *States and Sovereignty in the Global Economy*. London: Routledge.

Sbragia, Alberta (ed.) (1992). *Euro-Politics*. Washington, DC: Brookings Institution.

Scharpf, Fritz W. (1977). *Politische Immobilismus und ökonomische Krise. Aufsätze zu den politischen Restriktionen der Wirtschaftspolitik in der Bundesrepublik*. Königstein/Ts: Athenaeum.

—— (1988). 'The Joint-Decision Trap: Lessons from German Federalism and European Integration'. *Public Administration*, 66: 239–78.

—— (1991). *Crisis and Choice in European Social Democracy*. Ithaca, NY: Cornell University Press.

—— (1996). 'Negative and Positive Integration in the Political Economy of European Welfare States', in G. Marks *et al.* (eds), *Governance in the European Union*. London: Sage.

—— (1997a). 'Economic Integration, Democracy and the Welfare state'. *Journal of European Public Policy*, 4/1: 18–36.

—— (1997b). *Games Real People Play: Actor-Centered Institutionalism in Policy Research*. Boulder, CO: Westview.

Scharpf, Fritz W. (1997c). *Combating Unemployment in Continental Europe: Policy Options under Internationalization* (RSC Policy Paper 3). Florence: Robert Schuman Centre.

—— (2000a). *Governing in Europe*. Oxford: Oxford University Press.

—— (2000b). 'Economic Changes, Vulnerabilities, and Institutional Capabilities', in Fritz W. Scharpf and Vivien A. Schmidt (eds), *Welfare and Work In the Open Economy. Vol. I: From Vulnerability to Competitiveness*. Oxford: Oxford University Press.

—— and Schmidt, Vivien A. (eds) (2000). *Welfare and Work in the Open Economy. Vol. I: From Vulnerability to Competitiveness. Vol. II: Diverse Responses to Common Challenges*. Oxford: Oxford University Press.

—— —— and Vad, Torben (1998). 'The Adjustment of National Employment and Social Policy to Economic Internationalization'. Manuscript. Cologne: Max Planck Institute for the Study of Societies.

Schenk, C. R. (1994). *Britain and the Sterling Area: From Devaluation to Converibitlity in the 1950s*. London: Routledge.

Schmidt, Susanne K. (1998). 'Commission Activism: Subsuming Telecommunications and Electricity under European Competition Law'. *Journal of European Public Policy*, 5/1: 169–84.

Schmidt, Vivien A. (1986). 'Four Approaches to Scientific Rationality'. *Methodology and Science*, 19: 207–32.

—— (1987). 'Four Approaches to Science and their Implications for Organizational Theory and Research'. *Knowledge*, 9/1: 19–41.

—— (1988a). 'Four Models of Explanation'. *Methodology and Science*, 21/3: 174–201.

—— (1988b). 'The Historical Approach to Philosophy of Science: Toulmin in Perspective'. *Metaphilosophy*, 19: 223–36.

—— (1990). *Democratizing France: The Political and Administrative History of Decentralization*. New York: Cambridge University Press.

—— (1996). *From State to Market? The Transformation of French Business and Government*. New York and London: Cambridge University Press.

—— (1997a). 'Discourse and Disintegration in Europe: The Cases of France, Great Britain, and Germany'. *Daedalus*, 126/3: 167–98.

—— (1997b). 'European Integration and Democracy: The Differences among Member States'. *Journal of European Public Policy*, 4/1: 128–45.

—— (1997c). 'Economic Policy, Political Discourse, and Democracy in France'. *French Politics and Society*, 15/2: 37–48.

—— (1997d). 'Running on Empty: The End of Dirigisme in French Economic Leadership'. *Modern and Contemporary France*, 5: 229–41.

—— (1999a). 'European "Federalism" and its Encroachments on National Institutions'. *Publius*, 29/1: 19–44.

—— (1999b). 'National Patterns of Governance under Siege: The Impact of European Integration', in Beate Kohler-Koch and Rainer Eising (eds), *The Transformation of Governance in the European Union*. London: Routledge.

—— (1999c). 'The Changing Dynamics of State–Society Relations in the Fifth Republic'. *West European Politics*, 22: 141–65.

—— (2000a). 'Democracy and Discourse in an Integrating Europe and a Globalizing World'. *European Law Journal*, 6/3: 277–300.

—— (2000b). 'Values and Discourse in the Politics of Welfare State Adjustment', in Fritz W. Scharpf and Vivien A. Schmidt (eds), *Welfare and Work in the Open Economy. Vol. 1: From Vulnerability to Competitiveness*. Oxford: Oxford University Press.

—— (2001a). 'The Politics of Adjustment in France and Britain: When Does Discourse Matter?'. *Journal of European Public Policy*, 8: 247–64.

—— (2001b). 'Discourse and the Legitimation of Economic and Social Policy Change', in Steven Weber (ed.), *Globalization and the European Political Economy*. New York: Columbia University Press.

—— (2002a, forthcoming). 'Does Discourse Matter in the Politics of Welfare State Adjustment?' *Comparative Political Studies*.

—— (2002b). 'The Effects of European Integration on National Forms of Governance: Reconstructing Practices and Reconceptualizing Democracy', in Jürgen Gröte and Bernard Gbikpi (eds), *Participatory Governance: Theoretical, Political, and Societal Implications*. Opladen: Leske and Budruch.

Schmitter, Philippe C. and Lehmbruch, Gerhard (eds) (1979). *Trends Toward Capitalist Intermediation*. Beverly Hills: Sage Publications.

Schneider, Volker (2001). 'Institutional Reform in Telecommunications: The European Union in Transnational Policy Diffusion', in Maria Green Cowles, James Caporaso, and Thomas Risse (eds), *Europeanization and Domestic Change*. Ithaca, NY: Cornell University Press.

Schön, D. A. and Rein, M. (1994). *Frame Reflection: Toward the Resolution of Intractable Policy Controversies*. New York: Basic Books.

Schwartz, Herman (2000). 'Internationalization and Two Liberal Welfare States: Australia and New Zealand', in Fritz W. Scharpf and Vivien A. Schmidt (eds), *Welfare and Work in the Open Economy. Vol. II: Diverse Responses to Common Challenges*. Oxford: Oxford University Press.

Schwok, René (1999). 'La France et l'Intégration Européenne: Une Évaluation du "Paradigme Identitariste"'. *French Politics and Society*, 17/1: 56–69.

Serfati, Claude (2001). *La Mondialisation Armée*. Paris: Textuel.

Servan-Schreiber, Jean-Jacques (1967). *Le Défi Américain*. Paris: Éditions de Noel.

Shonfield, Andrew (1958). *British Economic Policy since the War*. London: Penguin.

—— (1965). *Modern Capitalism: The Changing Balance of Public and Private Power*. Oxford: Oxford University Press.

Sikkink, Kathryn (1986). 'Codes of Conduct for Transnational Corporations: The Case of the WHO/UNICEF Code'. *International Organization*, 40: 815–40.

—— (1991). *Ideas and Institutions: Developmentalism in Argentina and Brazil*. Ithaca, NY: Cornell University Press.

Silvia, Stephen (1988). 'The West German Labor Law Controversy: A Struggle for the Factory of the Future'. *Comparative Politics*, 20: 155–73.

Simmons, Beth (1998). 'The Internationalization of Capital', in Herbert Kitschelt *et al.* (eds), *Continuity and Change in Contemporary Capitalism*. New York: Cambridge University Press.

Sinclair, Timothy H. (1994a). 'Passing Judgment: Credit Rating Processes as Regulatory Mechanisms of Governance in the Emerging World Order'. *Review of International Political Economy*, 1: 133–59.

Sinclair, Timothy H. (1994*b*). 'Between State and Market: Hegemony and Institutions of Collective Action under Conditions of International Capital Mobility'. *Policy Sciences*, 27: 139–74.

Singer, Otto (1990). 'Policy Communities and Discourse Coalitions: The Role of Policy Analysis in Economic Policy-Making'. *Knowledge: Creation, Diffusion, Utilization* 11: 428–58.

Skinner, Quentin (1988). 'Meaning and Understanding in the History of Ideas', in James Tully (ed.), *Meaning and Context: Quentin Skinner and his Critics*. Princeton: Princeton University Press.

Skocpol, Theda (1985). 'Bringing the State Back In', in Peter Evans, Dietrich Rueschemeyer, and Theda Skocpol (eds), *Bringing the State Back In*. Cambridge: Cambridge University Press.

Smith, Mitchell P. (1996). 'Integration in Small Steps: The European Commission and Member-State Aid to Industry'. *West European Politics*, 19: 563–82.

—— (1998). 'Autonomy by the Rules: The European Commission and the Development of State Aid Policy'. *Journal of Common Market Studies*, 36: 55–78.

—— (2001*a*). 'In Pursuit of Selective Liberalization: Single Market Competition and its Limits'. *Journal of European Public Policy*, 8: 519–40.

—— (2001*b*). 'Europe and the German Model: Growing Tensions or Symbiosis?'. *German Politics*, 10/3: 119–40.

Smith, W. Rand (1988). *Crisis in the French Labor Movement: A Grassroots Perspective*. New York: St Martin's Press.

—— (1998). *The Left's Dirty Job. The Politics of Industrial Restructuring in France and Spain*. Pittsburgh, PA: University of Pittsburgh Press.

Smyser, W. R. (1992). *The Economy of United Germany*. London: Hurst.

Sobel, Andrew (1994). *Domestic Choices, International Markets; Dismantling National Barriers and Liberalizing Securities Markets*. Ann Arbor: University of Michigan Press.

Sofres (1995). *L'État de l'Opinion*. Paris: Sofres.

—— (1996). *L'État de l'Opinion*. Paris: Sofres.

—— (1998). *L'État de l'Opinion*. Paris: Sofres.

Soskice, David (1991). 'The Institutional Infrastructure for International Competitiveness: A Comparative Analysis of the U.K. and Germany', in A. B. Atkinson and R. Brunetta (eds), *The Economies of the New Europe*. London: Macmillan.

—— (1994). 'Reconciling Markets and Institutions: The German Apprenticeship System', in Lisa M. Lynch (ed.), *Training and the Private Sector: International Comparisons*. Chicago: Chicago University Press.

—— (1997*a*). 'The Future Political Economy of EMU. Rethinking the Effects of Monetary Integration on Europe'. Mss. Wissenschaftszentrum, Berlin.

—— (1997*b*). 'German Technology Policy, Innovation, and National Institutional Frameworks'. *Industry and Innovation*, 4/1: 75–96.

—— (1998). 'The Political Economy of the EMU'. Presentation at Harvard University, Cambridge, MA, 21 April.

—— (1999). 'Divergent Production Regimes: Coordinated and Uncoordinated Market Economies in the 1980s and 1990s', in Herbert Kitschelt *et al.* (eds), *Continuity and Change in Contemporary Capitalism*. New York: Cambridge University Press.

—— and Schettkat, Ronald (1993). 'West German Labor Market Institutions and East German Transformation', in Lloyd Ulman, Barry Eichengreen, and William T. Dickens (eds), *Labor in an Integrated Europe*. Washington, DC: Brookings Institution.

Sperling, James (1994). 'German Foreign Policy after Unification: The End of Cheque Book Diplomacy?' *West European Politics*, 17: 73–97.

Spicker, P. (1997). 'Concepts of Welfare and Solidarity in Britain and France', in J. Edwards and J.-P. Révauger (eds), *Discourse on Inequality in France and Britain*. Aldershot: Ashgate.

Stephens, John, Huber, Evelyne, and Ray, Leonard (1999). 'The Welfare State in Hard Times', in Herbert Kitschelt *et al.* (eds), *Continuity and Change in Contemporary Capitalism*. New York: Cambridge University Press.

Stone Sweet, Alec (2000). 'Islands of Transnational Governance'. Paper presented at the conference Beyond Center-Periphery or the Unbundling of Territoriality, Florence, European University Institute, 19–20 May.

Stopford, J. and Strange, S. (1991). *Rival States, Rival Firms: Competition for World Market Shares*. Cambridge: Cambridge University Press.

Story, Jonathan (1996). 'Finanzplatz Deutschland: National or European Response to Internationalisation?' *German Politics*, 5: 373–94.

Strange, Susan (1971). *Sterling and British Policy*. London: Oxford University Press.

—— (1986). *Casino Capitalism*. Oxford: Blackwell.

—— (1995). 'The Defective State'. *Daedalus*, 124: 55–74.

—— (1996). 'The Limits of Politics'. *Government and Opposition*, 30: 291–311.

—— (1998). 'Who are EU? Ambiguities in the Concept of Competitiveness'. *Journal of Common Market Studies*, 36/2: 101–14.

Stråth, Bo (1994). 'Modes of Governance in the Shipbuilding Sector in Germany, Sweden, and Japan', in Roger Hollingsworth, Philippe Schmitter, and Wolfgang Streeck (eds), *Governing Capitalist Economies*. Oxford: Oxford University Press.

Streeck, Wolfgang (1984). *Industrial Relations in West Germany: A Case Study of the Car Industry*. New York: St Martin's Press.

—— (1993). 'The Rise and Decline of Neo-Corporatism', in Lloyd Ulman, Barry Eichengreen, and William T. Dickens (eds), *Labor in an Integrated Europe*. Washington, DC: Brookings Institution.

—— (1994). 'Pay Restraint without Incomes Policy: Institutionalized Monetarism and Industrial Unionism in Germany', in Ronald Dore, Robert Boyer, and Zoe Mars (eds), *The Return to Incomes Policy*. London: Pinter.

—— (1996). 'Lean Production in the German Automobile Industry: A Test Case for Convergence Theory', in Suzanne Berger and Ronald Dore (eds), *National Diversity and Global Capitalism*. Ithaca, NY: Cornell University Press.

—— (1997). 'German Capitalism: Does It Exist? Can It Survive?', in Colin Crouch and Wolfgang Streeck (eds), *Modern Capitalism or Modern Capitalisms*. London: Pinter.

—— and Visser, Jelle (1997). 'The Rise of Conglomerate Unions'. *European Journal of Industrial Relations*, 3: 305–32.

—— and Yamamura, K. (2001). *The Origins of Nonliberal Capitalism: Germany and Japan*. Ithaca, NY: Cornell University Press.

Suleiman, Ezra and Courty, Guillaume (1996). *L'Age d'Or de l'État. Une Métamorphose Annoncée*. Paris: Seuil.

Sun, J.-M. and Pelkmans, Jacques (1995). 'Regulatory Competition in the Single Market'. *Journal of Common Market Studies*, 33: 67–89.

Surel, Yves (1995). 'Les Politiques Publiques comme Paradigme', in Alain Faure, Gilles Pollet, and Philippe Warin (eds), *La Construction du Sens dans les Politiques Publiques: Débats autour de la notion de Référentiel*. Paris: L'Harmattan.

Swank, Duane (1998). 'Funding the Welfare State: Globalization and the Taxation of Business in Advanced Market Economies'. *Political Studies*, 46: 671–92.

—— (2000). 'Globalisation, Democratic Institutions and the Welfare State'. Paper presented at the American Political Science Association National Meetings, Washington, DC, 30 August–3 September.

—— (2002). 'Withering Welfare? Globalization, Political Economic Institutions, and Contemporary Welfare States', in Linda Weiss (ed.), *States in the Global Economy: Bringing Domestic Institutions Back In*. Cambridge: Cambridge University Press.

Taylor, Paul (1983). *The Limits of European Integration*. New York: Columbia University Press.

—— (1991). 'The European Community and the State: Assumptions, Theories and Propositions'. *Review of International Studies*, 17: 109–25.

Taylor-Gooby, Peter (1991). 'Attachment to the Welfare State', in R. Jowell (ed.), *British Social Attitudes: The 8th Report*. Aldershot: Dartmouth.

Teles, Steve (1998). 'The Dialectics of Trust: Ideas, Finance and Pensions Privatization in the US and UK'. Paper prepared for presentation for the conference Varieties of Welfare Capitalism in Europe, North America and Japan, Cologne, Max Planck Institute, 11–13 June.

Temperton, Paul (1997). *The Euro*. Chichester: John Wiley.

Thatcher, Margaret (1989). *The Revival of Britain: Speeches on Home and European Affairs 1975–1988* (compiled by Alistair Cooke). London: Aurum Press.

—— (1993). *The Downing Street Years*. London: HarperCollins.

Thatcher, Mark (1998). 'Institutions, Regulation, and Change: New Regulatory Agencies in the British Privatised Utilities'. *West European Politics*, 21: 120–47.

—— (1999). *Politics of Telecommunications*. Oxford: Oxford University Press.

—— (2000). 'The National Politics of European Regulation: Institutional Reform in Telecommunications'. *Current Politics and Economics of Europe*, 9: 387–405.

Thelen, Kathleen (1993). 'West European Labor in Transition: Sweden and Germany Compared'. *World Politics*, 46: 23–49.

—— (2001). 'Varieties of Labor Politics in the Developed Democracies', in Peter A. Hall and David Soskice (eds), *Varieties of Capitalism: The Institutional Foundations of Comparative Advantage*. Oxford: Oxford University Press.

—— and Kume, Ikuo (1999). 'The Effects of Globalization on Labor Revisited: Lessons from Germany and Japan'. *Politics and Society*, 27: 477–505.

Thiel, Elke (1982). 'Deutschmark between the Dollar and the EMS'. *Aussenpolitik* (English edition), 33/1.

—— and Schroeder, Ingeborg (1998). 'Germany', in James Forder and Anand Menon (eds), *The European Union and National Macroeconomic Policy*. London: Routledge.

Tilly, Charles (1995). 'Globalization Threatens Labor's Rights'. *International Labor and Working-Class History*, 47/Spring: 1–23.

Timmins, Nicholas (1995). *The Five Giants*. London: HarperCollins.

Tiratsoo, Nick and Tomlinson, Jim (1998). *The Conservatives and Industrial Efficiency, 1951–1964: Thirteen Wasted Years?* London: Routledge.

Treu, Tiziano (1994). 'Procedures and Institutions of Incomes Policies in Italy', in Ronald Dore, Robert Boyer, and Zoe Mars (eds), *The Return to Incomes Policy*. London: Pinter.

Todd, Emanuel (1998). *L'Illusion Économique*. Paris: Gallimard.

Tomlinson, Jim (1990). *Public Policy and the Economy since 1900*. Oxford: Clarendon Press.

Toulmin, Stephen (1972). *Human Understanding*. Princeton: Princeton University Press.

Trachtman, Joel P. (1993). 'International Regulatory Competition, Externalization, and Jurisdiction'. *Harvard International Law Journal*, 34: 47–104.

Tsebelis, George (1995). 'Decision-making in Political Systems: Veto Players in Presidentialism, Parliamentarism, Multicameralism, and Multipartyism'. *British Journal of Political Science*, 25: 289–326.

Turner, Lowell (1991). *Democracy at Work: Changing World Markets and the Future of Labor Unions*. Ithaca, NY: Cornell University Press.

Tylecote, Andrew and Conesa, Emmanuelle (1999). *Industry and Innovation*, 6/1: 27–50.

UNCTAD (United Nations Conference on Trade and Development) (various years). *World Investment Report*. Geneva: Division on Transnational Corporations and Investment, UNCTAD.

Useem, Michael (1996). *Investor Capitalism: How Money Managers are Changing the Face of America*. New York: Basic Books.

Vail, Mark (1999). 'The Better Part of Valor: The Politics of French Welfare Reform'. *Journal of European Social Policy*, 9: 311–29.

Van Ypersele, Jacques (1985). *The European Monetary System: Origins, Operation and Outlook*. Chicago: St James Press.

Verdun, Amy (1996). 'An "Asymmetrical" Economic and Monetary Union in the EU: Perceptions of Monetary Authorities and Social Partners'. *Journal of European Integration*, 20/1: 59–82.

—— (1999). 'The Role of the Delors Committee in the Creation of EMU: An Epistemic Community?'. *Journal of European Public Policy*, 6: 308–28.

Vernon, Raymond (1971). *Sovereignty at Bay*. New York: Basic Books.

—— (1985). 'Sovereignty at Bay: Ten Years After', in T. Moran (ed.), *Multinational Corporations: The Political Economy of Foreign Direct Investment*. Lexington, MA: D. C. Heath.

Visser, Jelle and Hemerijck, Anton (1997). *'A Dutch Miracle': Job Growth, Welfare Reform and Corporatism in the Netherlands*. Amsterdam: Amsterdam University Press.

Vitols, Sigurt (1999). 'The Reconstructing of German Corporate Governance: Capital Market Pressures or Managerial Initiatives?' Paper prepared for the conference, The Political Economy of Corporate Governance in Europe and Japan, Florence, European University Institute, 10–11 June.

—— (2000). 'Germany's Neuer Markt: Radical Transformation or Incremental Change in a National Innovation System?' Paper presented to the Annual Conference of the Society for the Advancement of Socio-Economics, London, July.

Vitols, Sigurt (2001). 'Varieties of Corporate Governance: Comparing Germany and the UK', in Peter A. Hall and David Soskice (eds), *Varieties of Capitalism: The Institutional Foundations of Comparative Advantage*. Oxford: Oxford University Press.

Vogel, David (1995). *Trading Up: Consumer and Environmental Regulation in a Global Economy*. Cambridge, MA: Harvard University Press.

Vogel, Steven K. (1996). *Freer Markets, More Rules: Regulatory Reform in Advanced Industrial Countries*. Ithaca, NY: Cornell University Press.

—— (1997). 'International Games with National Rules: How Regulation Shapes Competition in "Global" Markets'. *Journal of Public Policy*, 17/2: 169–93.

Waddington, Jeremy and Hoffmann, Reiner (eds) (2001). *Trade Unions in Europe: Facing Challenges and Searching for Solutions*. Brussels: European Trade Union Institute.

Wade, Robert (1996). 'Globalization and its Limits: Reports of the Death of the National Economy are Grossly Exaggerated', in Suzanne Berger and Ronald Dore (eds), *National Diversity and Global Capitalism*. Ithaca, NY: Cornell University Press.

Waine, Barbara (1995). 'A Disaster Foretold? The Case of Personal Pensions'. *Social Policy and Administration*, 29: 317–34.

Wallace, Helen (1996). 'Relations between the European Union and the British Administration', in Yves Mény, Pierre Muller, and Jean-Louis Quermonne (eds), *Adjusting to Europe: The Impact of the European Union on National Institutions and Policies*. London: Routledge.

—— (2000). 'The Domestication of Europe and the Limits to Globalization'. Paper prepared for the International Political Science Association Meetings, Quebec, 1–5 August.

Walsh, James I. (2000a). *European Monetary Integration and Domestic Politics: Britain, France, and Italy*. Boulder, CO: Lynne Rienner.

—— (2000b). 'When do Ideas Matter? Explaining the Successes and Failures of Thatcherite Ideas'. *Comparative Political Studies*, 33: 483–516.

Waters, Malcolm (1995). *Globalization*. London: Routledge.

Webb, Michael C. (1991). 'International Economic Structures, Government Interests, and International Coordination of Macroeconomic Adjustment Processes'. *International Organization*, 45: 309–42.

Weiner, Martin J. (1981). *English Culture and the Decline of the Industrial Spirit, 1850–1980*. Cambridge: Cambridge University Press.

Weiss, Linda (1997). 'Globalization and the Myth of a Powerless State', *New Left Review*, 225: 3–27.

—— (1998). *The Myth of the Powerless State: Governing the Economy in a Global Era*. Cambridge: Polity Press.

—— (1999a). 'Globalization and National Governance: Antinomy or Interdependence?'. *Review of International Studies*, 25/December (Special Issue).

—— (1999b). 'State Power and the Asian Crisis'. *New Political Economy*, 4: 317–42.

—— (ed.) (2002). *States in the Global Economy: Bringing Domestic Institutions Back In*. Cambridge: Cambridge University Press.

Wendt, Alexander (1999). *Social Theory of International Politics*. Cambridge: Cambridge University Press.

Wessels, Wolfgang (1998). 'Comitology: Fusion in Action'. *Journal of European Public Policy*, 5: 209–34.

Wilding, Paul (1994). 'Government and Poverty in the 1980s: An Exercise in the Management of a Political Issue', in W. Jones (ed.), *Political Issues in Britain Today*. Manchester: Manchester University Press.

Wilkinson, Bruce W. (1993). 'Trade Liberalization, the Market Ideology, and Morality: Have We a Sustainable System?', in Ricardo Grinspun and Maxwell A. Cameron (eds), *The Political Economy of North American Free Trade*. New York: St Martin's Press.

Wincott, Daniel (1994). 'Between Economic Union and Political Union: European Monetary Union, Federalism and the "Bundesbank Analogy"', in A. Mullins and C. Saunders (eds), *Economic Union in Federal Systems*. Sydney: Federation Press.

Windolf, P. and Beyer, J. (1996). 'Co-operative Capitalism: Corporate Networks in Germany and Britain', *British Journal of Sociology*, 47: 205–31.

Winkler, J. T. (1976). 'Corporatism'. *European Journal of Sociology*, 17/1: 100–36.

Wittrock, Björn, Wagner, Peter, and Wollmann, Hellmut (1991). 'Social Science and the Modern State: Knowledge, Institutions, and Societal Transformations', in Peter Wagner, Carol Hirschon Weiss, and Hellmut Wollmann (eds), *Social Sciences and Modern States: National Experiences and Theoretical Crossroads*. Cambridge: Cambridge University Press.

Wolin, Sheldon (1968). 'Paradigms and Political Theories', in Preston King and B. C. Parekh (eds), *Politics and Experience*. Cambridge: Cambridge University Press.

Womack, J. P., Jones, D. T., and Roos, D. (1991). *The Machine that Changed the World: The Story of Lean Production*. New York: Harper.

Wood, Stewart (2001). 'Business, Government, and Patterns of Labor Market Policy in Britain and the Federal Republic of Germany', in Peter A. Hall and David Soskice (eds), *Varieties of Capitalism: The Institutional Foundations of Comparative Advantage*. Oxford: Oxford University Press.

World Competitiveness Yearbook (2000). Lausanne: International Institute for Management Development.

Wright, Vincent (1994). 'Conclusion', in Wolfgang C. Müller and Vincent Wright (eds), *The State in Western Europe: Retreat or Redefinition*. London: Frank Cass.

Wriston, Walter (1998). 'Dumb Networks and Smart Capital'. *Cato Journal*, 17: 333–44.

Woo-Cumings, Yung-en (ed.) (1999). *The Developmental State*. Ithaca, NY: Cornell University Press.

Zaller, John R. (1992). *The Nature and Origins of Mass Opinion*. Cambridge: Cambridge University Press.

Ziegler, J. Nicholas (1997). *Governing Ideas: Strategies in Innovation for France and Germany*. Ithaca, NY: Cornell University Press.

—— (2000). 'Corporate Governance and the Politics of Property Rights in Germany'. *Politics and Society*, 28/2: 195–221.

Zinsou, Lionel (1985). *Le Fer de Lance*. Paris: Olivier.

Zysman, John (1983). *Governments, Markets, and Growth: Financial Systems and the Politics of Industrial Change*. Ithaca, NY: Cornell University Press.

—— (1996). 'The Myth of a "Global" Economy: Enduring National Foundations and Emerging Regional Realities'. *New Political Economy*, 1/1: 157–84.

Index